ABHIJÑĀNA-ŚĀKUNTALA
OF
KĀLIDĀSA

Edited with an Exhaustive Introduction, Translation and Critical and Explanatory Notes

BY

C. R. DEVADHAR, M. A.
AND
N. G. SURU, M. A.

MOTILAL BANARSIDASS
DELHI :: PATNA :: VARANASI

Indological Publishers and Booksellers

Head Office : BUNGALOW ROAD, JAWAHARNAGAR, DELHI-7

Branches : 1. CHOWK, VARANASI (U.P.)

2. ASHOK RAJ PATH (OPP. PATNA COLLEGE), PATNA-4 (BIHAR)

First Edition 1934

Reprinted 1946, 1966, 1972

Printed in India

BY MOHAMMAD AHMAD, JAYYAD PRESS AND PUBLISHED BY SUNDARLAL JAIN FOR MOTILAL BANARSIDASS, BUNGALOW ROAD, JAWAHARNAGAR, DELHI-7

PREFACE

"The tastes of men differ as much as their sentiments and passions, and in feeling the beauties of art as in smelling flowers, tasting fruits, viewing prospects and hearing a melody, every individual must be guided by his own sensations and the incommunicable association of his own ideas." This is what Sir William Jones, the first to translate and interpret to Europe this great classic of India, remarks regarding the appreciation of a work of art. The charm of a great classic as a work of art, in common with all great works of art, lies in its eternal freshness and novelty; and to each and every mind a great work will reveal a new meaning and a new charm which alone are the source of all the enjoyment one derives from reading it.

How far it has been possible for us to reveal all the manifold charm of this great work of classical antiquity, it is for the reader to judge. We have spared no pains in bringing together all the accessaries to his enjoyment, selecting the best of all possible variants, giving a rendering in English of the original which is as literal as the idiom allows and adding critical, exegetical and rhetorical notes to aid the readers' understanding of the text. This is all that we have done; and if the reader does his part well, he will surely be able to understand and enjoy the book. For after all "We receive only what we give."

In preparing this edition, we have in the main followed the Devanāgarī recension of the text as represented by Monier Williams. We are, indeed, very greatly indebted to that scholarly edition of the classic. We have further availed ourselves of all printed texts and translations, notably those of Sir William

Jones, Ryder, and also of the stage version of the Śākuntala prepared by Das Gupta and Laurence Binyon, with its illuminating introduction by India's greatest living poet. We have further consulted much of the vast literature on the subject and we here make our grateful acknowledgments to all these.

14th June, 1934

C. R. DEVADHAR
N. G. SURU

INTRODUCTION

Kālidāsa, his aate, life and works.

Howsoever overlaid with fantasies or encrusted with a mass of isolated events separated in time and place, a widely circulated literary tradition contains within itself a germ of historical truth and can be set aside on pain of doing serious harm to that truth. Thus it is with king Vikramāditya of Ujjain, the liberal patron of learning and arts, of whom the great poet Kālidāsa was a contemporary. This tradition forms the starting point and the basis of the numerous theories regarding the age of Kālidāsa. Of these two rival theories may here be stated as those deserving of consideration. According to one held by most European scholars, the Vikramāditya of the tradition is no other than the Gupta king Candragupta II who assumed the title of Vikramāditya and succeeded his father Samudragupta 375 A.D. and made Ujjain his capital. Vincent Smith in his early history of India (P. 304, foot-note) expresses the view that the earlier works of Kālidāsa were composed before 413 A. D. during the regime of Candragupta and his later works were written under Kumārgupta I (413 A. D. to 455 A. D.) and that possibly his literary career extended even into the reign of Skandagupta (453 A. D. to 480 A. D.).

Some are inclined to suggest from the reference to the conquest of the Huns by Raghu in his Digvijaya, that Kālidāsa must have lived after the victory of Skandagupta over the Huns half a century later than the date suggested. But the evidence has no probative value. "There is nothing to indicate any reference to reality in this account of the exploits of a king of long ago, and if Kālidāsa had lived in the reign of Skandagupta when the fortune of the royal house was evidently tottering to a fall, it would be difficult to understand the calm contentment with the established order which marks all his works."

The other view held by many Indian scholars puts Kālidāsa in the first century before our era, and makes him a contemporary and a protege of King Vikramāditya the founder of the Saṁvat Era—57 B.C. That there is nothing implausible in the assumption is clear when on the strong testimony of Patañjali's Mahābhāṣya it has been possible to put back the beginnings of court poetry in general by a few centuries of the Christian Era. And "Epigraphy not merely confirms the evidence of the Mahābhāṣya that artificial poetry originated before the commencement of our era, but shows that that poetry continued to be cultivated throughout the succeeding centuries." Already in the days of Kaniṣka (78 A.D.) Aśvaghoṣa wrote his Buddhacarita in the artificial style and called it a Mahākāvya.

In connexion with this writer it is interesting to observe that there is a striking resemblance between his poetry and the poetry of Kālidāsa. Not only is there a close parallelism between a few isolated passages and descriptions, but between ideas and expressions fairly distributed over the poem. As Prof. R. N. Apte has observed these close resemblances warrant the conclusion that "one of the poets is using the other." It must be remembered that Aśvaghoṣa is a philosopher first and a poet afterwards; while Kālidāsa is an original poet. The probability, therefore, is that Aśvaghoṣa is the borrower and Kālidāsa his original. Cowell's theory of Kālidāsa's indebtedness to Aśvaghoṣa rests upon the view that Kālidāsa belongs to the Gupta period. The hollowness of this view, has, however, been shown by Prof. Shembavnekar in an article on 'the Date of Kālidāsa' contributed to "the Journal of the University of Bombay" (Vol. I, Part VI, pp. 232-246) who points out that the Gupta theory is based on the assumption that Chandragupta II was the first monarch who bore the name Vikramāditya, whereas on the testimony of the Rajput Chronicles and the Kathāsaritsāgara the first king to bear that appellation was King Vikramāditya of the Paramāra dynasty, the hero of countless legends, the ruler of Ujjayinī in Kālidāsa's day. It is held by many that the title 'Vikramorvaśīya' is chosen by the poet in order to glorify and immortalize his patron's name. According to Kathāsaritsāgara the father of Vikramāditya was Mahendrāditya. It is curious to note that the word Mahendra as an epithet of Indra is repeated by the poet no less than fourteen times in the play and in one place it is particularly significant to find the names of the father and son linked up : (दिष्ट्या महेंद्रोपकार्यासेन विक्रममहिम्ना वर्धते भवान् ।) It is possible, as Prof. Shembavnekar suggests, that the play was written at the time of the intended retirement of Mahendra from active life, and the coronation of Vikrama as king (Kathāsaritsāgara XVIII. 59-60). The last act of the play, therefore, where prince Āyus is installed as the young king is but a poetic reflex of the actual course of events of the times.

There is nothing in the arguments adduced by European scholars which is repugnant to this theory that Kālidāsa lived in the 1st century before our era at the court of King Vikrama of Ujjayinī who founded the Saṁvat era. Prof. Keith's view that 'the conclusive evidence displayed in the works preserved to us of elaborate training in all the learning available to a Brahmin student of the Gupta era from the science of politics to astrology and the Kāmasūtra....everything points to his flourishing in the time of Gupta glory" is only a dogmatic assertion. With regard to the astronomical terms, such as the names of the signs of the Solar Zodiac which are supposed to be of Greek origin and on which European critics lay so much emphasis, it has already been proved by scholars like S. P. Pandit, R. N. Apte, that there is nothing to show that they were unknown to the people of India a few centuries before the Christian Era. While the occurrence of un-Pāṇinian expressions and grammatical forms such as पातयां प्रथममास;प्रभ्रंशयां यो नहुषं चकार, दाश्वान् कामयान, in Kālidāsa can be satisfactorily explained only on the assumption that he belonged to a time when the Pāṇinian grammar nad not obtained a complete vogue.

The foregoing discussion is enough to justify the truth and the vitality of the age-long tradition that the poet belongs to the days of the glorious King Vikramāditya of Ujjayinī—the founder of the Saṁvat era (57 B. C.).

With regard to the external details of the poet's life, we know next to nothing; the numerous legends told about him are but empty figments, and only bear testimony to the greatness and extreme popularity of the poet in the land of his birth. "The truly great stand upon no middle ledge; they are either famous or unknown." But Kālidāsa is both famous and unknown. We look in vain in his works for knowledge about the facts of his life. The impression that we gather about him from them is that of a man, deeply learned in literature and philosophy and other traditional lore of the times, and more deeply learned in the book of nature. Ujjayinī was the city of his heart and he is delighted to sing of her glories and of the romantic loves of her maidens. He sings of this Gem of Avantī, rich with the storied legends of Udayana and the consecrated past, this radiant bit of heaven, with her flower-sweet balconies, and black-eyed maidens; of the dread shrine of Śiva, Mahākāla, of her rich gardens and lotus-lakes that send their fugitive sweetness through the dark; and his fondness for the city is so evident in his loving and lingering description of her varied charms that one might legitimately conclude that the poet must have spent at least a part of his life in this city. Further he was a widely-travelled man and was a keen observer of nature—not only of her sublime and wild aspects, but also of her mild and minute manifestations. "Rarely has a man walked our earth who observed the phenomena of living nature as accurately as he, though his accuracy was of course that of a poet, not that of the scientist."

He was essentially an eclectic in his religion and philosophy for if the Kumārasaṁbhava is distinctly Śivaistic, the Raghuvaṁśa is no less distinctly Viṣṇuite in tendency ; while Vedāntic monism or Sāṁkhya dualism, or the active devotion of Yoga equally engaged his regard ; so that, as Ryder says, "Kālidāsa moved among the jarring sects with sympathy for all, fanaticism for none." A pleasing trait of his personality is his modesty which Coleridge recognises as a sure sign of great genius. Above all, his writings are coloured with the suffusion of a charmed equanimity and give the impression of a man who walked the earth with a serene and god-like tread, with mind and senses keenly responsive to every form of beauty, and accepting life and the good things it offers in a spirit of sublime acquiescence.

Of his seven works which have come down to us, three are dramas, two epics, one a lyrical piece and one a descriptive poem. It is possible to fix the chronology of his dramas, the Mālavikāgnimitra being the composition of his salad days, the Vikramorvaśīya coming next, and the Śākuntala composed when he was in the prime of his manhood. There can be no reasonable doubt that the Ṛtusaṁhāra was a juvenile piece ; while with regard to the two epics Raghuvaṁśa and Kumārasaṁbhava, opinions differ, for whereas the introductory stanzas of the Raghu suggest that it was written before Kumāra, the abrupt and undignified ending of it suggests that the hand that wrote it was cold before it was finished ; but then we have to remember the tradition that in its original form it consisted of twenty-five cantos, of which only nineteen have come down to us. In general it would be only reasonable to assume that the great works on which his fame chiefly rests—the Śākuntala, the Raghuvaṁśa, the Kumārasaṁbhava and the Meghadūta—belong to a period of his life when his genius had attained to the fullest maturity of its powers.

The Story of Śākuntala in the Mahābhārata.

We shall now proceed to give the original story in full in order to realise how wonderfully baser metal is transmuted into gold by passing through the crucible of the poet's imagination.

Once upon a time that strong-armed king accompanied by a large army entered a thick wood. There he chased various beasts and killed them by the hundred. Then pursuing a deer, he came to a beautiful hermitage on the banks of the river Mālinī. He left his army on the skirt of that tranquil resort, and laying aside the insignia of royalty, entered the place alone, and sought the sage Kaṇva ; but finding no one there he cried aloud " Who is there ? " until the forest resounded with his cry. Hearing his voice, a beautiful maiden, dressed in hermit's garb came out and hailed him with words of welcome. On being asked his purpose he told her that he had come to pay reverence to the holy saint Kaṇva. Did she know where he had gone ?

Śakuntalā said, " My blessed father is gone to gather fruits in the forest. Please wait awhile : you shall see him when he returns."

Then, in the absence of the sage, the king seeing this lovely maiden of the fair hips and charming smiles, shining in her radiant beauty and youth, and her penance and self-restraint, said to her, " Who are you ? Whose are you lovely maid ? Why have you come to the forest ? You stole my heart at the first glance. I wish to know more of you. Lovely maid, answer me."

Thus asked the maiden smiling said in her sweet voice, "O Duṣyanta, I am the daughter of the sage Kaṇva, the high-souled, austere, and self-possessed saint."

Duṣyanta said, "But he is chaste, gentle maid, pure and holy in the world's regard. Even virtue may swerve from its course, but he would never swerve from his hard vow. How were you born his daughter, for you are so fair? I am filled with doubt about this. Pray answer me."

She then told him the story of her birth as she had heard it from the saint. Once, Indra, afraid of the austerities of the sage Viśvāmitra, sent the nymph Menakā to tempt him. She went to the sage and made reverence to him and while she was sportively moving about the hermitage her garment was carried away by the wind; the sage was disturbed and called her to him. They stayed together for a long time and a daughter was born of the union. Menakā deserted her on the banks of the Mālinī and returned to Indra's court. The child was cared for by Śakuntas (birds) and hence was called Śakuntalā. The saint found her there and reared her up as his foster-child.

Then Duṣyanta said, "So you are a princess, auspicious maiden; be my loving bride. Tell me what I may do for you. Let the whole of my realm be yours today; be mine by rites of Gāndharva marriage; become my wife, sweet maid."

Śakuntalā answered, "Promise me truly what I ask you in secret. If the son that will be born to me becomes king after you, then, O Duṣyanta, I will marry you."

"So be it," the king said without thinking and added "O my bride of the charming smile, I will take you to my city." He, then, married her duly according to the Gāndharva rite and dwelt with her. Then on the day of parting, he comforted her and repeatedly promised her that he would send a large army to bring his sweet smiling bride to his capital.

Having thus promised her, the king returned to his capital, his mind filled with thoughts of the sage Kaṇva, and wondering what he might do on hearing the news. Sometime after he had left, Kaṇva came back to the hermitage, and Śakuntalā durst not approach him for shame. But the great saint knew it through his divine vision and he was pleased and said, "Dear child, that you lived secretly with a man, forgetting me, is as I see it, not against the law; for the Gāndharva form of marriage is declared to be the best for a Kṣatriya, when both love one another, and no consecration by holy chants is deemed necessary. Duṣyanta is the best among the men, noble and law-abiding; and since you have found a loving husband, you shall give birth to a noble son, mighty in the world."

Śakuntalā then begged of the sage to think kindly of Duṣyanta, her husband.

She gave birth to a boy of unmeasured powers in the hermitage; his hands were marked with the quoit, and he quickly grew to be a splendid boy. When he was only six years old he rode on the back of lions, tigers and bears near about the hermitage and tamed them and sported with them; so that they gave him the name 'Sarvadamana' the 'All-tamer.' Then seeing the child and his more than human deeds, Kaṇva said that it was time the child was consecrated as Yuvaraja and calling to him his pupils he bade them take Śakuntalā and her boy to her husband's home. For people do not like a married woman to stay long among her relatives, as it is against the law, and destroys their character and reputation.

They then set out with Śakuntalā and her son for Hastināpura, and drawing near the king who instantly recognised her, they led her into his presence. She bowed to him and said, " This is your son, O king, install him as Yuvarāja, even as you promised before, when we met."

Hearing those words, the king, although he remembered everything, said, " I know not whose you are, you vile hermit-woman ; I do not remember to have wedded you for duty, pleasure or wealth. Stay or leave as you choose ; do what you like."

Having heard those words Śakuntalā was nigh fainting for shame and grief and stood motionless like a pillar. Her eyes became red with grief and anger ; her lips quivered, and she looked obliquely at the king seeming to consume him with her glances. Concealing her feelings and controlling her anger she held in check the magic power that her penance had given her. She thought for a while and looked at her husband in rage and grief, and said passionately to him, " How do you say " I do not know " like any ordinary person when you know everything, O king ? "

" I do not remember the son born of you, O Śakuntalā. Women are ever such liars. Who will believe your words ? Are you not ashamed to talk to me such incredible things ? Go, you vile hermit-woman."

Śakuntalā made answer, "King, remember truth is the highest divinity ; do not break your promise. But if you cling to a lie and believe not your own self, I must go away. There is no union with a man like you. Even without you my son shall protect the foursquare earth adorned with the lofty mountains."

So saying, Śakuntalā started, when a bodiless voice spoke to Duṣyanta, " Take your child, Duṣyanta, do not scorn your wife Śakuntalā. You are indeed the father of her boy. Śakuntalā tells the truth." Having heard thus, the king joyfully said to his chaplain and ministers : " Hear these words of the angels. For if I were to receive my son, solely relying on her words, he would be suspected by the people, he would not be pure."

Then he received the boy and lovingly embraced him. He then honoured his wife and comforting her, said, "Our marriage was a secret one ; so to save your reputation, I hesitated thus, my Queen ; for the people would have thought that it was a woman's passion that brought you to me. I gladly forgive you the harsh words which in an excess of passion you spoke to me, because you love me." Then Duṣyanta gave the name 'Bharata' to Śakuntalā's son, and made him crown prince (Yuvarāja).

The changes introduced by the poet.

Such is the story in its original form set forth with a considerable concision of all extraneous elements. Into the dry bones of this bare and unromantic tale, the poet has breathed the life of poetry and lifted it from a story of sordid passion into one of the most moving and ideal of loves. Into this matrix of the old the poet's dramatic imagination has fitted in such new elements, transforming, adding and reshaping it as to sublimate it into the very essence of poetry.

The fatal flaw in the original story is the rejection of Śakuntalā by Duṣyanta for reasons which are anything but convincing. They give him the character of a rake who would fain hide the folly of his youth, and degrade his love into lust, rank and disgusting—a mere diversion in the enforced separation from his harem-love. Thus the Duṣyanta of the epic is decidedly contemptible.

So the first great change which the poet introduces into the story is the curse of Durvāsas which clouds the king's memory—a supernatural element whose influence is of a compulsive kind and we feel it has removed the king's capacity or responsibility for dealing with the situation ; so that what is base and unconscionable betrayal of trustful innocence becomes only a tragic error involving no conscious breach of right—but on the other hand accompanied by a full conviction of right. We thus feel that "Men fight blindly in the dark 'themselves the authors of their proper woe,' and the power that works through them makes them the instrument of a design not their own". This influence of the supernatural thus saves the king from moral responsibility in his repudiation of Śakuntalā. But the recognition-ring which Duṣyanta gave to Śakuntalā might have saved the situation ; so the play of chance which has such an appreciable influence at the most critical point in the action. It is just an accident that Śakuntalā drops her ring in the holy water at Śakrāvatāra, before that fatal moment of her encounter with the king. The curse, however, is so modified as to exert its baneful influence for a time only until the king sees the ring—so miraculously recovered from the maw of a carp which a fisherman opened. Here perhaps—in the matter of the curse and its modification which to the Indian mind are matters of frequent occurrence—a foreigner will have to exercise what Coleridge happily describes as "that willing suspension of disbelief which constitutes poetic faith" ; although it must be remembered that "the poet has so delicately managed the matter as not to shock even a Modern and Western reader with a feeling of strong improbability."

Śakuntalā is certainly charming in the epic ; she is direct in her simplicity and fearful innocence. So also is the king's proposal of marriage a direct one—he is not troubled by those doubts by which a lover's heart is assailed. Straightway they go to the job, Śakuntalā feels no qualms in telling the king the story of her birth ; and like practically minded parents who arrange the dowries and the destinies of their children, she bargains with the king for the destiny of her offspring and only after she has secured the promise does she yield to his importunities. How drab, how prosaic is this tale of the wooing and winning of the bride! And how wonderfully has the poet transfused it into the very quintessence of romance and poetry! Their meeting, the story of her birth, the rapid growth of a mutual passion, the ecstasy of his adoration, the rapturous confession of their mutual love, and the final winning—how the minds of both are followed through passion, doubt, despair to exaltation and intense love. And yet "the ardour of love is not allowed to go beyond aesthetic bounds." The story of Śakuntalā's birth is most skilfully woven into the conversation of the king with her two friends, and the promise as to Śakuntalā's future destiny comes spontaneously from the king and is not extracted from him as the condition of their union. And both these have been managed with absolute delicacy and grace, Śakuntalā with a maiden's exquisite modesty and shyness playing the part of an interested listener.

Thirdly Śakuntalā leaves her forest-home for the palace before her son is born; and lastly the final union takes place after a long period of suffering and remorse.

Besides these changes, the poet has added largely from his imagination some very beautiful scenes and characters. As Ryder points out "only acts one and five, with a part of Act VII rest upon the ancient text, while acts two, three, four and six with most of seven, are a creation of the poet." It is obvious that a drama cannot be successfully written with such a meagre number of characters as in the epic—Duṣyanta, Śakuntalā and Kaṇva with the small boy somewhere in the background. To these Kālidāsa has added from the hermitage, the palace and the street, and finally from the "Elysian region which is represented with vague precision in the last act."

And yet it is interesting to note how minutely the poet has utilised his sources, how many are the epic suggestions which he has incorporated into his play. These it is worth listing together "to show how keen is the eye of genius." A careful student will not fail to notice for instance that the king lays aside the insignia of royal office, that Śakuntalā appears in a bark dress, and the name Śakuntalā itself is used in a very beautiful and effective way in the recognition scene in Act VII. Kaṇva's power of divination which saved the heroine from telling herself of her union with the king, the marks of imperial birth on the hand of the child, his rough play with the wild animals which earned him his nick-name "All-tamer" these and many others have not only been preserved but utilised with very great skill and delicacy.

Construction and analysis of the plot.

As Tagore remarks there are two unions in Śākuntala and the central motif of the play is the progress from the earlier union of the first three acts with its youthful beauty and romance through an interval of separation and intense and speechless agony to the ultimate union in the Elysian regions of eternal bliss described in the last act. The play, therefore, naturally falls into three divisions each having a distinct atmosphere of its own—the first four acts constituting the first division, the fifth and sixth the second, and the seventh act the last.

For the first four acts the scene is laid in the hermitage. The poet has already in the prelude intimated that it was the time of pleasant summer, and even within the precincts of the sacred grove every tree and plant is touched by its magic fingers so that "the wild-wood bloom outglows the garden flowers." No poet had a richer and fuller sense of sensuous loveliness or a more masterly command of the resources of suggestive incidents, imagery and pictorial phrasing such as would reveal that loveliness in words. Thus along with the exquisite peace of the place, the king feels what the throbbing of his arm has intimated to him, the presence of "Beauty that takes all peace away."

Then come the maidens on the scene, with the lovely Śakuntalā in the centre, delicate as a jasmine blossom, who waters her leafy sisters and takes delight in that duty : whose dawning youth is slyly suggested by her friend remarking that it was youth that had given her bosom its lovely swell. The Kesara tree is beckoning to her with his leafy fingers as if he means to speak to her and as she approaches him she looks a lovely vine that twines about him ; her breath-taking beauty is observed by the king who remarks how " youth with all its magic charm blossoms within her blood." How lovely was the season for the union of 'the moonlight of the forest', " all flowers now, all youth, and like a bridegroom newly dressed the mango takes and holds her to his breast."

Thus as Tagore has remarked the poet " has fully painted all the blandishments, playfulness and fluttering of the intoxicating sense of youth, the struggle between deep bashfulness and strong self-expression." Nature is not something outside of man with a life-spirit and purpose of its own ; but it is a background for reflecting human emotion. This which is felicitously described as " atmospheric subjectivity " is one feature of Kālidāsa's nature poetry.

How skilfully is the king introduced to the heroine ; the bee has left the jasmine and is trying to settle on Śakuntalā's face ; she calls for help and her friend playfully suggests that she had better call on Duṣyanta, the king, whose duty it was to protect the hermitage. This gives Duṣyanta, who so long had been eagerly watching them, his cue. He enters, and Śakuntalā feels a strange flutter in her heart at sight of him. She had not known Cupid before ; and hence 'her heart was bare of armour ; she could not distrust either the sentiment of love or the character of her lover ; but there was no need to arm herself against the sentiment or to distrust the lover's character. For in the subsequent conversation between her friends and the king, it has been very artistically revealed that he was in every way worthy of her, and her friends too feel that if father Kaṇva were present he would do honour to the guest and offer him the one possession he prized most. Duṣyanta's doubts regarding her birth are stilled when urged by him Śakuntalā's friends narrate to him how she was the daughter of Viśvāmitra and Menakā and is being reared not for the religious life but for marriage with some one worthy of her. Śakuntalā in feigned anger rises to leave when Priyaṁvadā detains her saying she had promised her the watering of two trees and she could not leave before she had paid her debt ; at which the king most gallantly gives her the ring to redeem her debt. This is the fatal ring which failed Śakuntalā just at the critical moment, and whose recovery restored the king's memory. The ring episode has indeed been very skilfully woven into the texture of the play and forms a sort of an organic filament in the whole fabric.

Their conversation is disturbed by the alarm of the elephant, which very beautifully signalises the storming of the peaceful and serene forest-retreat by the importunate forces of love and the outside world.

Act II shows how the king now pines for love, which allows him no rest at night and deprives him of all his zest for the pleasures of hunting. He recounts his feelings to his unsympathetic friend, the Vidūṣaka, and gratefully receives the request of the young hermit to protect the hermitage against the attacks of the demons. Then comes a messenger from the palace requesting the king's presence at a festival there, and this gives the king the opportunity to dismiss all his retinue and the Vidūṣaka, assuring him, to prevent a scandal, that his remarks about Śakuntalā were not made in earnest.

The third Act intimates to us in its introductory scene the love-stricken condition of Śakuntalā. The king has already driven off the powers of evil, and dismissed by the hermits, now seeks his love who spends those hours of midday heat with her friends on the vine-wreathed banks of the Mālinī. There she is discovered reclining on a bed of lotus-leaves, writing at her friend's suggestion a love-missive to the king. How careful is the poet to show that Śakuntalā in her maiden shame has not revealed her passion even to the friends of her bosom for long; it is only now when importuned by them that she talks of the desperate state to which she has been driven by love. Then follows a scene of ideal passion which is enshrined in syllables of imperishable fire; Śakuntalā has composed a song which breathes of the keen anguish that fills her heart, and the king who has overheard all comes on the scene and assures them of his deep devotion for the fair Śakuntalā. With rare skill, the poet makes Śakuntalā jealously remark that they should not tax the great king's courtesy—is he not separated from the fair eyes that long await his return to the palace? Upon which comes the confession of his passionate love for her. But they have heard that kings are prodigal of their love to many, Anasūyā remarks—whereupon the king assures them that in spite of many a wife in the palace courts, henceforth this dear friend of theirs shall be the chief glory of his throne. The friends now make excuses and leave and the lovers are left to themselves. How gracefully, how delicately is the love-scene drawn; "a kiss unkissed is the climax beyond which the affair does not pass." As already remarked the poet does not allow love to go beyond aesthetic bounds. The scene is ended by the arrival of Gautamī who comes to take away Śakuntalā to the hermitage.

The fourth act is full of the shadows of the coming doom. Anasūyā expresses her fears that surrounded by the bright ladies with their courtly ways, the king may not remember Śakuntalā or the hermitage. Priyaṁvadā, however, assures her that persons so noble are not changeable; what troubles her on the other hand is to know what Father Kaṇva will say when he knows of the union. Then comes the dread Durvāsas to the Āśrama. Poor Śakuntalā is far too deeply burdened to notice him. Care has already come and nested in her bosom; then like a knife on the innocent lamb falls the fierce imprecation of the choleric sage, which, however, is modified through the intercession of the agitated Priyaṃvadā. He graciously grants that although Śakuntalā shall be clean razed from her husbands memory, yet at the sight of the recognition ring the spell shall break. Happily the king has given Śakuntalā his signet-ring that the friends feel will save her; they decide to tell no one of the incident; for poor Śakuntalā ought not to be troubled; who would sprinkle boiling water on the jasmine flower and scald it?

The next scene opens in the tearful glimmer of the languid dawn, where in a very suggestive stanza a pupil of Kaṇva compares with the simultaneous rise and fall of heaven's brightest luminaries, the strange mutations of human life. Kaṇva by now has returned, and a divine voice has informed him of the marriage of Śakuntalā and her approaching maternity. He decides to send her under the escort of his trusty pupils and Gautamī to the king. And now follows the scene of leaving-taking which is drenched through and through in the heavy dew of long and living sorrow at the severence from a Paradise of love, innocence and vital memories— a Paradise which for ever vanishes from the picture. Hard of heart must he be who can read the act without mist in his eyes or catch in his voice! What tender leave-taking of the trees and plants, of the deer and peacock of the Vanajyotsnā, of the doe that is slow by the weight of her young, of the fawn, her foster-child, that would fain prevent her going and catches the end of her garment, and lastly of the friends of her girlhood and her father. What lingering farewell! Who can tear the fond parent from his beloved child! How the truth of the Prākṛt verse comes home to us चुम्बिज्जई सअहुत्तं अवरुन्धिज्जई सहस्सहुत्तम्मि ....पिओ जणो णत्थि पुनरुत्तं ॥ चुम्ब्यते शतकृत्वोऽवरुध्यते सहस्रकृत्वः । ...प्रियो जनो नास्ति पुनरुक्तम् ॥ With a mind galled and bleeding Śakuntalā finds herself between two worlds the one now lost to her, and the other dark and uncertain. The friends are already filled with apprehensions and tell Śakuntalā to show the ring in case the king is slow to recognise her, and with her father's words of consolation and advice in her ears, and with a heart heavy with grief she bids fare-well to the forest-world.

Here the lyrical element of the play reaches its climax. It is a most luminous picture of a great experience of life passed through the recreative process of expression and its pathos is profound and almost lacerating. And here again nature not only echoes the feelings of the persons and even the progress of their thought—but actively partakes of man's joys and sorrows and gives a foreboding of the approaching catastrophe.

We now come to the second division of the play. "In passing from the Fourth Act to the fifth we suddenly enter a new atmosphere"—as Tagore remarks, "from the ideal world of the hermitage we go forth to the royal court with its hard hearts, crooked ways of love-making, difficulties of union. Now the poet momentarily draws aside the curtain from the king's love affairs; we hear a woman's voice singing in an impassioned strain: it is a taunt to the king for his forgetting of Haṁsapadikā, on account of queen Vasumatī. Tagore describes it as "a small rent in the veil through which we can get an idea of the royal sin". Of course, he is judging from present day standards, imputing moral obliquity to Duṣyanta when nothing of the kind is ever intended. What he calls "the tear-strained song of a stricken-heart" is nothing more than a part of the give and take between the king and the women of the harem. It gives us a rude shock without doubt. The beauteous dream of the hermitage has already vanished. The two hermits who are escorting Śakuntalā at once feel that they have entered an altogether new world, "a house lapped in flames of fire," peopled with folk "who are unclean and manacled and fettered as slaves." By such touches as these does the poet prepare us for the crisis, for which he has now secured an effective setting.

Haṁsapadikā's song has caused a strange disturbance in Duṣyanta's soul, as if it sought something it could not find—the shadow of something dearly loved in a former and forgotten birth. And in this mood, with a heart, filled with a longing like sweet pain, he comes to face Śakuntalā and the hermits. What a fine and moving irony is there in that sweet song which tells of the effect of music, and of beauty.

The repudiation scene is one of the most masterly scenes in the whole range of literature, and we clearly feel how the avalanche is loosed and is coming inch by inch until gathering force it hurtles down with a tremendous force and crashes upon the dear head of the devoted Śakuntalā. The king denies having had anything to do with Śakuntalā, he does not recognize her when her veil is removed ; and by a most fatal chance the ring of recognition has already been lost. Thus when direct evidence (प्रत्यक्ष प्रमाण) fails the poor Śakuntalā makes the pathetic attempt of reviving his memory by verbal testimony (शाब्द प्रमाण) The irony of the king's remark श्रोतव्यं इदानीं संवृत्तम् cuts like a sharp knife, when everything fails her, with a mind torn between the pangs of despised love and the anguish of remorse, she bewails that in the innocence of her heart she should have given her honour to a man whose mouth drops honey, but whose heart is filled with poison! Śārangarava has a few spars with the king, and roundly abusing both Duṣyanta and Śakuntalā, bids them leave. "With rare poetic insight Kālidāsa has declined to restore Śakuntalā to Kaṇva's hermitage. It was impossible for her to live in harmony with that hermitage in the way she had done before. .A mighty silence was now needed, worthy of the mighty grief of the mourner."

The fifth Act with its painful and tense tragedy has strained our nerves to the utmost, and we stand in need of relief. So with a rare judgment the poet gives us at the beginning of the sixth act, a scene drawn almost raw from life, but one which is of vital importance to the play. For it describes the recovery of the ring from the maw of a carp which a fisherman had opened, and in the main act the poet describes how the king recognizes the wrong unwittingly done and of his heart-wrenching agony at loss of his beloved wife. He seeks to console himself with a portrait he had himself drawn of his love, when the jealous queen Vasumati is reported to be coming to him; but her presence would have been altogether out of place in a scene of severe penitence and tenderness, and the poet very skilfully avoids it by making the thoughtful queen give precedence to affairs of state. The minister obtains from the king the decision of a law-point involving the right of inheritance—an episode which only deepens the King's regret by reminding him of his childlessness.

The screams of the Vidūṣaka, who has been roughly handled by Mātali, awaken the king from his despair. This is necessary as Mātali explains "for bringing the king back to the realization that there are duties superior to private feeling." Indra requires his help in quelling the demons—the brood of Kālanemi.

We come to the last division of the play ; and from the gross and stifling atmosphere of the court and the capital, we escape into a divine and rarified atmosphere. What a contrast does it present with Kaṇva's hermitage. "We have there a hermit's daughter in the exuberance of youth, her two companions running over with playfulness. .the bee intoxicated with perfume. ." From this Eden of bliss, Śakuntalā, one of Eve's daughter, is exiled in disgrace. "But far different was the aspect of the other hermitage where Śakuntalā the mother of Bharata and the incarnation of goodness took refuge.... There a single boy fills the loving bosom of the entire forest-world ; he absorbs all the liveliness of the trees, creepers, flowers and foliage". Now as before when he was about to enter Kaṇva's Āśrama, the arm of the king throbs presaging his approaching fortune. He hears the matrons chiding the unruly boy and finds him dragging at the touselled mane of a lion's cub. The anagnorisis is the most skilfully and delicately managed of scenes. "What fire is in the child!" the king remarks. His heart goes out to him ; then as he stretches his hand, the marks of imperial birth are revealed. And then as the matrons say to him "Is not the Śākuntala lovely"—the most wonderful and effective use of word-play ever met with in literature—the child begins to look about for his mother Śakuntalā. When at last, in despair they call him to help them with the unruly boy, they are amazed at the "Speaking likeness" between him and the child, and tell him that the child belonged to Puru's line, that he had a heavenly nymph for mother who was cruelly abandoned by her heartless husband—a very beautiful instance of the use of irony in Kālidāsa—yet all this is not enough for the king. It is only when he touches the magic amulet, and is told by the matrons that none but his father or mother can touch it with impunity, that he realises that his dearest hope has come true. Then comes Śakuntalā on the scene who may be described in the words of Bhavabhūti as करुणस्य मूर्तिरथवा शरीरिणी विरहव्यथैव– "Pathos incarnate or the very pain of severence embodied;" the heart of the loving wife is full of understanding, of forgiveness; she blames only her fate which had been fixed for her by some former transgression of hers, and under the auspices of the divine pair Śakuntalā and her boy are united to Duṣyanta; and even if "there is one Paradise lost" yet there is "another Paradise regained."

Śākuntala, its inner meaning :

Starting with Goethe's words that the Śākuntala "blends together the young year's blossoms and the fruits of its decline, that it combines heaven and earth in one, Dr. Tagore remarks that the Śākuntala according to Goethe "contains the history of a development—the development of flower into fruit, of earth into heaven, of matter into spirit." The drama "was meant for translating the whole subject from one world to another—to elevate love from the sphere of physical beauty to the eternal heaven of moral beauty." "One sudden gust of youthful impulse had in a moment given her up to Duṣyanta, but that was not the true the full winning of her; the best means of winning is by devotion, by *Tapasya*. Therefore, the poet has made the two lovers undergo a long and austere *tapasya* that they may gain each other truly, eternally." "In this drama Kalidāsa has extinguished the volcanic fire of tumultuous passion by means of the tears of the penitent heart."

Here is a poet's interpretation of a poet, and howsoever beautiful it may be, it should not blind us to its central defect —it regards the first union of the lovers as a moral lapse. There is nothing to show that the poet ever regards the lovers as sinners, nor do any of the characters in the stage so regard it. On the other hand, every one commends the union and blesses it. Love is a beautiful passion of the soul, and youth a stuff that will not endure; do not, therefore, despise love; cherish it, and cherish the noble, and generous impulses of youth. Ah! but youth and love are not all; the gods are jealous; "like flies to wanton boys are we to the gods, they kill us for their sport." This tragic circumstance of our being is illustrated in the drama. Śakuntalā is happy and apparently secure; but suddenly a total reverse of fortune comes upon her—the calamity descending on her from the clouds with lightning swiftness. It makes us feel that man is blind and helpless, the plaything of an inscrutable power.

Character.

As already remarked, the poet has added to the meagre number of characters in the epic tale very largely from the grove, the city and the heavenly regions. It is remarkable that with great insight the poet gives but little part to the conventional Vidūṣaka in this play than in the others; he has absoutely very little place in so serious a play. In the Mālavikā, he plays a principal part and arranges all the intrigues; in the Vikramorvasiya, although he plays secondary role, yet his presence contributes greatly to the humour of the play and also to the complication of the plot. In the Śākuntala, however, he sinks into utter insignificance. Yes, he knows the love-affair in the grove; but addlepatted that he is, he believes what the king says at the moment, viz. that his love for Śakuntalā was all a joke—and never again speaks to the king about it. Here is irony—a literary expedient which Kālidāsa has very skilfully used in the play. Had he been present at the repudiation he would have spoken, and the tragedy averted. He is very cleverly dismissed on other business in Act II, as his presence would have spoilt the beautiful love idyll.

The two companions of Śakuntalā are drawn with delicate taste. How well are they differentiated, Anasūyā grave and sensible, Priyaṁvadā playful, vivacious, and yet both are equally devoted to Śakuntalā ; so also are the two pupils Śārangarava and Śāradvata skilfully distinguished—one proud and haughty, not afraid to rebuke the king severely, and the other more reserved and calm. Kaṇva, the loving hermit, and the motherly Gautamī, too, both brimful of affection for Śakuntalā are excellent creations. While the divine pair Mārica and Aditi are wonderfully contrasted with them with their solemn majesty, and with their unwearied contemplation of the world, intervening to set it right whenever necessary with disinterested zeal. " The small boy in the last act " as Ryder remarks "has magically become an individual in Kālidāsa's hands."

The fisherman and the policemen are drawn with no less skill in the opening scene of Act VI. They are drawn " raw from life " ; their unjust, overbearing conduct to the fisherman representing the spirit of those in office generally, who are made giddy by power.

Very grave injustice is done to Duṣyanta by representing him as a bee that ever seeks fresh honey. The fact that he had many wives in his harem, and therefore, as is natural, there are intrigues in the palace to win him and oust the rival from his affection does not necessarily show moral depravity when it is remembered that polygamy was so common in those days and is current to this day in India. Dhanamitra, the seafaring merchant was a rich man; " he must have many wives," Duṣyanta remarks. This shows that polygamy was quite an accepted fact in those days. Kālidāsa has taken very great pains to save him "from his epic shabbiness." He is a worthy hero, the ornament of the Purus, full of noble impulses, and careful to see that there is nothing in his conduct that is against the law. He is very brave and exerts himself nobly in the interest of his subjects. He is commended on all hands, by the hermits, by Kaṇva, by Mārica, the divine father of creation, and by the officers in the palace—and this is no mere flattery of the king. With scrupulous care does Kālidāsa show that he would not entertain any immoral thought about women. We have only to think of the apprehensions that filled his heart when he realised that Śakuntalā had already captured it. His intuition was infallible ; no unworthy thought would receive quarter in his mind. And it turns out that what he feared "as fire was the jewel of his desire." He relies upon the genial sense of youth. To him "love is an unerring light, and joy its own security." His later rejection of Śakuntalā also is not due to the fact that he despises her, but his fear that in accepting her whom he does not remember to have married, he would have committed an egregious sin.

And what words, will adequately describe the noblest and the loveliest of poetic creations the sweet Śakuntalā ? She "dominates the whole play. She is actually on the stage in five of the acts, and her spirit pervades the other two, the second and the sixth." "So noble a union of sweetness with strength is one of the miracles of art." Bred in the hermitage, amid the plants and trees, there is an innate simplicity and purity in her character. She yields to the impulse of love, and yet with a maiden's modesty would rather suffer in silence than speak of her passion. There is struggle in her soul "between deep bashfulness and strong self-expression." She is trustful ; that gives her strength in her distress—the rigid, tearless endurance of the blows of circumstance. She is forgiving, and kind to her husband, in spite of the cruellest breach of her confidence.

Her character grows under our very eyes—from the sweet loving girl she has been developed into "the model of a devoted wife, with her reserve, endurance of sorrow, and a life of rigid spiritual discipline." She has passed through great experiences of life—love, friendship, motherhood, most cruel humiliation and suspicion, and finally reunion with her husband. Like a flower meshed with the grey dew to the end she appears as a vision of sweetness, purity and strength.

The Title of the play.

Like the ornaments of Vasantsenā in the Mṛcchakatika, the signet ring has been used as a dominant motif in the play. In the first act Duṣyanta offers it to Śakuntalā's friend to redeem the debt she owes her ; and in the fourth act, after the curse of Durvāsas, when Anasūyā goes to appease his anger and he modifies his curse by saying that the spell shall break at the sight of some token of recognition, Priyaṃvadā tells us how the king at time of parting put the ring, engraved with his own name, in Śakuntalā's finger to remember him by ; and that will save Śakuntalā. Here Kālidāsa has most skilfully employed dramatic irony ; the well-meaning friends, with the desire to spare the feelings of Śakuntalā decide not to speak to any one of the episode of the curse, although towards the end of act IV they merely drop a hint by saying to Śakuntalā that should the king be slow to recognize her, she should show him the ring. Supposing they had explained, the tragedy of Śakuntalā's cruel rejection would well have been averted. "Our deeds are ours their ends none of our own." We know how the fatal ring fails Śakuntalā at the most critical moment in the court scene in the fifth act ; and in the opening scene of act VI we hear of its miraculous recovery from the maw of a carp-fish opened by the fisherman. At its sight, memory is revived, and Duṣyanta is now consumed with remorse. He reviles the ring ; but the Vidūṣaka consoles the king by pointing to the ring as one that shows that incredible meetings do take place. Finally in the seventh act when Śakuntalā sees the ring, the king tells her how at the sight of the ring his memory returned. He offers to put it on her finger, but Śakuntalā would not trust it; she would rather have the king wear it.

Thus it will be seen that this episode of the ring whose loss prevents the immediate recognition of Śakuntalā is very effectively conceived and woven into the texture of the play. Aptly, therefore, is the play given the name "Abhijñāna-Śākuntala."

Kālidāsa repeats himself.

If we compare the three plays of Kālidāsa, it will be seen how many incidents are repeated in the three plays; but in the Śākuntala these incidents are handled with far more perfect art. Thus the pretty idea of the king concealing himself and listening to the confidential talk of Śakuntalā and her friends is found in Act III of the Mālavikāgnimitra. When leaving Śakuntalā makes the pretext that her foot is pricked by a sharp blade of grass, and casts a stolen glance at the king; even so does Urvaśī in the Vikramorvaśīya pretend that her garment is caught in the branches to delay her going. Both express their love by letters. While Āyus has a peacock to play with, Bharata is given a clay peacock to induce him to give up his rough play with the lion's cub. The love-intrigues in the harem which figure so largely in the Vikramorśīya and Mālavikagnimitra are simply hinted at in the Śākuntala. Haṁsapadikā sings her song hinting at the king's inconstancy and queen Vasumatī in a jealous fit snatches the box of paint-brushes from Caturikā, the maid, who was taking them to the king. However, these are never brought on the stage. With true poetic insight Kālidāsa has avoided the temptation of bringing any other woman into competition with Śakuntalā.

Śākuntala, its recensions.

There is no wonder that several recensions of the play should have become current in India. Of these four are generally distinguished from one another, the Bengālī, Devanāgarī, Kāśmirī, and south Indian; but in point of fact we need take into account only two recensions the longer one being the Bengālī, with 221 stanzas with the commentaries of Śankara and Candraśekhara, and the Devanágarī with 194 stanzas with Rāghavabhatta's commentary; the Kāśmirī gives an introductory scene to act VII, but is no more than a combined version of these two, while the south Indian with the commentary of Kāṭayavema, closely follows the Devanāgarī. The text represented by Sir William Jone's translation as also that of Ryder is the Bengālī, and Ryder remarks "I find it hard to believe that any lesser artist could pad such a masterpiece and pad it all over, without making the fraud apparent on almost every page. The briefer version, on the other hand might easily grow out of the longer, either as an acting text, or as a schoolbook." This is also the view of Bollensen. Pischel lays stress on the more correct Prākrit of the Bengālī, but, as Keith points out, this argument from the Prākrit is not conclusive, for it may be due to the superior knowledge of the copyists in Bengal from whom the Bengālī version ultimately issued. Nothing conclusive can be said in regard to which of these recensions gives Kālidāsa's text correctly. However, the erotic passages in Act III in the Bengālī recensions are out of taste and mar the delicacy of the love-scene and as Weber points out, some of the Devanāgarī readings are distinctly better, and some of the Bengālī stanzas are mere repetitions of others found in both the versions. We are, therefore, inclined to give priority to the Devanāgarī text.

The law of inheritance.

From the VI act of the Śākuntala we get some idea of the law of inheritance prevailing in the days of Kālidāsa. The prime minister, the noble Piśuna, sends the following report of a case which he refers to the king for decision :—"A seafaring merchant named Dhanamitra has been lost in shipwreck. He dies childless, and his immense property becomes by law forfeited to the king". Now the king's reply is "As he had great riches, he must have several wives. Let inquiry be made. There may be a wife who is with child." And when he is told that one of his wives the daughter of a merchant from Sāketa is soon to become a mother, the king decides that the child shall receive the inheritance. The unborn child has a title to his father's property.

From this passage it is clear that in the days of Kālidāsa a widow was not entitled to inherit her husband's propery. The king directs an inquiry to be made, not whether there are widows of the merchant but whether there is a child in the womb which is entitled to its father's estate. The prime minister had simply inquired if there was a living child, and not whether a child was conceived, and thus a very nice point of law has been raised. This shows the poet's acquaintance with the laws prevailing in his time, and it follows, therefore, that in his days a widow was not entitled to her husband's property, though the right of the unborn child was admitted.

The widow's right to inherit as Prof. R. N. Apte shows, was gradually recognized. "Manu, Āpastamba and Vasiṣṭha do not recognise her as heir. Narada makes provision for her maintenance. .Bṛhaspati seems to admit her right for the first time. .Śaṅkha, Likhita and Yajñavalkya also admit her right. If this is the gradual development of the right of a widow, and this right is not recognized in the case before Duṣyanta, we may place Śākuntala before Bṛhaspati and after Manu or Āpastamba." So Prof. R. N. Apte concludes, that as the probable date of Bṛhaspati is the 1st century A.D. Kālidāsa must be placed before this date—a conclusion which accords well with the date of Kālidāsa already suggested.

The law of theft.

The opening scene of the VI act is a scene of rollicking humour in Kālidāsa. The fisherman is handcuffed and led by two guards and the officer; for they find the king's signet-ring in his possession. The punishment for theft is death and already the fingers of one of the guards are itching to kill this cutpurse. Thus, it would appear, that for theft of a gem there was capital punishment in Kālidāsa's days. So also in the Vikramorvaśīya the vulture who has carried away the Saṅgamanīya jewel is spoken of as आत्मनो वधमाहर्ता विहगतस्करः। "The winged thief that courts his own death."

Prof. Apte observes: "Tracing the law of theft from the times of Manu down to those of Yājñavalkya we find the punishment for theft of a gem has gradually been reduced from death to fine". Manu and Āpastamba say that such an offender shall suffer capital punishment. Bṛhaspati recommends that a fine shall be imposed equal to the value of the property stolen, or double the amount, or the thief shall be executed to prevent the repetition of the offence. Yājñavalkya does not give any hard and fast rules, and says that capital punishment may be inflicted, but all circumstances of time, place, age and health of the offender should be taken into consideration in giving the punishment. Here again there is a gradual tendency to lighten the punishment from death in the times of Manu and Āpastamba to an option between fine and death according to circumstances in the days of Bṛhaspati. "It appears therefore, that the law of our poet's days had not reached this stage of which the representative is the smṛti of Bṛhaspati."

अभिज्ञानशाकुन्तलम् ।

ABHIJÑĀNAŚĀKUNTALA

अथ

अभिज्ञानशाकुन्तलम् ।

या सृष्टिः स्रष्टुराद्या वहति विधिहुतं या हविर्या च होत्री
ये द्वे कालं विधत्तः श्रुतिविषयगुणा या स्थिता व्याप्य विश्वम् ।
यामाहुः सर्वबीजप्रकृतिरिति यया प्राणिनः प्राणवन्तः
प्रत्यक्षाभिः प्रपन्नस्तनुभिरवतु वस्ताभिरष्टाभिरीशः ॥ १ ॥

(नान्द्यन्ते)

सूत्रधारः—(नेपथ्याभिमुखमवलोक्य ।) आर्ये, यदि नेपथ्यविधानमवसितम्, इतस्तावदागम्यताम् ।

(प्रविश्य)

नटी—अज्जउत्त, इयं म्हि । आणवेदु अज्जो को णिओओ अणुचिट्ठीअदु त्ति । आर्यपुत्र, इयमस्मि । आज्ञापयत्वार्यः को नियोगोऽनुष्ठीयतामिति ।

सूत्रधारः—आर्ये, अभिरूपभूयिष्ठा परिषदियम् । अद्य खलु कालिदासग्रथितवस्तुना नवेनाभिज्ञानशाकुन्तलाख्येन नाटकेनोपस्थातव्यमस्माभिः । तत्प्रतिपात्रमाधीयतां यत्नः ।

नटी—सुविहिदप्पओअदाए अज्जस्स ण किं पि परिहाइस्सदि ।
सुविहितप्रयोगतयार्यस्य न किमपि परिहास्यते ।

सूत्रधारः—आर्ये, कथयामि ते भूतार्थम् ।

आ परितोषाद्विदुषां न साधु मन्ये प्रयोगविज्ञानम् ।
बलवदपि शिक्षितानामात्मन्यप्रत्ययं चेतः ॥ २ ॥

ABHIJÑĀNAŚĀKUNTALA

That which is the first creation of the Creator ; that which bears the offering made according to due rites ; that which is the offerer ; those two which make time ; that which pervades all space, having for its quality what is perceived by the ear ; that which is the womb of all seeds ; that by which all living beings breathe ; endowed with these eight visible forms, may the supreme Lord protect you ! (1)

(*At the end of the benediction*)

THE STAGE-DIRECTOR (*Looking towards the dressing-room*). My lady, if you have finished with your dressing, pray, come here.

(*Entering*)

AN ACTRESS. Here I am, my lord ; let my lord direct what I am to do.

STAGE-DIRECTOR. My lady, this audience is for the most part composed of learned men. To-day, we are indeed to entertain them with a new play, composed by Kālidāsa ; so please bestow great care on every part.

ACTRESS. As your arrangements are well-made, nothing will be wanting.

STAGE-DIRECTOR. My lady, I will tell you the truth :

Until the wise are satisfied, I cannot feel that my knowledge of acting is sound ; the mind of even the best-trained (persons) is loth to trust itself. (2)

नटी—अज्ज, एवं णेदम्। अणन्तरकरणिज्जं दाव अज्जो आणवेदु। आर्य, एवमेतत्। अनन्तरकरणीयं तावदार्य आज्ञापयतु।

सूत्रधारः—किमन्यदस्याः परिषदः श्रुतिप्रसादनतः। तदिममेव तावदचिरप्रवृत्तमुपभोगक्षमं ग्रीष्मसमयमधिकृत्य गीयताम्। संप्रति हि

सुभगसलिलावगाहाः पाटलसंसर्गसुरभिवनवाताः।
प्रच्छायसुलभनिद्रा दिवसाः परिणामरमणीयाः॥ ३॥

नटी—तह। तथा। (इति गायति।)

ईसीसिचुम्बिआइं भमरेहिं सुउमारकेसरसिहाइं।
ओदंसयन्ति दअमाणा पमदाओ सिरीसकुसुमाइं॥ ४॥

ईषदीषच्चुम्बितानि भ्रमरैः सुकुमारकेसरशिखानि।
अवतंसयन्ति दयमानाः प्रमदाः शिरीषकुसुमानि॥ ४॥

सूत्रधारः—आर्ये, साधु गीतम्। अहो रागबद्धचित्तवृत्तिरालिखित इव सर्वतो रङ्गः। तदिदानीं कतमत्प्रकरणमाश्रित्यैनमाराधयामः।

नटी—णं अज्जमिस्सेहिं पढमं एव्व आणत्तं अहिण्णाणसउन्दलं णाम अपुव्वं णाडअं पओएण अधिकरीअदुत्ति। नन्वार्यमिश्रैः प्रथममेवाज्ञसमभिज्ञानशाकुन्तलं नामापूर्वं नाटकं प्रयोगेणाधिक्रियतामिति।

सूत्रधारः—आर्ये, सम्यगनुबोधितोऽस्मि। अस्मिन्क्षणे विस्मृतं खलु मया। कुतः।

तवास्मि गीतरागेण हारिणा प्रसभं हृतः।
एष राजेव दुष्यन्तः सारङ्गेणातिरंहसा॥ ५॥

(निष्क्रान्तौ।)

इति प्रस्तावना।

ACTRESS. So it is. Let my lord now command what is to be done next.

STAGE-DIRECTOR. What other than to please the ears of this audience? Therefore, sing about this very summer-season, (so) enjoyable, which has just begun. For now,

> Come the days so delightful towards their close, when a plunge in water is so grateful; when the fresh-breeze is fragrant from contact with the Pāṭala flower; and when sleep is easily induced in deep shady places. (3)

ACTRESS. Right. (*Sings.*)

> Tender-hearted ladies make ear-ornaments of the Śirīṣa-blossoms with delicate filament-points, that are very gently kissed by bees. (4)

STAGE-DIRECTOR. Well-sung, my lady. The theatre on all sides has its mental activity arrested by your melody and sits as if painted in a picture. So now what play shall we give to entertain them?

ACTRESS. Why, the noble audience has already given the command that a new play called Abhijñāna-Śākuntala should be staged.

STAGE-DIRECTOR. My lady, well have you reminded me. For the moment I had quite forgotten. For,

> I was forcibly carried away by the charming melody of your song like king Duṣyanta here by the very fleet deer. (5)

(*Exeunt.*)

Here ends the Prologue

(ततः प्रविशति मृगानुसारी सशरचापहस्तो राजा रथेन सूतश्च ।)

सूतः—(राजानं मृगं चावलोक्य ।) आयुष्मन्,

कृष्णसारे ददच्चक्षुस्त्वयि चाधिज्यकार्मुके ।
मृगानुसारिणं साक्षात्पश्यामीव पिनाकिनम् ॥ ६ ॥

राजा—सूत, दूरममुना सारङ्गेण वयमाकृष्टाः । अयं पुनरिदानीमपि

ग्रीवाभङ्गाभिरामं मुहुरनुपतति स्यन्दने बद्धदृष्टिः
पश्चार्धेन प्रविष्टः शरपतनभयाद्भूयसा पूर्वकायम् ।
दर्भैरर्धावलीढैः श्रमविवृतमुखभ्रंशिभिः कीर्णवर्त्मा
पश्योदग्रप्लुतत्वाद्वियति बहुतरं स्तोकमुर्व्यां प्रयाति ॥ ७ ॥

(सविस्मयम् ।) कथमनुपतत एव मे प्रयत्नप्रेक्षणीयः संवृत्तः ।

सूतः—आयुष्मन्, उद्घातिनी भूमिरिति मया रश्मिसंयमनाद्रथस्य मन्दीकृतो वेगः । तेन मृग एष विप्रकृष्टान्तरः संवृत्तः । संप्रति समदेशवर्तिनस्ते न दुरासदो भविष्यति ।

राजा—तेन हि मुच्यन्तामभीशवः ।

सूतः—यदाज्ञापयत्यायुष्मान् । (रथवेगं निरूप्य) आयुष्मन्, पश्य पश्य ।

मुक्तेषु रश्मिषु निरायतपूर्वकाया
निष्कम्पचामरशिखा निभृतोर्ध्वकर्णाः ।

(Then enter king in a chariot, pursuing an antelope, bow and arrow in hand, and his charioteer.)

CHARIOTEER *(Looking at the king and the antelope)*. O long-lived one,

When I cast my eye on that black antelope and on you with your braced bow, I see (before me) as it were the Pināka-wielder in person, chasing a deer. (6)

KING. Charioteer, the antelope has given us a long chase. Even now he from time to time,

Looking back gracefully by the bending of his neck, at the car which follows him; now, through fear of a descending shaft, by his haunches drawing himself mostly into the fore-part of his body, strewing his track with grass, half-chewed, which drops from his mouth, kept open from exhaustion, mark, how by reason of his lofty boundings, he moves much more through the air, and but lightly skims the ground. (7)

(Wonderingly). How now the deer is scarce discernible to me though I have been pursuing him?

CHARIOTEER. Long-lived one, seeing that the ground was uneven, I pulled up the reins and slackened the speed of the chariot. But now that you are on level ground, you will not find it difficult to overtake him.

KING. Well, then, loosen the reins.

CHARIOTEER. As the long-lived one commands.

(Exhibiting by gesticulation the speed of the car). Long-lived one! look! look!

the reins being loosed, the chariot-horses run along as if impatient of the speed of the deer,

आत्मोद्धतैरपि रजोभिरलङ्घनीया
धावन्त्यमी मृगजवाक्षमयेव रथ्याः ॥ ८ ॥

राजा—(सहर्षम् ।) सत्यम् । अतीत्य हरितो हरींश्च वर्तन्ते वाजिनः । तथा हि

यदालोके सूक्ष्मं व्रजति सहसा तद्विपुलतां
यदर्धे विच्छिन्नं भवति कृतसंधानमिव तत् ।
प्रकृत्या यद्वक्रं तदपि समरेखं नयनयो-
र्न मे दूरे किंचित्क्षणमपि न पार्श्वे रथजवात् ॥ ९ ॥

सूत, पश्यैनं व्यापाद्यमानम् । (इति शरसंधानं नाटयति ।)

(नेपथ्ये ।)

भो भो राजन्, आश्रममृगोऽयं न हन्तव्यो न हन्तव्यः ।

सूतः—(आकर्ण्यावलोक्य च ।) आयुष्मन्, अस्य खलु ते बाणपथवर्तिनः कृष्णसारस्यान्तरे तपस्विन उपस्थिताः ।

राजा—(ससंभ्रमम् ।) तेन हि प्रगृह्यन्तां वाजिनः ।

सूतः—तथा । (इति रथं स्थापयति ।)

(ततः प्रविशत्यात्मना तृतीयो वैखानसः ।)

वैखानसः—(हस्तमुद्यम्य ।) राजन्, आश्रममृगोऽयं न हन्तव्यो न हन्तव्यः ।

न खलु न खलु बाणः सन्निपात्योऽयमस्मिन्
मृदुनि मृगशरीरे पुष्पराशाविवाग्निः ।
क्व बत हरिणकानां जीवितं चातिलोलं
क्व च निशितनिपाताः वज्रसाराः शरास्ते ॥ १० ॥

with the fore-part of their bodies well stretched out, with the chowrie-crests motionless, with ears erect and steady, not to be overtaken even by the dust that they themselves raise. (8)

KING (*With joy*). Truly, the horses are outstripping the horses of the sun and those of Indra.

For,

Objects which to my sight appeared minute suddenly become large; what was really divided, seems united; and what was in truth bent appears straight to my eyes. So swift the motion of the chariot, that nothing even for a moment seems either near or distant. (9)

CHARIOTEER. Behold him as I kill him. (*Acts fixing an arrow in his bowstring.*)

(*Behind the scenes*)

O king, that is a deer of the hermitage : he must not be slain, he must not be slain.

CHARIOTEER (*Listening and looking*). Long-lived one, here have hermits advanced between you and the antelope that presents a fair mark for your arrows.

KING (*Hastily*). Well, then, rein in the horses.

CHARIOTEER. Very well. (*Stops the chariot.*)

(*Then enter a hermit with two others.*)

HERMIT (*Raising his hand*). This is a deer of the hermitage; this must not be slain, this must not be slain.

Not indeed, not indeed, must this arrow be allowed to fall upon this tender body of the deer, like fire upon a heap of flowers. Compared with thy sharp-falling adamantine shafts, how weak must be the very frail existence of fawns! (10)

तत्साधुकृतसंधानं प्रतिसंहर सायकम् ।
आर्तत्राणाय वः शस्त्रं न प्रहर्तुमनागसि ॥ ११ ॥

राजा—एष प्रतिसंहृतः । (इति यथोक्तं करोति ।)

वैखानसः—सदृशमेतत्पुरुवंशप्रदीपस्य भवतः ।

जन्म यस्य पुरोर्वंशे युक्तरूपमिदं तव ।
पुत्रमेवंगुणोपेतं चक्रवर्तिनमाप्नुहि ॥ १२ ॥

इतरौ—(बाहू उद्यम्य ।) सर्वथा चक्रवर्तिनं पुत्रमाप्नुहि ।

राजा—(सप्रणामम् ।) प्रतिगृहीतम् ।

वैखानसः—राजन्, समिदाहरणाय प्रस्थिता वयम् । एष खलु कण्वस्य कुलपतेरनुमालिनीतीरमाश्रमो दृश्यते । न चेदन्यकार्यातिपातः, तत्प्रविश्य प्रतिगृह्यतामातिथेयः सत्कारः । अपि च ।

रम्यास्तपोधनानां प्रतिहतविघ्नाः क्रियाः समवलोक्य ।
ज्ञास्यसि कियद्भुजो मे रक्षति मौर्वीकिणाङ्क इति ॥ १३ ॥

राजा—अपि संनिहितोऽत्र कुलपतिः ।

वैखानसः—इदानीमेव दुहितरं शकुन्तलामतिथिसत्काराय नियुज्य दैवमस्याः प्रतिकूलं शमयितुं सोमतीर्थं गतः ।

राजा—भवतु । तामेव द्रक्ष्यामि । सा खलु विदितभक्तिं मां महर्षेः कथयिष्यति ।

वैखानसः—साधयामस्तावत् । (इति सशिष्यो निष्क्रान्तः ।)

राजा—सूत, चोदयाश्वान् । पुण्याश्रमदर्शनेन तावदात्मानं पुनीमहे ।

Replace, therefore, thy well-aimed arrow. Thy weapon is designed for the relief of the distressed, not for the destruction of the guiltless. (11)

KING. Well, it is replaced. (*Does as said.*)

HERMIT. This is worthy of thee—the light of the race of Puru.

This is exceedingly worthy of thee, who art descended from Puru. Mayest thou have a son, adorned with like virtues, sovereign of the world. (12)

OTHERS (*Raising their hands*). Oh, by all means, mayest thou have a son, the sovereign of the world !

KING (*Bowing*). It is accepted.

HERMIT. King, we have set out to collect wood for solemn rites. And this, on the bank of the Mālinī, is, in truth, the religious domicile of the great sage Kaṇva. If no other duty is interfered with, then enter and accept the rights of hospitality. And, moreover,

Beholding the pleasing rites of those whose wealth is their piety, performed without any hindrances, thou wilt know how much thy arm marked with the scar of the bow-string defends. (13)

KING. Is the patriarch of the family at home ?

HERMIT. Just now, charging his daughter Śakuntalā to perform the rights of hospitality, he is gone to Somatīrtha, in hopes of deprecating her adverse fate.

KING. Well, I will see her ; and she, having observed my devotion, will report it to the venerable sage.

HERMIT. Well, we will now depart. (*Exit with his pupils.*)

KING. Charioteer, drive on the horses. By visit-

सूतः—यदाज्ञापयत्यायुष्मान्। (इति भूयो रथवेगं निरूपयति।)

राजाः—(समन्तादवलोक्य।) सूत, अकथितोऽपि ज्ञायत एव यथायमाभोगस्तपोवनस्येति।

सूतः—कथमिव।

राजा—किं न पश्यति भवान्। इह हि

नीवाराः शुकगर्भकोटरमुखभ्रष्टास्तरूणामधः
प्रस्निग्धाः क्वचिदिङ्गुदीफलभिदः सूच्यन्त एवोपलाः।
विश्वासोपगमादभिन्नगतयः शब्दं सहन्ते मृगा-
स्तोयाधारपथाश्च वल्कलशिखानिष्यन्दरेखाङ्किताः ॥१४॥

अपि च।

कुल्यांभोभिः पवनचपलैः शाखिनो धौतमूला
भिन्नो रागः किसलयरुचामाज्यधूमोद्गमेन।
एते चार्वागुपवनभुवि च्छिन्नदर्भाङ्कुरायां
नष्टाशङ्का हरिणशिशवो मन्दमन्दं चरन्ति ॥ १५ ॥

सूतः—सर्वमुपपन्नम्।

राजा—(स्तोकमन्तरं गत्वा।) तपोवननिवासिनामुपरोधो मा भूत्। अत्रैव रथं स्थापय। यावदवतरामि।

सूतः—धृताः प्रग्रहाः। अवतरत्वायुष्मान्।

ing the abode of holiness, we shall purify ourselves.

CHARIOTEER. As the long-lived one commands.

(*Again gesticulates swift movement of the chariot.*)

KING (*Looking around*). Charioteer, even without being told, it may be known indeed that these are the precincts of the sacred grove.

CHARIOTEER. How indeed?

KING. Don't you see? For here,

Under (yonder) trees are the grains of wild rice fallen from the openings of the hollow-trunks filled with parrots; in other places are seen the polished stones which have bruised the fruit of the Ingudī; and the fawns, too, from having acquired confidence bear the sound (of our approach) without varying their course; and the paths of the reservoirs are marked with lines by the drippings from the fringes of bark-garments. (14)

Moreover,

The roots of yon trees are bathed in the waters of canals which quiver as the wind plays upon them; the glowing lustre of the fresh leaves is partially obscured by the smoke that rises from (oblations of) clarified butter; and here in front, these young fawns are leisurely grazing without fear on the garden-lawns where the sprouts of Darbha-grass have been cut away. (15)

CHARIOTEER. All is indeed true.

KING (*Going a little way*). Let the dwellers of the sacred grove be not disturbed. Stop the chariot just here, that I may descend.

CHARIOTEER. The reins are held in. Let the long-

राजा—(अवतीर्यात्मानमवलोक्य च ।) सूत, विनीतवेषेण प्रवेष्टव्यानि तपोवनानि नाम । इदं तावद्गृह्यताम् । (इति सूतस्याभरणानि धनुश्चोपनीय ।) सूत, यावदाश्रमवासिनः प्रत्यवेक्ष्याहमुपावर्ते तावदार्द्रपृष्ठाः क्रियन्तां वाजिनः ।

सूतः—तथा । (इति निष्क्रान्तः ।)

राजा—(परिक्रम्यावलोक्य च ।) इदमाश्रमद्वारम् । यावत्प्रविशामि । (प्रविश्य । निमित्तं सूचयन् ।)

शान्तमिदमाश्रमपदं स्फुरति च बाहुः कुतः फलमिहास्य ।
अथवा भवितव्यानां द्वाराणि भवन्ति सर्वत्र ॥ १६ ॥

(नेपथ्ये ।)

इदो इदो सहीओ । इत इतः सख्यौ ।

राजा—(कर्णं दत्वा ।) अये, दक्षिणेन वृक्षवाटिकामालाप इव श्रूयते । यावदग्रे गच्छामि । (परिक्रम्यावलोक्य च ।) अये, एतास्तपस्विकन्यकाः स्वप्रमाणानुरूपैः सेचनघटैर्बालपादपेभ्यः पयो दातुमित एवाभिवर्तन्ते । (निपुणं निरूप्य ।) अहो, मधुरमासां दर्शनम् ।

शुद्धान्तदुर्लभमिदं वपुराश्रमवासिनो यदि जनस्य ।
दूरीकृताः खलु गुणैरुद्यानलता वनलताभिः ॥ १७ ॥

यावदिमां छायामाश्रित्य प्रतिपालयामि । (इति विलोकयन्स्थितः ।)

lived one descend.

KING (*Having descended, and looking at himself*). Charioteer, sacred groves must indeed be entered in humble habiliments; therefore take these. (*Giving his ornaments and bow to the charioteer*). Charioteer, by the time I return after visiting the inmates of this holy sanctuary, let the horses be washed and refreshed.

CHARIOTEER. Very well. (*Exit.*)

KING (*Walking round and looking*). This is the entrance to the hermitage. Let me enter. (*Entering and acting as if he perceived an omen*).

> Tranquil is this hermitage, and yet my arm throbs; whence can there rise the fruit of this in such a place? But yet the gates of predestined events are in all places open. (16)

(*Behind the scenes*)

Come hither, my friends, come hither.

KING (*Listening*). Ha! I seem to hear voices to the right of the grove of trees. So I will proceed. (*Walking about and observing*). There are some damsels belonging to the hermits' family coming in this direction, to water the young plants from water-pots of different sizes proportioned to their strength. (*Eyeing them closely*) How lovely they look;

> If such the beauty of maids, who dwell in woodland retreats, the like of which is not easily to be found in the recesses of a palace, then indeed are the garden-plants well surpassed in merit by the woodland creepers. (17)

So I will stand in this shade and await (them).

(*He stands gazing at them.*)

[ततः प्रविशति यथोक्तव्यापारा सह सखीभ्यां शकुन्तला ।]

शकुन्तला—इदो इदो सहीओ । इत इतः सख्यौ ।

अनसूया—हला सउन्दले, तुवत्तो वि तादकस्सवस्स अस्समरुक्खआ पिअदरत्ति तक्केमि । जेण णोमालिआकुसुमपेलवा वि तुमं एदाणं आलवालपूरणे णिउत्ता । हला शकुन्तले, त्वत्तोऽपि तातकाश्यपस्याश्रमवृक्षकाः प्रियतरा इति तर्कयामि । येन नवमालिकाकुसुमपेलवा त्वमप्येतेषामालवालपूरणे नियुक्ता ।

शकुन्तला—ण केअलं तादणिओओ एव्व । अत्थि मे सोदरसिणेहो वि एदेसु । (इति वृक्षसेचनं रूपयति ।) न केवलं तातनियोग एव । अस्ति मे सोदरस्नेहोऽप्येतेषु ।

राजा—कथमियं सा कण्वदुहिता । असाधुदर्शी खलु तत्रभवान्काश्यपः, य इमामाश्रमधर्मे नियुङ्क्ते ।

इदं किलाव्याजमनोहरं वपु-
स्तपःक्षमं साधयितुं य इच्छति ।
ध्रुवं स नीलोत्पलपत्रधारया
शमीलतां छेत्तुमृषिर्व्यवस्यति ॥ १८ ॥

भवतु । पादपान्तरित एव विश्वस्तां तावदेनां पश्यामि । (इति तथा करोति ।)

शकुन्तला—सहि अणसूए, अदिपिणद्धेण वक्कलेण पिअंवदाए णिअन्तिदम्हि । सिढिलेहि दाव णं । सखि अनसूये, अतिपिनद्धेन वल्कलेन प्रियंवदया नियन्त्रितास्मि । शिथिलय तावदेतत् ।

अनसूया—तह । (इति शिथिलयति ।) तथा ।

प्रियंवदा—(सहासम् ।) **एत्थ पओहरवित्थारइत्तअं अत्तणो जोव्वणं उवालह । मं किं उवालम्भेसि ।** अत्र पयोधरविस्तारयितृ आत्मनो यौवनमुपालभस्व । मां किमुपालभसे ।

(*Then enter Sakuntalā occupied in the manner described and her two friends.*)

ŚAKUNTALĀ. Come hither, my friends, come hither.

ANASŪYĀ. Friend Śakuntalā, I think the trees in the hermitage are dearer to father Kāśyapa than your own self, since he has appointed even you, who are soft like a Navamālikā flower, to fill their basins.

ŚAKUNTALĀ. It is not only in obedience to our father, but I really feel the affection of a sister for them.

(*Acts watering the plant.*)

KING. How ! Is this Kaṇava's daughter ? Truly the venerable Kāśyapa has but little discrimination, since he has allotted her the duties of the hermitage.

> The sage who would make this artlessly-charming form capable of enduring penance would attempt, I suppose, to cleave the Śamī tree with the edge of the blue lotus-leaf. (18)

Well, concealed by the trees even as I am, I will gaze on her without diminishing her confidence. (*Does so.*)

ŚAKUNTALĀ. Friend Anasūyā, I feel quite tied down by the bark-garment which Priyaṁvadā has too tightly fastened. Pray loosen it.

ANASŪYĀ. Very well. (*Loosens it.*)

PRIYAṀVADĀ (*Laughing*). In this, you better revile your youthful prime which gives your bosom such a swell ; why do you blame me.

राजा—सम्यगियमाह ।

इदमुपहितसूक्ष्मग्रन्थिना स्कन्धदेशे
स्तनयुगपरिणाहाच्छादिना वल्कलेन ।
वपुरभिनवमस्याः पुष्यति स्वां न शोभां
कुसुममिव पिनद्धं पाण्डुपत्रोदरेण ॥ १९ ॥

अथवा काममननुरूपमस्या वपुषो वल्कलं न पुनरलंकारश्रियं न पुष्यति । कुतः ।

सरसिजमनुविद्धं शैवलेनापि रम्यं
मलिनमपि हिमांशोर्लक्ष्म लक्ष्मीं तनोति ।
इयमधिकमनोज्ञा वल्कलेनापि तन्वी
किमिव हि मधुराणां मण्डनं नाकृतीनाम् ॥ २० ॥

शकुन्तला—(अग्रतोऽवलोक्य ।) एसो वादेरिदपल्लवङ्गुलीहिं तुवरेदि विअ मं केसररुक्खओ । जाव णं संभावेमि । (इति परिक्रामति ।) एष वातेरितपल्लवाङ्गुलीभिस्त्वरयतीव मां केसरवृक्षकः । यावदेनं संभावयामि ।

प्रियंवदा—हला सउन्दले एत्थ एव्व दाव मुहुत्तअं चिट्ठ । हला शकुन्तले, अत्रैव तावन्मुहूर्तं तिष्ठ ।

शकुन्तला—किंणिमित्तं । किंनिमित्तम् ।

प्रियंवदा—जाव तुए उवगदाए लदासणाधो विअ अअं केसररुक्खओ पडिभादि । यावत्त्वयोपगतया लतासनाथ इवायं केसरवृक्षकः प्रतिभाति ।

शकुन्तला—अदो क्खु पिअंवदा सि तुमं । अतः खलु प्रियंवदासि त्वम् ।

राजा—प्रियमपि तथ्यमाह शकुन्तलां प्रियंवदा । अस्याः खलु

अधरः किसलयरागः कोमलविटपानुकारिणौ बाहू ।
कुसुममिव लोभनीयं यौवनमङ्गेषु संनद्धम् ॥ २१ ॥

KING. She speaks well.

This her youthful body, by reason of the bark garment tied with delicate knots upon the shoulder, and covering the expanse of her twin breasts, does not exhibit its own charms, like a flower enfolded by a pale leaf. (19)

Or rather, granted that the bark-garment suits but ill her figure, yet it really does possess the charm of an ornament. For,

The lotus, though moss may overlay it, is, nevertheless, beautiful ; the spot on the moon, for all its darkness, heightens the charm of the moon ; this slender (maiden) is more lovely even in her dress of bark : for what indeed is not an embellishment of sweet forms ? (20)

ŚAKUNTALĀ (*Looking before her*). This Kesara-tree with its fingers of leaves, which the gale gently agitates, bids me hasten as it were (towards it). I will just attend to it. (*Moves about.*)

PRIYAMVADĀ. Friend Śakuntalā, just stand where you are for a moment.

ŚAKUNTALĀ. Why ?

PRIYAṀVADĀ. For, with you standing near it, the Kesara appears as though possessed of a creeper.

ŚAKUNTALĀ. Hence indeed are you properly named Priyaṁvadā.

KING. Though agreeable, still it is the truth which Priyaṁvadā says to Śakuntalā.

Truly, her lower lip glows like a tender leaf, her arms resemble flexible stalks. And youth, bewitching like a blossom, shines in all her lineaments. (21)

अनसूया—हला सउन्दले, इअं सअंवरवहू सहआरस्स तुए किदणामहेआ वणजोसिणित्ति णोमालिआ। णं विसुमरिदा सि। हला शकुन्तले, इयं स्वयंवरवधूः सहकारस्य त्वया कृतनामधेया वनज्योत्स्नेति नवमालिका। एनां विस्मृतवत्यसि।

शकुन्तला—तदा अत्ताणं वि विसुमरिस्सं। (लतामुपेत्यावलोक्य च सहर्षम्।) हला, रमणीए क्खु काले इमस्स लदापाअवमिधुणस्स वइअरो संवुत्तो। णवकुसुमजोव्वणा वणजोसिणी, बद्धपल्लवदाए उवभोअक्खमो सहआरो। (इति पश्यन्ती तिष्ठति।) तदात्मानमपि विस्मरिष्यामि। हला, रमणीये खलु काल एतस्य लतापादपमिथुनस्य व्यतिकरः संवृत्तः। नवकुसुमयौवना वनज्योत्स्ना, स्निग्धपल्लवतयोपभोगक्षमः सहकारः।

प्रियंवदा—(सस्मितम्।) अणसूए, जाणासि किंणिमित्तं सउन्दला वणजोसिणिं अदिमेत्तं पेक्खदित्ति। अनसूये, जानासि किंनिमित्तं शकुन्तला वनज्योत्स्नामतिमात्रं पश्यतीति।

अनसूया—ण क्खु विभावेमि। कहेहि। न खलु विभावयामि। कथय।

प्रियंवदा—जधा वणजोसिणी अणुरूवेण पाअवेण संगदा अवि णाम एव्वं अहं वि अत्तणो अणुरूवं वरं लहेअंति। यथा वनज्योत्स्नानुरूपेण पादपेन संगता, अपि नामैवमहमप्यात्मनोऽनुरूपं वरं लभेयेति।

शकुन्तला—एसो णूणं तुह अत्तगदो मणोरधो। (इति कलशमावर्जयति।) एष नूनं तवात्मगतो मनोरथः।

राजा—अपि नाम कुलपतेरियमसवर्णक्षेत्रसंभवा स्यात्। अथवा कृतं संदेहेन।

असंशयं क्षत्रपरिग्रहक्षमा
 यदार्यमस्यामभिलाषि मे मनः।
सतां हि संदेहपदेषु वस्तुषु
 प्रमाणमन्तःकरणप्रवृत्तयः॥ २२॥

तथापि तत्त्वत एनामुपलप्स्ये।

Anasūyā. Oh, Śakuntalā! Here is the Navamālikā, named by you the Light of the Grove, the self-elected bride of the mango tree. Have you forgotten her?

ŚAKUNTALĀ. Then I shall forget even my own self! (*Approaching the creeper and looking at it*). Friend, at a charming season, indeed, has the union between the pair—the creeper and the tree—taken place. Vanajyotsnā shows her youth in her fresh blossoms; and the Sahakāra his readiness to enjoy, in his sprouting young leaves.

PRIYAMVADĀ (*Smiling*). Do you know, my Anasūyā, why Śakuntalā is gazing so intently at Vanajyotsnā?

ANASŪYĀ. No, I cannot guess. Pray, tell me.

PRIYAMVADĀ. "As the Vanajyotsnā is united to a suitable tree, thus, may I, too, hope for a bridegroom to my mind."

ŚAKUNTALĀ. This is, indeed what you want for yourself.

(*She tips her water-pot.*)

KING. May I hope that she is the daughter of the patriarch by a wife of a different caste? But have done with doubt.

> Surely, she cannot but be fit to be wedded to a Kṣatriya, since my noble soul has longing towards her: for in matters beset with doubts, the promptings of the heart are to the good an authoritative guide. (22)

Nevertheless, I will ascertain the truth about her.

शकुन्तला—(ससंभ्रमम् ।) अम्मो । सलिलसेअसंभमुग्गदो णोमालिअं उज्झिअ वअणं मे महुअरो अहिवट्टइ । (इति भ्रमरबाधां रूपयति ।) अम्मो । सलिलसेकसंभ्रमोद्गतो नवमालिकामुज्झित्वा वदनं मे मधुकरोऽभिवर्तते ।

राजा—(सस्पृहं विलोक्य ।)

यतो यतः षट्चरणोऽभिवर्तते
ततस्ततः प्रेरितलोललोचना ।
विवर्तितभ्रूरियमद्य शिक्षते
भयादकामापि हि दृष्टिविभ्रमम् ॥ २३ ॥

अपि च । (सासूयमिव ।)

चलापाङ्गां दृष्टिं स्पृशसि बहुशो वेपथुमतीं
रहस्याख्यायीव स्वनसि मृदु कर्णान्तिकचरः ।
करौ व्याधुन्वत्याः पिबसि रतिसर्वस्वमधरं
वयं तत्त्वान्वेषान्मधुकर हतास्त्वं खलु कृती ॥ २४ ॥

शकुन्तला—ण एसो धिट्ठो विरमदि । अण्णदो गमिस्सं । (पदान्तरे स्थित्वा सदृष्टिक्षेपम् ।) कधं इदो वि आअच्छदि । हला, परित्ताअध मं इमिणा दुव्विणीदेण दुट्ठमहुअरेण अहिहूअमाणं । न एष धृष्टो विरमति । अन्यतो गमिष्यामि । कथमितोऽप्यागच्छति । हला, परित्रायेथां मामनेन दुर्विनीतेन दुष्टमधुकरेणाभिभूयमानाम् ।

उभे—(सस्मितम् ।) काओ अम्हे परित्तादुं । दुस्सन्दं अक्कन्द । राअरक्खिदव्वाइं तवोवणाइं णाम । के आवां परित्रातुम् । दुष्यन्तमाक्रन्द । राजरक्षितव्यानि तपोवनानि नाम ।

राजा—अवसरोऽयमात्मानं प्रकाशयितुम् । न भेतव्यं (इत्यर्धोक्ते । स्वगतम् ।) राजभावस्त्वभिज्ञातो भवेत् । भवतु । एवं तावदभिधास्ये ।

शकुन्तला—(पदान्तरे स्थित्वा । सदृष्टिक्षेपम् ।) कधं इदोवि मं अणुसरदि । कथमितोऽपि मामनुसरति ।

ŚAKUNTALĀ (*Excitedly*). Ah! Rising through the disturbance caused by the sprinkling of water, a bee has left the Navamālikā and is fluttering round my face.

(*She shows herself annoyed by the bee.*)

KING (*Looking longingly*).

In whichever direction the bee turns, in that direction she turns her rolling eyes. Arching her brows, she is learning to day coquettish play of her eyes through fright (only) and not from love. (23)

Moreover, (*A bit jealously*).

Frequently dost thou touch her throbbing eye with its outer corner trembling; approaching her ear, thou murmurest softly, as if thou wert whispering a secret of love; and while she waves her hands, thou sippest her lower lip which contains all the treasure of delight; whilst we, O bee, through search after truth are disappointed, thou hast gained thy wish! (24)

ŚAKUNTALĀ. This importunate bee does not stop I will remove to another place. (*Stepping aside, and looking about her*). How, now! He is coming this way too! Save me, friends, save me from this ill-mannered bee which hath quite baffled me.

BOTH (*Smiling*). What power have we to deliver you? Call upon Duṣyanta. Indeed holy groves are to be protected by the king.

KING. A good opportunity this to discover myself; fear not (*When half through these words to himself*). But my royal character will be known to them. Well, I will speak thus.

ŚAKUNTALĀ (*Stepping aside and looking about*). How even here he follows me!

राजा—(सत्वरमुपसृत्य ।) आः ।

कः पौरवे वसुमतीं शासति शासितरि दुर्विनीतानाम् ।
अयमाचरत्यविनयं मुग्धासु तपस्विकन्यासु ॥ २५ ॥

(सर्वा राजानं दृष्ट्वा किंचिदिव संभ्रान्ताः ।)

अनसूया—**अज्ज, ण क्खु किंपि अच्चाहिदं । इअं णो पिअसही महुअरेण अहिहूअमाणा कादरीभूदा ।** (इति शकुन्तलां दर्शयति ।) आर्य, न खलु किमप्यत्याहितम् । इयं नः प्रियसखी मधुकरेणाभिभूयमाना कातरीभूता ।

राजा—(शकुन्तलाभिमुखो भूत्वा ।) **अपि तपो वर्धते ।**

(शकुन्तला साध्वसादवचना तिष्ठति ।)

अनसूया—**दाणिं अदिधिविसेसलाहेण । हला सउन्दले, गच्छ उडअं । फलमिस्सं अग्घं उवहर । इदं पादोदअं भविस्सदि ।** इदानीमतिथिविशेषलाभेन । हला शकुन्तले, गच्छोटजम् । फलमिश्रमर्घमुपहर । इदं पादोदकं भविष्यति ।

राजा—**भवतीनां सूनृतयैव गिरा कृतमातिथ्यम् ।**

प्रियंवदा—**तेण हि इमस्सिं पच्छाअसीदलाए सत्तवण्णवेदिआए मुहुत्तअं उवविसिअ परिस्समविणोदं करेदु अज्जो ।** तेन हि अस्यां प्रच्छायशीतलायां सप्तपर्णवेदिकायां मुहूर्तमुपविश्य परिश्रमविनोदं करोत्वार्यः ।

राजा—**नूनं यूयमप्यनेन कर्मणा परिश्रान्ताः ।**

अनसूया—**हला सउन्दले, उइदं णो पज्जुवासणं अदिधीणं । एत्थ उवविसम्ह ।** (इति सर्वा उपविशन्ति ।) हला शकुन्तले, उचितं नः पर्युपासनमतिथीनाम् । अत्रोपविशामः ।

शकुन्तला—(आत्मगतम् ।) **किं णु क्खु इमं पेक्खिअ तवोवणविरोहिणो विआरस्स गमणीअम्हि संवुत्ता ।** किं नु खल्विमं प्रेक्ष्य तपोवनविरोधिनो विकारस्य गमनीयास्मि संवृत्ता ।

राजा—(सर्वा विलोक्य ।) **अहो समवयोरूपरमणीयं भवतीनां सौहार्दम् ।**

KING (*Quickly advancing.*)

While a descendent of Puru, a chastiser of
the ill-behaved, governs the world, who is this
that is so rude to these artless hermit-girls ? (25)

(*All are slightly confused at sight of the king.*)

ANASŪYĀ. It is nothing very dreadful, gentle sir; but this our dear friend was teased and frightened by a bee. (*Indicates Śakuntalā.*)

KING (*Turning to Śakuntalā*). I trust your devotion prospers.

(*Śakuntalā stands speechless through embarrassment.*)

ANASŪYĀ. Now through the arrival of a distinguished guest. Go to the cottage, Śakuntalā, and fetch an offering mixed with fruits. This will serve as water for the feet.

KING. The rites of hospitality have been performed by your sweet and sincere words.

PRIYAMVADĀ. Then, sir, pray sit down for a while on the raised-seat under the Saptaparṇa tree which is cool and deeply shady, and beguile your fatigue.

KING. You, too, must all be fatigued by this work.

ANASŪYĀ. Friend Śakuntalā, it is proper for us to wait upon our guests. Let us be seated here. (*All sit down.*)

ŚAKUNTALĀ (*To herself*). How is it, that at the sight of this person, I feel an emotion scarce consistent with a grove devoted to piety ?

KING (*Looking at them all*). How delightful is your friendship with the (charming) equality of your ages and of your beauty.

प्रियंवदा—(जनान्तिकम् ।) **अणसूए, को णु क्खु एसो चउरगम्भीराकिदी महुरं आलवन्तो पहाववन्तो विअ लक्खीअदि।** अनसूये, को नु खल्वेष चतुरगम्भीराकृतिर्मधुरमालपन्प्रभाववानिव लक्ष्यते ।

अनसूया—**सहि, मम वि अत्थि कोदूहलं। पुच्छिस्सं दाव णं।** (प्रकाशम् ।) **अज्जस्स महुरालावजणिदो वीसम्भो मं मन्तावेदि। कदमो अज्जेण राएसिणो वंसो अलंकरीअदि, कदमो वा विरहपज्जुस्सुअजणो किदो देसो, किंणिमित्तं वा सुउमारदरो वि तवोवणगमणपरिस्समस्स अत्ता पदं उवणीदो।** सखि, ममाप्यस्ति कौतूहलम् । पृच्छामि तावदेनम् । आर्यस्य मधुरालापजनितो विश्रम्भो मां मन्त्रयते । कतम आर्येण राजर्षेर्वंशोऽलंक्रियते, कतमो वा विरहपर्युत्सुकजनः कृतो देशः, किंनिमित्तं वा सुकुमारतरोऽपि तपोवनगमनपरिश्रमस्यात्मा पदमुपीतः ।

शकुन्तला—(आत्मगतम्) **हिअअ, मा उत्तम्म । एसा तुए चिन्तिदाइं अणसूआ मन्तेदि ।** हृदय, मोत्ताम्य । एषा त्वया चिन्तितान्यनसूया मन्त्रयते ।

राजा—(आत्मगतम् ।) **कथमिदानीमात्मानं निवेदयामि, कथं वात्मापहारं करोमि। भवतु। एवं तावदेनां वक्ष्ये ।** (प्रकाशम् ।) **भवति, यः पौरवेण राज्ञा धर्माधिकारे नियुक्तः सोऽहमविघ्नक्रियोपलम्भाय धर्मारण्यमिदमायातः ।**

अनसूया—**सणाधा दाणिं धम्मआरिणो।** सनाथा इदानीं धर्मचारिणः ।

(शकुन्तला शृङ्गारलज्जां रूपयति ।)

सख्यौ—(उभयोराकारं विदित्वा । जनान्तिकम् ।) **हला सउन्दले, जइ एत्थ अज्ज तादो संणिहिदो भवे।** हला शकुन्तले, यद्यत्राद्य तातः संनिहितो भवेत् ।

शकुन्तला—**तदो किं भवे।** ततः किं भवेत् ।

सख्यौ—**इमं जीविदसव्वस्सेण वि अदिधिविसेसं किदत्थं करिस्सदि ।** इमं जीवितसर्वस्वेनाप्यतिथिविशेषं कृतार्थं करिष्यति ।

PRIYAṂVADĀ (*Aside*). Who can this be, my Anasūyā, who combines liveliness with dignity in his mien, and seems to be endowed with majesty while speaking to us sweetly?

ANASŪYĀ. Friend, I am curious, too. I shall just ask him. (*Aloud*). Your sweet speech gives me the confidence to speak to you. What house of royal sages is embellished by your honour? And what country has its people grieving at your absence? On what account has your person, though very delicate, been submitted to the weary journey into our pious grove?

ŚAKUNTALĀ (*Aside*). O my heart! be not uneasy. This Anasūyā speaks your very thoughts.

KING (*To himself*). How shall I reveal, or how shall I disguise myself now? Well, I will speak to her thus. (*Aloud*). Lady, I am the person appointed by the king, the descendent of Puru, to supervise religious rites, and have arrived at this grove of piety to ascertain whether the religious rites suffer no obstruction.

ANASŪYĀ. Then the people engaged in acts of piety have now found some one to take care of them.

(*Śakuntalā acts amorous bashfulness.*)

THE TWO FRIENDS (*Observing the demeanour of the two, aside*). Śakuntalā, dear, if only father were here today—

ŚAKUNTALĀ (*With anger*). What would happen then?

THE TWO FRIENDS. He would make this distinguished guest happy, even if it took the most valuable possession of his life.

शकुन्तला—तुह्मे अवेध । किं पि हिअए कदुअ मन्तेध । ण वो वअणं सुणिस्सं । युवामपेतम् । किमपि हृदये कृत्वा मन्त्रयेथे । न युवयोर्वचनं श्रोष्यामि ।

राजा—वयमपि तावद्भवत्योः सखीगतं किमपि पृच्छामः ।

सख्यौ—अज्ज, अणुग्गहो विअ इअं अब्भत्थणा । आर्य, अनुग्रह इवेयमभ्यर्थना ।

राजा—भगवान्काश्यपः शाश्वते ब्रह्मणि स्थित इति प्रकाशम् । इयं च वः सखी तदात्मजेति कथमेतत् ।

अनसूया—सुणादु अज्जो । अत्थि को वि कोसिओत्ति गोत्तणामहेओ महाप्पहावो राएसी । शृणोत्वार्यः । अस्ति कोऽपि कौशिक इति गोत्रनामधेयो महाप्रभावो राजर्षिः ।

राजा—अस्ति । श्रूयते ।

अनसूया—तं णो पिअसहीए पहवं अवगच्छ । उज्झिदाए सरीरसंवड्ढणादीहिं तादकस्सवो से पिदा । तमावयोः प्रियसख्याः प्रभवमवगच्छ । उज्झितायाः शरीरसंवर्धनादिभिस्तातकाश्यपोऽस्याः पिता ।

राजा—उज्झितशब्देन जनितं मे कौतूहलम् । आ मूलाच्छ्रोतुमिच्छामि ।

अनसूया—सुणादु अज्जो । गोदमीतीरे पुरा किल तस्स राएसिणो उग्गे तवसि वट्टमाणस्स किंपि जादसङ्केहिं देवेहिं मेणआ णाम अच्छरा पेसिदा णिअमविग्घकारिणी । शृणोत्वार्यः । गौतमीतीरे पुरा किल तस्य राजर्षेरुग्रे तपसि वर्तमानस्य किमपि जातशङ्कैर्देवैर्मेनका नामाप्सराः प्रेषिता नियमविघ्नकारिणी ।

राजा—अस्त्येतदन्यसमाधिभीरुत्वं देवानाम् ।

अनसूया—तदो वसन्तोदारसमए से उम्मादइत्तअं रूवं पेक्खिअ—(इत्यर्धोक्ते लज्जया विरमति) ततो वसन्तोदारसमये तस्या उन्मादयितृ रूपं प्रेक्ष्य—

राजा—परस्तादवगम्यत एव । सर्वथाप्सरःसंभवैषा ।

अनसूया—अह इं । अथ किम् ।

ŚAKUNTALĀ. Go to! you form some (absurd) notion in your mind and speak. I will not listen to you.

KING. We, too, would like to ask something about your friend.

THE TWO FRIENDS. Sir, your request is as a favour to us.

KING. The revered Kāśyapa lives in the constant practice of continence; how then can this friend of yours be, as it is said, his daughter?

ANASŪYĀ. Listen, sir. There is a certain royal sage of great majesty whose family name is Kauśika.

KING. Ah, yes, I have heard (of him).

ANASŪYĀ. Know him to be the source of our dear friend's being; but father Kāśyapa is her father, through his having taken care of her person and such like acts when she was abandoned.

KING. The word 'abandoned' has wakened my curiosity. I would like to hear from the beginning.

ANASŪYĀ. Listen, sir. Formerly, while the royal sage was leading a life of stern austerities on the banks of the Gautamī, the gods, becoming somehow alarmed, sent the nymph Menakā to disturb him.

KING. Yes, there is this jealousy of the gods towards the austerities of others.

ANASŪYĀ. Then at the advent of spring, having beheld her intoxicating beauty—(*She stops through bashfulness when this is half said.*)

KING. What followed is quite plain. So, she is sprung from a nymph.

ANASŪYĀ. Exactly so.

राजा—उपपद्यते।

मानुषीषु कथं वा स्यादस्य रूपस्य संभवः।
न प्रभातरलं ज्योतिरुदेति वसुधातलात्॥ २६॥

(शकुन्तलाधोमुखी तिष्ठति।)

राजा—(आत्मगतम्।) लब्धावकाशो मे मनोरथः। किंतु सख्याः परिहासोदाहृतां वरप्रार्थनां श्रुत्वा धृतद्वैधीभावकातरं मे मनः।

प्रियंवदा—(सस्मितं शकुन्तलां विलोक्य नायकाभिमुखी भूत्वा।) पुणो वि वत्तुकामो विअ अज्जो। पुनरपि वक्तुकाम इवार्यः।

(शकुन्तला सखीमङ्गुल्यातर्जयति।)

राजा—सम्यगुपलक्षितं भवत्या। अस्ति नः सच्चरितश्रवणलोभादन्यदपि प्रष्टव्यम्।

प्रियंवदा—अलं विआरिअ। अणिअन्तणाणुओओ तवस्सिअणो णाम। अलं विचार्य। अनियन्त्रणानुयोगस्तपस्विजनो नाम।

राजा— इति सखीं ते ज्ञातुमिच्छामि।

वैखानसं किमनया व्रतमाप्रदाना-
व्द्यापाररोधि मदनस्य निषेवितव्यम्।
अत्यन्तमात्मसदृशेक्षणवल्लभाभि-
राहो निवत्स्यति समं हरिणाङ्गनाभिः॥ २७॥

प्रियंवदा—अज्ज, धम्मचरणे वि परवसो अअं जणो गुरुणो उण से अणुरूववरप्पदाणे संकप्पो। आर्य, धर्मचरणेऽपि परवशोऽयं जनः। गुरोः पुनरस्या अनुरूपवरप्रदाने संकल्पः।

राजा—(आत्मगतं सहर्षम्।) न दुरवापेयं खलु प्रार्थना।

भव हृदय साभिलाषं संप्रति संदेहनिर्णयो जातः।
आशङ्कसे यदग्निं तदिदं स्पर्शक्षमं रत्नम्॥ २८॥

KING. That is, as it should be.

Or how could any woman give birth to such a lovely form? The light that sparkles with tremulous beams does not rise from the surface of the earth. (26)

(*Śakuntalā hangs her head.*)

KING (*To himself*). My desire has found scope. Nevertheless having heard of her desire for a husband, mentioned in pleasantry by her friend, my heart is filled with suspense and anxiety.

PRIYAṀVADĀ (*Looking with a smile at Śakuntalā and turning to the hero*). Sir, it seems as if you had more to say.

(*Śakuntalā threatens her friend with her finger.*)

KING. You have rightly observed. From an eagerness to know more of a virtuous life, I have another question to ask.

PRIYAṀVADĀ. Do not hesitate. For hermits may indeed be questioned without any reserve.

KING. I wish to know your friend.

Is this monastic vow, so opposed to the ways of love, to be observed by her till her marriage only, or is she destined to reside for life along with the female deer, her favourites from having eyes like her own? (27)

PRIYAṀVADĀ. Sir, even in the practice of religious duties this person is dependent on another. But it is her father's intention to give her to a suitable bridegroom.

KING (*To himself, with joy*). This desire indeed is not difficult to obtain.

My heart, be hopeful; for now all doubt is done; what you dreaded as fire, the same is a

शकुन्तला—(सरोषमिव ।) **अणसूए, गमिस्सं अहं ।** अनसूये, गमिष्याम्यहम् ।

अनसूया—किंणिमित्तं । किंनिमित्तम् ।

शकुन्तला—इमं असंबद्धप्पलाविणिं पिअंवदं अज्जाए गोदमीए णिवेदइस्सं । इमामसंबद्धप्रलापिनीं प्रियंवदामार्यायै गौतम्यै निवेदयिष्यामि ।

अनसूया—सहि, ण जुत्तं अकिदसक्कारं अदिधिविसेसं विसज्जिअ सच्छन्ददो गमणं । सखि, न युक्तमकृतसत्कारमतिथिविशेषं विसृज्य स्वच्छन्दतो गमनम् ।

(शकुन्तला न किंचिदुक्त्वा प्रस्थितैव)

राजा—(ग्रहीतुमिच्छन्निगृह्यात्मानम् । आत्मगतम् ।) **अहो चेष्टाप्रतिरूपिका कामिजनमनोवृत्तिः । अहं हि**

अनुयास्यन्मुनितनयां सहसा विनयेन वारितप्रसरः ।
स्थानादनुच्चलन्नपि गत्वेव पुनः प्रतिनिवृत्तः ॥ २९ ॥

प्रियंवदा—(शकुन्तलां निरुध्य ।) **हला, ण दे जुत्तं गन्तुं ।** हला, न ते युक्तं गन्तुम् ।

शकुन्तला—(सभ्रूभङ्गम्) **किं णिमित्तं ।** किंनिमित्तम् ।

प्रियंवदा—रुक्खसेअणे दुवे धारेसि मे । एहि दाव । अत्ताणं मोचिअ तदो गमिस्ससि । (इति बलादेनां निवर्तयति) वृक्षसेचने द्वे धारयसि मे । एहि तावत् । आत्मानं मोचयित्वा ततो गमिष्यसि ।

राजा—भद्रे, वृक्षसेचनादेव परिश्रान्तामत्रभवतीं लक्षये । तथा ह्यस्याः

स्रस्तांसावतिमात्रलोहिततलौ बाहू घटोत्क्षेपणा-
दद्यापि स्तनवेपथुं जनयति श्वासः प्रमाणाधिकः ।

gem capable of being touched. (28)

ŚAKUNTALĀ (*Feigning anger*). Anasūyā, I am going.

ANASŪYĀ. What for?

ŚAKUNTALĀ. I am going to tell the venerable Gautamī how impertinently Priyaṁvadā has been prattling.

ANASŪYĀ. It is not proper, my friend, for you to leave at will, before the rites of hospitality are done to an honoured guest.

(*Śakuntalā has already started without saying anything.*)

KING (*Wishing to detain her, then checking himself, aside*). Ah! the state of a lover's mind is an exact reflection of bodily movement; for

Thinking of following the hermit's daughter, all at once I have been held back from advancing by decorum; although not moving from my place it seems as if I had gone and turned back again. (29)

PRIYAṀVADĀ (*Detaining Śakuntalā*). Dear, it is not proper for you to leave.

ŚAKUNTALĀ (*Knitting her eyebrows*). Why not?

PRIYAṀVADĀ. You owe me the watering of two trees. Come then, you will pay your debt and then you can leave.

(*She forces her to turn back.*)

KING. Good lady, it is only by watering trees that the lady, I imagine, is wearied. For,

Her shoulders droop, and the palms of her hands are excessively reddened by lifting up the watering-jar; even now her breathing which is heavier than usual causes a heaving of her breasts; on her face a collection of the drops of sweat has broken out, impeding (the

बद्धं कर्णशिरीषरोधि वदने घर्माम्भसां जालकं
बन्धे स्रंसिनि चैकहस्तयमिताः पर्याकुला मूर्धजाः ॥ ३० ॥

तदहमेनामनृणां करोमि। (इत्यङ्गुलीययं दातुमिच्छति।)

(उभे नाममुद्राक्षराण्यनुवाच्य परस्परमवलोकयतः।)

राजा—अलमस्मानन्यथा संभाव्य। राज्ञः परिग्रहोऽयमिति राजपुरुषं मामवगच्छथ।

प्रियंवदा—तेण हि णारिहदि एदं अङ्गुलीअअं अङ्गुलीविओअं। अज्जस्स वअणेण अणिरिणा दाणिं एसा। (किंचिद्विहस्य।) हला सउन्दले, मोइदासि अणुअम्पिणा अज्जेण, अधवा महाराएण। गच्छ दाणिं। तेन हि नार्हत्येतदङ्गुलीयकमङ्गुलीवियोगम्। आर्यस्य वचनेनानृणेदानीमेषा। हला शकुन्तले, मोचितास्यनुकम्पिनार्येण, अथवा महाराजेन। गच्छेदानीम्।

शकुन्तला—(आत्मगतम्।) जइ अत्तणो पहविस्सं। (प्रकाशम्।) का तुमं विसज्जिदव्वस्स रुन्धिदव्वस्स वा। यद्यात्मनः प्रभविष्यामि। का त्वं विसर्जितव्यस्य रोद्धव्यस्य वा।

राजा—(शकुन्तलां विलोक्य, आत्मगतम्।) किं नु खलु यथा वयमस्यामेवमियमप्यस्मान्प्रति स्यात्। अथवा लब्धावकाशा मे प्रार्थना। कुतः।

वाचं न मिश्रयति यद्यपि मद्वचोभिः
कर्णं ददात्यभिमुखं मयि भाषमाणे।
कामं न तिष्ठति मदाननसंमुखीयं
भूयिष्ठमन्यविषया न तु दृष्टिरस्याः ॥ ३१ ॥

(नेपथ्ये।)

भो भोस्तपस्विनः, संनिहितास्तपोवनसत्त्वरक्षायै भवत। प्रत्यासन्नः किल मृगयाविहारी पार्थिवो दुष्यन्तः।

play of) the Śirīsa flower in her ear ; and the braid getting loose, her dishevelled hair are held together with one hand. (30)

So I will pay back her debt. (*Desires to give a ring.*)

(*Both reading the letters of the name on the seal look at each other.*)

KING. Do not take me to be different (from what I am) ; this is a present from the king ; so, know me to be the king's officer.

PRIYAṀVADĀ. Then indeed this ring does not deserve to be separated from your finger. Your word has already remitted her debt. (*Smiling a little*). Well, Śakuntalā, you are set free by the kind gentleman--or rather by the king himself. So you can go.

ŚAKUNTALĀ (*To herself*). If I have power over myself ! (*Aloud*). Who are you to send me away or hold me back ?

KING (*Looking at Śakuntalā ; to himself*). Is it possible that she feels towards me as I do towards her ? Or rather there is ground for hope. For

Although she mingles not her speech with mine, yet when I speak she turns her ear directly opposite to me. Granted that she does not stand with her face turned towards mine, nevertheless, her eyes for the most part are not turned to any other object. (31)

(*Behind the scenes*). Ye hermits, keep close at hand to defend the creatures in the pious grove. For they say king Duṣyanta is diverting himself with the chase in the neighbourhood.

तुरगखुरहतस्तथा हि रेणु-
विटपविषक्तजलार्द्रवल्कलेषु।
पतति परिणतारुणप्रकाशः
शलभसमूह इवाश्रमद्रुमेषु॥ ३२॥

अपि च।

तीव्राघातप्रतिहततरुः स्कन्धलग्नैकदन्तः
पादाकृष्टव्रततिवलयासङ्गसंजातपाशः।
मूर्तो विघ्नस्तपस इव नो भिन्नसारङ्गयूथो
धर्मारण्यं प्रविशति गजः स्यन्दनालोकभीतः॥ ३३॥

(सर्वाः कर्णं दत्वा किंचिदिव संभ्रान्ताः।)

राजा—(आत्मगतम्।) अहो धिक्। पौरा अस्मदन्वेषिणस्तपोवनमुपरुन्धन्ति। भवतु। प्रतिगमिष्यामस्तावत्।

सख्यौ—अज्ज, इमिणा आरण्णअवुत्तन्तेण पज्जाउलम्ह। अणुजाणाहि णो उडअगमणस्स। आर्य, अनेनारण्यकवृत्तान्तेन पर्याकुलाः स्मः। अनुजानीहि न उटजगमनाय।

राजा—(ससंभ्रमम्।) गच्छन्तु भवत्यः। वयमप्याश्रमपीडा यथा न भवति तथा प्रयतिष्यामहे।

(सर्वे उत्तिष्ठन्ति।)

सख्यौ—अज्ज, असंभाविदअदिहिसक्कारं भूओ वि पेक्खणणिमित्तं लज्जेमो अज्जं विण्णविदुं। आर्य, असंभावितातिथिसत्कारं भूयोऽपि प्रेक्षणनिमित्तं लज्जावहे आर्यं विज्ञापयितुम्।

राजा—मा मैवम्। दर्शनेनैव भवतीनां पुरस्कृतोऽस्मि।

शकुन्तला—अणसूए अहिणवकुससूईए परिक्खदं मे चलणं। कुरवअसाहापरिलग्गं च वक्कलं। दाव परिपालेध मं जाव णं मोआवेमि।

The dust raised by the hoofs of his horses, red as the evening twilight, falls like a locust-swarm on the trees of the hermitage having bark-garments, moist with water, suspended on the boughs. (32)

Moreover,

An elephant, alarmed at the appearance of a car, enters the pious grove, scaring the herd of deer, with fetters formed by the clinging of Vratati coils dragged along by his feet ; having one of his tusks fixed in a tree-trunk, struck by a cruel blow, a very interruption incarnate of our penance. (33).

(*All listen and are a little bewildered.*)

KING (*To himself*). Alas ! my officers are disturbing the holy grove in their search for me. Well I must go back.

THE TWO FRIENDS. Noble sir, this alarm of the wild (elephant) has greatly frightened us. Give us leave to return to the cottage.

KING (*excitedly*). Yes, you go ; and it shall be my care that no disturbance happens in your hermitage.

(*All rise.*)

THE TWO FRIENDS. Noble sir, we are ashamed to request that you will give us the pleasure of seeing you once again, since you have not now been received with the hospitality due to a guest.

KING. Nay, not so ; I feel honoured by the mere sight of you.

ŚAKUNTALĀ. Anasūyā, my foot is cut by the point of a fresh Kuśa-blade ; and my bark-dress is caught on a Kurabaka twig. Wait for me while I loosen it.

अनसूये, अभिनवकुशसूच्या परिक्षतं मे चरणम्। कुरबकशाखापरिलग्नं च वल्कलम्। तावत् परिपालयतं मां यावदेतन्मोचयामि।

(इति राजानमवलोकयन्ती सव्याजं विलम्ब्य सह सखीभ्यां निष्क्रान्ता।)

राजा—मन्दौत्सुक्योऽस्मि नगरगमनं प्रति। यावदनुयात्रिकान्समेत्य नातिदूरे तपोवनस्य निवेशयेयम्। न खलु शक्नोमि शकुन्तलाव्यापारादात्मानं निवर्तयितुम्। मम हि

गच्छति पुरः शरीरं धावति पश्चादसंस्तुतं चेतः।
चीनांशुकमिव केतोः प्रतिवातं नीयमानस्य॥ ३४॥

(इति निष्क्रान्ताः सर्वे।)

इति प्रथमोऽङ्कः।

(*She casts a glance at the king alone and delaying under pretexts goes out with the two friends.*)

KING. I am not very eager now to return to the city. Meanwhile I will join my followers and encamp at no great distance from the holy grove. I cannot, in truth, divert my mind from occupying itself with (thoughts about) Śakuntalā ;

for my

Body moves onward, but my heart, (as if) unrelated (with the former) runs back, like the silken cloth of a banner borne against the wind. (34).

(*Exeunt Omnes.*)

Here Ends Act One.

द्वितीयोऽङ्कः ।

(ततः प्रविशति विषण्णो विदूषकः ।)

विदूषकः—(निःश्वस्य ।) भो दिट्ठं । एदस्स मिअआसीलस्स रण्णो वअस्सभावेण णिव्विण्णो म्हि । अअं मिओ अअं वराहो अअं सद्दूलो त्ति मज्झण्णे वि गिम्हविरलपाअवच्छाआसु वणराईसु आहिण्डीअदि अडवीदो अडविं । पत्तसंकरकसाआइं कडुआइं गिरिणईजलाइं पीअन्ति । अणिअदवेलं सुल्लमंसभूइट्ठो आहारो अण्हीअदि । तुरगाणुधावणकण्डिदसंधिणो रत्तिम्मि वि णिकामं सइदव्वं णत्थि । तदो महन्ते एव्व पच्चूसे दासीएपुत्तेहिं सउणिलुद्धएहिं वणग्गहणकोलाहलेण पडिबोधिदोम्हि । एत्तिएण दाणिं पि पीडा ण णिक्कमदि । तदो गण्डस्स उवरि पिण्डिआ संवुत्ता । हिओ किल अम्हेसु ओहीणेसु तत्तहोदो मिआणुसारेण अस्समपदं पविट्ठस्स तावसकण्णआ सउन्दला णाम मम अधण्णदाए दंसिदा । संपदं णअरगमणस्स मणं कहं वि ण करेदि । अज्ज वि से तं एव्व चिन्तअन्तस्स अच्छीसु पभादं आसि । का गदी । जाव णं किदाचारपरिक्कमं पेक्खामि । (इति परिक्रम्यावलोक्य च ।) एसो बाणासणहत्थाहिं जवणीहिं वणपुप्फमालाधारिणीहिं परिवुदो इदो एव्व आअच्छदि पिअवअस्सो । होदु । अङ्गभङ्गविअलो विअ भविअ चिट्ठिस्सं । जइ एव्वं वि णाम विस्समं लहेअं । (इति दण्डकाष्ठमवलम्ब्य स्थितः) भो दृष्टम् । एतस्य मृगयाशीलस्य राज्ञो वयस्यभावेन निर्विण्णोऽस्मि । अयं मृगोऽयं वराहोऽयं शार्दूल इति मध्याह्नेऽपि ग्रीष्मविरलपादपच्छायासु वनराजीष्वाहिण्ड्यतेऽटवीतोऽटवीम् । पत्रसंकरकषायाणि कटूनि गिरिनदीजलानि पीयन्ते । अनियतवेलं शूल्यमांसभूयिष्ठ आहारो भुज्यते । तुरगानुधावनकण्डितसंधे रात्रावपि निकामं शयितव्यं नास्ति । ततो महत्येव प्रत्यूषे दास्याः पुत्रैः शकुनिलुब्धकैर्वनग्रहणकोलाहलेन प्रतिबोधितोऽस्मि । इयतेदानीमपि पीडा न निष्क्रामति । ततो गण्डस्योपरि पिण्डिका संवृत्ता । ह्यः किलास्मास्ववहीनेषु तत्रभवतो मृगानुसारेणाश्रमपदं प्रविष्टस्य तापसकन्यका

ACT II.

(*Then Enter Vidūṣaka dejected.*)

VIDŪṢAKA (*Sighing*). Oh my fate! I am tired of being friends with this king who is so addicted to the chase. 'Here's a deer,' 'There's a boar,' 'Yonder's a tiger,' thus, even at mid-day, we wander about from forest to forest, amid rows of woods with summer-thinned tree-shades. We drink hot, stinking waters of mountain-torrents, astringent from the mixture of leaves. At irregular hours, we get our meal (consisting) chiefly of meat roasted on spits. And even in the night, I cannot have enough sleep, as my joints are all dislocated by riding on horseback (after the chase). Then at the very earliest dawn, the sons of slave-girls—the fowlers, wake me up with the din of taking the forest. And yet even with all this, my troubles do not end; (for) then there is a (new) pimple growing on the old boil. For, indeed, yesterday, while we were left behind, his Majesty had entered the grounds of the religious domicile, when as my ill-luck would have it, a hermit's daughter named Śakuntalā was presented to his view. And now he has not even a thought of going back to the city. Even to-day, while he was thinking only of her, the (light of) dawn broke upon his eyes. What help! Well, I will see him when he will have performed his usual toilet. (*Walking round and observing*). Ah, here comes my dear friend in this very direction, surrounded by Yavana-girls holding bows in their hands, and wearing garlands of wild-flowers; well, then, I will stand as if crippled by paralysis of my limbs, if even thus I may know (some) respite. (*Stands leaning on a staff.*)

शकुन्तला नाम ममाधन्यतया दर्शिता । सांप्रतं नगरगमनस्य मनः कथमपि न करोति । अद्यापि तस्य तामेव चिन्तयतोऽक्ष्णोः प्रभातमासीत् । का गतिः । यावत्तं कृताचारपरिक्रमं पश्यामि । एष बाणासनहस्ताभिर्यवनीभिर्वनपुष्पमालाधारिणीभिः परिवृत इत एवागच्छति प्रियवयस्यः । भवतु । अङ्गभङ्गविकल इव भूत्वा स्थास्यामि । यद्येवमपि नाम विश्रमं लभेय ।

(ततः प्रविशति यथानिर्दिष्टपरिवारो राजा ।)

राजा—

कामं प्रिया न सुलभा मनस्तु तद्भावदर्शनाश्वासि ।
अकृतार्थेऽपि मनसिजे रतिमुभयप्रार्थना कुरुते ॥ १ ॥

(स्मितं कृत्वा ।) **एवमात्माभिप्रायसंभावितेष्टजनचित्तवृत्तिः प्रार्थयिता विडम्ब्यते । तद्यथा**

स्निग्धं वीक्षितमन्यतोऽपि नयने यत्प्रेरयन्त्या तया
यातं यच्च नितम्बयोर्गुरुतया मन्दं विलासादिव ।
मा गा इत्युपरुद्धया यदपि सा सासूयमुक्ता सखी
सर्वं तत्किल मत्परायणमहो कामी स्वतां पश्यति ॥ २ ॥

विदूषकः—(तथा स्थित एव ।) **भो वअस्स, ण मे हत्थपाआ पसरन्ति । ता वाआमेत्तएण जीआवइस्सं ।** भो वयस्य, न मे हस्तपादं प्रसरति । तद्वाङ्मात्रेण जापयिष्यामि ।

राजा—कुतोऽयं गात्रोपघातः ।

विदूषकः—कुदो किल सअं अच्छीइं आउलीकरिअ अस्सुकारणं पुच्छसि । कुतः किल स्वयमक्षीण्याकुलीकृत्याश्रुकारणं पृच्छसि ।

राजा—न खल्ववगच्छामि । भिन्नार्थमभिधीयताम् ।

विदूषकः—भो वअस्स, जं वेदसो खुज्जलीलं विडम्बेदि तं किं अत्तणो पहावेण । णं णईवेअस्स । वयस्य, यद्वेतसः कुब्जलीलां विडम्बयति, तत्किमात्मनः प्रभावेण । ननु नदिवेगस्य ।

(*Enter king with attendants as described.*)

KING. True, my darling is not easily attainable; yet my heart assumes confidence from observing the manner in which she seems affected. Even though our love has not hitherto prospered, yet our mutual longing causes delight. (1)

(*Smiling*). Thus is the lover beguiled, who judges of the state of his beloved's feeling by his own desires. It is thus

The tender look she cast, even while she directed her eyes elsewhere; her slow movement caused by the heaviness of her hips, as if for grace's sake; the angry words she spoke to her friend who detained her saying 'Do not go;'—all this was, no doubt, on my account! Ah! how does a lover discover his own (everywhere)! (2)

VIDŪṢAKA (*Still in the same position*). O friend, my hands are incapable of movement; therefore, by words merely I will wish you victory.

KING. Whence this palsy of limbs?

VIDŪṢAKA. How, indeed, having yourself troubled my eyes, you ask what makes them weep?

KING. Indeed, I know not what you mean; speak intelligibly.

VIDŪṢAKA. Well, my friend, when the reed imitates the character of the Kubja plant, is it by its own act, or by the force of the stream?

राजा—नदीवेगस्तत्र कारणम् ।

विदूषकः—मम वि भवं । ममापि भवान् ।

राजा—कथमिव ।

विदूषकः—एव्वं राअकज्जाणि उज्झिअ एदारिसे आउलप्पदेसे वणचरवुत्तिणा तुए होदव्वं । जं सच्चं पच्चहं सावदाणुसरणेहिं संखोहिअसंधिबन्धाणं मम गत्ताणं अणीसो म्हि संवुत्तो । त्ता पसादइस्सं विसज्जिदुं मं एक्काहं वि दाव विस्समिदुं । एवं राजकार्याण्युज्झित्वैतादृश आकुलप्रदेशे वनचरवृत्तिना त्वया भवितव्यम् । यत्सत्यं प्रत्यहं श्वापदानुसरणैः संक्षोभितसंधिबन्धानां मम गात्राणामनीशोऽस्मि संवृत्तः । तत्प्रसादयिष्यामि विसर्जितुं मामेकाहमपि तावद्विश्रमितुम् ।

राजा—(स्वगतम् ।) अयं चैवमाह । ममापि काश्यपसुतामनुस्मृत्य मृगयाविक्लवं चेतः । कुतः ।

न नमयितुमधिज्यमस्मि शक्तो
धनुरिदमाहितसायकं मृगेषु ।
सहवसतिमुपेत्य यैः प्रियायाः
कृत इव मुग्धविलोकितोपदेशः ॥ ३ ॥

विदूषकः—(राज्ञो मुखं विलोक्य ।) अत्तभवं किं वि हिअए करिअ मन्तेदि । अरण्णे मए रुदिअं आसि । अत्रभवान्किमपि हृदये कृत्वा मन्त्रयते । अरण्ये मया रुदितमासीत् ।

राजा—(सस्मितम् ।) किमन्यत् । अनतिक्रमणीयं मे सुहृद्वाक्यमिति स्थितोऽस्मि ।

विदूषकः—चिरं जीअ । (इति गन्तुमिच्छति) चिरं जीव ।

राजा—वयस्य, तिष्ठ । सावशेषं मे वचः ।

विदूषकः—आणवेदु भवं । आज्ञापयतु भवान् ।

राजा—विश्रान्तेन भवता ममाप्यनायासे कर्मणि सहायेन भवितव्यम् ।

विदूषकः—किं मोदअखण्डिआए । तेण हि अअं सुगहीदो खणो । किं मोदकखण्डिकायाम् । तेन ह्ययं सुगृहीतः क्षणः ।

KING. The force of the stream is the cause of it.

VIDŪṢAKA. So are you, of my (troubles).

KING. How indeed?

VIDŪṢAKA. That you should leave the affairs of your empire, and live like a forester in a wild and unfrequented region like this! So that, truth to say, I am become no longer master of my own limbs whose joints are all shaken up by my daily running after wild animals. I, therefore, entreat you to favour me with your permission to repose but a single day.

KING (*To himself*). He says this; and I, too, when I think of Kaṇva's daughter, have little relish for hunting. For

I am not able to bend this strung bow, with the arrow fixed upon it, against the fawns, who, abiding with my darling, have taught her those beautiful glances! (3)

VIDŪṢAKA (*Looking at the king's face*). You have something in your mind and have been deliberating. Mine is a cry in the wilderness.

KING (*Smilingly*). What else? I ought not to disregard a friend's advice; and so I stand here.

VIDŪṢAKA. May you live long! (*Desires to leave.*)

KING. Stay, friend, I have not done.

VIDŪṢAKA. Let the king command.

KING. When you have taken repose, I, too, shall want your assistance in another business, that will cause you no fatigue.

VIDŪṢAKA. Eating a few sweetmeats? Well, then, I accept the engagement.

राजा—यत्र वक्ष्यामि । कः कोऽत्र भोः ।

(प्रविश्य ।)

दौवारिकः—[प्रणम्य ।] आणवेदु भट्टा । आज्ञापयतु भर्ता ।

राजा—रैवतक, सेनापतिस्तावदाहूयताम् ।

दौवारिकः—तह । (इति निष्क्रम्य सेनापतिना सह पुनः प्रविश्य ।) एसो अण्णावअणुक्कण्ठो भट्टा इदो दिण्णदिट्ठी एव्व चिट्ठदि । उवसप्पदु अज्जो । तथा । एष आज्ञावचनोत्कण्ठो भर्तेतो दत्तदृष्टिरेव तिष्ठति । उपसर्पत्वार्यः ।

सेनापतिः—(राजानमवलोक्य ।) दृष्टदोषापि स्वामिनि मृगया केवलं गुण एव संवृत्ता । तथा हि देवः

अनवरतधनुर्ज्यास्फालनक्रूरपूर्वं
रविकिरणसहिष्णु क्लेशलेशैरभिन्नम् ।
अपचितमपि गात्रं व्यायतत्वादलक्ष्यं
गिरिचर इव नागः प्राणसारं बिभर्ति ॥ ४ ॥

(उपेत्य ।) जयतु स्वामी । गृहीतश्वापदमरण्यम् । किमिति स्थीयते ।

राजा—मन्दोत्साहः कृतोऽस्मि मृगयापवादिना माठव्येन ।

सेनापतिः—(जनान्तिकम् ।) सखे, स्थिरप्रतिबन्धो भव । अहं तावत्स्वामिनश्चित्तवृत्तिमनुवर्तिष्ये । (प्रकाशम् ।) प्रलपत्येष वैधेयः । ननु प्रभुरेव निदर्शनम् ।

मेदश्छेदकृशोदरं लघु भवत्युत्थानयोग्यं वपुः
सत्त्वानामपि लक्ष्यते विकृतिमच्चित्तं भयक्रोधयोः ।

KING. I will tell you where. Hola! Who is there?

(*Entering*) DOOR-KEEPER. Let my sovereign command me.

KING. Raivataka, bid the General attend.

DOOR-KEEPER. I obey—(*He goes out and returns with the General*). There is his Majesty eager to give (some) command, looking in this very direction; sir, you will draw near.

GENERAL (*Looking at the king*). Though reckoned a vice, hunting has proved only an advantage in our King. Thus his Majesty

> Like a mountain-roving elephant possesses a body, whose forepart is hardened by the ceaseless friction of the bow-string, which is capable of enduring the sun's rays, and is not affected by the slightest fatigue; though reduced in bulk yet is not marked (as such) by reason of its muscular development, and is all life and vitality. (4)

(*Approaching*). May our monarch ever be victorious. The forest has its beasts of prey tracked; why then delay?

KING. My ardour has been all damped by Māṭhavya who has been preaching against hunting.

GENERAL (*Aside*). Friend, be firm in your opposition. I will humour the king for a while. (*Aloud*). This fool talks nonsense. Why, our king himself is an example. Consider, your Majesty;

> The (hunter's) body, with the waist attenuated by the removal of fat becomes light and fit

उत्कर्षः स च धन्विनां यदिषवः सिध्यन्ति लक्ष्ये चले
मिथ्यैव व्यसनं वदन्ति मृगयामीदृग्विनोदः कुतः ॥ ५ ॥

विदूषकः—(सरोषम्) अवेहि रे उच्छाहहेतुअ । अत्तभवं पकिदिं आपण्णो । तुमं दाव अडवीदो अडविं आहिण्डन्तो णरणासिआलोलुवस्स जिण्णरिच्छस्स कस्स वि मुहे पडिस्ससि । अपेहि रे उत्साहहेतुक । अत्रभवान्प्राकृतिमापन्नः । त्वं तावदटवीतोऽटवीमाहिण्डमानो नरनासिकालोलुपस्य जीर्णऋक्षस्य कस्यापि मुखे पतिष्यसि ।

राजा—भद्र सेनापते, आश्रमसंनिकृष्टे स्थिताः स्मः । अतस्ते वचो नाभिनन्दामि । अद्य तावत्

गाहन्तां महिषा निपानसलिलं शृङ्गैर्मुहुस्ताडितं
छायाबद्धकदम्बकं मृगकुलं रोमन्थमभ्यस्यतु ।
विश्रब्धं क्रियतां वराहततिभिर्मुस्ताक्षतिः पल्वले
विश्रामं लभतामिदं च शिथिलज्याबन्धमस्मद्धनुः ॥ ६ ॥

सेनापतिः—यत्प्रभविष्णवे रोचते ।

राजा—तेन हि निवर्तय पूर्वगतान्वनग्राहिणः । यथा न मे सैनिकास्तपोवनमुपरुन्धन्ति तथा निषेद्धव्याः । पश्य ।

शमप्रधानेषु तपोवनेषु
गूढं हि दाहात्मकमस्ति तेजः ।
स्पर्शानुकूला इव सूर्यकान्ता-
स्तदन्यतेजोऽभिभवाद्वमन्ति ॥ ७ ॥

for exertion; besides, the spirit of even the beasts is observed to be affected with various emotions, through fear and anger; and that is the glory of the archers, when their arrows hit the mark as it flies; falsely indeed do they call hunting a vice; no recreation, surely, can be compared with it. (5)

VIDŪṢAKA (*Angrily*): Away, you inciter. His Majesty has come to his senses; but you chasing from forest to forest, will surely fall into the jaws of some old bear greedy after a man's nose!

KING. Good General, we are staying in the vicinity of a hermitage. I cannot, therefore, approve your words. So for to-day,

Let the buffaloes plunge into the waters of tanks struck repeatedly with their horns; let the deer herding together underneath the shade chew the cud ; let herds of boar, undisturbed, bruise the Mustā grass in the pool; and let this my bow, take repose with a slackened string. (6)

GENERAL. As it pleases your Majesty.

KING. Well, then recall the forest-beaters that have already left, and forbid my soldiers to vex this hallowed grove. Remember,

Holy men, pre-eminent in the virtue of quietism, conceal within their bosom a scorching flame, which, like sun-crystals which are grateful to the touch, they emit when assailed by some foreign lustre. (7)

सेनापतिः—यदाज्ञापयति स्वामी ।

विदूषकः—गच्छ भो दासीएपुत्त । धंसदु दे उच्छाहवुत्तन्तो । गच्छ भो दास्याःपुत्र । ध्वंसतां त उत्साहवृत्तान्तः ।

(निष्क्रान्तः सेनापतिः ।)

राजा—(परिजनं विलोक्य ।) अपनयन्तु भवत्यो मृगयावेषम् । रैवतक, त्वमपि स्वं नियोगमशून्यं कुरु ।

परिजनः—जं देवो आणवेदि । (इति निष्क्रान्तः ।) यद्देव आज्ञापयति ।

विदूषकः—किदं भवदा णिम्मच्छिअं । संपदं एदस्सि पादवच्छाआए विरइदलदाविदाणदंसणीआए आसणे णिसीददु भवं जाव अहं वि सुहासीणो होमि । कृतं भवता निर्मक्षिकम् । सांप्रतमेतस्यां पादपच्छायायां विरचितलतावितानदर्शनीयायामासने निषीदतु भवान्, यावदहमपि सुखासीनो भवामि ।

राजा—गच्छाग्रतः ।

विदूषकः—एदु भवं । एतु भवान् ।

(इत्युभौ परिक्रम्योपविष्टौ ।)

राजा—माठव्य, अनवाप्तचक्षुःफलोऽसि । येन त्वया दर्शनीयं न दृष्टम् ।

विदूषकः—णं भवं अग्गदो मे वट्टदि । ननु भावनग्रतो मे वर्तते ।

राजा—सर्वः कान्तमात्मीयं पश्यति । तामाश्रमललामभूतां शकुन्तलामधिकृत्य ब्रवीमि ।

विदूषकः—(स्वगतम्) होदु । से अवसरं ण दाइस्सं । (प्रकाशम्) भो वअस्स, ते तावसकण्णआ अब्भत्थणीआ दीसदि । भवतु । अस्यावसरं न दास्ये । भो वयस्य, ते तापसकन्यकाभ्यर्थनीया दृश्यते ।

राजा—सखे, न परिहार्ये वस्तुनि पौरवाणां मनः प्रवर्तते ।

GENERAL. As your Majesty commands.

VIDŪṢAKA. Get away, you son of a slave-girl! You have talked in vain about exertion (in the chase.)

(*Exit General.*)

KING (*Looking to his attendants*). Put off your hunting apparel; and thou, Raivataka, return to thy post of duty.

ATTENDANTS. As our lord bids. (*Exit.*)

VIDŪṢAKA. So you have now cleared the stage. Now be seated on this stone-slab, over which the trees spread their beautiful, canopy of shade; so that I, too, will sit at mine ease.

KING. Lead the way.

VIDŪṢAKA. Come along, sir.

(*They walk about and sit down.*)

KING. Māthavya, you have not obtained the fruit of your eyes, since you have not beheld the fairest of all objects.

VIDŪṢAKA. Why, you are there in front of me.

KING. Every one thinks his own as beautiful; but I am speaking in reference to that same Śakuntalā, who is the ornament of the hermitage.

VIDŪṢAKA (*Aside*). Well, I will give him no chance. (*Aloud*). Well, my friend, it appears she is a hermit's daughter whom you love.

KING. Friend, the thoughts of Puru's descendants will never dwell on any forbidden object.

सुरयुवतिसंभवं किल मुनेरपत्यं तदुज्झिताधिगतम् ।
अर्कस्योपरि शिथिलं च्युतमिव नवमालिकाकुसुमम् ॥ ८ ॥

विदूषकः—(विहस्य)—जह कस्स वि पिण्डखज्जूरेहिं उव्वेजिदस्स तिन्तिणीए अहिलासो भवे, तह इत्थिआरदणपरिभाविणो भवदो इअं अब्भत्थणा । यथा कस्यापि पिण्डखर्जूरैरुद्वेजितस्य तिन्तिण्यामभिलाषो भवेत्, तथा स्त्रीरत्नपरिभाविनो भवत इयमभ्यर्थना ।

राजा—न तावदेनां पश्यसि येनैमवादीः ।

विदूषकः—तं क्खु रमणिज्जं जं भवदो वि विम्हअं उप्पादेदि । तत्खलु रमणीयं यद्भवतोऽपि विस्मयमुत्पादयति ।

राजा—वयस्य, किं बहुना ।

चित्रे निवेश्य परिकल्पितसत्त्वयोगा
रूपोच्चयेन मनसा विधिना कृता नु ।
स्त्रीरत्नसृष्टिरपरा प्रतिभाति सा मे
धातुर्विभुत्वमनुचिन्त्य वपुश्च तस्याः ॥ ९ ॥

विदूषकः—जइ एव्वं पच्चादेसो दाणिं रूववदीणं । यद्येवं प्रत्यादेश इदानीं रूपवतीनाम् ।

राजा—इदं च मे मनसि वर्तते ।

अनाघ्रातं पुष्पं किसलयमलूनं कररुहै-
रनाविद्धं रत्नं मधु नवमनास्वादितरसम् ।
अखण्डं पुण्यानां फलमिव च तद्रूपमनघं
न जाने भोक्तारं कमिह समुपस्थास्यति विधिः ॥ १० ॥

Sprung from a nymph of heaven, so it is said, this sage's child was found by him when she deserted her; like a Navamallikā flower loosened and flung upon the Sun-plant. (8)

VIDŪṢAKA (*Laughing*). This desire of yours, who scorn the bright gems of women in your palace, is like the fancy of a man who has lost his relish for dates, and longs for the (sour) tamarind.

KING. You have not seen her; and, therefore, you speak thus.

VIDŪṢAKA. That indeed must be charming, which excites even your admiration.

KING. Friend, what need is there of many words?

Was she delineated in a picture and then endowed with life? Or was she moulded in the Creator's mind from an assemblage (selection) of all lovely forms? When I meditate on the power of the creator, and on her lineaments, she appears to me like a matchless creation of the loveliest of women. (9)

VIDŪṢAKA. If that is so, she must render all other handsome women contemptible.

KING. This, moreover, is in my thought:

This immaculate beauty is like a flower not yet smelt, a delicate shoot not torn by the nails; an unperforated diamond; or fresh honey whose sweetness is yet untasted; or the full reward of meritorious deeds. I know not whom Destiny will approach as the enjoyer here (of this form). (10)

विदूषकः—तेण हि लहु परित्ताअदु णं भवं । मा कस्स वि तवस्सिणो इङ्गुदीतेल्लचिक्कणसीसस्स हत्थे पडिस्सदि । तेन हि लघु परित्रायतामेनां भवान् । मा कस्यापि तपस्विन इङ्गुदीतैलमिश्रचिक्कणशीर्षस्य हस्ते पतिष्यति ।

राजा—परवती खलु तत्रभवती । न च संनिहितोऽत्र गुरुजनः ।

विदूषकः—अध भवन्तं अन्तरेण कीदिसो से दिट्ठिराओ । अथ भवन्तमन्तरेण कीदृशस्तस्या दृष्टिरागः ।

राजा—निसर्गादेवाप्रगल्भस्तपस्विकन्याजनः । तथापि तु

अभिमुखे मयि संहृतमीक्षितं
हसितमन्यनिमित्तकृतोदयम् ।
विनयवारितवृत्तिरतस्तया
न विवृतो मदनो न च संवृतः ॥ ११ ॥

विदूषकः—णं क्खु दिट्ठमेत्तस्स तुह अङ्कं आरोहदि । ननु खलु दृष्टमात्रस्य तवाङ्कमारोहति ।

राजा—मिथःप्रस्थाने पुनः शालीनतयापि काममाविष्कृतो भावस्तत्रभवत्या । तथा हि ।

दर्भाङ्कुरेण चरणः क्षत इत्यकाण्डे
तन्वी स्थिता कतिचिदेव पदानि गत्वा ।
आसीद्विवृत्तवदना च विमोचयन्ती
शाखासु वल्कलमसक्तमपि द्रुमाणाम् ॥ १२ ॥

विदूषकः—तेण हि गहीदपाधेओ होहि । किदं तुए उववणं तवोवणं त्ति पेक्खामि । तेन हि गृहीतपाथेयो भव । कृतं त्वयोपवनं तपोवनमिति पश्यामि ।

VIDŪṢAKA. Let your Highness make haste, then, to rescue her, lest she should fall into the hands of some hermit whose head shines with the oil of Ingudi.

KING. She is not her own mistress; and her father is not here.

VIDŪṢAKA. Well, what kind of feeling did her eyes betray towards your Honour?

KING. The daughters in a hermit's family are naturally (so) reserved; yet,

> She averted her eyes, when I stood facing her and she smiled (as it were) from some other cause (than love); hence love, whose course was checked by modesty was neither fully displayed (by her) nor yet wholly concealed. (11)

VIDŪṢAKA. Surely you did not expect her to climb into your lap the moment she saw you!

KING. But, at our mutual parting, she did betray her feeling towards me, though with modesty.

> For when the slim (girl) had proceeded but a few steps, she stopped all of a sudden, saying, "My foot is hurt by the points of the Kuśa grass;" and then she turned back her face (towards me), whilst (pretending to be occupied with) disentangling her bark-dress from the branches of the shrubs in which it had not really been caught. (12)

VIDŪṢAKA. Well, then, provide yourself with a stock of provender; you have made a pleasure-garden of the penance-grove, I find.

राजा—सखे, तपस्विभिः कैश्चित्परिज्ञातोऽस्मि। चिन्तय तावत्केनापदेशेन सकृदप्याश्रमे वसामः।

विदूषकः—को अवरो अवदेसो। णं तुमं राआ। णीवारच्छट्ठभाअं अम्हाणं उपहरन्तु त्ति। कोऽपरोऽपदेशः। ननु त्वं राजा। नीवारषष्ठभागमस्माकमुपहरन्त्विति।

राजा—मूर्ख, अन्यद्भागधेयमेतेषां रक्षणे निपतति, यद्रत्नराशीनपि विहायाभिनन्द्यम्। पश्य।

यदुत्तिष्ठति वर्णेभ्यो नृपाणां क्षयि तत्फलम्।
तपःषड्भागमक्षय्यं ददत्यारण्यका हि नः॥ १३॥

(नेपथ्ये।)

हन्त, सिद्धार्थौ स्वः।

राजा—(कर्णं दत्त्वा।) अये, धीरप्रशान्तस्वरैस्तपस्विभिर्भवितव्यम्।

(प्रविश्य।)

दौवारिकः—जेदु भट्टा। एदे दुवे इसिकुमारआ पडिहारभूमिं उवट्ठिदा। जयतु भर्ता। एतौ द्वौ ऋषिकुमारौ प्रतीहारभूमिमुपस्थितौ।

राजा—तेन ह्यविलम्बितं प्रवेशय तौ।

दौवारिकः—एसो पवेसेमि। (इति निष्क्रम्य ऋषिकुमाराभ्यां सह प्रविश्य।) इदो इदो भवन्ता। एष प्रवेशयामि। इत इतो भवन्तौ।

(उभौ राजानं विलोकयतः।)

प्रथमः—अहो दीप्तिमतोऽपि विश्वसनीयतास्य वपुषः। अथवोपपन्नमेतदृषिभ्यो नातिभिन्ने राजनि। कुतः।

KING. Friend, a few hermits have recognized me; find out, therefore, some pretext for our entering into that religious domicile once again.

VIDŪṢAKA. What (need of any) other pretext? Are you not the king? (You can enter saying) "Bring us our sixth part of your grain."

KING. Fool, these hermits pay quite a different tribute, which is welcomed more than heaps of jewels; see,

> The wealth of princes, collected from the (four) classes (of their subjects) is perishable; but these hermits give us a sixth part of (the fruits of their) piety which is imperishable. (13)

(*Behind the scenes.*)

O joy! We have now attained the object of our desire.

KING (*Listening*). Oh! These must be hermits (to judge) by their grave and (yet) calm voices.

(*Entering*) DOOR-KEEPER. May the king be victorious! Here are two hermit-boys arrived at the door.

KING. Well, then, introduce them without delay.

DOOR-KEEPER. Well, I will bring them. (*He goes out and then returns with the young hermits.*) This way, sir, this way.

(*Both look at the king.*)

FIRST. Oh! A majestic presence, and yet what confidence it inspires! Or this is quite proper in a king who is very little inferior to a sage. For

अध्याक्रान्ता वसतिरमुनाप्याश्रमे सर्वभोग्ये
रक्षायोगादयमपि तपः प्रत्यहं संचिनोति ।
अस्यापि द्यां स्पृशति वशिनश्चारणद्वन्द्वगीतः
पुण्यः शब्दो मुनिरिति मुहुः केवलं राजपूर्वः ॥ १४ ॥

द्वितीयः—गौतम, अयं स बलभित्सखो दुष्यन्तः ।

प्रथमः—अथ किम् ।

द्वितीयः—तेन हि

नैतच्चित्रं यदयमुदधिश्यामसीमां धरित्री-
मेकः कृत्स्नां नगरपरिघप्रांशुबाहुर्भुनक्ति ।
आशंसन्ते सुरसमितयो बद्धवैरा हि दैत्यै-
रस्याधिज्ये धनुषि विजयं पौरुहूते च वज्रे ॥ १५ ॥

उभौ—(उपगम्य ।) विजयस्व राजन् ।

राजा—(आसनादुत्थाय ।) अभिवादये भवन्तौ ।

उभौ—स्वस्ति भवते ।

(इति फलान्युपहरतः ।)

राजा—(सप्रणामं परिगृह्य ।) आज्ञापयितुमिच्छामि ।

उभौ—विदितो भवानाश्रमसदामिहस्थः । तेन भवन्तं प्रार्थयन्ते ।

राजा—किमाज्ञापयन्ति ।

उभौ—तत्रभवतः कण्वस्य महर्षेरसांनिध्याद्रक्षांसि न इष्टिविघ्नमुत्पादयन्ति । तत्कतिपयरात्रं सारथिद्वितीयेन भवता सनाथीक्रियतामाश्रम इति ।

He, too, now abides in that stage of life which is open to the enjoyment of everyone; and through his exertions for (our) safety he has been accumulating the merit of penance from day to day; and the sacred title of Muni preceded by the (word) Rāja of this king, too, who has conquered his passions, frequently ascends to heaven, being chanted by pairs of bards. (14)

SECOND. Gautama, so this is Duṣyanta, the friend of Indra.

FIRST. Yes, it is.

SECOND. Then, indeed,

It is not wonderful that he whose arm is long as the bar of a city (gate) alone protects the whole earth bounded by the dark (green) ocean. For the Gods, rooted in their enmity with the demons, rely for victory in battles on his braced bow and Indra's thunder-bolt. (15)

BOTH (*Advancing*). O king, be victorious!

KING (*Rising from his seat*). I salute you.

BOTH. Blessings on you! (*They offer fruit.*)

KING (*Receiving it with a bow*). I desire (to know) your command.

BOTH. Your Highness is known by the dwellers of the hermitage to be staying here; and they, therefore, implore your Highness—

KING. What is their command?

BOTH. In the absence of his Reverence, the great sage Kaṇva, some evil demons are disturbing our sacrificial

राजा—अनुगृहीतोऽस्मि ।

विदूषकः—(अपवार्य ।) एसा दाणिं अणुऊला ते अब्भत्थणा। एषेदानीमनुकूला तेऽभ्यर्थना ।

राजा—(स्मितं कृत्वा ।) रैवतक, मद्वचनादुच्यतां सारथिः सबाणासनं रथमुपस्थापयेति ।

दौवारिकः—जं देवो आणवेदि । (इति निष्क्रान्तः ।) यद्देव आज्ञापयति ।

उभौ—(सहर्षम् ।)

अनुकारिणि पूर्वेषां युक्तरूपमिदं त्वयि ।
आपन्नाभयसत्रेषु दीक्षिताः खलु पौरवाः ॥१६॥

राजा—(सप्रमाणम् ।) गच्छतां पुरो भवन्तौ । अहमप्यनुपदमागत एव ।

उभौ—विजयस्व । (इति निष्क्रान्तौ ।)

राजा—माठव्य, अप्यस्ति शकुन्तलादर्शने कुतूहलम् ।

विदूषकः—पढमं सपरीवाहं आसि । दाणिं रक्खसवुत्तन्तेण बिन्दूवि णावसेसिदो । प्रथमं सपरीवाहमासीत् इदानीं राक्षसवृत्तान्तेन बिन्दुरपि नावशेषितः ।

राजा—मा भैषीः । ननु मत्समीपे वर्तिष्यसे ।

विदूषकः—एस रक्खसादो रक्खिदो म्हि । एष राक्षसाद्रक्षितोऽस्मि ।

(प्रविश्य ।)

दौवारिकः—सज्जो रधो भट्टिणो विजअप्पत्थाणं अवेक्खदि । एस उण णअरादो देवीणं आणत्तिहरओ करभओ आअदो । सज्जो रथो भर्तुर्विजयप्रस्थानमपेक्षते । एष पुनर्नगराद्देवीनामाज्ञप्तिहरः करभक आगतः ।

राजा—(सादरम् ।) किमम्बाभिः प्रेषितः ।

दौवारिकः—अह इं । अथ किम् ।

राजा—ननु प्रवेश्यताम् ।

rites. Deign, therefore, accompanied by your charioteer to be master of the hermitage, for a few nights.

KING. I am highly favoured.

VIDŪṢAKA (*Aside*). Here is now a request favourable to you!

KING (*Smiling*). Raivataka, say to the charioteer in my name, "Bring my car and my bow."

DOOR-KEEPER. As your Majesty commands. (*Exit.*)

BOTH. (*With joy*).

This well becomes you, who emulate your ancestors; truly the descendants of Puru are the officiating priests in the sacrifices of delivering from fear the distressed. (16)

KING (*Bowing*). Go first, sirs; I too will follow instantly.

BOTH. Be ever victorious. (*Exeunt.*)

KING. Māṭhavya, have you any curiosity to see Śakuntalā?

VIDŪṢAKA. At first it was full to overflowing; but now by this talk of the demons, not even a drop is left.

KING. Oh, fear nothing: you will be with me.

VIDŪṢAKA. I am protected from the demons.

(*Entering*) DOOR-KEEPER. The car is ready, and awaits my Lord's advance to victory; but here is Karabhaka, just arrived from the city, bearing a message from the Queen-mother.

KING. (*Respectfully*). What, sent by my mother?

DOOR-KEEPER. Yes.

KING. Well, bring him to me.

दौवारिकः—तह। (इति निष्क्रम्य करभकेण सह प्रविश्य।) **एसो भट्टा। उवसप्प।** तथा। एष भर्ता। उपसर्प।

करभकः—जेदु भट्टा। देवी आणवेदि। आआमिणि चउत्थदिअहे पुत्तपिण्डपालणो णाम उववासो भविस्सदि। तहिं दीहाउणा अवस्सं संभाविदव्वा त्ति। जयतु भर्ता। देव्याज्ञापयति। आगामिनि चतुर्थदिवसे पुत्रपिण्डपालनो नाम उपवासो भविष्यति। तत्र दीर्घायुषावश्यं संभावनीयेति।

राजा—इतस्तपस्विकार्यम्। इतो गुरुजनाज्ञा। द्वयमनतिक्रमणीयम्। किमत्र प्रतिविधेयम्।

विदूषकः—तिसङ्कु विअ अन्तराले चिट्ठ। त्रिशङ्कुरिवान्तराले तिष्ठ।

राजा—सत्यमाकुलीभूतोऽस्मि।

कृत्ययोर्भिन्नदेशत्वाद्द्वैधीभवति मे मनः।
पुरः प्रतिहतं शैले स्रोतः स्रोतोवहो यथा॥ १७॥

(विचिन्त्य।) **सखे, त्वमम्बया पुत्र इति प्रतिगृहीतः। अतो भवानितः प्रतिनिवृत्य तपस्विकार्यव्यग्रमानसं मामावेद्य तत्रभवतीनां पुत्रकृत्यमनुष्ठातुमर्हति।**

विदूषकः—णं क्खु मं रक्खोभीरुअं गणेसि। ननु खलु मां रक्षोभीरुकं गणयसि।

राजा—(सस्मितम्) **कथमेतद्भवति संभाव्यते।**

विदूषकः—जह राआणुएण गन्तव्वं तह गच्छामि। यथा राजानुजेन गन्तव्यं तथा गच्छामि।

राजा—ननु तपोवनोपरोधः परिहरणीय इति सर्वानानुयात्रिकांस्त्वयैव सह प्रस्थापयामि।

DOOR-KEEPER. Yes. (*Goes out and returns with Karabhaka.*) Here is his Majesty. Advance.

KARABHAKA. Victory to your Majesty. The royal mother sends this command: On the fourth day from to-day, falls the fast named "Putra-pinda-pālana;" and on that occasion the long-lived one ought not fail to honour us with his presence.

KING. On one hand is a commission from holy hermits; on the other, a command from my revered parent: neither may be neglected; what is the remedy?

VIDŪṢAKA. Stay suspended (between them both) like Triṣanku.

KING. In truth I am (greatly) perplexed.

My mind is distracted by the difference of the two places where the two duties have to be performed, as the stream of a river is split in two by rocks lying before it. (17)

(*Musing*). You have been treated by the Queen-mother as a son. Do you, therefore, return from hence and tell her how my mind is intent on this commission of the hermits, and have the goodness to perform yourself the offices of a son.

VIDŪṢAKA. But you will not really suppose that I was afraid of the demons.

KING (*Smilingly*). How is this possible in your Honour?

VIDŪṢAKA. But I would go, as befits a younger brother of the king.

KING. Surely, I will dispatch my whole train to attend you, for the pious grove must not be disturbed.

विदूषकः—तेण हि जुवराओ म्हि दाणिं संवुत्तो। तेन हि युवराजोऽस्मीदानीं संवृत्तः।

राजा—(आत्मगतम् ।) चपलोऽयं बटुः । कदाचिदस्मत्प्रार्थनामन्तःपुरेभ्यः कथयेत्। भवतु। एनमेवं वक्ष्ये। (विदूषकं हस्ते गृहीत्वा। प्रकाशम् ।) वयस्य, ऋषिगौरवादाश्रमं गच्छामि। न खलु सत्यमेव तापसकन्यकायां ममाभिलाषः। पश्य।

क्व वयं क्व परोक्षमन्मथो
मृगशावैः सममेधितो जनः।
परिहासविजल्पितं सखे
परमार्थेन न गृह्यतां वचः ॥ १८ ॥

(इति निष्क्रान्ताः सर्वे ।)

इति द्वितीयोऽङ्कः।

VIDŪṢAKA (*Proudly*). Then indeed I am the young prince.

KING. (*To himself*). The fellow is a chatterbox. He might disclose my present pursuit to the ladies in the palace. Good, then ; I will say this to him. (*He takes Vidūṣaka by the hand. Aloud*). Friend, I shall enter the hermitage (only) through respect for the sages. Do not think that I have any real inclination for the hermit-girl Śakuntalā. Just think :

Where are we, and where a person bred with the fawns, and a stranger to love ! O friend ! let not the light words spoken in jest be taken in earnest. (18)

VIDŪṢAKA. Yes, to be sure.

(*All go out.*)

End of act II.

तृतीयोऽङ्कः ।

(ततः प्रविशति कुशानादाय यजमानशिष्यः ।)

शिष्यः—अहो, महानुभावः पार्थिवो दुष्यन्तः । प्रविष्टमात्र एवाश्रमं तत्रभवति राजनि निरुपप्लवानि नः कर्माणि संवृत्तानि ।

का कथा बाणसंधाने ज्याशब्देनैव दूरतः ।
हुंकारेणेव धनुषः स हि विघ्नानपोहति ॥ १ ॥

यावदिमान्वेदिसंस्तरणार्थं दर्भानृत्विग्भ्य उपनयामि (परिक्रम्यावलोक्य च । आकाशे ।) प्रियंवदे, कस्येदमुशीरानुलेपनं मृणालवन्ति च नलिनीपत्राणि नीयन्ते । (श्रुतिमभिनीय ।) किं ब्रवीषि । आतपलङ्घनाद्बलवदस्वस्था शकुन्तला । तस्याः शरीरनिर्वापणायेति । तर्हि त्वरितं गम्यताम् । सा खलु भगवतः कण्वस्य कुलपतेरुच्छ्वसितम् । अहमपि तावद्वैतानिकं शान्त्युदकमस्यै गौतमीहस्ते विसर्जयिष्यामि । (इति निष्क्रान्तः ।)

विष्कम्भकः ।

(ततः प्रविशति कामयमानावस्थो राजा ।)

राजा—(निःश्वस्य ।)

जाने तपसो वीर्यं सा बाला परवतीति मे विदितम् ।
न च निम्नादिव सलिलं निवर्तते मे ततो हृदयम् ॥ २ ॥

ACT III.

(Then enter the sacrificer's pupil bearing Kuśa-grass.)

PUPIL. How great is the power of king Duṣyanta! Since his Highness had no sooner entered the hermitage than we could continue our holy rites undisturbed.

> Why talk of aiming the shaft? For by the
> mere sound of the bow-string from afar, as if
> by the angry murmur of his bow, he disperses
> (at once) our obstacles. (1)

Now, then, I shall deliver to the priests this Kuśa-grass to be scattered round the altar. *(Moving about and observing; in the air)*. Ah! Priyaṁvadā, for whom are you carrying this Uśīra ointment and these lotus-leaves with stalks? *(Acting as if he has heard)*. What say you? "That Śakuntalā is extremely disordered from injury caused by the Sun's heat, and these are for cooling her body." Well, then, go quickly; for she is the very life-breath of the venerable Kaṇva, the head of our society. I, too, will send to Gautamī for her some healing water consecrated in the sacrificial rites.

(Exit.)

Here ends the prelude.

(Enter Duṣyanta, expressing the distraction of a lover.)

KING. *(With a sigh)*.

> I know the power of penance: and I am fur-
> ther aware that the maiden is not her own mis-
> tress; and yet my heart can no more turn back
> from her, than water can from a slope. (2)

भगवन्कुसुमायुध, त्वया चन्द्रमसा च विश्वसनीयाभ्यामतिसंधीयते कामिजनसार्थः । कुतः ।

तव कुसुमशरत्वं शीतरश्मित्वमिन्दो-
र्द्वयमिदमयथार्थं दृश्यते मद्विधेषु ।
विसृजति हिमगर्भैरग्निमिन्दुर्मयूखै-
स्त्वमपि कुसुमबाणान्वज्रसारीकरोषि ॥ ३ ॥

(मदनबाधां निरूप्य । सासूयम् ।) भगवन्मन्मथ । कुतस्ते कुसुमायुधस्य शरतैक्ष्ण्यमेतत् । (स्मृत्वा ।) आं ज्ञातम् ।

अद्यापि नूनं हरकोपवह्नि-
स्त्वयि ज्वलत्यौर्व इवाम्बुराशौ ।
त्वमन्यथा मन्मथ मद्विधानां
भस्मावशेषः कथमेवमुष्णः ॥ ४ ॥

अथवा—

अनिशमपि मकरकेतुर्मनसो रुजमावहन्नभिमतो मे ।
यदि मदिरायतनयनां तामधिकृत्य प्रहरतीति ॥ ५ ॥

(सखेदं परिक्रम्य ।) क्व नु खलु संस्थिते कर्मणि सदस्यैरनुज्ञातः श्रमक्लान्तमात्मानं विनोदयामि । (निःश्वस्य ।) किं नु खलु मे प्रियादर्शनादृते शरणमन्यत् । यावदेनामन्विष्यामि । (सूर्यमवलोक्य ।) इमामुग्रातपां वेलां प्रायेण लतावलयवत्सु मालिनीतीरेषु ससखीजना शकुन्तला गमयति । तत्रैव तावद्गच्छामि ।

O divine flower-armed god, by you and by the Moon, though each of you seems worthy of confidence, the whole company of lovers is (cruelly) deceived. For

> Your having flowery shafts and the Moon's having cool beams—both these are observed to be untrue for such as me. For the Moon sheds fire (on them) with her dewy rays; and you make your flowery-darts hard as adamant. (3)

(*Acting as if he is afflicted by love; angrily*). Whence this sharpness of yours who are flower-armed? (*Remembering*). Ah, I know.

> Verily the fire of Hara's wrath even now burns in you like the submarine fire in the ocean; how else could you, O agitator of the soul, who were consumed to ashes, be so scorching to such as me? (4)

Nevertheless,

> This God, who bears a fish on his banner, and who is incessantly giving pain to my mind, will give me real delight, if he strikes me because of her whose eyes are large and bewitching. (5)

(*Moving about in anguish*).

Where indeed can I recreate my afflicted soul, being permitted by those who took part (in the sacrifice) at the conclusion of the rite? (*Sighing*). What else, indeed, can bring me relief but a sight of my beloved? So I will find her out. (*Looking at the sun.*) Śakuntalā and her friends are probably passing this intensely hot noon on the creeper-wreathed banks of the Mālini. So I will advance thither.

(परिक्रम्य स्पर्शं रूपयित्वा ।) अहो प्रवातसुभगोऽयमुद्देशः ।

शक्यमरविन्दसुरभिः कणवाही मालिनीतरङ्गाणाम् ।
अङ्गैरनङ्गतप्तैरविरलमालिङ्गितुं पवनः ॥ ६ ॥

(परिक्रम्यावलोक्य च ।) अस्मिन्वेतसपरिक्षिप्ते लतामण्डपे संनिहितया तया भवितव्यम् । तथा हि । (अधो विलोक्य ।)

अभ्युन्नता पुरस्तादवगाढा जघनगौरवात्पश्चात् ।
द्वारेऽस्य पाण्डुसिकते पदपङ्क्तिर्दृश्यतेऽभिनवा ॥ ७ ॥

यावद्विटपान्तरेणावलोकयामि । (परिक्रम्य तथा कृत्वा सहर्षम् ।) अये, लब्धं नेत्रनिर्वाणम् । एषा मे मनोरथप्रियतमा सकुसुमास्तरणं शिलापट्टमधिशयाना सखीभ्यामन्वास्यते । भवतु । श्रोष्याम्यासां विश्रम्भकथितानि । (इति विलोकयन्स्थितः ।)

(ततः प्रविशति यथोक्तव्यापारा सहसखीभ्यां शकुन्तला ।)

सख्यौ—(उपवीज्य सस्नेहम् ।) हला सउन्दले, अवि सुहेदि दे णलिणीपत्तवादो । हला शकुन्तले, अपि सुखयति ते नलिनीपत्रवातः ।

शकुन्तला—किं वीअअन्ति मं सहीओ । किं वीजयतो मां सख्यौ ।

(सख्यौ विषादं नाटयित्वा परस्परमवलोकयतः ।)

राजा—बलवदस्वस्थशरीरा शकुन्तला दृश्यते । (सवितर्कम् ।) तत्किमयमातपदोषः स्यात् । उत यथा मे मनसि वर्तते । (साभिलाषं निर्वर्ण्य ।) अथवा कृतं संदेहेन ।

(*Moving about and gesticulating that he feels touch*).

Ah! this is a pleasant spot, with the fresh breeze blowing!

It is possible to embrace closely, with my limbs which are inflamed by the bodiless god, the breeze fragrant with the lotuses and wafting the spray from the waves of the Mālinī. (6)

(*Moving about and observing*). She must be somewhere in this bower of creepers encircled by reeds. For, (*looking down*).

On the white sand at its door is discerned a fresh line of footsteps, raised in front, and depressed behind by the weight of her hips. (7)

So I will look through the branches. (*Walking and doing so, with joy*). Ah! my eyes have been fully gratified. The darling of my thoughts, reposing on a flat stone-slab strewn with flowers, is attended by her two friends. Well, I will hear what they say to each other in all confidence. (*He stands gazing.*)

(*Enter Śakuntalā as described with her two friends.*)

FRIENDS (*Fanning affectionately*). Dear Śakuntalā, is the breeze from the lotus leaves refreshing to you?

ŚAKUNTALĀ. What? Are my friends fanning me?

(*The two friends look sorrowfully at one another.*)

KING. Śakuntalā appears to be seriously indisposed. (*Guessing*). Is it the fault of the heat, or is it what my heart suggests? (*Looking longingly*). Or, I need have no doubt.

स्तनन्यस्तोशीरं शिथिलितमृणालैकवलयं
प्रियायाः साबाधं किमपि कमनीयं वपुरिदम् ।
समस्तापः कामं मनसिजनिदाघप्रसरयो-
र्न तु ग्रीष्मस्यैवं सुभगमपराद्धं युवतिषु ॥ ८ ॥

प्रियंवदा—(जनान्तिकम्) अणसूए, तस्स राएसिणो पढमदंसणादो आरहिअ पज्जुस्सुआ विअ सउन्दला । किंणु क्खु से तण्णिमित्तो अअं आतङ्को भवे । अनसूये तस्य राजर्षेः प्रथमदर्शनादारभ्य पर्युत्सुकेव शकुन्तला । किं नु खलु तस्यास्तन्निमित्तोऽयमातङ्को भवेत् ।

अनसूया—सहि, ममवि ईदिसी आसङ्का हिअअस्स । होदु । पुच्छिस्सं दाव णं । (प्रकाशम्) सहि, पुच्छिदव्वासि किंपि । बलवं क्खु दे संदावो । सखि, ममापीदृश्याशङ्का हृदयस्य । भवतु । प्रक्ष्यामि तावदेनाम् । सखि, प्रष्टव्यासि किमपि । बलवान्खलु ते संतापः ।

शकुन्तला—(पूर्वार्धेन शयनादुत्थाय ।) हला, किं वत्तुकामासि । हला, किं वक्तुकामासि ।

अनसूया—हला सउन्दले, अणब्भन्तरा क्खु अम्हे मदणगदस्स वुत्तन्तस्स । किंदु जादिसी इतिहासणिबन्धेसु कामअमाणाणं अवत्था सुणीअदि तादिसीं दे पेक्खामि । कहेहि किंणिमित्तं दे संदावो । विआरं क्खु परमत्थदो अजाणिअ अणारम्भो पडिआरस्स । हला शकुन्तले, अनभ्यन्तरे खल्वावां मदनगतस्य वृत्तान्तस्य । किंतु यादृशीतिहासनिबन्धेषु कामयमानानामवस्था श्रूयते तादृशीं तव पश्यामि । कथय किंनिमित्तं ते संतापः । विकारं खलु परमार्थतोऽज्ञात्वानारम्भः प्रतीकारस्य ।

राजा—अनसूयामप्यनुगतो मदीयस्तर्कः ।

शकुन्तला—(आत्मगतम् ।) बलिअं क्खु मे अहिणिवेसो । दाणिं वि सहसा एदाणं ण सक्कणोमि णिवेदिदुं । बलवान्खलु मेऽभिनिवेशः इदानीमपि सहसैतयोर्न शक्नोमि निवेदयितुम् ।

प्रियंवदा—सहि सउन्दले, सुट्ठु एसा भणादि । किं अत्तणो आतङ्कं उवेक्खसि । अणुदिअहं क्खु परिहीअसि अङ्गेहिं । केवलं लावण्णमई छाआ तुमं ण मुञ्चदि । सखि शकुन्तले, सुष्ठ्वेषा भणति ।

The Uśīra salve has been applied to her bosom, and her only bracelet of lotus-stalks is hanging loose; thus this form of my beloved (thus) disordered is yet exquisitely beautiful. True it is that love and the influence of summer inflame (us) equally: still the disorder brought about by the hot weather does not affect maidens in such a charming manner. (8)

PRIYAṀVADĀ (*Aside*). Anasūyā, Śakuntalā appears to have been greatly affected since she first saw the pious monarch. May it be that this her malady is due to him?

ANASŪYĀ. Friend, the same suspicion has risen in my mind. Well. I will just ask her. (*Aloud*). My dear, I must ask you something. You are, indeed, greatly troubled.

ŚAKUNTALĀ (*Rising from her bed with the upper half.*) My dear, what would you ask?

ANASŪYĀ. Śakuntalā, dear, we are indeed perfectly ignorant about matters relating to love. But I suspect your case to be like that of love-sick persons described in legendary tales. Tell us what causes your illness. For without knowing the exact nature of a disorder, there can be no application of the remedy.

KING. Anasūyā too has guessed my thoughts.

ŚAKUNTALĀ (*To herself*). Great indeed is my attachment; even now I am unable to disclose it to them all at once.

PRIYAṀVADĀ. She speaks the truth, dear Śakuntalā. Why do you neglect your malady? Your

किमात्मन आतङ्कमुपेक्षसे। अनुदिवसं खलु परिहीयसेऽङ्गैः। केवलं लावण्यमयी छाया त्वां न मुञ्चति।

राजा—अवितथमाह प्रियंवदा। तथा हि।

क्षामक्षामकपोलमाननमुरः काठिन्यमुक्तस्तनं
मध्यः क्लान्ततरः प्रकामविनतावंसौ छविः पाण्डुरा।
शोच्या च प्रियदर्शना च मदनक्लिष्टेयमालक्ष्यते
पत्राणामिव शोषणेन मरुता स्पृष्टा लता माधवी॥ ९॥

शकुन्तला—सहि, कस्स वा अण्णस्स कहइस्सं। आआसइत्तिआ दाणिं वो भविस्सं। सखि, कस्य वान्यस्य कथयिष्यामि। आयासयित्रीदानीं वां भविष्यामि।

उभे—अदो एव्व क्खु णिब्बन्धो। सिणिद्धजणसंविभत्तं हि दुक्खं सज्झवेदणं होदि। अत एव खलु निर्बन्धः। स्निग्धजनसंविभक्तं हि दुःखं सह्यवेदनं भवति।

राजा—

पृष्टा जनेन समदुःखसुखेन बाला
नेयं न वक्ष्यति मनोगतमाधिहेतुम्।
दृष्टो विवृत्य बहुशोऽप्यनया सतृष्ण-
मत्रान्तरे श्रवणकातरतां गतोऽस्मि॥ १०॥

शकुन्तला—सहि, जदो पहुदि मम दंसणपहं आअदो सो तवोवणरक्खिदा राएसी, (इत्यर्धोक्तेन लज्जां नाटयति।) सखि, यतः प्रभृति मम दर्शनपथमागतः स तपोवनरक्षिता राजर्षिः—

उभे—कथेदु पिअसही। कथयतु प्रियसखी।

शकुन्तला—तदो आरहिअ तग्गदेण अहिलासेण एतदवत्थम्हि संवुत्ता। तत आरभ्य तद्गतेनाभिलाषेणैतदवस्थास्मि संवृत्ता।

राजा—(सहर्षम्।) **श्रुतं श्रोतव्यम्।**

limbs are wasting away every day, though your exquisite beauty has not forsaken you.

KING. Priyaṁvadā speaks the truth. For indeed

Her face has its cheeks excessively emaciated, her bosom has lost the firmness of its breasts; her waist is more slender (than before); her shoulders are very much drooping; her complexion is wan; thus tormented by love, she appears both deplorable and charming, like the Mādhavī creeper when touched by the wind that dries up its leaves. (9)

ŚAKUNTALĀ. Friend, to whom else shall I relate? But I shall now be the occasion of your sorrow.

BOTH. For that very reason are we (so) importunate. For grief shared with affectionate friends becomes bearable pain.

KING.

Being questioned by the persons who share her sorrows as well as joys, she cannot fail to disclose the cause of her malady now hidden in her breast. Although she turned round again and again and looked upon me with longing, nevertheless, at the present moment I am filled with nervous fear to hear her (answer). (10)

ŚAKUNTALĀ. Friend, from the very instant the pious king who guards our hallowed forest met my eye—(*She breaks off and looks abashed.*)

BOTH. Speak on, beloved friend.

ŚAKUNTALĀ. From that instant, my love for him has reduced me to this plight.

KING. (*With joy*). I have heard what is worth hearing.

स्मर एव तापहेतुर्निर्वापयिता स एव मे जातः ।
दिवस इवाभ्रश्यामस्तपात्यये जीवलोकस्य ॥ ११ ॥

शकुन्तला—तं जइ वो अणुमदं ता तह वट्टह जह तस्स राएसिणो अणुकम्पणिज्जा होमि । अण्णहा अवस्सं सिञ्चध मे तिलोदअं। तद्यदि वामनुमतं तदा तथा वर्तेथां यथा तस्य राजर्षेरनुकम्पनीया भवामि। अन्यथावश्यं सिञ्चतं मे तिलोदकम् ।

राजा—संशयच्छेदि वचनम् ।

प्रियंवदा—(जनान्तिकम् ।) अणसूये, दूरगअवम्महा अक्खमा इअं कालहरणस्स । जस्सिं बद्धभावा एसा सो ललामभूदो पोरवाणं। ता जुत्तं से अहिलासो अहिणन्दिदुं । अनसूये, दूरगतमन्मथाक्षमेयं कालहरणस्य । यस्मिन्बद्धभावैषा स ललामभूतः पौरवाणाम् । तद्युक्तमस्या अभिलाषोऽभिनन्दितुम् ।

अनसूया—तह जह भणसि । तथा यथा भणसि ।

प्रियंवदा—(प्रकाशम् ।) सहि, दिट्ठिआ अणुरूवो दे अहिणिवेसो । साअरं उज्झिअ कहिं वा महाणई ओदरइ । को दाणिं सहआरं अन्तरेण अदिमुत्तलदं पल्लविदं सहेदि । सखि, दिष्ट्यानुरूपस्तेऽभिनिवेशः । सागरमुज्झित्वा कुत्र वा महानद्यवतरति । क इदानीं सहकारमन्तरेणातिमुक्तलतां पल्लवितां सहते ।

राजा—किमत्र चित्रं यदि विशाखे शशाङ्कलेखामनुवर्तेते ।

अनसूया—को उण उवाओ भवे जेण अविलम्बिअं णिहुअं अ सहीए मणोरमं संपादेम्ह । कः पुनरुपायो भवेद्येनाविलम्बितं निभृतं च सख्या मनोरथं संपादयावः ।

प्रियंवदा—णिहुअंत्ति चिन्तणिज्जं भवे । सिग्घंत्ति सुअरं । निभृतमिति चिन्तनीयं भवेत् । शीघ्रमिति सुकरम् ।

अनसूया—कहं विअ । कथमिव ।

प्रियंवदा—णं सो राएसी इमस्सिं सिणिद्धदिट्ठीए सूइदाहिलासो इमाइं दिअहाइं पजाअरकिसो लक्खीअदि । ननु स राजर्षिरेतस्यां स्निग्धदृष्ट्या सूचिताभिलाष एतान्दिवसान्प्रजागरकृशो लक्ष्यते ।

It was, indeed, love that caused my fever, and it is love alone that (now) allays it ; as, at the end of summer, a day, grown black with clouds, relieves the living world from the heat which itself had caused. (11)

ŚAKUNTALĀ. Then if you approve (of it) so contrive that the good king takes pity on me. Otherwise most certainly (you will) sprinkle for me water with sesasum-seed.

KING. Her words end all doubt.

PRIYAṀVADĀ (*Aside*). Anasūyā, she is far gone in love and cannot endure any delay. He on whom she has fixed her affection is the ornament of the Pauravas; it is, therefore, proper that her love finds our approval.

ANASŪYĀ. Just as you say.

PRIYAṀVADĀ (*Aloud*). My dear, fortunately your affection is placed on one worthy of yourself. Or rather where could a great river flow if not into the sea ? What other tree except the Mango can support the Atimukta creeper with new sprouts ?

KING. What wonder if the two Viśākhā stars follow the crescent-moon ?

ANASŪYĀ. But by what expedient can we accomplish the desire of our friend quickly and secretly ?

PRIYAṀVADĀ. Your "secretly" will have to be thought about ; the "quickly" is not hard.

ANASŪYĀ. How do you mean ?

PRIYAṀVADĀ. Why, the good king who has shown himself to be enamoured of her by his tender glances has been observed, during these days, to be wasting through sleeplessness.

राजा—सत्यमित्थंभूत एवास्मि । तथाहि ।

इदमशिशिरैरन्तस्तापाद्विवर्णमणीकृतं
निशि निशि भुजन्यस्तापाङ्गप्रसारिभिरश्रुभिः ।
अनभिलुलितज्याघाताङ्कं मुहुर्मणिबन्धना-
त्कनकवलयं स्रस्तं स्रस्तं मया प्रतिसार्यते ॥ १२ ॥

प्रियंवदा—(विचिन्त्य ।) **हला, मअणलेहो से करीअदु । इमं देवदासेसावदेसेण सुमणोगोविदं करिअ से हत्थअं पावइस्सं** हला, मदनलेखोऽस्य क्रियताम् । इमं देवताशेषापदेशेन सुमनोगोपितं कृत्वा तस्य हस्तं प्रापयिष्यामि ।

अनसूया—**रोअइ मे सुउमारो पओओ । किं वा सउन्दला भणादि ।** रोचते मे सुकुमारः प्रयोगः । किं वा शकुन्तला भणति ।

शकुन्तला—**सहीणिओओवि विकप्पीअदि ।** सखीनियोगोऽपि विकल्प्यते ।

प्रियंवदा—**तेण हि अत्तणो उवण्णासपुव्वं चिन्तेहि दाव किंपि ललिअपदबन्धणं ।** तेन ह्यात्मन उपन्यासपूर्वं चिन्तय तावत् किमपि ललितपदबन्धनम् ।

शकुन्तला—**हला, चिन्तेमि अहं । अवहीरणभीरुअं पुणो वेवइ मे हिअअं ।** हला, चिन्तयाम्यहम् । अवधीरणभीरु पुनर्वेपते मे हृदयम् ।

राजा—(सहर्षम् ।)

अयं स ते तिष्ठति संगमोत्सुको
विशङ्कसे भीरु यतोऽवधीरणाम् ।
लभेत वा प्रार्थयिता न वा श्रियं
श्रिया दुरापः कथमीप्सितो भवेत् ॥ १३ ॥

सख्यौ—**अत्तगुणावमाणिणि, को दाणिं सरीरणिव्वावत्तिअं सारदिअं जोसिणिं पडन्तेण वारेदि ।** आत्मगुणावमानिनि, क इदानीं शरीरनिर्वापयित्रीं शारदीं ज्योत्स्नां पटान्तेन वारयति ।

KING. True it is that I have become just so. For

This golden bracelet, which has its gems sullied by tears which are hot from internal pain, and nightly flow from the corner of my eye that rests upon my arm, slipping every now and then from the wrist without touching the scars made by the friction of the bow-string, is constantly being pushed back by me. (12)

PRIYAṀVADĀ (*Reflecting*). Well, she should write him a love-letter. And I will hide it in flowers and deliver it into his hands under the pretext of their being the remains of an offering presented to some deity.

ANASŪYĀ. A pretty plan and I like it; but what says Śakuntalā to this?

ŚAKUNTALĀ. What? How may I doubt my friend's injunction?

PRIYAṀVADĀ. Well, then, think of some pretty composition in verse beginning with an allusion to yourself.

ŚAKUNTALĀ. Friend, I will think out; but then my heart flutters for fear he will despise me.

KING (*With joy*).

Here stands the man eager for union with you from whom, O timid one, you are apprehensive of a refusal. The seeker may or may not find fortune; but could fortune, seeking, fail to find? (13)

FRIENDS. O scorner of your own merits, who now would ward off with the edge of his garments the moonlight of autumn which can allay the fever of his body?

शाकुन्तला—(सस्मितम् ।) **णिओइदा दाणिं म्हि ।** (इत्युपविष्टा चिन्तयति ।) नियोजितेदानीमस्मि ।

राजा—स्थाने खलु विस्मृतनिमेषेण चक्षुषा प्रियामवलोकयामि । यतः

उन्नमितैकभ्रूलतमाननमस्याः पदानि रचयन्त्याः ।
कण्टकितेन प्रथयति मय्यनुरागं कपोलेन ॥ १४ ॥

शाकुन्तला—हला, चिन्तिदं मए गीदवत्थु । ण क्खु सण्णिहिदाणि उण लेहणसाहणाणि । हला, चिन्तितं मया गीतवस्तु । न खलु संनिहितानि पुनर्लेखनसाधनानि ।

प्रियंवदा—इमस्सिं सुओदरसुउमारे णलिणीपत्ते णहेहिं णिक्खित्तवण्णं करेहि । एतस्मिञ्छुकोदरसुकुमारे नलिनीपत्रे नखैर्निक्षिप्तवर्णं कुरु ।

शाकुन्तला—(यथोक्तं रूपयित्वा ।) **हला, सुणुह दाणिं संगदत्थं ण वेत्ति ।** हला शृणुतमिदानीं संगतार्थं न वेति ।

उभे—अवहिद म्ह । अवहिते स्वः ।

शाकुन्तला—(वाचयति ।)

तुज्झ ण आणे हिअअं मम उण कामो दिवावि रत्तिंपि ।
णिग्घिण तवेइ बलिअं तुइ वुत्तमणोरहाइं अङ्गाइं ॥ १५ ॥

तव न जाने हृदयं मम पुनः कामो दिवापि रात्रावपि ।
निर्घृण तपति बलीयस्त्वयि वृत्तमनोरथान्यङ्गानि ॥

राजा—(सहसोपसृत्य ।)

तपति तनुगात्रि मदनस्त्वामनिशं मां पुनर्दहत्येव ।
ग्लपयति यथा शशाङ्कं न तथा हि कुमुद्वतीं दिवसः ॥ १६ ॥

सख्यौ—(सहर्षम् ।) **साअदं अविलम्बिणो मणोरधस्स ।** स्वागतमविलम्बिनो मनोरथस्य ।

ŚAKUNTALĀ (*Smilingly*). So now I have been directed.

(*She sits up and meditates.*)

KING. It is only proper that I should gaze at my darling with eyes that forget to wink! For

As she is composing words (for her song), her face, with one creeper-like eye-brow lifted, reveals her passion for me by her thrilling cheeks. (14)

ŚAKUNTALĀ. Well, I have thought out a little song. But we haven't any writing-materials.

PRIYAṀVADĀ. Here on this lotus-leaf smooth as a parrot's breast, do you engrave the letters with your nails.

ŚAKUNTALĀ (*Acting as said*). Friends, listen (and say) if it makes sense.

BOTH. We are attentive.

ŚAKUNTALĀ (*Reads*).

Thy heart I know not: but Love, O cruel one, fiercely inflames both by day and by night my limbs, whose desires are centred on thee. (15)

KING (*Hastily Advancing*).

Thee, O slender maid, Love only inflames incessantly, but me he quite consumes: for the day does not cause the lotus to fade so much as it does the Moon. (16)

FRIENDS (*With joy*). Welcome to (the object of your) desire which presents itself without delay.

(शकुन्तलाभ्युत्थातुमिच्छति)

राजा—अलमलमायासेन ।

संदष्टकुसुमशयनान्याशुक्लान्तबिसभङ्गसुरभीणि ।
गुरुपरितापानि न ते गात्राण्युपचारमर्हन्ति ॥ १७ ॥

अनसूया—इदो सिलातलेक्कदेसं अलंकरेदु वअस्सो । इत शिलातलैकदेशमलंकरोतु वयस्यः ।

(राजोपविशति । शकुन्तला सलज्जा तिष्ठति ।)

प्रियंवदा—दुवेणं पि वो अण्णोण्णाणुराओ पच्चक्खो । सहीसिणेहो मं पुणरुत्तवादिणीं करेदि । द्वयोरपि युवयोरन्योन्यानुरागः प्रत्यक्षः । सखीस्नेहो मां पुनरुक्तवादिनीं करोति ।

राजा—भद्रे, नैतत्परिहार्यम् । विवक्षितं ह्यनुक्तमनुतापं जनयति ।

प्रियंवदा—आवण्णस्स विसअणिवासिणो जणस्स अत्तिहरेण रण्णा होदव्वं त्ति एसो वो धम्मो । आपन्नस्य विषयनिवासिनो जनस्यार्तिहरेण राज्ञा भवितव्यमित्येष युष्माकं धर्मः ।

राजा— नास्मात्परम् ।

प्रियंवदा—तेण हि इअं णो पिअसही तुमं उद्दिसिअ इमं अवत्थन्तरं भअवदा मअणेण आरोविदा । ता अरुहसि अब्भुववत्तीए जीविदं से अवलम्बिदुं । तेन हीयमावयोः प्रियसखी त्वामुद्दिश्येदमवस्थान्तरं भगवता मदनेनारोपिता । तदर्हस्यभ्युपपत्त्या जीवितं तस्या अवलम्बितुम् ।

राजा—भद्रे, साधारणोऽयं प्रणयः । सर्वथानुगृहीतोऽस्मि ।

शकुन्तला—(प्रियंवदामवलोक्य ।) **हला, किं अन्तेउरविहरपज्जुस्सुअस्स राएसिणो उवरोहेण ।** हला, किमन्तःपुरविरहपर्युत्सुकस्य राजर्षेरुपरोधेन ।

(*Śakuntalā expresses an inclination to rise.*)

KING. Give yourself no pain.

Your limbs, which closely press the couch of flowers, and bear the fragrance of pieces of lotus-stalks which have quickly faded, being grievously inflamed, must not be fatigued by ceremony. (*Lit.* do not deserve to perform the customary salutation). (17)

ANASŪYĀ. Let our friend favour a part of this stone-slab here (by sitting upon it).

(*The king sits; Śakuntalā feels bashful.*)

PRIYAṀVADĀ. Your mutual love is (quite) evident. But affection for my friend prompts me to speak something superfluous.

KING. Excellent damsel, that ought not to be suppressed. For to leave unsaid what was intended to be said produces subsequent regret.

PRIYAṀVADĀ. A king ought to remove the sufferings of the distressed people living in his kingdom—such is your duty.

KING. No other than this.

PRIYAṀVADĀ. Then (understand that) this our dear friend has been brought to this altered condition by the divinity Love on your account. It is, therefore, proper that you favour her and preserve her life.

KING. Excellent damsel, our passion is reciprocal. I feel favoured in every way.

ŚAKUNTALĀ (*Looking at Priyaṁvadā*). Why should you detain the pious king who must be afflicted by separation from his royal-consorts?

राजा—

इदमनन्यपरायणमन्यथा
हृदयसंनिहिते हृदयं मम।
यदि समर्थयसे मदिरेक्षणे
मदनबाणहतोऽस्मि हतः पुनः ॥ १८ ॥

अनसूया—वअस्स, बहुवल्लहा राआणो सुणीअन्ति। जह णो पिअसही बन्धुअणसोअणिज्जा ण होई तह णिव्वत्तेहि। वयस्य, बहुवल्लभा राजानः श्रूयन्ते। यथा नौ प्रियसखी बन्धुजनशोचनीया न भवति तथा निर्वर्तय।

राजा—भद्रे, किं बहुना।

परिग्रहबहुत्वेऽपि द्वे प्रतिष्ठे कुलस्य मे।
समुद्रवसना चोर्वी सखी च युवयोरियम् ॥ १९ ॥

उभे—णिव्वुद म्ह। निर्वृते स्वः।

प्रियंवदा—(सदृष्टिक्षेपम्।) **अणसूए, जह एसो इदोदिण्णदिट्ठी उत्सुओ मिअपोदओ मादरं अण्णेसदि। एहि। संजोएम णं।** (इत्युभे प्रस्थिते।) अनसूये, यथैष इतोदत्तदृष्टिरुत्सुको मृगपोतको मातरमन्विष्यति। एहि। संयोजयाव एनम्।

शकुन्तला—हला, असरण म्हि। अण्णदरा वो आअच्छदु। हला, अशरणास्मि। अन्यतरा युवयोरागच्छतु।

उभे—पुहवीए जो सरणं सो तुह समीवे वट्टइ। (इति निष्क्रान्ते।) पृथिव्या यः शरणं स तव समीपे वर्तते।

शकुन्तला—कहं गदाओ एव्व। कथं गते एव।

राजा—अलमावेगेन। नन्वयमाराधयिता जनस्तव समीपे वर्तते।

KING.

Thou, with bewitching eyes, that art near my heart, if this heart of mine, which is devoted to no other, thou judgest to be otherwise, then I who was slain by Love's arrow, am slain once again ! (18).

ANASŪYĀ. Friend, kings are said to have many favourite consorts. You must, therefore, act in such a way that our dear friend may not become a cause of grief to her kinsmen.

KING. Good damsel, what need is there of many words ?

Let there be ever so many wives of mine,
there will be but two chief glories of my race—
the sea-clad Earth, and this friend of yours. (19)

BOTH. We are content.

PRIYAṀVADĀ (*Casting a glance*). Anasūyā, there is the eager young antelope turning his eyes in this direction and seeking his mother ; so come, let us help him to join his mother.

(*Both start.*)

ŚAKUNTALĀ. Dear, I am in such a helpless state. Let one of you come back.

BOTH. The protector of the Earth is with you ! (*Exeunt.*)

ŚAKUNTALĀ. How ! they are already gone !

KING. Do not be anxious. Is not this person, your adorer, near you ?

किं शीतलैः क्लमविनोदिभिरार्द्रवातान्
संचारयामि नलिनीदलतालवृन्तैः ।
अङ्के निधाय करभोरु यथासुखं ते
संवाहयामि चरणावुत पद्मताम्रौ ॥ २० ॥

शकुन्तला—ण माणणीएसु अत्ताणं अवराहइस्सं । (इत्युत्थाय गन्तुमिच्छति ।) न माननीयेष्वात्मानमपराधयिष्ये ।

राजा—सुन्दरि, अपरिनिर्वाणो दिवसः । इयं च ते शरीरावस्था ।

उत्सृज्य कुसुमशयनं नलिनीदलकल्पितस्तनावरणम् ।
कथमातपे गमिष्यसि परिबाधापेलवैरङ्गैः ॥ २१ ॥

(इति बलादेनां निवर्तयति ।)

शकुन्तला—पोरव, रक्ख अविणअं । मअणसंतत्तावि ण हु अत्तणो पहवामि । पौरव, रक्षाविनयम् । मदनसंतप्तापि न खल्वात्मनः प्रभवामि ।

राजा—भीरु, अलं गुरुजनभयेन । दृष्ट्वा ते विदितधर्मा तत्रभवान्नात्र दोषं ग्रहीष्यति कुलपतिः । अपि च ।

गान्धर्वेण विवाहेन बह्व्यो राजर्षिकन्यकाः ।
श्रूयन्ते परिणीतास्ताः पितृभिश्चाभिनन्दिताः ॥ २२ ॥

शकुन्तला—मुञ्च दाव मं । भूओ वि सहीजणं अणुमाणइस्सं । मुञ्च तावन्माम् । भूयोऽपि सखीजनमनुमानयिष्ये ।

राजा—भवतु । मोक्ष्यामि ।

शकुन्तला—कदा । कदा ।

Shall I set in motion moist breezes by means of fans of cool lotus-leaves to dissipate your languor, or shall I, O round-thighed (maiden), lay those feet red as lotuses in my lap and press them so as to relieve your pain? (20)

ŚAKUNTALĀ. I will not offend against those whom I am bound to respect.

(*Rises up and desires to leave.*)

KING. The day is not yet cool, beautiful one, and such is your condition.

Leaving the couch of flowers where lotus-leaves formed the covering of your bosom, how will you go in the sun, with your limbs rendered so languid by suffering? (21)

(*He forcibly draws her back.*)

ŚAKUNTALĀ. O descendant of Puru, keep within the bounds of modesty. For although I am inflamed by Love, yet I have not the power of disposing of myself.

KING. Timid one, do not fear your elders. For the revered Father of your society, who knows the law, will not take exception to it when he sees it. Moreover

Many daughters of royal sages are heard to have been married by the ceremony called Gāndharva, and (even) their fathers have approved them. (22)

ŚAKUNTALĀ. Leave me awhile; I will again take counsel with my friends.

KING. Yes, I will leave you.

ŚAKUNTALĀ. When?

राजा—

अपरिक्षतकोमलस्य याव-
त्कुसुमस्येव नवस्य षट्पदेन ।
अधरस्य पिपासता मया ते
सदयं सुन्दरि गृह्यते रसोऽस्य ॥ २३ ॥

(इति मुखमस्याः समुन्नमयितुमिच्छति । शकुन्तला परिहरति नाट्येन ।)

(नेपथ्ये ।)

चक्कवाकवहुए, आमन्तेहि सहअरं । उवट्ठिदा रअणी । चक्रवाकवधूः आमन्त्रयस्व सहचरम् । उपस्थिता रजनी ।

शकुन्तला—(ससंभ्रमम् ।) **पोरव, असंसअं मम सरीरवुत्तन्तोवलम्भस्स अज्जा गोदमी इदो एव्व आअच्छदि । जाव विडवन्तरिदो होहि ।** पौरव, असंशयं मम शरीरवृत्तान्तोपलम्भायार्या गौतमीत एवागच्छति । यावद्विटपान्तरितो भव ।

राजा—तथा । (इत्यात्मानमावृत्य तिष्ठति ।)

(ततः प्रविशति पात्रहस्ता गौतमी सख्यौ च ।)

सख्यौ—इदो इदो अज्जा गोतमी । इत इत आर्या गौतमी ।

गौतमी—(शकुन्तलामुपेत्य ।) **जादे, अवि लहुसंदाबाइं दे अङ्गाइं ।** जाते, अपि लघुसंतापानि तेऽङ्गानि ।

शकुन्तला—अज्जे, अत्थि मे विसेसो । आर्ये, अस्ति मे विशेषः ।

गौतमी—इमिणा दब्भोदएण णिराबाधं एव्व दे सरीरं भविस्सदि । (शिरसि शकुन्तलामभ्युक्ष्य) **वच्छे, परिणदो दिअहो । एहि । उडजं एव्व गच्छम्ह ।** अनेन दर्भोदकेन निराबाधमेव ते शरीरं भविष्यति ॥ वत्से, परिणतो दिवसः । एहि । उटजमेव गच्छामः ।

(इति प्रस्थिताः ।)

शकुन्तला—(आत्मगतम् ।) **हिअअ, पढमं एव्व सुहोवणदे मणोरहे कादरभावं ण मुञ्चसि । साणुसअविहडिअस्स महं दे संपदं संदाबो ।** (पदान्तरे स्थित्वा । प्रकाशम् ।) **लादावलअ संदा-**

KING.

When the nectar of your lower lip, O fair one, is gently stolen by me thirsting (for it), as by the bee the honey of the fresh and untouched flower. (23)

(*Desires to raise her face. Śakuntalā gesticulates as if she repels him. Behind the Scenes*)

O female Cakrawāka, bid farewell to thy mate : (for) the night approaches.

ŚAKUNTALĀ (*Hurriedly*). Paurava, surely this is mother Gautamī come to inquire after my health. Hide yourself, therefore, behind the branches.

KING. I will do so. (*Remains in hiding; enter Gautami with a vessel in her hand, and friends.*)

FRIENDS. This way, venerable Gautamī, this way.

GAUTAMĪ (*Approaching Śakuntalā*). Child, is the fever of your body a little abated ?

ŚAKUNTALĀ. Venerable mother, there is a change for the better in me.

GAUTAMĪ. With this water mixed with Kuśa-grass, your body will assuredly be relieved of pain. (*Sprinkling water on Śakuntalā's head*) Child, the day is departing ; come let us both go to the cottage.

(*They start*).

ŚAKUNTALĀ (*To herself*). O my heart, even before, when the object of your desire came of itself so readily, you did not find courage (to accept it) ; why then this anguish now when separated and (consequently) filled with repentence ? (*Taking a step and standing still; aloud*), O bower of creepers that removed my suffering,

वहारअ, आमन्तेमि तुमं भूओ वि परिमोअस्स । (इति दुःखेन निष्क्रान्ता शकुन्तला सहेतराभिः ।) हृदय, प्रथममेव सुखोपनते मनोरथे कातरभावं न मुञ्चसि । सानुशयविघटितस्य कथं ते सांप्रतं संतापः । लतावलय संतापहारक, आमंत्रये त्वां भूयोऽपि परिभोगाय ।

राजा—(पूर्वस्थानमुपेत्य । सनिःश्वासम् ।) अहो विघ्नवत्यः प्रार्थितार्थसिद्धयः । मया हि

मुहुरङ्गुलिसंवृताधरोष्ठं
प्रतिषेधाक्षरविक्लवाभिरामम् ।
मुखमंसविवर्ति पक्ष्मलाक्ष्याः
कथमप्युन्नमितं न चुम्बितं तु ॥ २४ ॥

क्व नु खलु संप्रति गच्छामि । अथवा । इहैव प्रियापरिभुक्तमुक्ते लतावलये मुहुर्तं स्थास्यामि । (सर्वतोऽवलोक्य)

तस्याः पुष्पमयी शरीरलुलिता शय्या शिलायामियं
क्रान्तो मन्मथलेख एष नलिनीपत्रे नखैरर्पितः ।
हस्ताद्भ्रष्टमिदं बिसाभरणमित्यासज्यमानेक्षणो
निर्गन्तुं सहसा न वेतसगृहाच्छक्नोमि शून्यादपि ॥ २५ ॥

(आकाशे ।)

राजन्,

सायंतने सवनकर्मणि संप्रवृत्ते
वेदीं हुताशनवतीं परितः प्रकीर्णाः ।
छायाश्चरन्ति बहुधा भयमादधानाः
संध्यापयोदकपिशाः पिशिताशनानाम् ॥ २६ ॥

राजा—अयमयमागच्छामि । (इति निष्क्रान्तः ।)

इति तृतीयोऽङ्कः ।

I bid you farewell (hoping) to be once more happy (under your shade). (*Śakuntalā departs in pain, with others.*

THE KING. (*Returning to the former spot; heaving a sigh*). How the accomplishment of one's wishes is beset with obstacles!

For the face of that (maiden) with soft eye-lashes, which had the lower lip repeatedly covered by her fingers, which looked beautiful as it stammered words of denial and which was turned on one side, was somehow raised by me but not kissed! (24)

Where, indeed, shall I go now? Or rather, I will remain for a little while in this bower of creepers where my beloved lay, but which is now deserted by her.

(*Looking all around*).

Here lies on the stone-slab her flowery couch crushed by her form; here is the faded love-missive committed to the lotus-leaf with her nails; and here the bracelet of lotus-stalk dropped down from her arm—as I fix my eyes on these (objects) I have no power to tear myself away from this reedy bower, even though deserted by her. (25)

(*In the air*). O king!

As the evening sacrifice is commenced, the shadows of the flesh-eating demons, brown as evening clouds, and scattered around the blazing altar, are flitting about and creating terror in a variety of ways. (26)

KING. Here I am coming. (*Exit.*)

End of Act III.

चतुर्थोऽङ्कः ।

(ततः प्रविशतः कुसुमावचयं नाटयन्त्यौ सख्यौ ।)

अनसूया—हला पिअंवदे, जइ वि गन्धव्वेण विवाहविहिणा णिव्वुत्तकल्लाणा सउन्दला अणुरूवभत्तुगामिणी संवुत्तेत्ति णिव्वुदं मे हिअअं, तह वि पत्तिअं चिन्तणिज्जं । हला प्रियंवदे, यद्यपि गान्धर्वेण विवाहविधिना निर्वृत्तकल्याणा शकुन्तलानुरूपभर्तृगामिनी संवृत्तेति निर्वृतं मे हृदयम्, तथाप्येतावच्चिन्तनीयम् ।

प्रियंवदा—कहं विअ । कथमिव ।

अनसूया—अज्ज सो राएसी इट्ठिं परिसमाविअ इसीहिं विसज्जिदो अत्तणो णअरं पविसिअ अन्तेउरसमागदो इदोगदं वुत्तन्तं सुमरदि वा ण वेत्ति । अद्य स राजर्षिरिष्टिं परिसमाप्य ऋषिभिर्विसर्जित आत्मनो नगरं प्रविश्यान्तःपुरसमागत इतोगतं वृत्तान्तं स्मरति वा न वेति ।

प्रियंवदा—वीसद्धा होहि । ण तादिसा आकिदिविसेसा गुणविरोहिणो होन्ति । किंदु तादो दाणिं इमं वुत्तन्तं सुणिअ ण आणे किं पडिवज्जिस्सदि त्ति । विस्रब्धा भव । न तादृशा आकृतिविशेषा गुणविरोधिनी भवन्ति । किंतु तात इदानीमिमं वृत्तान्तं श्रुत्वा न जाने किं प्रतिपत्स्यत इति ।

अनसूया—जह अहं देक्खामि, तह तस्स अणुमदं भवे । यथाहं पश्यामि, तथा तस्यानुमतं भवेत् ।

प्रियंवदा—कहं विअ । कथमिव ।

अनसूया—गुणवदे कण्णआ पडिबादणिज्जेत्ति अअं दाव पढमो संकप्पो । तं जइ देव्वं एव्व संपादेदि, णं अप्पआसेण किदत्थो गुरुअणो । गुणवते कन्यका प्रतिपादनीयेत्ययं तावत्प्रथमः संकल्पः । तं यदि दैवमेव संपादयति नन्वप्रयासेन कृतार्थो गुरुजनः ।

प्रियंवदा—(पुष्पभाजनं विलोक्य ।) **सहि, अवइदाहं बलिकम्मपज्जत्ताइं कुसुमाइं ।** सखि, अवचितानि बलिकर्मपर्याप्तानि कुसुमानि ।

ACT IV

(*Then enter the two friends, acting the gathering of flowers.*)

ANASŪYĀ. O my Priyaṁvadā, although my heart is comforted by the thought that Śakuntalā has her nuptials celebrated according to the Gāndharva form and has now been united to a husband worthy of her, yet there is still some cause for uneasiness.

PRIYAṀVADĀ. How do you mean ?

ANASŪYĀ. Whether the pious king, who is dismissed to-day by the hermits at the completion of the sacrifice, will remember things here, when after entering his capital he will be surrounded by his ladies in the recesses of the palace.

PRIYAṀVADĀ. You need have no anxiety (about that). Such distinguished forms as these can never be opposed to virtue. But I cannot tell now what reply the father will make when he shall have heard what has passed.

ANASŪYĀ. As I see it, he will approve.

PRIYAṀVADĀ. Why do you think so ?

ANASŪYĀ.. One can desire nothing better than that one's daughter is married to a virtuous husband ; and if fate brings this about of itself, then indeed the father has his desire accomplished without effort.

PRIYAṀVADĀ (*Looking at the flower-basket*). My friend, we have gathered flowers enough for the offering.

अनसूया—णं पिअसहीए सउन्दलाए सोहग्गदेवआ अच्चणीआ। ननु प्रियसख्याः शकुन्तलायाः सौभाग्यदेवतार्चनीया।

प्रियंवदा—जुज्जदि। युज्यते।

(इति तदेव कर्मारभेते।)

(नेपथ्ये।)

अयमहं भोः।

अनसूया—(कर्णं दत्त्वा।) **सहि, अदिधीणं विअ णिवेदिदं।** सखि अतिथीनामिव निवेदितम्।

प्रियंवदा—णं उडजसंणिहिदा सउन्दला। (आत्मगतम्।) **अज्ज उण हिअएण असंणिहिदा।** ननूटजसंनिहिता शकुन्तला। अद्य पुनर्हृदयेनासंनिहिता।

अनसूया—होदु। अलं एत्तिएहिं कुसुमेहिं। भवतु। अलमेतावद्भिः कुसुमैः।

(इति प्रस्थिते।)

(नेपथ्ये।)

आः अतिथिपरिभाविनी,

विचिन्तयन्ती यमनन्यमानसा
तपोधनं वेत्सि न मामुपस्थितम्।
स्मरिष्यति त्वां न स बोधितोऽपि स-
न्कथां प्रमत्तः प्रथमं कृतामिव॥ १॥

प्रियंवदा—हद्धी हद्धी। अप्पिअं एव्व संवुत्तं। कस्सिं पि पूआरुहे अवरद्धा सुण्णहिअआ सउन्दला। (पुरोऽवलोक्य।) **ण हु जस्सिं कस्सिं पि। एसो दुव्वासो सुलहकोवो महेसी। तह सविअ वेअबलुप्फुल्लाए दुव्वाराए गईए पडिणिवुत्तो। को अण्णो हुदवहादो दहिदुं पहविस्सदि।** हा धिक् हा धिक्। अप्रियमेव संवृत्तम्। कस्मिन्नपि पूजार्हेऽपराद्धा शून्यहृदया शकुन्तला। न खलु यस्मिन्कस्मिन्नपि। एष दुर्वासाः सुलभकोपो महर्षिः। तथा शप्त्वा वेगबलोत्फुल्लया दुर्वारया गत्या प्रतिनिवृत्तः। कोऽन्यो हुतवहाद्दग्धुं प्रभविष्यति।

ANASŪYĀ. But surely the deity that watches over the fortune of our dear friend Śakuntalā will have to be honoured (by us).

PRIYAṀVADĀ. Very well. (*They act doing the same.*)

(*Behind the scenes*)

It is I—Hola!

ANASŪYĀ (*Listening*). My dear, it sounds like some guest announcing himself.

PRIYAṀVADĀ. Well, Śakuntalā is near the cottage. (*To herself*). But not near with her heart to day.

ANASŪYĀ. Well, these flowers will do.

(*They start away.*)

(*Behind the scenes*). Ah, thou that art disrespectful to a guest,

> He on whom thou art meditating with a mind that is regardless of everything else, while thou perceivest not me, rich in penance, to have arrived, will not remember thee, though reminded, like a drunken man the words previously spoken. (1)

PRIYAṀVADĀ. Alas! alas! a very unpleasant thing has indeed occurred. Śakuntalā has, through absence of mind, offended some one deserving reverence. (*Looking ahead*). Not, indeed, any ordinary person! This is the great sage Durvāsas, so quick-tempered. After uttering such an imprecation, he is striding away with a step bounding and irresistible through its impetuosity. Who besides fire has power to consume?

अनसूया—गच्छ । पादेसु पणमिअ णिवत्तेहि णं, जाव अहं अग्घोदअं उवकप्पेमि । गच्छ । पादयोः प्रणम्य निवर्तयैनं, यावदहमर्घोदकमुपकल्पयामि ।

प्रियंवदा—तह । (इति निष्क्रान्ता ।) तथा ।

अनसूया—(पदान्तरे स्खलितं निरूप्य ।) **अम्मो ! आवेअक्खलिदाए गईए पब्भट्ठं मे अग्गहत्थादो पुप्फभाअणं ।** (इति पुष्पोच्चयं रूपयति ।) अहो । आवेगस्खलितया गत्या प्रभ्रष्टं ममाग्रहस्तात्पुष्पभाजनम् ।

(प्रविश्य ।)

प्रियंवदा—सहि, पकिदिवक्को सो कस्स अणुणअं पडिगेण्हदि । किं पि उण साणुक्कोसो किदो । सखि, प्रकृतिवक्रः स कस्यानुनयं प्रतिगृह्णाति । किमपि पुनः सानुक्रोशः कृतः ।

अनसूया—(सस्मितम् ।) **तस्सिं बहु एदं पि । कहेहि ।** तस्मिन्बह्वेतदपि । कथय ।

प्रियंवदा—जदा णिवत्तिदुं ण इच्छदि तदा विण्णविदो मए । भअवं, पढमं त्ति पेक्खिअ अविण्णादतवप्पहावस्स दुहिदुजणस्स भअवदा एक्को अवराहो मरिसिदव्वोत्ति । यदा निवर्तितुं नेच्छति तदा विज्ञापितो मया । भगवन्, प्रथम इति प्रेक्ष्याविज्ञाततपःप्रभावस्य दुहितृजनस्य भगवतैकोऽपराधो मर्षितव्य इति ।

अनसूया—तदो तदो । ततस्ततः ।

प्रियंवदा—तदो मे वअणं अण्णहाभविदुं णारिहदि । किंदु अहिण्णाणाभरणदंसणेण सावो णिवत्तिस्सदि त्ति मन्तअन्तो सअं अन्तरिहिदो । ततो मे वचनमन्यथाभवितुं नार्हति । किंत्वभिज्ञानाभरणदर्शनेन शापो निवर्तिष्यत इति मन्त्रयन्स्वयमन्तर्हितः ।

ANASŪYĀ. Go, fall at his feet, and bring him back, whilst I prepare a propitiatory offering and water.

PRIYAṀVADĀ. I will. (*Exit.*)

ANASŪYĀ (*Showing that she stumbles at the next step*). As I stumbled in my excitement, the flower-baskets fell out from my hands.

(*She acts the gathering up of the flowers.*)

(*Entering*) PRIVAṀVADĀ. Whose entreaties would this ill-tempered person accept? However, I softened him a little.

ANASŪYĀ (*Smiling*). Even that is a good deal for him : tell me.

PRIYAṀVADĀ. When he would not return, I prayed to him : "Holy sir, considering it is the first time, this one offence of the daughter, who did not recognize the potency of penance, should be forgiven her by your reverence."

ANASŪYĀ. And then—

PRIYAṀVADĀ. And then saying, "My word must not be recalled : but the curse shall be lifted at the sight of the ornament (given her) for a token," he vanished from sight.

अनसूया—सक्कं दाणिं अस्ससिदुं । अत्थि तेण राएसिणा संपत्थिदेण सणामहेअङ्किअं अङ्गुलीअअं सुमरणीअंत्ति सअं पिणद्धं । तस्सिं साहीणोबाआ सउन्दला भविस्सदि । शक्यमिदानीमाश्वसितुम् । अस्ति तेन राजर्षिणा संप्रस्थितेन स्वनामधेयाङ्कितमङ्गुलीयकं स्मरणीयमिति स्वयं पिनद्धम् । तस्मिन्स्वाधीनोपाया शकुन्तला भविष्यति ।

प्रियंवदा—सहि, एहि । देवकज्जं दाव णिव्वत्तेम्ह । सखि, एहि । देवकार्यं तावन्निर्वर्तयावः ।

(इति परिक्रामतः ।)

प्रियंवदा—(विलोक्य ।)**अणसूए, पेक्ख दाव । वामहत्थोवहिदवअणा आलिहिदा विअ पिअसही । भत्तुगदाए चिन्ताए अत्ताणं पि ण एसा विभावेदि । किं उण आअन्तुअं** । अनसूये, पश्य तावत् । वामहस्तोपहितवदनालिखितेव प्रियसखी । भर्तृगतया चिन्तयात्मानमपि नैषा विभावयति । किं पुनरागन्तुकम् ।

अनसूया—पिअंवदे, दुवेणं एव्व णं णो मुहे एसो वुत्तन्तो चिट्ठदु । रक्खिदव्वा क्खु पकिदिपेलवा पिअसही । प्रियंवदे, द्वयोरेव ननु नौ मुख एष वृत्तान्तस्तिष्ठतु । रक्षितव्या खलु प्रकृतिपेलवा प्रियसखी ।

प्रियंवदा—को णाम उण्होदएण णोमालिअं सिञ्चेदि । को नामोष्णोदकेन नवमालिकां सिञ्चति ।

(इत्युभे निष्क्रान्ते ।)

विष्कम्भः ।

(ततः प्रवशति सुप्तोत्थितः शिष्यः ।)

शिष्यः—वेलोपलक्षणार्थमादिष्टोऽस्मि तत्रभवता प्रवासादुपावृत्तेन काश्यपेन । प्रकाशं निर्गतस्तावदवलोकयामि कियदवशिष्टं रजन्या इति । (परिक्रम्यावलोक्य च ।) **हन्त प्रभातम् । तथा हि**

यात्येकतोऽस्तशिखरं पतिरोषधीना-
माविष्कृतारुणपुरःसर एकतोऽर्कः ।

ANASŪYĀ. We can now feel confident: at his departure the good king himself put a ring, engraved with his own name, (on her finger) as a souvenir. In that Śakuntalā will be possessed of a remedy in her own power.

PRIYAṀVADĀ. Come, dear, let us worship the gods.

(*They walk about.*)

PRIYAṀVADĀ (*Gazing*). See, my Anasūyā, there is the dear girl, with her face resting on her left hand, looking like a painted picture. With her mind so intent on her husband, she is not conscious of even her own self, much less of a stranger.

ANASŪYĀ. Priyaṁvadā, let this incident remain in the mouth of us two only; we must spare the dear girl, who is naturally (so) delicate.

PRIYAṀVADĀ. Who would sprinkle the jasmine with boiling water?

(*Both go out.*)

End of the introductory scene.

(*Then enter a pupil of Kaṇva, just risen from sleep*).

PUPIL. I am bidden by the venerable Kāśyapa, who is returned from his pilgrimage, to find out what time it is. I will go into the open air and see how much of the night remains. (*Walking about and observing.*) See! It is the break of day. For

On one side, the lord of herbs is sinking to the summit of the western mount, while on the other the Sun heralded by Aruṇa has just become visible. By the contemporaneous rise

तेजोद्वयस्य युगपद्व्यसनोदयाभ्यां
लोको नियम्यत इवात्मदशान्तरेषु ॥ १ ॥

अपि च ।

अन्तर्हिते शशिनि सैव कुमुद्वती मे
दृष्टिं न नन्दयति संस्मरणीयशोभा ।
इष्टप्रवासजनितान्यबलाजनस्य
दुःखानि नूनमतिमात्रसुदुःसहानि ॥ २ ॥

अनसूया—(प्रविश्यापटीक्षेपेण ।)—एवं णाम विसअपरम्मुहस्स वि जणस्स ण एदं ण विदिअं जधा तेण रण्णा सउन्दलाए अणज्जं आआरिदं । एवं नाम विषयपराङ्मुखस्यापि जनस्य नैतन्न विदितं यथा तेन राज्ञा शकुन्तलायामनार्यमाचरितम् ।

शिष्यः—यावदुपस्थितां होमवेलां गुरवे निवेदयामि । (इति निष्क्रान्तः ।)

अनसूया—पडिबुद्धा वि किं करिस्सं । ण मे उइदेसु वि णिअकरणिज्जेसु हत्थपाआ पसरन्ति । कामो दाणिं सकामो होदु । जेण असच्चसंधे जणे सुद्धहिअआ सही पदं कारिदा । अहवा दुव्वाससाबो एसो विआरेदि । अण्णहा कहं सो राएसी तारिसाणि मन्तिअ एत्तिअस्स कालस्स लेहमेत्तं पि ण विसज्जेदि । ता इदो अहिण्णाणं अङ्गुलीअअं से विसज्जेम । दुक्खसीले तवस्सिजणे को अब्भत्थीअदु । णं सहीगामी दोसो त्ति ववसिदा वि ण पारेमि पवासपडिणिउत्तस्स तादकस्सवस्स दुस्सन्तपरिणीदं आवण्णसत्तं सउन्दलं णिवेदिदुं । इत्थंगए अम्हेहिं किं करणिज्जं । प्रतिबुद्धापि किं करिष्ये । न म उचितेष्वपि निजकार्येषु हस्तपादं प्रसरति । काम इदानीं सकामो भवतु । येनासत्यसंधे जने शुद्धहृदया सखी पदं कारिता । अथवा दुर्वासःशाप एष विकारयति । अन्यथा कथं स राजर्षिस्तादृशानि मन्त्रयित्वैतावत्कालस्य लेखमात्रमपि न विसर्जयति । तदितोऽभिज्ञानमङ्गुलीयकं तस्य विसर्जयावः । दुःखशीले तपस्विजने कोऽभ्यर्थ्यताम् । ननु सखीगामी दोष इति

and fall of these twin lights of heaven, people are as it were instructed regarding the vicissitudes of their life. (1)

And again,

When the Moon is hidden, the same night-lotus no longer pleases the eye, its beauty being now only a matter of remembrance. Surely the sorrows of a tender girl produced by the absence of the loved one are beyond all measure very hard to bear. (2)

ANASŪYĀ (*Entering with a hurried toss of the curtain*). However withdrawn from all worldly concerns this person (I) may be, yet it is not unknown to her that Śakuntalā has been treated shamefully by the king.

PUPIL. I will just tell the preceptor that the hour of sacrifice is come. (*Exit*)

ANASŪYĀ. Although wide-awake, what shall I do? My hands and feet move not readily to the usual occupations of the morning. Let Love now enjoy his triumph, who persuaded the pure-minded girl to repose confidence in that perfidious man. Or does the imprecation of Durvāsas cause the change? How else could the good king say such (sweet) things and then not send so much as a letter for such a (long) time? Therefore, we must send him from here the ring he has left as a token. And who, among the ascetics inured to hardship, should be implored? And because the blame lies with my friend, I cannot, although I have made up my mind, summon up courage to tell father Kāśyapa who has returned from his pilgrimage that Śakuntalā

व्यवसितापि न पारयामि प्रवासप्रतिनिवृत्तस्य तातकाश्यपस्य दुष्यन्तपरिणीतामापन्नसत्त्वां शकुन्तलां निवेदयितुम् । इत्थंगतेऽस्माभिः किं करणीयम् ।

प्रियंवदा—(प्रविश्य सहर्षम् ।) **सहि, तुवर तुवर सउन्दलाए पत्थाणकोदुअं णिव्वत्तिदुं** । सखि, त्वरस्व त्वरस्व शकुन्तलायाः प्रस्थानकौतुकं निर्वर्तयितुम् ।

अनसूया—सहि, कहं एदं । सखि, कथमेतत् ।

प्रियंवदा—सुणाहि दाणिं । सुहसइदपुच्छिआ सउन्दलासआसं गदम्हि । तदो जाव एणं लज्जावणदमुहिं परिस्सजिअ सअं तादकस्सवेण एव्वं अहिणन्दिदं । दिट्ठिआ धूमाउलिददिट्ठिणो वि जअमाणस्स पाअए एव्व आहुदी पडिदा । वच्छे, सुसिस्सपरिदिण्णा विज्जा विअ असोअणिज्जा संवुत्ता । अज्ज एव्व इसिरक्खिदं तुमं भत्तुणो सआसं विसज्जेमि त्ति । श्रृणु इदानीम् । सुखशयितपृच्छिका शकुन्तलासकाशं गतास्मि । ततो यादवेनां लज्जावनतमुखीं परिष्वज्य स्वयं तातकाश्यपेनैवमभिनन्दितम् । दिष्ट्या धूमाकुलितदृष्टेरपि यजमानस्य पावक एवाहुतिः पतिता । वत्से, सुशिष्यपरिदत्ता विद्येवाशोचनीया संवृत्ता । अद्यैव ऋषिरक्षितां त्वां भर्तुः सकाशं विसर्जयामीति ।

अनसूया—अह केण सूइदो तादकस्सवस्स वुत्तन्तो । अथ केन सूचितस्तातकाश्यपस्य वृत्तान्तः ।

प्रियंवदा—अग्गिसरणं पविट्ठस्स सरीरं विणा छन्दोमईए वाणिआए । अग्निशरणं प्रविष्टस्य शरीरं विना छन्दोमय्या वाण्या ।

अनसूया—(सविस्मयं) **कहेहि** । कथय ।

प्रियंवदा—(संस्कृतमाश्रित्य ।)

दुष्यन्तेनाहितं तेजो दधानां भूतये भुवः ।
अवेहि तनयां ब्रह्मन्नग्निगर्भां शमीमिव ॥ ३ ॥

अनसूया—(प्रियंवदामाश्लिष्य ।) **सहि, पिअं मे । किंदु अज्ज एव्व सउन्दला णीअदित्ति उक्कण्ठासाधारणं परितोसं अणुहोमि ।** सखि, प्रियं मे । किंत्वद्यैव शकुन्तला नीयत इत्युत्कण्ठासाधारणं परितोषमनुभवामि ।

is married to Duṣyanta and is pregnant. What shall we do then under the circumstances?

PRIYAṀVADĀ (*Entering; with joy*). Hasten, my dear, hasten to perform the festive solemnities at Śakuntalā's departure.

ANASŪYĀ. How is this, my dear?

PRIYAṀVADĀ. Hear me. I just went to Śakuntalā to inquire if she had slept well. And then father Kāśyapa having of his own accord embraced her, while she hung her head in shame, congratulated her thus: "O joy! the offering of the sacrificer fell straight into the fire, albeit his sight was impeded by the smoke. My child, like knowledge imparted to an excellent pupil, thou art not to be sorrowed for. This very day I will send thee to thy husband escorted by hermits."

ANASŪYĀ. But who told father Kāśyapa what had passed?

PRIYAṀVADĀ. An incorporeal metrical speech, when he had entered the fire-sanctuary.

ANASŪYĀ (*Astonished*). Tell me.

PRIYAṀVADĀ. (*Speaking in Sanskrit*).

> Know, Brāhmaṇa, that your daughter bears, for earth's prosperity, the glorious seed implanted by Duṣyanta, as the Śamī tree is pregnant with fire. (3)

ANASŪYĀ (*Hugging Priyaṁvadā*). I am so glad, my dear; and yet my joy is mingled with sorrow when I think that Śakuntalā is going to be taken away only to-day.

प्रियंवदा—सहि, अम्हे दाव उक्कण्ठं विणोदइस्सामो । सा वस्सिणी णिव्वुदा होदु । सखि, आवां तावदुत्कण्ठां विनोदयिष्यावः । सा तपस्विनी निर्वृता भवतु ।

अनसूया—तेण हि एदस्सिं चूदसाहावलम्बिदे णारिएरसमुग्गए एतण्णिमित्तं एव्व कालन्तरक्खमा, णिक्खित्ता मए केसरमालिआ । ता इमं हत्थसंणिहिदं करेहि । जाव अहंपि से मिअलोअणं तित्थमित्तिअं दुव्वाकिसलआणित्ति मङ्गलसमालम्भणाणि विरएमि । तेन ह्येतस्मिंश्चूतशाखावलम्बिते नारिकेलसमुद्गक एतन्निमित्तमेव कालान्तरक्षमा निक्षिप्ता मया केसरमालिका । तदिमां हस्तसंनिहितां कुरु । यावदहमपि तस्यै मृगरोचनां तीर्थमृत्तिकां दूर्वाकिसलयानीति मङ्गलसमालम्भनानि विरचयामि ।

प्रियंवदा—तह करीअदु । तथा क्रियताम् ।

(अनसूया निष्क्रान्ता । प्रियंवदा नाट्येन सुमनसो गृह्णाति ।)

(नेपथ्ये ।)

गौतमि, आदिश्यन्तां शार्ङ्गरवमिश्राः शकुन्तलानयनाय ।

प्रियंवदा—(कर्णं दत्त्वा ।) **अणसूए, तुवर तुवर । एदे क्खु हत्थिणाउरगामिणो इसीओ सद्दावीअन्ति ।** अनसूये, त्वरस्व त्वरस्व । एते खलु हस्तिनापुरगामिन ऋषय शब्दाय्यन्ते ।

(प्रविश्य समालम्भनहस्ता ।)

अनसूया—सहि, एहि । गच्छम्ह । सखि, एहि । गच्छावः ।

(इति परिक्रामतः ।)

प्रियंवदा—(विलोक्य ।) **एसा सुज्जोदय एव्व सिहामज्जिदा पडिच्छिदणीवारहत्थाहिं सोत्थिवाअणकाहिं तावसीहिं अहिणन्दीअमाणा सउन्दला चिट्ठइ । उवसप्पम्ह णं ।** एषा सूर्योदय एव शिखामज्जिता प्रतिष्ठितनीवारहस्ताभिः स्वस्तिवाचनिकाभिस्तापसीभिरभिनन्द्यमाना शकुन्तला तिष्ठति । उपसर्पाव एताम् ।

(इत्युपसर्पतः ।)

PRIYAṀVADĀ. Well, my dear, we will dissipate all anxiety. Only let the poor-girl be made happy.

ANASŪYĀ. Well, then, in this cocoa-nut casket, hanging on the branch of the mango-tree I have put a Keśara-garland which is capable of keeping fresh for a time, with this very object. Therefore take it in your hand: while I prepare for her auspicious decorations such as yellow orpiment, holy earth and Durvā sprouts.

PRIYAṀVADĀ. Be it so done.

(*Exit Anasūyā. Priyaṁvadā acts the gathering of flowers. Behind the Scenes.*)

Gautamī, bid the worthy Śārṇgarava and others escort Śakuntalā.

PRIYAṀVADĀ (*Listening*). Hurry, Anasūyā, hurry. They are calling the hermits who are to go to Hastināpura.

(*Entering, with the decorations in her hand*).

Anasūyā Come, dear, let us go. (*They walk round.*)

PRIYAṀVADĀ (*Observing*). There stands our Śakuntalā, after bathing overhead at earliest sunrise, while the hermit-women, who are congratulating her, have the hallowed grains in their hands, and are invoking blessings on her. Let us advance to her. (*They advance.*)

(ततः प्रविशति यथोद्दिष्टव्यापारासनस्था शकुन्तला ।)

तापसीनामन्यतमा—(शकुन्तलां प्रति ।) **जादे, भत्तुणो बहुमाणसूअअं महादेईसद्दं लहेहि** । जाते, भर्तुर्बहुमानसूचकं महादेवीशब्दं लभस्व ।

द्वितीया—वच्छे, वीरप्पसविणी होहि । वत्से, वीरप्रसविनी भव ।

तृतीया—वच्छे, भत्तुणो बहुमदा होहि । वत्से, भर्तुर्बहुमता भव ।

(इत्याशिषो दत्त्वा गौतमीवर्जं निष्क्रान्ताः ।)

सख्यौ—(उपसृत्य ।) **सहि सुहमज्जणं दे होदु** । सखि, सुखमज्जनं ते भवतु ।

शकुन्तला—साअदं मे सहीणं । इदो णिसीदह । स्वागतं मे सख्योः । इतो निषीदतम् ।

उभे—(मङ्गलपात्राण्यादाय । उपविश्य ।) **हला, सज्जा होहि । जाव मङ्गलसमालम्भणं विरएम** । हला, सज्जा भव । यावन्मङ्गलसमालम्भनं विरचयावः ।

शकुन्तला—एदं पि बहु मन्तव्वं । दुलहं दाणिं मे सहीमण्डणं भविस्सदि त्ति । (इति बाष्पं विसृजति ।) एतदपि बहु मन्तव्यम् । दुर्लभमिदानीं मे सखीमण्डनं भविष्यतीति ।

उभे—सहि, उइअं ण दे मङ्गलकाले रोइदुं । (इत्यश्रूणि प्रमृज्य नाट्येन प्रसाधयतः ।) सखि, उचितं न ते मङ्गलकाले रोदितुम् ।

प्रियंवदा—आहरणोइदं रूवं अस्समसुलहेहिं पसाहणेहिं विप्पआरीअदि । आभरणोचितं रूपमाश्रमसुलभैः प्रसाधनैर्विप्रकार्यते ।

(प्रविश्योपायनहस्तौ ।)

ऋषिकुमारकौ—इदमलंकरणम् । अलंक्रियतामत्रभवती ।

(सर्वा विलोक्य विस्मिताः ।)

गौतमी—वच्छ णारअ, कुदो एदं । वत्स नारद, कुत एतत् ।

प्रथमः—तातकाश्यपप्रभावात् ।

गौतमी—किं माणसी सिद्धी । किं मानसी सिद्धिः ।

(*Enter Śakuntalā seated, and engaged as described.*)

ONE OF THE HERMIT-WOMEN. (*To Śakuntalā*). My child, mayst thou receive the title of 'Great Queen' showing how well thy husband honours thee!

SECOND. Child, mayest thou be delivered of a hero!

THIRD. Child, mayest thou be highly esteemed by thy husband!

(*Having blessed her thus, exeunt all except Gautamī.*)

FRIENDS (*Approaching*). Friend, may it prove to thee a happy ablution!

ŚAKUNTALĀ. My friends, are welcome : sit here.

BOTH (*Taking up the vessels containing the auspicious materials, and seating themselves*). Get ready, dear, while we put on (you) the auspicious decorations.

ŚAKUNTALĀ. Even this ought to be highly valued : adornment at the hands of my friends will be ever so rare to me. (*She sheds tears.*)

BOTH. You ought not to weep, dear, at this happy time. (*Wiping off her tears, they act adorning her*).

PRIYAṀVADĀ. Your beauty which deserves (richer) ornaments is disfigured by such decorations as we could procure in the hermitage.

(*Entering with presents in hand.*)

TWO HERMIT-LADS. Here are ornaments. Let her ladyship put them on.

(*All are amazed on seeing them.*)

GAUTAMĪ. Child Nārada, whence come these things?

FIRST. From the holy power of father Kāśyapa.

GAUTAMĪ. A creation of his mind?

द्वितीयः—न खलु । श्रूयताम् । तत्रभवता वयमाज्ञप्ताः शकुन्तलाहेतोर्वनस्पतिभ्यः कुसुमान्याहरतेति । तत इदानीं

क्षौमं केनचिदिन्दुपाण्डु तरुणा माङ्गल्यमाविष्कृतं
निष्ठ्यूतश्चरणोपभोगसुलभो लाक्षारसः केनचित् ।
अन्येभ्यो वनदेवताकरतलैरापर्वभागोत्थितै-
र्दत्तान्याभरणानि तत्किसलयोद्भेदप्रतिद्वन्द्विभिः ॥ ४ ॥

प्रियंवदा—हला, इमाए अब्भुववत्तीए सूइआ दे भत्तुणो गेहे अणुहोदव्वा राअलच्छित्ति । हला, अनयाभ्युपपत्त्या सूचिता ते भर्तुर्गेहेऽनुभवितव्या राजलक्ष्मीरीति ।

(शकुन्तला व्रीडां रूपयति ।)

प्रथमः—गौतम, एह्येहि । अभिषेकोत्तीर्णाय काश्यपाय वनस्पतिसेवां निवेदयावः ।

द्वितीयः—तथा ।

(इति निष्क्रान्तौ ।)

सख्यौ—अए, अणुवजुत्तभूसणो अअं जणो । चित्तकम्मपरिअएण अङ्गेसु दे आहरणविणिओअं करेम्ह । अये, अनुपयुक्तभूषणोऽयं जनः । चित्रकर्मपरिचयेनाङ्गेषु ते आभरणविनियोगं कुर्वः ।

शकुन्तला—जाणे वो णेउणं । जाने वां नैपुणम् ।

(उभे नाट्येनालंकुरुतः ।)

(ततः प्रविशति स्नानोत्तीर्णः काश्यपः ।)

काश्यपः—

यास्यत्यद्य शकुन्तलेति हृदयं संस्पृष्टमुत्कण्ठया
कण्ठः स्तम्भितबाष्पवृत्तिकलुषश्चिन्ताजडं दर्शनम् ।
वैक्लव्यं मम तावदीदृशमपि स्नेहादरण्यौकसः
पीड्यन्ते गृहिणः कथं न तनयाविश्लेषदुःखैर्नवैः ॥ ५ ॥

SECOND. Not, indeed. Listen. The venerable (sage) gave us his order "Bring hither flowers for Śakuntalā from the trees." And then

> by a certain tree was exhibited an auspicious silken garment white as the moon; another distilled the lac-dye so excellent to stain her feet; and from others were presented ornaments by fairy-hands extending as far as the wrist that rivalled the first sproutings of delicate leaves of those trees. (4)

PRIYAṀVADĀ. This favour is a presage of the royal fortune which you are to enjoy in your husband's home.

(*Śakuntalā looks bashful.*)

FIRST. Come, my Gautama, come. We shall tell father Kāśyapa (who must have) returned from bathing, of the service done by the trees.

SECOND. All right (*Exeunt.*)

FRIENDS. My dear, we are never used to ornaments; but our acquaintance with the art of painting will help us to adjust these ornaments on your limbs.

ŚAKUNTALĀ. I know how clever you are. (*Both act adorning her.*)

(*Enter Kāśyapa returning after bathing.*)

> This day will Śakuntalā depart: at such (a thought) my heart is smitten with anguish; my voice is choked by suppressing the flow of tears; and my senses paralysed by anxious thought. If such, through affection, is the affliction even of me a hermit, O with what pangs must they who are fathers of families be afflicted at the first parting with their daughters? (5)

(इति परिक्रामति)

सख्यौ—हला सउन्दले अवसिदमण्डणासि । परिधेहि संपदं खोमजुअलं । हला शकुन्तले, अवसितमण्डनासि । परिधत्स्व सांप्रतं क्षौमयुगलम् ।

(शकुन्तलोत्थाय परिधत्ते ।)

गौतमी—जादे, एसो दे आणन्दपरिवाहिणा चक्खुणा परिस्सजन्तो विअ गुरू उवट्ठिदो । आआरं दाव पडिवज्जस्स । जाते, एष त आनन्दपरिवाहिणा चक्षुषा परिष्वजमान इव गुरुरुपस्थितः । आचारं तावत्प्रतिपद्यस्व ।

शकुन्तला—(सव्रीडम् ।) **ताद, वन्दामि ।** तात वन्दे ।

काश्यपः--वत्से,

ययातेरिव शर्मिष्ठा भर्तुर्बहुमता भव ।
सुतं त्वमपि सम्राजं सेव पूरुमवाप्नुहि ॥ ६ ॥

गौतमी—भअवं, वरो क्खु एसो ण आसिसा । भगवन्, वरः खल्वेषो नाशीः ।

काश्यपः—वत्से, इतः सद्योहुताग्नीन्प्रदक्षिणीकुरुष्व ।

[सर्वे परिक्रामन्ति ।]

काश्यपः—(ऋक्छन्दसाशास्ते ।)

अमी वेदिं परितः क्लृप्तधिष्ण्याः
समिद्वन्तः प्रान्तसंस्तीर्णदर्भाः ।
अपघ्नन्तो दुरितं हव्यगन्धै-
र्वैतानास्त्वां वह्नयः पावयन्तु ॥ ७ ॥

प्रतिष्ठस्वेदानीम् । (सदृष्टिक्षेपम् ।) **क्व ते शार्ङ्गरवमिश्राः ।**

(प्रविश्य ।)

शिष्यः--भगवन्, इमे स्मः ।

काश्यपः--भगिन्यास्ते मार्गमादेशय ।

(*Walks about.*)

FRIENDS. Dear Śakuntalā, your decoration is completed. Now put on the pair of silken garments.

(*Śakuntalā rises and puts them on.*)

GAUTAMĪ. My child, here comes your father, whose eyes overflow with tears of joy, as if (already) embracing you. Just, therefore, do him the customary reverence.

ŚAKUNTALĀ (*Bashfully*). Father, I salute you.

KĀŚYAPA. My child,

Mayest thou be cherished by thy husband, as Śarmiṣṭhā was cherished by Yayāti. And mayest thou bear a son, as she did Puru, who shall be the sovereign of the world. (6)

GAUTAMĪ. Holy sir, this is indeed a boon, not a mere benediction.

KĀŚYAPA. My child, this way go round the fires in which the offerings have just been thrown.

(*All walk about.*)

KĀŚYAPA. (*Pronounces a blessing in the metre of the Ṛgveda*).

Let these sacrificial fires, whose places are fixed round the altar, fed with holy wood, having the Darbha grass strewn around their margins, removing sin by the perfume of the oblations, purify thee. (7)

Now set out (on thy journey.) (*Looking round*). Where are Śārṅgarava and others?

(*Entering*) PUPIL. Holy sire, here we are.

KĀŚYAPA. Show thy sister her way.

शार्ङ्गरवः—इत इतो भवती ।

(सर्वे परिक्रामन्ति ।)

काश्यपः—भो भोः संनिहितास्तपोवनतरवः,

पातुं न प्रथमं व्यवस्यति जलं युष्मास्वपीतेषु या
नादत्ते प्रियमण्डनापि भवतां स्नेहेन या पल्लवम् ।
आद्ये वः कुसुमप्रसूतिसमये यस्या भवत्युत्सवः
सेयं याति शकुन्तला पतिगृहं सर्वैरनुज्ञायताम् ॥ ८ ॥

(कोकिलरवं सूचयित्वा)

अनुमतगमना शकुन्तला
तरुभिरियं वनवासबन्धुभिः ।
परभृतविरुतं कलं यथा
प्रतिवचनीकृतमेभिरीदृशम् ॥ ९ ॥

(आकाशे ।)

रम्यान्तरः कमलिनीहरितैः सरोभि-
श्छायाद्रुमैर्नियमितार्कमयूखतापः ।
भूयात्कुशेशयरजोमृदुरेणुरस्याः
शान्तानुकूलपवनश्च शिवश्च पन्थाः ॥ १० ॥

(सर्वे सविस्मयमाकर्णयन्ति ।)

गौतमी—जादे, णादिजणसिणिद्धाहिं अणुण्णादगमणासि तवोवणदेवदाहिं । पणम भअवदीणं । जाते, ज्ञातिजनस्निग्धाभिरनुज्ञातगमनासि तपोवनदेवताभिः । प्रणम भगवतीभ्यः ।

शकुन्तला—(सप्रणामं परिक्रम्य । जनान्तिकम् ।) हला पिअंवदे, णं अज्जउत्तदंसणुस्सुआए वि अस्समपदं परिच्चअन्तीए दुक्खेण मे चलणा पुरदो पवट्टन्ति । हला प्रियंवदे, नन्वार्यपुत्रदर्शनोत्सुकाया अप्याश्रमपदं परित्यजन्त्या दुःखेन मे चरणौ पुरतः प्रवर्तेते ।

ŚĀRNGARAVA. This way, this way, lady.

(*They all walk about.*)

KĀŚYAPA. Ye neighbouring trees of the pious grove!

She who would not drink water first, before you were watered; she who cropped not through affection for you one of your fresh leaves, though she is so fond of ornaments: she whose chief delight was in the season of the first appearance of your bloom; even that same Śakuntalā is going to the palace of her wedded lord. Let all give their consent. (8)

(*Acting as if he heard the note of a Koil.*)

Śakuntalā is given leave to depart by the trees, the companions of her forest—life; since a song to this effect, a sweet Koil-song was employed as an answer by them. (9)

(*In the air*)

May her path, pleasant at intervals with lakes that are green with lotus-beds, where the heat of the sun's rays is mitigated by shady-trees, where the dust is soft as the pollen from the lotuses, be cheered by gentle and pleasant breezes and be (altogether) prosperous. (10)

(*All listen with wonderment.*)

GAUTAMĪ. Child, the deities of the holy forest, who are dear to thee as thy own kinsfolk, have given thee leave to depart. Pay reverence to the holy ones.

ŚAKUNTALĀ (*She walks round bowing; aside*). Priyaṁvadā, dear, long as I may to see my husband, yet in leaving this hermitage, my feet can hardly move forward.

प्रियंवदा—ण केवलं तवोवणविरहकादरा सही एव्व । तुए उवट्ठिदविओअस्स तवोवणस्स वि दाव समवत्था दीसइ । न केवलं तपोवनविरहकातरा सख्येव । त्वयोपस्थितवियोगस्य तपोवनस्यापि तावत्समवस्था दृश्यते ।

उग्गलिअदब्भकवला मिआ परिच्चत्तणच्चणा मोरा ।
ओसरिअपण्डुपत्ता मुअन्ति अस्सू विअ लदाओ ॥ ११ ॥

उद्गलितदर्भकवला मृग्यः परित्यक्तनर्तना मयूराः ।
अपसृतपाण्डुपत्रा मुञ्चन्त्यश्रूणीव लताः ॥

शकुन्तला—(स्मृत्वा ।) ताद, लदाबहिणिअं वणजोसिणिं दाव आमन्तइस्सं । तात, लताभगिनीं वनज्योत्स्नां तावदामन्त्रयिष्ये ।

काश्यपः—अवैमि ते तस्यां सोदर्यस्नेहम् । इयं तावद्दक्षिणेन ।

शकुन्तला—(लतामुपेत्य । **) वणजोसिणी, चूदसंगता वि मं पच्चालिङ्ग इदोगदाहिं साहाबाहाहिं । अज्जप्पहुदि दूरपरिवत्तिणी दे खु भविस्सं ।** वनज्योत्स्ने, चूतसंगतापि मां प्रत्यालिङ्गेतोगताभिः शाखाबाहाभिः । अद्यप्रभृति दूरपरिवर्तिनी ते खलु भविष्यामि ।

काश्यपः—

संकल्पितं प्रथममेव मया तवार्थे
भर्तारमात्मसदृशं सुकृतैर्गता त्वम् ।
चूतेन संश्रितवती नवमालिकेय-
मस्यामहं त्वयि च संप्रति वीतचिन्तः ॥ १२ ॥

इतः पन्थानं प्रतिपद्यस्व ।

शकुन्तला—(सख्यौ प्रति । **) हला, एसा दुवेणं वो हत्थे णिक्खेवो ।** हला, एषा द्वयोर्युवयोर्हस्ते निक्षेपः ।

सख्यौ—अअं जणो कस्स हत्थे समप्पिदो । (इति बाष्पं विहरतः ।) अयं जनः कस्य हस्ते समर्पितः ।

PRIYAMVADĀ. My friend is not the only one to feel distressed at this separation from the pious grove. One may observe the same condition even of the grove now when the time of your departure approaches.

The deer let fall the morsels of Darbha-grass,
the peacocks stop their dancing, and the cree-
pers, whose pale leaves fall (to the ground),
appear to shed tears. (11)

ŚAKUNTALĀ (*Remembering*). Father, I will just say good-bye to Vanajyotsnā, my sister among the creepers.

KĀŚYAPA. I know thou lovest her as thy sister. Here she is now to the right.

ŚAKUNTALĀ (*Approaching the creeper*). O Vanajyotsnā, although wedded to the mango-tree, yet embrace me, too, with your arms, these branches, which are turned in this direction. I shall be far away from you after this day.

KĀŚYAPA.

Thy merits have gained thee a husband equal
to thyself, who had already been originally de-
termined upon by me for thee ; this Navamā-
likā has resorted to the mango-tree, so that
now my solicitude for thee and for her is at
an end. (12)

From here, proceed on thy journey.

ŚAKUNTALĀ (*To her friends*). Friends, this (creeper) is a deposit in your hands.

FRIENDS. (But) into whose hands shall we be left? (*they shed tears.*)

काश्यपः—अनसूये, अलं रुदित्वा । ननु भवतीभ्यामेव स्थिरीकर्तव्या शकुन्तला ।

(सर्वे परिक्रामन्ति ।)

शकुन्तला—ताद, एसा उडजपज्जन्तचारिणी गब्भमन्थरा मिअवहू जदा अणघप्पसवा होइ तदा मे कंपि पिअणिवेदइत्तअं विसज्जइस्सह । तात एषोटजपर्यंतचारिणी गर्भमन्थरा मृगवधूर्यदानघप्रसवा भवति तदा मह्यं कमपि प्रियनिवेदयितृकं विसर्जयिष्यथ ।

काश्यपः—नेदं विस्मरिष्यामः ।

शकुन्तला—(गतिभङ्गं रूपयित्वा ।) को णु क्खु एसो णिवसणे मे सज्जइ । (इति परावर्तते ।) को नु खल्वेष निवसने मे सज्जते ।

काश्यपः—वत्से,

यस्य त्वया व्रणविरोपणमिङ्गुदीनां
तैलं न्यषिच्यत मुखे कुशसूचिविद्धे ।
श्यामाकमुष्टिपरिवर्धितको जहाति
सोऽयं न पुत्रकृतकः पदवीं मृगस्ते ॥ १३ ॥

शकुन्तला—वच्छ, किं सहवासपरिच्चाइणिं मं अणुसरसि । अचिरप्पसूदाए जणणीए विणा वड्ढिदो एव्व । दाणिं पि मए विरहिदं तुमं तादो चिन्तइस्सदि । णिवत्तेहि दाव । (इति रुदती प्रस्थिता ।) वत्स, किं सहवासपरित्यागिनीं मामनुसरसि । अचिरप्रसूतया जनन्या विना वर्धित एव । इदानीमपि मया विरहितं त्वां तातश्चिन्तयिष्यति । निवर्तस्व तावत् ।

काश्यपः—

उत्पक्ष्मणोर्नयनयोरुपरुद्धवृत्तिं
बाष्पं कुरु स्थिरतया विरतानुबन्धम् ।

KĀŚYAPA. Anasūyā, enough of weeping! It is you, surely, who must cheer Śakuntalā.

(*All walk round.*)

ŚAKUNTALĀ. Father, when yon female antelope grazing about near the hut, who now moves slowly from the weight of her young, shall be safely delivered of it, then you will send me some one to announce the happy event.

KĀŚYAPA. I shall not forget it.

ŚAKUNTALĀ (*Showing her movement is obstructed.*) Ah! who is it that clings to my dress?

(*She turns round.*)

KĀŚYAPA. My darling,

It is thy adopted child, the (little) fawn whose mouth, when the sharp points of Kuśa grass wounded it, was sprinkled by thee with the healing oil of Ingudī, who has been tenderly reared by thee with handfuls of Śyāmāka grains; and who now will not leave thy footsteps. (13)

ŚAKUNTALĀ. My child, why should you follow me who must leave your company? You were indeed brought up by me when bereft of your mother shortly after she was delivered of you; now also, when separated from me, will father attend you with anxious care; go back then. (*She walks on weeping.*)

KĀŚYAPA.

Be firm and check the rising tears, that obstruct the free action of thy eyes, with their upturned eyelashes. For here on this path

अस्मिन्नलक्षितनतोन्नतभूमिभागे
मार्गे पदानि खलु ते विषमीभवन्ति ॥ १४ ॥

शार्ङ्गरवः—भगवन्, ओदकान्तं स्निग्धो जनोऽनुगन्तव्य इति श्रूयते। तदिदं सरस्तीरम्। अत्र संदिश्य प्रतिगन्तुमर्हसि।

काश्यपः—तेन हीमां क्षीरवृक्षच्छायामाश्रयामः।

(सर्वे परिक्रम्य स्थिताः।)

काश्यपः—(आत्मगतम्।) किं नु खलु तत्रभवतो दुष्यन्तस्य युक्तरूपमस्माभिः संदेष्टव्यम्। (इति चिन्तयति।)

शकुन्तला—(जनान्तिकम्।) हला, पेक्ख। णलिणीपत्तन्तरिदं वि सहअरं अदेक्खन्ती आदुरा चक्कवाई आरडदि दुक्करं अहं करेमि त्ति। हला, पश्य नलिनीपत्रान्तरितमपि सहचरमपश्यन्त्यातुरा चक्रवाक्यारौति दुष्करमहं करोमीति।

अनसूया—सहि, मा एव्वं मन्तेहि। सखि, मैवं मन्त्रयस्व।

एसा वि पिएण विणा गमेइ रअणिं विसाअदीहअरं।
गरुअं पि विरहदुक्खं आसाबन्धो सहावेदि ॥ १५ ॥

एषापि प्रियेण विना गमयति रजनीं विषाददीर्घतराम्।
गुर्वपि विरहदुःखमाशाबन्धः साहयति ॥

काश्यपः—शार्ङ्गरव, इति त्वया मद्वचनात्स राजा शकुन्तलां पुरस्कृत्य वक्तव्यः।

शार्ङ्गरवः—आज्ञापयतु भवान्।

काश्यपः—

अस्मान्साधु विचिन्त्य संयमधनानुच्चैः कुलं चात्मन-
स्त्वय्यस्याः कथमप्यबान्धवकृतां स्नेहप्रवृत्तिं च ताम्।

where the undulations of ground are not discernible, they footsteps must needs be unequal. (14)

ŚĀRṄGARAVA. It is a sacred rule, holy father, that one should accompany a loved person as far as the water's brink. Give us your message here, and be pleased to return.

KĀŚYAPA. Let us, then rest in the shade of this Kṣīra-tree.

(*All walk around and stop.*)

KĀŚYAPA (*To himself*). What message should be sent by me that would be most appropriate for the noble Duṣyanta? (*He reflects.*)

ŚAKUNTALĀ (*Aside*). Look, friend, the female Cakravāka, not perceiving her dear mate when only hidden behind lotus-leaves is crying in her anguish How hard is my lot!'

ANASŪYĀ. Friend, do not say so.

Even she, without her beloved, passes away the night made too long by grief. The bond of hope makes the pain of severence, however keen, supportable. (15)

KĀŚYAPA. Śārṅgarava, when you present Śakuntalā to the king, address him thus in my name.

ŚĀRṄGARAVA. Give your commands, holy father.

KĀŚYAPA.

Having well considered us as rich in devotion, thy own exalted birth and the free flow of affection of this (girl) towards thee, which arose in her without any interference of her kindred,

सामान्यप्रतिपत्तिपूर्वकमियं दारेषु दृश्या त्वया
भाग्यायत्तमतःपरं न खलु तद्वाच्यं वधूबन्धुभिः ॥ १६ ॥

शार्ङ्गरवः—गृहीतः संदेशः ।

काश्यपः—वत्से, त्वमिदानीमनुशासनीयासि । वनौकसोऽपि सन्तो लौकिकज्ञा वयम् ।

शार्ङ्गरवः—न खलु धीमतां कश्चिदविषयो नाम ।

काश्यपः—सा त्वमितः पतिकुलं प्राप्य

शुश्रूषस्व गुरून्कुरु प्रियसखीवृत्तिं सपत्नीजने
भर्तुर्विप्रकृतापि रोषणतया मा स्म प्रतीपं गमः ।
भूयिष्ठं भव दक्षिणा परिजने भाग्येष्वनुत्सेकिनी
यान्त्येवं गृहिणीपदं युवतयो वामाः कुलस्याधयः ॥ १७ ॥

कथं वा गौतमी मन्यते ।

गौतमी—एत्तिओ वहूजणस्य उवदेसो । जादे, एदं क्खु सव्वं ओधारेहि । एतावान्वधूजनस्योपदेशः । जाते, एतत्खलु सर्वमवधारय ।

काश्यपः—वत्से, परिष्वजस्व मां सखीजनं च ।

शकुन्तला—ताद, इदो एव्व किं पिअंवदामिस्साओ सहीओ णिवत्तिस्सन्ति । तात, इत एव किं प्रियंवदामिश्राः सख्यो निवर्तिष्यन्ते ।

look on her among thy wives with the same respect (kindness) which they experience: more than that depends upon the will of heaven, and should, not indeed, be demanded by the bride's kinsfolk. (16)

ŚĀRṄGARAVA. I have (well) comprehended your message.

KĀŚYAPA. My child, I must now give thee my advice. Though I live in the forest, yet well do I know the ways of the world.

ŚĀRṄGARAVA. Nothing, indeed, to the wise is out of reach.

KĀŚYAPA. When thou wilt have gone from here to thy husband's home,

Pay respectful attention to thy elders; treat thy rivals as thy dear friends; should thy husband wrong thee, let not thy resentment lead thee to disobedience. Be ever courteous towards thy servants; not puffed with pride in thy fortune. By such behaviour, young women become honoured wives; but perverse wives are the bane of a family. (17)

But what does Gautamī say?

GAUTAMĪ. This is the advice to be given to a young bride. My child, be sure to remember it all.

KĀŚYAPA. Come, my child, embrace me and thy friends.

ŚAKUNTALĀ. O my father, must my friends turn back from here?

काश्यपः—इमे अपि प्रदेये। न युक्तमनयोस्तत्र गन्तुम्। त्वया सह गौतमी यास्यति।

शकुन्तला—(पितरमाश्लिष्य।) कहं दाणिं तादस्स अङ्कादो परिब्भट्ठा मलअतडुम्मूलिआ चन्दणलदा विअ देसन्तरे जीविअं धारइस्सं। कथमिदानीं तातस्याङ्कात्परिभ्रष्टा मलयतटोन्मूलिता चन्दनलतेव देशान्तरे जीवितं धारयिष्ये।

काश्यपः—वत्से, किमेवं कातरासि।

अभिजनवतो भर्तुः श्लाघ्ये स्थिता गृहिणीपदे
विभवगुरुभिः कृत्यैस्तस्य प्रतिक्षणमाकुला।
तनयमचिरात्प्राचीवार्कं प्रसूय च पावनं
मम विरहजां न त्वं वत्से शुचं गणयिष्यसि॥ १८॥

(शकुन्तला पितुः पादयोः पतति।)

काश्यपः—यदिच्छामि ते तदस्तु।

शकुन्तला—(सख्यावुपेत्य।) हला, दुवे वि मं समं एव्व परिस्सजह। हला, द्वे अपि मां सममेव परिष्वजेथाम्।

सख्यौ—(तथा कृत्वा।) सहि, जइ णाम सो राआ पच्चहिण्णाणमन्थरो भवे तदो से इमं अत्तणामहेअङ्किअं अङ्गुलीअअं दंसेहि। सखि, यदि नाम स राजा प्रत्यभिज्ञानमन्थरो भवेत्ततस्तस्येदमात्मनामधेयाङ्कितमङ्गुलीयकं दर्शय।

शकुन्तला—इमिणा संदेहेण वो आकम्पिदम्हि। अनेन संदेहेन वामाकम्पितास्मि।

सख्यौ—मा भाआहि। अदिसिणेहो पावसङ्की। मा भैषीः। अतिस्नेहः पापशङ्की।

KĀŚYAPA. These, too, are to be given away in marriage. It would not be proper for them to go there, but Gautamī will accompany thee.

ŚAKUNTALĀ (*Embracing her father*). Removed from the lap of my father, like a young sandal tree, rent from the slopes of the Malaya, how shall I exist in a strange soil ?

KĀŚYAPA. My child, why shouldst thou be so anxious ?

When thou shalt be occupying the honoured position of the consort of a nobly-born husband ; engrossed every moment in his affairs important through his greatness ; and when before long thou wilt have given birth to a child that will purify (his race) as the East brings forth the Sun, then wilt thou think but lightly of this affliction caused by severence from me. (18)

(*Śakuntalā falls at the feet of her father.*)

KĀŚYAPA. My darling, mayest thou have all that I desire for thee !

ŚAKUNTALĀ (*Advancing to her friends*). Come, friends ; embrace me, both of you together.

FRIENDS (*So doing*). Friend, should the king be slow to recognize you, show him this ring on which his own name is engraved.

ŚAKUNTALĀ. My heart flutters at the apprehension which you have raised.

FRIENDS. Do not be afraid. Excessive love is apt to suspect evil.

शार्ङ्गरवः—**युगान्तरमारूढः सविता । त्वरतामत्रभवती ।**

शकुन्तला—(आश्रमाभिमुखा स्थित्वा ।) **ताद, कदा णु भूओ तवोवणं पेक्खिस्सं ।** तात, कदा नु भूयस्तपोवनं प्रेक्षिष्ये ।

काश्यपः—**श्रूयताम् ।**

भूत्वा चिराय चतुरन्तमहीसपत्नी
दौष्यन्तमप्रतिरथं तनयं निवेश्य ।
भर्त्रा तदर्पितकुटुम्बभरेण सार्धं
शान्ते करिष्यसि पदं पुनराश्रमेऽस्मिन् ॥ १९ ॥

गौतमी—**जादे, परिहीअदि गमणवेला । णिवत्तेहि पिदरं । अहवा चिरेण वि पुणो पुणो एसा एव्वं मन्तइस्सदि । णिवत्तदु भवं ।** जाते, परिहीयते गमनवेला । निवर्तय पितरम् । अथवा चिरेणापि पुनः पुनरेषैवं मन्त्रयिष्यते । निवर्ततां भवान् ।

काश्यपः—**वत्से, उपरुध्यते तपोऽनुष्ठानम् ।**

शकुन्तला—(भूयः पितरमाश्लिष्य ।) **तवच्चरणपीडिदं तादसरीरं । ता मा अदिमेत्तं मम किदे उक्कण्ठिदुम् ।** तपश्चरणपीडितं तातशरीरम् । तन्मातिमात्रं मम कृत उत्कण्ठितुम् ।

काश्यपः—(सनिःश्वासम् ।)

शममेष्यति मम शोकः कथं नु वत्से त्वया रचितपूर्वम् ।
उटजद्वारविरूढं नीवारबलिं विलोकयतः ॥ २० ॥

गच्छ । शिवास्ते पन्थानः सन्तु ।

(निष्क्रान्ता शकुन्तला सहयायिनश्च ।)

सख्यौ—(शकुन्तलां विलोक्य ।) **हद्धी हद्धी । अन्तरिहिदा सउन्दला वणराईए ।** हा धिक्, हा धिक् । अन्तर्हिता शकुन्तला वनराज्या ।

ŚĀRṄGARAVA. The Sun has ascended to another quarter of the heavens. Let the worthy lady hasten.

ŚAKUNTALĀ (*Turning her face towards the hermitage*). Father, when shall I behold this pious grove again?

KĀŚYAPA. Listen.

When thou shalt long have been a co-wife of the Earth bounded by the four cardinal-points, and settled in marriage in Duṣyanta's son by thee, a matchless warrior ; then with thy husband who shall have transferred the burden of family-cares to him, thou shalt again set foot in this peaceful hermitage. (19)

GAUTAMĪ. My child, the (proper) hour of our journey is slipping by. Suffer thy father to return. Or since ever so long she will go on talking again and again in the same strain, let the holy father return.

KĀŚYAPA. Sweet child, the practice of devotions is interrupted.

ŚAKUNTALĀ (*Embracing her father again*). Father's body is already worn out by his devotion. Do not, therefore, grieve for me beyond measure.

KĀŚYAPA (*Sighing*). How, my child, will my grief cease, as I look at the hallowed rice-grains formerly offered by thee, germinating at the door of my cottage? (20)

Go, may thy journey prosper.

(*Exeunt Śakuntalā and her escort.*)

FRIENDS (*Gazing after Śakuntalā*). Alas! Alas! Śakuntalā is hidden by the thick trees.

काश्यपः—(सनिःश्वासम् ।) अनसूये, गतवती वां सहधर्मचारिणी । निगृह्य शोकमनुगच्छतं मां प्रस्थितम् ।

उभे—ताद, सउन्दलाविरहिदं सुण्णं विअ तवोवणं कहं पविसामो । तात, शकुन्तलाविरहितं शून्यमिव तपोवनं कथं प्रविशावः ।

काश्यपः—स्नेहप्रवृत्तिरेवंदर्शिनी । (सविमर्शं परिक्रम्य ।) हन्त भोः, शकुन्तलां पतिकुलं विसृज्य लब्धमिदानीं स्वास्थ्यम् । कुतः

अर्थो हि कन्या परकीय एव
तामद्य संप्रेष्य परिग्रहीतुः ।
जातो ममायं विशदः प्रकामं
प्रत्यर्पितन्यास इवान्तरात्मा ॥ २१ ॥

(इति निष्क्रान्ताः सर्वे ।)

चतुर्थोऽङ्कः ।

KĀŚYAPA (*Sighing*). Anasūyā, your companion is (at length) departed. Check your grief and follow me who am leaving.

BOTH. Father, how shall we enter the pious grove which without Śakuntalā seems a perfect vacuity?

KĀŚYAPA. So your love interprets. (*He walks round meditating*). Ah, dismissing Śakuntalā to her husband's home, I have regained my natural serenity of mind. For

In truth a daughter is another's property;
and having to-day sent her to her lord, I find
my soul has become quite clear as if after re-
storing a deposit. (21)

(*Exeunt All.*)

Here ends Act IV

पञ्चमोऽङ्कः ।

(ततः प्रविशत्यासनस्थो राजा विदूषकश्च ।)

विदूषकः—(कर्णं दत्त्वा ।) **भो वअस्स, संगीदसालन्तरे अवधाणं देहि । कलविसुद्धाए गीदीए सरसंजोओ सुणीअदि । जाणे तत्तहोदी हंसवदिआ वण्णपरिअअं करेदि त्ति ।** भो वयस्य, संगीतशालान्तरेऽवधानं देहि । कलविशुद्धाया गीतेः स्वरसंयोगः श्रूयते । जाने तत्रभवती हंसपदिका वर्णपरिचयं करोतीति ।

राजा—तूष्णीं भव । यावदाकर्णयामि ।

(आकाशे गीयते ।)

अहिणवमहुलोलुवो तुमं
तह परिचुम्बिअ चूअमञ्जरिं ।
कमलवसइमेत्तणिव्वुदो
महुअर विम्हरिओ सि णं कहं ॥ १ ॥

अभिनवमधुलोलुपस्त्वं तथा परिचुम्ब्य चूतमञ्जरीम् ।
कमलवसतिमात्रनिर्वृतो मधुकर विस्मृतोऽस्येनां कथम् ॥

राजा—अहो रागपरिवाहिनी गीतिः ।

विदूषकः—किं दाव गीदीए अवगदो अक्खरत्थो । किं तावद्गीत्या अवगतोऽक्षरार्थः ।

राजा—(स्मितं कृत्वा ।) **सकृत्कृतप्रणयोऽयं जनः । तदस्या देवीं वसुमतीमन्तरेण महदुपालम्भं गतोऽस्मि । सखे माठव्य, मद्वचनादुच्यतां हंसपदिका । निपुणमुपालब्धोऽस्मीति ।**

ACT V

(*Enter king seated and the Vidūṣaka.*)

VIDŪṢAKA (*Listening.*) O friend, turn your attention to the interior of the Music-hall. One hears harmonious notes blended in a sweet and clear song. I believe the lady Haṁsapadikā is practising singing.

KING. Be quiet, that I may listen.

(*A song is sung in the air.*)

O bee, how comes it that you who eagerly long for fresh-honey, after having kissed the mango-blossom in that way, should have forgotten it, being now satisfied with mere dwelling in the lotus ! (1)

KING. O, what an impassioned song ?

VIDŪṢAKA. But, do you understand the meaning of the words of the song ?

KING (*Smiling*). I was once in love with her, and am now reproved on account of the queen Vasumatī. Friend Māṭhavya inform Haṁsapadikā in my name that I am well reproved.

विदूषकः—जं भवं आणवेदि । (उत्थाय ।) भो वअस्स, गहीदस्स ताए परकीएहिं हत्थेहिं सिहण्डए ताडीअमाणस्स अच्छराए वीदराअस्स विअ णत्थि दाणिं मे मोक्खो । यद्भवानाज्ञापयति । भो वयस्य, गृहीतस्य तया परकीयैर्हस्तैः शिखण्डके ताड्यमानस्याप्सरसा वीतरागस्येव नास्तीदानीं मे मोक्षः ।

राजा—गच्छ । नागरिकवृत्त्या संज्ञापयैनाम् ।

विदूषकः—का गई । (इति निष्क्रान्तः ।) का गतिः ।

राजा—(आत्मगतम् ।) किं नु खलु गीतार्थमाकर्ण्येष्टजनविरहादृतेऽपि बलवदुत्कण्ठितोऽस्मि । अथवा ।

रम्याणि वीक्ष्य मधुरांश्च निशम्य शब्दा-
न्पर्युत्सुकीभवति यत्सुखितोऽपि जन्तुः ।
तच्चेतसा स्मरति नूनमबोधपूर्वं
भावस्थिराणि जननान्तरसौहृदानि ॥२ ॥

(इति पर्याकुलस्तिष्ठति ।)

(ततः प्रविशति कञ्चुकी ।)

कञ्चुकी—अहो नु खल्वीदृशीमवस्थां प्रतिपन्नोऽस्मि ।

आचार इत्यवहितेन मया गृहीता
या वेत्रयष्टिरवरोधगृहेषु राज्ञः ।
काले गते बहुतिथे मम सैव जाता
प्रस्थानविक्लवगतेरवलम्बनार्था ॥ ३ ॥

भोः, कामं धर्मकार्यमनतिपात्यं देवस्य । तथापीदानीमेव धर्मासनादुत्थिताय पुनरुपरोधकारि कण्वशिष्यागमनमस्मै नोत्सहे निवेदितुम् । अथवाविश्रमोऽयं लोकतन्त्राधिकारः । कुतः ।

VIDŪṢAKA. As your Majesty, commands. (*Rising*). But now there will be no liberation for me when seized by her with the hands of others by the crest-lock and belaboured, any more than for a sage whose passions are spent, if seized by a nymph.

KING. Go, tell her in a courtly style.

VIDŪṢAKA. What help! (*He goes out.*)

KING (*To himself*). Why am I filled with such deep sadness when I am in fact not separated from any real object of my affection, on hearing the meaning of the song? Or,

> When even a happy being is filled with wistful longings on seeing beautiful forms and listening to sweet sounds, then surely without being conscious of it, he remembers in his mind the friendships of a former birth deeply-rooted there in the form of impressions. (2)

(*He remains deeply troubled.*)

(*Then enter a chamberlain.*)

CHAMBERLAIN. Alas! To such a state am I reduced!

> This staff which I assumed as a matter of form for the discharge of my duties in the inner apartment of my king, has, now when much time has elapsed since then, become the support to aid my faltering steps. (3)

Ah, surely the king cannot neglect a religious duty. And yet I have not the heart to announce to him, who has just risen from his tribunal the arrival of Kaṇva's pupils which will again detain him. But, this office of supporting the world will not allow any repose. For

भानुः सकृद्युक्ततुरङ्ग एव
रात्रिंदिवं गन्धवहः प्रयाति ।
शेषः सदैवाहितभूमिभारः
षष्ठांशवृत्तेरपि धर्म एषः ॥ ४ ॥

यावन्नियोगमनुतिष्ठामि । (परिक्रम्यावलोक्य च ।) एष देवः

प्रजाः प्रजाः स्वा इव तन्त्रयित्वा
निषेवते श्रान्तमना विविक्तम् ।
यूथानि संचार्य रविप्रतप्तः
शीतं दिवा स्थानमिव द्विपेन्द्रः ॥ ५ ॥

(उपगम्य ।) जयतु जयतु देवः । एते खलु हिमगिरेरुपत्यकारण्यवासिनः काश्यपसंदेशमादाय सस्त्रीकास्तपस्विनः संप्राप्ताः । श्रुत्वा देवः प्रमाणम् ।

राजा—(सादरम् ।) किं काश्यपसंदेशहारिणः ।

कञ्चुकी—अथ किम् ।

राजा—तेन हि मद्वचनाद्विज्ञाप्यतामुपाध्यायः सोमरातः । अमूनाश्रमवासिनः श्रौतेन विधिना सत्कृत्य स्वयमेव प्रवेशयितुमर्हतीति । अहमप्यत्र तपस्विदर्शनोचिते प्रदेशे स्थितः प्रतिपालयामि ।

कञ्चुकी—यदाज्ञापयति देवः । (इति निष्क्रान्तः ।)

राजा—(उत्थाय ।) वेत्रवति, अग्निशरणमार्गमादेशय ।

The Sun has yoked his steeds but once, the gale breathes by night and by day : Śeṣa continually sustains the weight of the Earth ; this also is the duty of him whose subsistence arises from a sixth part (of his people's income). (4)

Let me then attend to my duty. (*Walking about and observing*). Here is his Majesty

Attending to his people as to his own children, he now, being wearied in mind, seeks seclusion ; as an elephant, the chief of his herds, after having taken them round, and being heated by the Sun, repairs to a cool place during (the oppressive heat of) the day. (5)

(*Advancing*) Victory, victory to your Majesty ! Here are hermits with some women, come from their abode in the forest at the foot of the snowy mountains, and they bring a message from Kāśyapa. Having heard, your Majesty will command.

KING (*Respectfully.*) Do they bring a message from Kāśyapa ?

CHAMBERLAIN. It is even so.

KING. Well then, order the priest Somarātā, in my name : It is proper that you should give them a reception in the form appointed by the scriptures, and bring them (into the palace). I, too, shall await (them) here in this place fit for the reception of hermits.

CHAMBERLAIN. As your Majesty commands. (*exit.*)

KING. (*Rising*). Vetravati, lead the way to the fire-sanctuary.

प्रतीहारी—इदो इदो देवो। इत इतो देवः।

राजा—(परिक्रामति। अधिकारखेदं निरूप्य।) सर्वः प्रार्थितमर्थमधिगम्य सुखी संपद्यते जन्तुः। राज्ञां तु चरितार्थता दुःखोत्तरैव।

औत्सुक्यमात्रमवसादयति प्रतिष्ठा
क्लिश्नाति लब्धपरिपालनवृत्तिरेव।
नातिश्रमापनयनाय यथा श्रमाय
राज्यं स्वहस्तधृतदण्डमिवातपत्रम्॥ ६॥

(नेपथ्ये।)

वैतालिकौ—विजयतां देवः।

प्रथमः—

स्वसुखनिरभिलाषः खिद्यसे लोकहेतोः
प्रतिदिनमथवा ते वृत्तिरेवंविधैव।
अनुभवति हि मूर्ध्ना पादपस्तीव्रमुष्णं
शमयति परितापं छायया संश्रितानाम्॥ ७॥

द्वितीयः—

नियमयसि विमार्गप्रस्थितानात्तदण्डः
प्रशमयसि विवादं कल्पसे रक्षणाय।
अतनुषु विभवेषु ज्ञातयः सन्तु नाम
त्वयि तु परिसमाप्तं बन्धुकृत्यं प्रजानाम्॥ ८॥

राजा—एते क्लान्तमनसः पुनर्नवीकृताः स्मः। (इति परिक्रामति।)

PORTRESS. This way, your Majesty, this way.

KING. (*Moves about ; betraying the cares of office*). Every one is happy on attaining his desire ; but to kings, the attainment of their desire is only followed by pain.

The attainment of one's ambition destroys only all eager longing ; but the task of retaining what has been secured gives extreme pain. A kingdom, like an umbrella, of which a man carries the staff in his own hand, does not so much remove fatigue as it causes fatigue. (6)

(*Behind the Scenes*)

TWO BARDS. May the king be victorious !

FIRST.

Thou seekest not thy own happiness, but for the people thou dost toil from day to day. Or thus is thy very nature made. For the Tree bears on his head the fierce heat (of day) while his shade allays the fever of those who seek shelter under him. (7)

SECOND.

Wielding the rod of justice, thou bringest to order all those who have set out on bad courses ; thou biddest contention cease ; and thou preservest thy people. One may have, in truth, a number of kinsmen, when wealth abounds ; but in thee the duty of your subjects' kinsmen towards them finds perfection. (8)

KING. Now, wearied in mind that I was, I feel refreshed. (*Walks round.*)

प्रतीहारी—अहिणवसम्मज्जणसस्सिरीओ सण्णिहिदहोमधेणू-अग्गिसरणालिन्दो । आरुहदु देवो । अभिनवसंमार्जनसश्रीकः संनिहित-होमधेनुरग्निशरणालिन्दः । आरोहतु देवः ।

राजा—(आरुह्य परिजनांसावलम्बी तिष्ठति ।) वेत्रवति, किमुद्दिश्य भगवता काश्यपेन मत्सकाशमृषयः प्रेषिताः स्युः ।

किं तावद्व्रतिनामुपोढतपसां विघ्नैस्तपो दूषितं
धर्मारण्यचरेषु केनचिदुत प्राणिष्वसच्चेष्टितम् ।
आहोस्वित्प्रसवो ममापचरितैर्विष्टम्भितो वीरुधा-
मित्यारूढबहुप्रतर्कमपरिच्छेदाकुलं मे मनः ॥ ९ ॥

प्रतीहारी—सुचरिदणन्दिणो इसीओ देवं सभाजइदुं आअदे त्ति तक्केमि । सुचरितनन्दिन ऋषयो देवं सभाजयितुमागता इति तर्कयामि ।

(ततः प्रविशन्ति गौतमीसहिताः शकुन्तलां पुरस्कृत्य मुनयः ।)

[पुरश्चैषां कञ्चुकी पुरोहितश्च ।]

कञ्चुकी —इत इतो भवन्तः ।

शार्ङ्गरवः—शारद्वत,

महाभागः कामं नरपतिरभिन्नस्थितिरसौ
न कश्चिद्वर्णानामपथमपकृष्टोऽपि भजते ।
तथापीदं शश्वत्परिचितविविक्तेन मनसा
जनाकीर्णं मन्ये हुतवहपरीतं गृहमिव ॥ १० ॥

PORTRESS. Here is the terrace of the fire sanctuary, which being newly-swept looks beautiful, and near it is the cow that yields the milk for sacrifice. Let the king ascend.

KING. (*Ascends and stands leaning on the shoulder of an attendant*). Vetravati, with what object has the revered Kāśyapa sent these sages to me?

May it be that the penance of those who have commenced a vow and stored up religious merit, has been defiled by obstacles? Or has any harm been inflicted by any one on the animals who graze in the hallowed forest? Or my sins have checked the flowering of the plants? Thus my mind which is assailed by many doubts, is perplexed on account of its inability to decide. (9)

PORTRESS. I imagine the pious men have come to pay homage to their king with whose pious rule they are pleased.

(*Then enter sages accompanied by Gautamī, leading Śakuntalā before them; and in front of them the chamberlain and the chaplain.*)

CHAMBERLAIN. This way, this way, sirs.

ŚĀRṄGARAVA. Śāradvata,

Granted that this glorious king does not swerve from rectitude; and that none of all the grades, not even the lowliest, seeks the path of wrong: nevertheless my mind having ever been accustomed to solitude, I consider this (place) thronged with men to be like a house all lapped about with flame. (10)

शारद्वतः—स्थाने भवान्पुरप्रवेशादित्थंभूतः संवृत्तः । अहमपि

अभ्यक्तमिव स्नातः शुचिरशुचिमिव प्रबुद्ध इव सुप्तम् ।
बद्धमिव स्वैरगतिर्जनमिह सुखसङ्गिनमवैमि ॥ ११ ॥

शाकुन्तला—(निमित्तं सूचयित्वा ।) अम्महे, किं मे वामेदरं णअणं विप्फुरदि । अहो, किं मे वामेतरन्नयनं विस्फुरति ।

गौतमी—जादे पडिहदं अमङ्गलं । सुहाइं दे भत्तुकुलदेवदाओ वितरन्दु । (इति परिक्रामति ।) जाते, प्रतिहतममङ्गलम् । सुखानि ते भर्तृकुलदेवता वितरन्तु ।

पुरोहितः—(राजानं निर्दिश्य ।) भो भोस्तपस्विनः असावत्रभवान्वर्णाश्रमाणां रक्षिता प्रागेव मुक्तासनो वः प्रतिपालयति । पश्यतैनम् ।

शार्ङ्गरवः—भो महाब्राह्मण, काममेतदभिनन्दनीयम् । तथापि वयमत्र मध्यस्थाः । कुतः ।

भवन्ति नम्रास्तरवः फलागमै-
र्नवाम्बुभिर्भूरिविलम्बिनो घनाः ।
अनुद्धताः सत्पुरुषाः समृद्धिभिः
स्वभाव एवैष परोपकारिणाम् ॥ १२ ॥

प्रतीहारी—देव, पसण्णमुहवण्णा दीसन्ति । जाणामि वीसद्धकज्जा इसीओ । देव, प्रसन्नमुखवर्णा दृश्यन्ते । जानामि विश्रब्धकार्या ऋषयः ।

राजा—(शकुन्तलां दृष्ट्वा ।) अथात्रभवती

ŚĀRADVATA. Rightly have you become thus on entering this city. I, too,

Look on these people here devoted to worldly joys as a man (just) bathed on a man smeared with oil, as the pure on the impure, as the waking on the sleeping, or as the free man on the captive. (11)

ŚAKUNTALĀ (*Indicating an omen*). Oh, why does my right eye throb?

GAUTAMĪ. May the evil be averted, my sweet child! May thy husband's household gods confer happiness upon thee!

(*She walks round.*)

CHAPLAIN. (*Indicating the king*). There, holy men, is he the protector of the four orders and classes, who having already quitted the seat (of justice) is awaiting you. Behold him.

ŚĀRṄGARAVA. O great Brahmin, this is surely commendable; yet we do not think much of it; for

These become bent down by the abundance of their fruit; clouds hang low when they teem with fresh rain; good men are never elated by riches; this is the very nature of the benefactors of others. (12)

PORTRESS. O king, the holy men appear to have placid looks; so I think they come on an errand about which they feel confident.

KING. (*Beholding Śakuntalā*).

Who is she, shrouded in the veil, the loveliness of whose person is not fully revealed,

काऽस्विदवगुण्ठनवती नातिपरिस्फुटशरीरलावण्या ।
मध्ये तपोधनानां किसलयमिव पाण्डुपत्राणाम् ॥ १३ ॥

प्रतीहारी—देव, कुदूहलगब्भोपहिदो ण मे तक्को पसरदि । णं दंसणीआ उण से आकिदी लक्खीअदि । देव, कुतूहलगर्भोपहितो न मे तर्कः प्रसरति । ननु दर्शनीया पुनरस्या आकृतिर्लक्ष्यते ।

राजा—भवतु । अनिर्वर्णनीयं परकलत्रम् ।

शकुन्तला—(हस्तमुरसि कृत्वा । आत्मगतम्) हिअअ, किं एव्वं वेवसि । अज्जउत्तस्स भावं ओधारिअ धीरं दाव होहि । हृदय, किमेवं वेपसे । आर्यपुत्रस्य भावमवधार्य धीरं तावद्भव ।

पुरोहितः—(पुरो गत्वा ।) एते विधिवदर्चितास्तपस्विनः । अस्ति कश्चिदेषामुपाध्यायसंदेशः । तं देवः श्रोतुमर्हति ।

राजा—अवहितोऽस्मि ।

ऋषयः—(हस्तानुद्यम्य) विजयस्व राजन् ।

राजा—सर्वानभिवादये ।

ऋषयः—इष्टेन युज्यस्व ।

राजा—अपि निर्विघ्नतपसो मुनयः ।

ऋषयः—

कुतो धर्मक्रियाविघ्नः सतां रक्षितरि त्वयि ।
तमस्तपति घर्मांशौ कथमाविर्भविष्यति ॥ १४ ॥

राजा—अर्थवान्खलु मे राजशब्दः । अथ भगवांल्लोकानुग्रहाय कुशली काश्यपः ।

ऋषयः—स्वाधीनकुशलाः सिद्धिमन्तः । स भवन्तमनामयप्रश्नपूर्वकमिदमाह ।

looking in the midst of hermits like a fresh bud
among yellow leaves? (13)

PORTRESS. Your Majesty, my reason, though impelled by curiosity, does not work; but she appears to have a lovely figure.

KING. Enough! One ought not to gaze upon another's wife.

ŚAKUNTALĀ (*Laying her hand on her bosom; to herself*). My heart, why dost thou palpitate so? Call to mind the love of thy lord and be firm.

CHAPLAIN (*Going forward*). The holy men have been duly honoured. They have some message from their preceptor. Let the king deign to hear it.

KING. I am attentive.

SAGES (*Raising their hands*). Victory to you, O king.

KING. I salute you all.

SAGES. May you attain your desires!

KING. Has the devotion of the hermits been uninterrupted?

SAGES. How could the pious rites be disturbed when thou art the preserver of the good? How, when the bright Sun blazes, should darkness make its appearance? (14)

KING. My royal title, indeed, is not an empty one. Is the holy Kāśyapa now all well, to bless the world?

SAGES. They who possess miraculous powers can command welfare. He first asks after your health and then addresses you in these words—

राजा—किमाज्ञापयति भगवान् ।

शार्ङ्गरवः—यन्मिथः समयादिमां मदीयां दुहितरं भवानुपायंस्त तन्मया प्रीतिमता युवयोरनुज्ञातम् । कुतः ।

त्वमर्हतां प्राग्रसरः स्मृतोऽसि नः
शकुन्तला मूर्तिमती च सत्क्रिया ।
समानयंस्तुल्यगुणं वधूवरं
चिरस्य वाच्यं न गतः प्रजापतिः ॥ १५ ॥

तदिदानीमापन्नसत्त्वा प्रतिगृह्यतां सहधर्मचरणायेति ।

गौतमी—अज्ज, किंपि वत्तुकामम्हि । ण मे वअणावसरो अत्थि । कहंत्ति । आर्य, किमपि वक्तुकामास्मि । न मे वचनावसरोऽस्ति । कथमिति ।

णावेक्खिओ गुरुअणो इमीअ ण तुए वि पुच्छिदो बन्धू ।
एक्कक्कमेव्व चरिए भणामि किं एक्कमेक्कस्स ॥ १६ ॥

नापेक्षितो गुरुजनोऽनया न त्वयापि पृष्टो बन्धुः ।
एकैकमेव चरिते भणामि किमेकैकम् ।

शकुन्तला—(आत्मगतम् ।) किं णु क्खु अज्जउत्तो भणादि । किं नु खल्वार्यपुत्रो भणति ।

राजा—किमिदमुपन्यस्तम् ।

शकुन्तला—(आत्मगतम् ।) पावओ क्खु एसो वअणोवण्णासो । पावकः खल्वेष वचनोपन्यासः ।

शार्ङ्गरवः—कथमिदं नाम । भवन्त एव सुतरां लोकवृत्तान्तनिष्णाताः ।

सतीमपि ज्ञातिकुलैकसंश्रयां
जनोऽन्यथा भर्तृमतीं विशङ्कते ।

KING. What does the holy one command?

ŚĀRṄGARAVA. By reciprocal agreement hast thou married this daughter of mine which I have with pleasure approved. For

> Thou art known, to us as the best of worthy men; while my Śakuntalā is virtue itself in human form; Brahman, who has now united a bride and bridegroom of equal merit, has after a long time incurred no censure. (15)

Therefore, now receive her, who is quick with child, that she may perform, in conjunction with thee, the duties prescribed by religion.

GAUTAMĪ. Noble sir, I wish to say something. And (yet) there is no occasion for my words. (If you ask) how so?

> Her elderly relatives were not regarded by her, nor were kinsmen consulted by thee. The affair being transacted solely by mutual (consent), what may one say to either? (16)

ŚAKUNTALĀ (*To herself*). What will my lord say now?

KING. What is (all) this brought before me?

ŚAKUNTALĀ (*To herself*). Like fire indeed are these words he has uttered.

ŚĀRṄGARAVA. How, indeed, is this? You yourself know the world's ways well enough.

> People suspect a married woman, living wholly in her kinsmen's family, although chaste, to be otherwise. Therefore, her kinsmen desire

अतः समीपे परिणेतुरिष्यते
तदप्रियापि प्रमदा स्वबन्धुभिः ॥ १७ ॥

राजा—किं चात्रभवती मया परिणीतपूर्वा ।

शकुन्तला—(सविषादम् । आत्मगतम् ।) हिअअ, संपदं दे आसङ्का । हृदय, सांप्रतं त आशङ्का ।

शार्ङ्गरवः—

किं कृतकार्यद्वेषाद्धर्मं प्रति विमुखतोचिता राज्ञः ।

राजा—कुतोऽयमसत्कल्पनाप्रश्नः ।

शार्ङ्गरवः—

मूर्च्छन्त्यमी विकाराः प्रायेणैश्वर्यमत्तेषु ॥ १८ ॥

राजा—विशेषेणाधिक्षिप्तोऽस्मि ।

गौतमी—जादे, मुहुत्तअं मा लज्ज । अवणइस्सं दाव दे ओउण्ठणं । तदो तुमं भट्टा अहिजाणिस्सदि । (इति यथोक्तं करोति ।) जाते, मुहूर्तं मा लज्जस्व । अपनेष्यामि तावत्तेऽवगुण्ठनम् । ततस्त्वां भर्ताभिज्ञास्यति ।

राजा—(शकुन्तलां निर्वर्ण्य । आत्मगतम् ।)

इदमुपनतमेवं रूपमक्लिष्टकान्ति
प्रथमपरिगृहीतं स्यान्न वेत्यव्यवस्यन् ।
भ्रमर इव विभाते कुन्दमन्तस्तुषारं
न खलु च परिभोक्तुं नैव शक्नोमि हातुम् ॥ १९ ॥

(इति विचारयन् स्थितः ।)

प्रतीहारी—अहो धम्मावेक्खिदा भट्टिणो । इदिसं णाम सुहोवणदं रूवं देक्खिअ को अण्णो विआरेदि । अहो धर्मापेक्षिता भर्तुः । ईदृशं नाम सुखोपनतं रूपं दृष्ट्वा कोऽन्यो विचारयति ।

a young woman to be with her husband even
though he love her not. (17)

KING. And, was this lady married to me before?

ŚAKUNTALĀ (*Sorrowfully; to herself*). O my heart, thy fears are justified!

ŚĀRṄGARAVA.

Does it become a king to depart from the
rules of justice, merely because of his aversion
to a deed done?

KING. What means this accusation based upon a false assumption?

ŚĀRṄGARAVA.

Such fickleness of disposition mostly takes
effect in those whom power intoxicates. (18)

KING. I am reproved with too great severity.

GAUTAMĪ. Child, forget thy shame for a while. I will just remove the veil, so that thy husband will then recognize thee. (*Does as said.*)

KING. (*Observing Śakuntalā; to himself.*)

While I am doubtful whether this unblemish-
ed beauty which is thus brought near to me
may or may not have been formerly married
by me, verily I neither can enjoy nor forsake
her like a bee at the close of night, the Kunda
flower filled with dew. (19)

(*Keeps reflecting.*)

PORTRESS. How greatly is virtue honoured by our lord! Would any other man hesitate when he saw such beauty presenting herself with ease?

शार्ङ्गरवः—भो राजन्, किमिति जोषमास्यते ।

राजा—भोस्तपोधनाः, चिन्तयन्नपि न खलु स्वीकरणमत्रभवत्याः स्मरामि । तत्कथमिमामभिव्यक्तसत्त्वलक्षणां प्रत्यात्मानं क्षेत्रिणमाशङ्कमानः प्रतिपत्स्ये ।

शकुन्तला—(अपवार्य ।) **अज्जस्स परिणए एव्व संदेहो । कुदो दाणिं मे दूराहिरोहिणी आसा ।** आर्यस्य परिणय एव संदेहः । कुत इदानीं मे दूराधिरोहिण्याशा ।

शार्ङ्गरवः—मा तावत्

कृताभिमर्शामनुमन्यमानः
सुतां त्वया नाम मुनिर्विमान्यः ।
मुष्टं प्रतिग्राहयता स्वमर्थं
पात्रीकृतो दस्युरिवासि येन ॥ २० ॥

शारद्वतः—शार्ङ्गरव, विरम त्वमिदानीम् । शकुन्तले, वक्तव्यमुक्तमस्माभिः । सोऽयमत्रभवानेवमाह । दीयतामस्मै प्रत्ययप्रतिवचनम् ।

शकुन्तला—(अपवार्य ।) **इमं अवत्थन्तरं गदे तारिसे अणुराए किं वा सुमराविदेण । अत्ता दाणिं मे सोअणीओ त्ति ववसिदं एदं ।** (प्रकाशम् ।) **अज्जउत्त,** (इत्यर्धोक्ते ।) **संसइदे दाणिं परिणए ण एसो समुदाआरो । पोरव, ण जुत्तं णाम दे तह पुरा अस्समपदे सहावुत्ताणहिअअं इमं जणं समअपुव्वं पतारिअ ईदिसेहिं अक्खरेहिं पच्चाचक्खिदुं ।** इदमवस्थान्तरं गते तादृशेऽनुरागे किं वा स्मारितेन । आत्मेदानीं मे शोचनीय इति व्यवसितमेतत् । आर्यपुत्र । संशयित इदानीं परिणये नैष समुदाचारः । पौरव, न युक्तं नाम ते तथा पुराश्रमपदे स्वभावोत्तानहृदयमिमं जनं समयपूर्वं प्रतार्येदृशैरक्षरैः प्रत्याख्यातुम् ।

राजा—(कर्णौ पिधाय ।) **शान्तं पापम् ।**

ŚĀRṄGARAVA. Why do you sit silent, O king?

KING. Ye holy men! I do not remember, much as I think of it, to have taken this lady in marriage. How then shall I receive her, bearing evident signs of pregnancy, when I have doubts about being her husband?

ŚAKUNTALĀ (*Aside*). My lord even casts doubt on our marriage. Where is now my high-soaring hope?

ŚĀRṄGARAVA. Do not indeed——

Would you insult the sage who approved
his daughter who had been seduced by you;
and who allowing his stolen property to be kept
by you has deemed you worthy of the gift; as
one would a robber by allowing him to retain
one's stolen goods? (20)

ŚĀRADVATA. Rest you, now, my Śārṅgarava. Śakuntalā, we have now said what was for us to say. His Honour has spoken thus. Let a convincing reply be given him.

ŚAKUNTALĀ (*Aside*). When such (great) affection has suffered this change, of what use will it be to recall his remembrance (of me)? It is settled now that I should deplore my own self. (*Aloud*). My noble Lord!—(*When half said*)—This is not the proper form of address, now that the very marriage is called in question. O, Son of Puru, it is not becoming in you that having formerly in the hermitage beguiled in that way this person (myself) naturally open-hearted, after making an agreement, you should reject me with such words.

KING. (*Stopping his ears*). Be the sin removed from my soul!

व्यपदेशमाविलयितुं किमीहसे जनमिमं च पातयितुम् ।
कूलंकषेव सिन्धुः प्रसन्नमम्भस्तटतरुं च ॥ २१ ॥

शकुन्तला—होदु । जइ परमत्थदो परपरिग्गहसङ्किणा तुए एव्वं पउत्तं ता अहिण्णाणेण इमिणा तुह आसङ्कं अवणइस्सं। भवतु । यदि परमार्थतः परपरिग्रहशङ्किना त्वयैवं प्रवृत्तं तदभिज्ञानेनानेन तवाशङ्कामपनेष्यामि ।

राजा—उदारः कल्पः ।

शकुन्तला—(मुद्रास्थानं परामृश्य) हद्धी । अङ्गुलीअअसुण्णा मे अङ्गुली । (इति सविषादं गौतमीमवेक्षते ।) हा धिक् । अङ्गुलीयकशून्या मेऽङ्गुलिः ।

गौतमी—णूणं दे सक्कावदारब्भन्तरे सचीतित्थसलिलं वन्दमाणाए पब्भट्टं अङ्गुलीअअं । नूनं ते शक्रावताराभ्यन्तरे शचीतीर्थसलिलं वन्दमानायाः प्रभ्रष्टमङ्गुलीयकम् ।

राजा—(सस्मितम् ।) इदं तत्प्रत्युत्पन्नमति स्त्रैणमिति यदुच्यते ।

शकुन्तला—एत्थ दाव विहिणा दंसिदं पहुत्तणं । अवरं दे कहिस्सं । अत्र तावद्विधिना दर्शितं प्रभुत्वम् । अपरं ते कथयिष्यामि ।

राजा—श्रोतव्यमिदानीं संवृत्तम् ।

शकुन्तला—णं एक्कस्सिं दिअहे णोमालिआमण्डवे णलिणीपत्तभाअणगदं उदअं तुह हत्थे संणिहिदं आसि । नन्वेकस्मिन्दिवसे नवमालिकामण्डपे नलिनीपत्रभाजनगतमुदकं तव हस्ते संनिहितमासीत् ।

राजा—शृणुमस्तावत् ।

शकुन्तला—तक्खणं सो मे पुत्तकिदओ दीहापङ्गो णाम मिअपोदओ उवट्ठिओ । तुए अअं दाव पढमं पिअउ त्ति अणुअम्पिणा उवच्छन्दिदो उअएण । ण उण दे अपरिचआदो हत्थब्भासं उगवदो । पच्छा तस्सिं एव्व मए गहिदे सलिले णेण किदो पणओ । तदा तुमं इत्थं पहसिदो सि । सव्वो सगन्धेसु विस्ससदि । दुवेवि एत्थ आरण्णआ त्ति । तत्क्षणे स मे पुत्रकृतको दीर्घापाङ्गो नाम मृगपोतक उपस्थितः । त्वयायं तावत्प्रथमं पिबत्वित्यनुकम्पिनोपच्छन्दित उदकेन ।

Why seek you to sully your family, and drag me down, as a stream, that eats away the bank, sullies its clear water and drags down the trees on its banks? (21)

ŚAKUNTALĀ. Well, if you act thus because you really think me to be another's wife, I will remove your doubts by this token of recognition.

KING. A capital suggestion.

ŚAKUNTALĀ (*Touching the place of the ring*). Alas! My finger is without the ring! (*She looks sadly at Gautamī.*)

GAUTAMĪ. The ring must have in all probability dropped (From thy finger) as thou worshippedst the Śacītīrtha at Śakrāvatāra.

KING (*Smiling*). This is an instance of the proverb "Women are ready-witted."

ŚAKUNTALĀ. Here now destiny has shown its power. I will tell you something else.

KING. Now it has come to something to be heard!

ŚAKUNTALĀ. One day, in the Navamālikā bower, you had in your hand water in a vase of lotus-leaves.

KING. Well, I am listening.

ŚAKUNTALĀ. At that moment the fawn Dīrghāpāṅga, my foster-child, came up. Then you took pity on him saying "Let him drink first", and coaxed him to drink; but as he did not know you, he would not come to drink water from your hand. But later, when I held the very same water, he liked it. Then you said in jest: "Every one trusts his own kindred. You are both foresters alike."

न पुनस्तेऽपरिचयाद्धस्ताभ्याशमुपगतः । पश्चात्तस्मिन्नेव मया गृहीते सलिलेऽनेन कृतः प्रणयः । तदा त्वमित्थं प्रहसितोऽसि । सर्वः सगन्धेषु विश्वसिति । द्वावप्यत्रारण्यकाविति ।

राजा—एवमादिभिरात्मकार्यनिर्वर्तिनीनामनृतमयवाङ्मधुभिराकृष्यन्ते विषयिणः ।

गौतमी—महाभाअ, ण अरुहसि एव्वं मन्तिदुं । तवोवणसंवड्ढिदो अणभिण्णो अअं जणो कइदवस्स । महाभाग, नार्हस्येवं मन्त्रयितुम् । तपोवनसंवर्धितोऽनभिज्ञोयं जनः कैतवस्य ।

राजा—तापसवृद्धे,

स्त्रीणामशिक्षितपटुत्वममानुषीषु
संदृश्यते किमुत याः प्रतिबोधवत्यः ।
प्रागन्तरिक्षगमनात्स्वमपत्यजात-
मन्यैर्द्विजैः परभृताः खलु पोषयन्ति ॥ २२ ॥

शकुन्तला—(सरोषम् ।) **अणज्ज, अत्तणो हिअआणुमाणेण पेक्खसि । को दाणिं अण्णो धम्मकञ्चुअप्पवेसिणो तिणच्छण्णकूवोवमस्स तव अणुकिदिं पडिवदिस्सदि ।** अनार्य, आत्मनो हृदयानुमानेन पश्यसि । क इदानीमन्यो धर्मकञ्चुकप्रवेशिनस्तृणच्छन्नकूपोपमस्य तवानुकृतिं प्रतिपत्स्यते ।

राजा—(आत्मगतम् ।) **संदिग्धबुद्धिं मां कुर्वन्नकैतव इवास्याः कोपो लक्ष्यते । तथा ह्यनया**

मय्येव विस्मरणदारुणचित्तवृत्तौ
वृत्तं रहः प्रणयमप्रतिपद्यमाने ।
भेदाद्भ्रुवोः कुटिलयोरतिलोहिताक्ष्या
भग्नं शरासनमिवातिरुषा स्मरस्य ॥ २३ ॥

(प्रकाशम् ।) **भद्रे, प्रथितं दुष्यन्तस्य चरितम् । तथापीदं न लक्षये ।**

शकुन्तला—सुट्ठु दाव अत्त सच्छन्दचारिणी किदम्हि जा अहं इमस्स पुरुवंसप्पच्चएण मुहमहुणो हिअअट्ठिअविसस्स हत्थब्भासं

KING. By such honeyed falsehoods are voluptuaries ensnared by (women) who seek to compass their own ends.

GAUTAMĪ. Worthy sir, forbear to speak thus. She was bred in the sacred grove, and she does not know guile.

KING. Old hermit-woman,

> The female's untaught cunning may be observed even in those that are not of the human race ; far more in those who are endowed with reason. The female cuckoos, it is well-known, allow their young ones to be reared by other birds, before they can soar in the sky. (22)

ŚAKUNTALĀ (*Angrily*). Wicked man, you measure (all this) by your own heart. What other man would act like you, who wearing the garb of virtue, resemble a grass-concealed well ?

KING. (*To himself*). Throwing my mind in doubt, her anger seems to be unfeigned. For

> When I, whose mental attitude was harsh (towards her) from the absence of all recollection, would not admit our secret love, it seemed that she, whose eyes were flashing red, bending her curved eyebrows, fiercely snapped Love's bow. (23)

(*Aloud*). Good woman, Duṣyanta's conduct is well known ; yet this is not found (in it).

ŚAKUNTALĀ. Well have I been made (to appear) a wanton woman, who trusting Puru's race put myself in the hands of one who had honey in his mouth, but

उवगदा । (इति पटान्तेन मुखमावृत्य रोदिति ।) सुष्ठु तावदत्र स्वच्छन्दचारिणी कृतास्मि याहमस्य पुरुवंशप्रत्ययेन मुखमधोर्हृदयस्थितविषस्य हस्ताभ्याशमुपगता ।

शार्ङ्गरवः—इत्थमात्मकृतमप्रतिहतं चापलं दहति ।

अतः परीक्ष्य कर्तव्यं विशेषात्संगतं रहः ।
अज्ञातहृदयेष्वेवं वैरीभवति सौहृदम् ॥ २४ ॥

राजा—अयि भोः, किमत्रभवतीप्रत्ययादेवास्मान्संभृतदोषैः क्षिणुथ ।

शार्ङ्गरवः—(सासूयम् ।) श्रुतं भवद्भिरधरोत्तरम् ।

आ जन्मनः शाठ्यमशिक्षितो य-
स्तस्याप्रमाणं वचनं जनस्य ।
परातिसंधानमधीयते यै-
र्विद्येति ते सन्तु किलाप्तवाचः ॥ २५ ॥

राजा—भोः सत्यवादिन् , अभ्युपगतं तावदस्माभिरेवम् । किं पुनरिमामतिसंधाय लभ्यते ।

शार्ङ्गरवः—विनिपातः ।

राजा—विनिपातः पौरवैः प्रार्थ्यत इति न श्रद्धेयम् ।

शारद्वतः—शार्ङ्गरव, किमुत्तरेण । अनुष्ठितो गुरोः संदेश । प्रतिनिवर्तामहे वयम् । (राजानं प्रति ।)

तदेषा भवतः कान्ता त्यज वैनां गृहाण वा ।
उपपन्ना हि दारेषु प्रभुता सर्वतोमुखी ॥ २६ ॥

गौतमि, गच्छाग्रतः ।

(इति प्रस्थिताः ।)

poison in his heart ! (*She covers her face with the end of her garment and weeps.*)

ŚĀRṄGARAVA. Thus does one's own levity, if not bridled, breed poignant remorse.

> Therefore, a union, especially, a secret one,
> ought to be formed with great circumspection ;
> with those who know not each other's heart,
> love thus turns to hate. (24)

KING. O sir, would you rely on her, and reproach me with accumulated faults ?

ŚĀRṄGARAVA (*Scornfully*). Have you heard (such a) perversion !

> The words of one who from birth has never
> learnt deceit are to receive no credit ; while
> they, forsooth, who make the deception of
> others their study, calling it a science, are to
> be considered as worthy of trust ! (25)

KING. Now, truth-teller, we admit it for a moment; but what would be gained by deceiving her ?

ŚĀRṄGARAVA. Damnation !

KING. It is unthinkable that damnation would be sought by Puru's line.

ŚĀRADVATA. Śārṅgarava, what avails you answer ? We have executed the commands of our preceptor, and we now return. (*To the king*).

> Here then is your wife, (whether you) desert
> her or acknowledge her. For the authority
> over wives is admitted to be absolute. (26).
> Gautamī, lead the way.

(*They start.*)

शकुन्तला—कहं इमिणा किदवेण विप्पलद्ध म्हि । तुम्हे वि मं परिच्चअध । (इत्यनुप्रतिष्ठते ।) कथमनेन कितवेन विप्रलब्धास्मि । यूयमपि मां परित्यजथ ।

गौतमी—(स्थित्वा) वच्छ सङ्गरव, अनुगच्छदि इअं क्खु णो करुणपरिदेविणी सउन्दला । पच्चादेसपरुसे भत्तरि किं वा मे पुत्तिआ करेदु । वत्स शार्ङ्गरव, अनुगच्छतीयं खलु नः करुणपरिदेविनी शकुन्तला । प्रत्यादेशपरुषे भर्तरि किं वा मे पुत्रिका करोतु ।

शार्ङ्गरवः—(सरोषं निवृत्य ।) किं पुरोभागिनि, स्वातंत्र्यमवलम्बसे ।

(शकुन्तला भीता वेपते ।)

शार्ङ्गरवः—शकुन्तले,

यदि यथा वदति क्षितिपस्तथा
त्वमसि किं पितुरुत्कुलया त्वया ।
अथ तु वेत्सि शुचि व्रतमात्मनः
पतिकुले तव दास्यमपि क्षमम् ॥ २७ ॥

तिष्ठ । साधयामो वयम् ।

राजा—भोस्तपस्विन् , किमत्रभवतीं विप्रलभसे । कुतः

कुमुदान्येव शशाङ्कः सविता बोधयति पङ्कजान्येव ।
वशिनां हि परपरिग्रहसंश्लेषपराङ्मुखी वृत्तिः ॥ २८ ॥

शार्ङ्गरवः—यदा तु पूर्ववृत्तमन्यसङ्गाद्विस्मृतो भवांस्तदा कथमधर्मभीरुः ।

राजा—भवन्तमेवात्र गुरुलाघवं पृच्छामि ।

ŚAKUNTALĀ. How have I been deceived by the perfidious man! But will you, too, leave me?

(*She starts to follow.*)

GAUTAMĪ (*Stopping*). Śārṅgarava, my son, Śakuntalā is indeed, following us, lamenting piteously; or what can my poor child do, when her husband is so ruthless in rejecting her?

ŚĀRṄGARAVA (*Turning back in anger*). Well, wanton girl, would you affect independence?

(*Śakuntalā trembles in fear.*)

ŚĀRṄGARAVA. Śakuntalā,

If you are what the king makes you out to be, what has father to do with you—a disgrace to your family? But if you know your (marriage) vow to be pure, it will become you to wait even as a handmaid in the mansion of your lord. (27)

STAY. We must return.

KING. O hermit, why deceive the lady? For

The Moon opens the night-lotuses only and the Sun the day-lotuses. The feelings of those who are self-controlled ever recoil from any connection with the wife of another. (28)

ŚĀRṄGARAVA. But when you have forgotten a former engagement on account of union with another (wife) how are you (to be regarded as) one who fears to offend virtue?

KING. I would ask your reverence which is the greater and which the lesser evil:

मूढः स्यामहमेषा वा वदेन्मिथ्येति संशये
दारत्यागी भवाम्याहो परस्त्रीस्पर्शपांसुलः ॥ २९ ॥

पुरोहितः—(विचार्य) यदि तावदेवं क्रियताम् ।

राजा—अनुशास्तु मां भवान् ।

पुरोहितः—अत्रभवती तावदाप्रसवादस्मद्गृहे तिष्ठतु । कुत इदमुच्यत इति चेत् । त्वं साधुभिरुद्दिष्टः प्रथममेव चक्रवर्तिनं पुत्रं जनयिष्यसीति । स चेन्मुनिदौहित्रस्तल्लक्षणोपपन्नो भविष्यति, अभिनन्द्य शुद्धान्तमेनां प्रवेशयिष्यसि । विपर्यये तु पितुरस्याः समीपनयनमवस्थितमेव ।

राजा—यथा गुरुभ्यो रोचते ।

पुरोहितः—वत्से, अनुगच्छ माम् ।

शकुन्तला—भअवदि वसुहे, देहि मे विवरं । भगवति वसुधे, देहि मे विवरम् । (इति रुदती प्रस्थिता । निष्क्रान्ता सह पुरोधसा, तपस्विभिश्च)

(राजा शापव्यवहितस्मृतिः शकुन्तलागतमेव चिन्तयति ।)

(नेपथ्ये ।)

आश्चर्यम् ।

राजा—(आकर्ण्य) किं नु खलु स्यात् ।

(प्रविश्य ।)

पुरोहितः—(सविस्मयम् ।) देव, अद्भुत खलु संवृत्तम् ।

राजा—किमिव ।

In a doubt as to whether I be infatuated or she speak falsely, shall I forsake my own wife, or defile myself by having intercourse with the wife of another? (29)

CHAPLAIN (*Deliberating*). Well, then, if this were done—

KING. Let the venerable one instruct me.

CHAPLAIN. Let the lady dwell till her delivery in my house. If you ask why I say this, (my answer is) you have been told by the sages that at the very first you will beget a son who will bear the mark of a discus (on his hand). If then the son of the hermit's daughter bears that mark, then greet her and introduce her to the female apartments. But if the reverse happens, it is evident enough that she must be taken to her father.

KING. As it pleases my worthy teacher.

CHAPLAIN. Daughter, follow me.

ŚAKUNTALĀ. Divine Earth, open (to receive me).

(*She is in tears as she starts; exit with the Chaplain and the hermits; the king, whose memory is still clouded by the curse, ponders on something regarding Śakuntalā herself*).

(*Behind the Scenes*).

A miracle!

KING. (*Listening*). What could it be?

(*Entering*) Chaplain (*in amazement*). Your Majesty, a wonderful thing has happened!

KING. What is it?

पुरोहितः—देव, परावृत्तेषु कण्वशिष्येषु

सा निन्दन्ती स्वानि भाग्यानि बाला
बाहूत्क्षेपं क्रन्दितुं च प्रवृत्ता ।

राजा—किं च ।

पुरोहितः—

स्त्रीसंस्थानं चाप्सरस्तीर्थमारा-
दुक्षिप्यैनां ज्योतिरेकं जगाम ॥ ३० ॥

(सर्वे विस्मयं रूपयन्ति ।)

राजा—भगवन् प्रागपि सोऽस्माभिरर्थः प्रत्यादिष्ट एव । किं वृथा तर्केणान्विष्यते । विश्राम्यतु भवान् ।

पुरोहितः—(विलोक्य ।) विजयस्व । (इति निष्क्रान्तः ।)

राजा—वेत्रवति, पर्याकुलोऽस्मि । शयनभूमिमार्गमादेशय ।

प्रतीहारी—इदो इदो देवो । (इति प्रस्थितः ।) इत इतो देवः ।

राजा—

कामं प्रत्यादिष्टां स्मरामि न परिग्रहं मुनेस्तनयाम् ।
बलवत्तु दूयमानं प्रत्याययतीव मां हृदयम् ॥ ३१ ॥

(इति निष्क्रान्ताः सर्वे ।)

पञ्चमोऽङ्कः ।

CHAPLAIN. Your Majesty, when Kaṇva's pupils had departed,

The young girl, blaming her fortunes, threw up her arms and started weeping—

KING. What then?

CHAPLAIN.

When a body of light, in a female shape, snatched her up from afar, and went to Apsaras-tīrtha. (30)

(*All betray astonishment.*)

KING. Revered sir, we have already dismissed that object from us. What need to reason more on it? Please rest you, sir.

CHAPLAIN (*Observing*). Victory to your Majesty! (*Goes out.*)

KING. Vetravati, I am troubled. Lead the way to the bed-chamber.

PORTRESS. This way, your Majesty, this way.

(*Starts.*)

KING.

True I do not recollect this daughter of the sage (now) repudiated to be my wife; nevertheless my heart being powerfully agitated almost persuades me to believe (her story). (31)

(*Exeunt Omnes.*)

End of Act V

षष्ठोऽङ्कः ।

(ततः प्रविशति नागरिकः श्यालः पश्चाद्बद्धपुरुषमादाय रक्षिणौ च ।)

रक्षिणौ—(ताडयित्वा ।) **अले कुम्भिलआ, कहेहि कहिं तुए एशे मणिबन्धणुक्किण्णणामहेए लाअकीए अङ्गुलीअए शमाशादिए ।** अरे कुम्भिलक, कथय कुत्र त्वयैतन्मणिबन्धनोत्कीर्णनामधेय राजकीयमङ्गुलीयकं समासादितम् ।

पुरुषः—(भीतिनाटितकेन ।) **पशीदन्तु भावमिश्शे । हगे ण ईदिशाकम्मकाली ।** प्रसीदन्तु भावमिश्राः । अहं नेदृशकर्मकारी ।

प्रथमः—**किं खु शोहणे बम्हणेत्ति कलिअ लण्णा पडिग्गहे दिण्णे ।** किं खलु शोभनो ब्राह्मण इति कृत्वा राज्ञा प्रतिग्रहो दत्तः ।

पुरुषः—**शुणध दाणिं । हगे शक्कावदालब्भन्तलवाशी धीवले ।** शृणुतेदानीम् । अहं शक्रावताराभ्यन्तरवासी धीवरः ।

द्वितीयः—**पाडच्चला, किं अम्हेहिं जादी पुच्छिदा ।** पाटच्चर, किमस्माभिर्जातिः पृष्टा ।

श्यालः—**सूअअ, कहेदु सव्वं अणुक्कमेण । मा णं अन्तरा पडिबन्धह ।** सूचक, कथयतु सर्वमनुक्रमेण । मैनमन्तरे प्रतिबन्धय ।

उभौ—**जं आवुत्ते आणवेदि । कहेहि ।** यदावुत्त आज्ञापयति । कथय ।

पुरुषः—**अहके जालुग्गालादीहिं मच्छबन्धणोवाएहिं कुडुम्बभलणं कलेमि ।** अहं जालोद्गालादिभिर्मत्स्यबन्धनोपायैः कुटुम्बभरणं करोमि ।

श्यालः—(विहस्य ।) **विसुद्धो दाणिं आजीवो ।** विशुद्ध इदानीमाजीवः ।

पुरुषः—

शहजे किल जे विणिन्दिए ण हु दे कम्म विवज्जणीअए ।
पशुमालणकम्मदालुणे अणुकम्पामिदु एव्व शोत्तिए ॥ १ ॥

ACT VI

(Enter the King's brother-in-law (as) the chief of the city-police with two policemen leading a man with his hands bound behind his back.)

THE TWO POLICEMEN (*Striking*). Now, thief, tell us where you found this royal ring the setting of which is engraven with his name.

THE MAN (*With a gesticulation of fear*). Be pleased, your honours. I would never do such an act.

FIRST. Was it, then, a present given by the king, thinking you were an illustrious Brahmin ?

THE MAN. Hear me, now. I am a fisherman dwelling at Śakrāvatāra.

SECOND. Thief, we did not ask about your caste.

ŚYĀLA. Let him tell the story in order, Sūcaka. Do not interrupt him in the middle.

BOTH. As the brother-in-law commands. Speak.

MAN. I support my family with things you catch fish with—nets and hooks and such like.

ŚYĀLA (*Smiling*). A virtuous way of gaining a livelihood !

MASTER. Do not say that, master.

> The occupation in which one was born, as they say, how low soever, must not be forsaken. The same learned Brahmin who is cruel in the act of killing animals (for the sacrifice), is yet soft with pity. (1)

सहजं किल यद्विनिन्दितं न खलु तत्कर्म विवर्जनीयम् ।
पशुमारणकर्मदारुणोऽनुकम्पामृदुरेव श्रोत्रियः ॥

श्यालः—तदो तदो । ततस्ततः ।

पुरुषः—एक्कर्शिश दिअशे खण्डशो लोहिअमच्छे मए कप्पिदे जाव तश्श उदलब्भन्तले एदं लदणभाशुलं अङ्गुलीअअं देक्खिजं । पच्छा अहके शे विक्कआअ दंशअन्ते गहिदे भावमिश्शेहिं । मालेह वा मुञ्चेह वा । अअं शे आअमवुत्तन्ते । एकस्मिन्दिवसे खण्डशो रोहितमत्स्यो मया कल्पितो यावत् तस्योदराभ्यन्तर इदं रत्नभासुरमङ्गुलीयं दृष्टम् । पश्चादहं तस्य विक्रयाय दर्शयन्गृहीतो भावमिश्रैः । मारयत वा मुञ्चत वा । अयमस्यागमवृत्तान्तः ।

श्यालः—जाणुअ, विस्सगन्धी गोहादी मच्छबन्धो एव्व णिस्संसअं । अङ्गुलीअअदंसणं से विमरिसिदव्वं । राउलं एव्व गच्छामो । जानुक, विस्रगन्धी गोधादी मत्स्यबन्ध एव निःसंशयम् । अङ्गुलीयकदर्शनमस्य विमर्शयितव्यम् । राजकुलमेव गच्छामः ।

रक्षिणौ—तह । गच्छ अले गण्ठिभेदअ । तथा । गच्छ अरे ग्रन्थिभेदक ।

(सर्वे परिक्रामन्ति ।)

श्यालः—सूअअ, इमं पुरदुआरे अप्पमत्ता पडिवालह । जाव इमं अङ्गुलीअअं जहागमणं भट्टिणो णिवेदिअ तदो सासणं पडिच्छिअ णिक्कमामि । सूचक, इमं पुरद्वारेऽप्रमत्तौ प्रतिपालयतम् । यावदिदमङ्गुलीयकं यथागमनं भर्तुर्निवेद्य ततः शासनं प्रतीक्ष्य निष्क्रमामि ।

उभौ—पविशदु आवुत्ते शामिपशादश्श । प्रविशत्वावुत्तः स्वामिप्रसादाय ।

(इति निष्क्रान्तः श्यालः ।)

प्रथमः—जाणुअ, चिलाअदि क्खु आवुत्ते । जानुक, चिरायते खल्वावुत्तः ।

द्वितीयः—णं अवशलोवशप्पणीआ लाआणो । नन्ववसरोपसर्पणीया राजानः ।

प्रथमः—जाणुअ, फुलन्ति मे हत्था इमश्श वज्झश्श शुमणो पिणद्धुं । (इति पुरुषं निर्दिशति ।) जानुक, स्फुरतो मम हस्तावस्य वध्यस्य सुमनसः पिनद्धुम् ।

ŚYĀLA. Go on, go on.

MAN. Well, one day I was cutting open a carp when in its maw I saw this ring, flashing with its gem. When later I offered it for sale, I was apprehended by your honours. Now kill me or leave me alone. (But) that is the way I got it.

ŚYĀLA. O Jānuka, he is doubtless a fisherman, stinking as he does of raw flesh—this eater of alligators. But the finding of the ring by him requires to be considered. Let us proceed to the palace itself.

THE TWO POLICEMEN. Just so; move on, you cutpurse.

(*All walk round.*)

ŚYĀLA. Sūcaka guard him carefully at the city-gate, while I tell the king how this ring was found, and receiving his commands, come out.

BOTH. Let the master enter to receive the king's favour.

(*Exit Śyāla.*)

FIRST. Jānuka, the chief is indeed taking too long a time.

SECOND. Well, kings can only be approached at their leisure.

FIRST. Jānuka, how my hands tingle to fasten flowers about the head of this victim! (*He points to the man.*)

पुरुषः—**ण अलुहदि भावे अकालणमालणे भविदुं** । नार्हति भावोऽकारणमारणो भवितुम् ।

द्वितीयः—(विलोक्य ।) **एशे अम्हाणं शामी पत्तहत्थे लाअशाशणं पडिच्छिअ इदोमुहे देक्खीअदि । गिद्धबली भविश्शशि । शुणो मुहं वा देक्खिश्शशि** । एष नौ स्वामी पत्रहस्तो राजशासनं प्रतीक्ष्येतोमुखो दृश्यते । गृध्रबलिर्भविष्यसि, शुनो मुखं वा द्रक्ष्यसि ।

(प्रविश्य ।)

श्यालः—**सूअअ, मुञ्चेदु एसो जालोअजीवी । उववण्णो क्खु अङ्गुलीअस्स आअमो** । सूचक, मुच्यतामेष जालोपजीवी । उपपन्नः खल्वङ्गुलीयस्यागमः ।

सूचकः—**जह आवुत्ते भणादि** । यथावुत्तो भणति ।

द्वितीयः—**एशे जमशदणं पविशिअ पडिणिवुत्ते** । (इति पुरुषं परिमुक्तबन्धनं करोति ।) एष यमसदनं प्रविश्य प्रतिनिवृत्तः ।

पुरुषः—(श्यालं प्रणम्य ।) **भट्टा, अह कीलिशे मे आजीवे** । भर्तः, अथ कीदृशो मे आजीवः ।

श्यालः—**एसो भट्टिणा अङ्गुलीअअमुल्लसम्मिदो पसादो विदाविदो** । (इति पुरुषायार्थं प्रयच्छति ।) एष भर्त्राङ्गुलीयकमूल्यसमितः प्रसादोऽपि दापितः ।

पुरुषः—(सप्रणामं प्रतिगृह्य ।) **भट्टा, अणुग्गहीदम्हि** । भर्तः, अनुगृहीतोऽस्मि ।

सूचकः—**एशे णाम अणुग्गहिदे जे शूलादो अवदालिअ हत्थिक्खन्धे पडिट्ठाविदे** । एष नामानुगृहीतो यच्छूलादवतार्य हस्तिस्कन्धे प्रतिष्ठापितः ।

जानुकः—**आवुत्त, पालिदोशिअं कहेदि तेण अङ्गुलीअएण भट्टिणो शम्मदेण होदव्वं** । आवुत्त, पारितोषिकं कथयति तेनाङ्गुलीयकेन भर्तुः संमतेन भवितव्यम् ।

MAN. You would not kill a man without reason, master.

SECOND (*Observing*). There is our chief, letter in hand, who is coming towards us after receiving the king's command. You will either be food for vultures or will see the face of a dog.

(*Entering*) ŚYĀLA. Sūcaka, let the fisherman be discharged. This finding of the ring is indeed explained.

SŪCAKA. As the chief says.

SECOND. Here he returns, after having entered the abode of the God of death.

(*Unbinds the prisoner.*)

MAN (*Bowing to Śyāla*). Master, how do you think is my profession?

ŚYĀLA. And the king has further given him a sum of money equal to the full value of the ring. (*Offers the man money.*)

MAN (*Accepting with a bow*). I am favoured by my master.

SŪCAKA. He has, indeed, been favoured, who after being taken down from the stake, has been set on the withers of an elephant.

JĀNUKA. My chief, the reward shows that the ring must be highly prized by the king.

श्यालः—ण तस्सिं महारुहं रदणं भट्टिणो बहुमदं त्ति तक्केमि। तस्स दंसणेण भट्टिणो अभिमदो जणो सुमराविदो। मुहुत्तअं पकिदिगम्भीरो वि पज्जुसुअणअणो आसि। न तस्मिन्महार्हं रत्नं भर्तुर्बहुमतमिति तर्कयामि। तस्य दर्शनेन भर्तुरभिमतो जनः स्मारितः। मुहूर्तं प्रकृतिगम्भीरोऽपि पर्युत्सुकनयन आसीत्।

सूचकः—शेविदं णाम आवुत्तेण। सेवितं नामावुत्तेन।

जानुकः—णं भणाहि। इमश्श कए मच्छिआभत्तुणोत्ति। (इति पुरुषमसूयया पश्यति।) ननु भण। अस्य कृते मात्स्यिकभर्तुरिति।

पुरुषः—भट्टालके, इदो अद्धं तुम्हाणं शुमणोमुल्लं होदु। भट्टारक, इतोऽर्धं युष्माकं सुमनोमूल्यं भवतु।

जानुकः—एत्तके जुज्जई। एतावद्युज्यते।

श्यालः—धीवर, महत्तरो तुमं पिअवअस्सओ दाणिं मे संवुत्तो। कादम्बरीसक्खिअं अम्हाणं पढमसोहिदं इच्छीअदि। ता सोण्डिआपणं एव्व गच्छामो। धीवर, महत्तरस्त्वं प्रियवयस्यक इदानीं मे संवृत्तः। कादम्बरीसाक्षिकमस्माकं प्रथमसौहृदमिष्यते। तच्छौण्डिकापणमेव गच्छामः। (इति निष्क्रान्ताः सर्वे।)

प्रवेशकः।

(ततः प्रविशत्याकाशयानेन सानुमती नामाप्सराः।)

सानुमती—णिव्वत्तिदं मए पज्जाअणिव्वत्तणिज्जं अच्छरातित्थसण्णिज्झं जाव साहुजणस्स अभिसेअकालो त्ति। संपदं इमस्स राएसिणो उदन्तं पच्चक्खीकरिस्सं। णं मेणआसंबन्धेण सरीरभूदा मे सउन्दला। ताए अ दुहिदुणिमित्तं आदिट्ठपुव्वम्हि। (समन्तादवलोक्य।) **किं णु क्खु उदुच्छवे वि णिरुच्छवारम्भं विअ राअउलं दीसइ। अत्थि मे विहवो पणिधाणेण सव्वं परिण्णादुं। किंदु सहीए आदरो मए माणइदव्वो। होदु। इमाणं एव्व उज्जाणपालिआणं तिरक्खरिणीपडिच्छण्णा पस्सवत्तिणी**

ŚYĀLA. I do not think that the costly gem in it was prized by the king; but, at its sight, the king remembered somebody he loves; and although naturally firm, he became for a moment agitated in mind.

SŪCAKA. Our master has given (the king) extreme pleasure.

JĀNUKA. Rather say, for the sake of this chief of fishermen. (*Eyes the man enviously*).

MAN. Let half of this be the price of your flower. master.

JĀNUKA. That is right.

ŚYĀLA. Fisherman, now you are the biggest and the best friend I have got. It is desirable that we pledge our first friendship over (some) wine. So let us get along to a wine-shop.

(*They all go out.*)

End of the introductory scene.

(*Then enter in an aerial car a nymph named Sānumatī.*)

SĀNUMATĪ. Attendance at Apsaras-tīrtha which is to be performed by turns, during the time the pious people have their ablutions, has been performed by me. I will now see with my own eyes what the good king is doing. Śakuntalā has, indeed, now become a part of myself, through my relation with Menakā. And she has already sent me on this commission on her daughter's account. (*Looking about*). How even at the festival of the season, no preparations for a celebration

भविअ उवलहिस्स। (इति नाट्येनावतीर्य स्थिता।) निर्वर्तितं मया पर्यायनिर्वर्तनीयमप्सरस्तीर्थसांनिध्यं यावत्साधुजनस्याभिषेककाल इति। सांप्रतमस्य राजर्षेरुदन्तं प्रत्यक्षीकरिष्यामि। ननु मेनकासंबन्धेन शरीरभूता मे शकुन्तला। तथा च दुहितृनिमित्तमादिष्टपूर्वास्मि। किं नु खलु ऋतूत्सवेऽपि निरुत्सवारम्भमिव राजकुलं दृश्यते। अस्ति मे विभवः प्रणिधानेन सर्वं परिज्ञातुम्। किं तु सख्या आदरो मया मानयितव्यः। भवतु। अनयोरेवोद्यानपालिकयोस्तिरस्करिणीप्रतिच्छन्ना पार्श्ववर्तिनी भूत्वोपलप्स्ये।

(ततः प्रविशति चूताङ्कुरमवलोयन्ती चेटी। अपरा च पृष्ठतस्तस्याः।)

प्रथमा—

आतम्महरिअपण्डुर वसन्तमासस्स जीअसव्वस्स।
दिट्ठो सि चूदकोरअ उदुमङ्गल तुमं पसाएमि॥ २॥

आताम्रहरितपाण्डुर वसन्तमासस्य जीवसर्वस्व।
दृष्टोऽसि चूतकोरक ऋतुमङ्गल त्वां प्रसादयामि॥

द्वितीया—परहुदिए, किं एआइणी मन्तेसि। परभृतिके, किमेकाकिनी मन्त्रयसे।

प्रथमा—महुअरिए, चूदकलिअं देक्खिअ उम्मत्तिआ परहुदिआ होदि। मधुकरिके, चूतकलिकां दृष्ट्वोन्मत्ता परभृतिका भवति।

द्वितीया—(सहर्षं त्वरयोपगम्य।) **कहं उवट्ठिदो महुमासो**। कथमुपस्थितो मधुमासः।

प्रथमा—महुअरिए, तव दाणिं कालो एसो मदविब्भमगीदाण। मधुकरिके, तवेदानीं काल एष मदविभ्रमगीतानाम्।

द्वितीया—सहि, अवलम्ब मं। जाव अग्गपादट्ठिआ भविअ चूदकलिअं गेण्हिअ कामदेवच्चणं करेमि। सखी, अवलम्बस्व मां यावदग्रपादस्थिता भूत्वा चूतकलिकां गृहीत्वा कामदेवार्चनं करोमि।

प्रथमा—जइ मम वि क्खु अद्धं अच्चणफलस्स। यदि ममापि खल्वर्धमर्चनफलस्य।

are to be seen at the palace ? I might learn everything by exerting my supernatural power. But respect must be shown to (the desire of) my friend. I will make myself invisible through my supernatural powers and standing near these girls who take care of the garden, will find out.

(*She acts descending, and stops*).

(*Then enter a maid gazing at the mango-blossom, and another behind her.*)

FIRST.

O mango-blossom, a little pink and green and pale, the very essence of the life of spring, thou art seen by me, and I beg thee to favour (me), thou blesssing of the season. (2)

SECOND. Parabhṛtikā, what are you talking about to yourself ?

FIRST. Madhukarikā, when a female kokil sees the mango-blossom, she goes crazy with delight.

SECOND (*Hastily advancing ; with joy*). What, is the spring really come ?

FIRST. Madhukarikā, this is the time for your wild and graceful songs.

SECOND. Hold me, dear, while I stand tip-toe and take the mango-blossom to worship God Kāma.

FIRST. If mine would be half the reward of the worship.

द्वितीया—अकहिदे वि एदं संपज्जइ जदो एक्कं एव्व णो जीविदं दुधा ट्ठिदं सरीरं। (सखीमवलम्ब्य स्थिता चूताङ्कुरं गृह्णाति।) अए, अप्पडिबुद्धो वि चूदप्पसवो एत्थ बन्धणभङ्गसुरभी होदि। अकथितेऽप्येतत्संपद्यते यत एकमेव नौ जीवितं द्विधा स्थितं शरीरम्। अये, अप्रतिबुद्धोऽपि चूतप्रसवोऽत्र बन्धनभङ्गसुरभिर्भवति।

(कपोतहस्तकं कृत्वा।)

तुं सि मए चूदङ्कुर दिण्णो कामस्स गहिदधणुअस्स।
पहिअजणजुवइलक्खो पञ्चब्भहिओ सरो होहि॥ ३॥

त्वमसि मया चूताङ्कुर दत्तः कामाय गृहीतधनुषे।
पथिकजनयुवतिलक्ष्यः पञ्चाभ्यधिकः शरो भव॥

(इति चूताङ्कुरं क्षिपति।)

(प्रविश्यापटीक्षेपेण कुपितः)

कञ्चुकी—मा तावत्। अनात्मज्ञे, देवेन प्रतिषिद्धे वसन्तोत्सवे त्वमाम्रकलिकाभङ्गं किमारभसे।

उभे—(भीते) पसीददु अज्जो। अग्गहीदत्थाओ अम्हे। प्रसीदत्वार्यः। अगृहीतार्थे आवाम्।

कञ्चुकी—न किल श्रुतं युवाभ्यां यद्वासन्तिकैस्तरुभिरपि देवस्य शासनं प्रमाणीकृतं तदाश्रयिभिः पत्रिभिश्च। तथाहि

चूतानां चिरनिर्गतापि कलिका बध्नाति न स्वं रजः
संनद्धं यदपि स्थितं कुरबकं तत्कोरकावस्थया।
कण्ठेषु स्खलितं गतेऽपि शिशिरे पुंस्कोकिलानां रुतं
शङ्के संहरति स्मरोऽपि चकितस्तूणार्धकृष्टं शरम्॥ ४॥

उभे—णत्थि संदेहो। महाप्पहावो राएसी। नास्ति संदेहः। महाप्रभावो राजर्षिः।

SECOND. That goes without saying, dear; for our life is but one, though our bodies stand apart. (*Stands leaning on her friend and takes the mango-blossom*). Ah, the mango-blossom though not opened, is yet fragrant as its stalk is cut. (*Joining her hands together*).

O mango-sprout, thou art offered by me to God Kāma, who has taken up his bow. Be an arrow more splendid than (his) five, having for thy marks the girls whose lovers are journeying. (3)

(*She throws down the mango-sprout.*)

(*Entering with a hurried toss of the curtain; angrily*)

CHAMBERLAIN. Don't, thoughtless girl; the king having forbidden the spring-festival, how have you started breaking off mango-buds?

BOTH (*frightened*). Please, sir, we did not know about it.

CHAMBERLAIN. You knew it not! When the king's command is obeyed even by the vernal trees, and the birds that dwell in them! Thus

The mango-buds, which have long appeared do not yet form their own pollen; the Kurabaka (flower) also though all-ready to bloom, remains in the state of a bud; the voice of the male-cuckoos, though the cold season is gone, falters in the throat; while I suspect even Smara, being awed, replaces the shaft half-drawn from his quiver. (4)

BOTH. There is no doubt of it. The pious king possesses great power.

प्रथमा—अज्ज कदि दिअहाइं अम्हाणं मित्तावसुणा रट्ठिएण भट्टिणो पाअमूलं पेसिदाणं। इत्थं अ णो पमदवणस्स पालणकम्म समप्पिदं। ता आअन्तुअदाए अस्सुदपुब्वो अम्हेहिं एसो वुत्तन्तो। आर्य, कति दिवसान्यावयोर्मित्रावसुना राष्ट्रीयेण भर्तुः पादमूलं प्रेषितयोः। इत्थं च नौ प्रमदवनस्य पालनकर्म समर्पितम्। तदागन्तुकतया-श्रुतपूर्व आवाभ्यामेष वृत्तान्तः।

कञ्चुकी—भवतु। न पुनरेवं प्रवर्तितव्यम्।

उभे—अज्ज, कोदूहलं णो। जदि इमिणा जणेण सोदव्वं कहेदु भवं किंणिमित्तं भट्टिणा वसन्तुस्सवो पडिसिद्धो। आर्य, कौतूहलं नौ। यद्यनेन जनेन श्रोतव्यं कथयतु भवान् किंनिमित्तं भर्त्रा वसन्तोत्सवः प्रतिषिद्धः।

सानुमती—उस्सवप्पिआ क्खु मणुस्सा। गुरुणा कारणेण होदव्वं। उत्सवप्रियाः खलु मनुष्याः। गुरुणा कारणेन भवितव्यम्।

कञ्चुकी—बहुलीभूतमेतत्किं न कथ्यते। किमत्रभवत्योः कर्ण-पंथ नायातं शकुन्तलाप्रत्यादेशकौलीनम्।

उभे—सुदं रट्ठिअमुहादो जाव अङ्गुलीअअदंसणं। श्रुतं राष्ट्रीयमुखाद्यावदङ्गुलीयकदर्शनम्।

कञ्चुकी—तेन ह्यल्पं कथयितव्यम्। यदैव खलु स्वाङ्गुलीयक-दर्शनादनुस्मृतं देवेन सत्यमूढपूर्वा मे तत्रभवती रहसि शकुन्तला मोहात्प्रत्यादिष्टेति। तदाप्रभृत्येव पश्चात्तापमुपगतो देवः। तथाहि।

रम्यं द्वेष्टि यथापुरा प्रकृतिभिर्न प्रत्यहं सेव्यते
शय्याप्रान्तविवर्तनैर्विगमयत्युन्निद्र एव क्षपाः।
दाक्षिण्येन ददाति वाचमुचितामन्तःपुरेभ्यो यदा
गोत्रेषु स्खलितस्तदा भवति च व्रीडाविलक्षश्चिरम्॥ ५॥

सानुमती—पिअं मे। प्रियं मे।

First. Noble sir, but a few days ago, we were sent to the feet of his Majesty, by Mitrāvasu, the king's brother-in-law, and were entrusted with the duty of keeping the pleasure-garden ; thus being strangers, we have heard nothing of this affair.

Chamberlain. Well, you must not do so again.

Both. Sir, we are curious. If we may know, pray tell us what induced our sovereign to forbid the spring festival ?

Sānumatī. Men are, indeed, fond of festivals ; there must be some weighty reason.

Chamberlain. Why should I not tell it, when it is generally known ? Have not your ladyships heard the scandal concerning Śakuntalā's rejection ?

Both. We have heard it from the mouth of the king's brother-in-law up to the point of the recovery of the ring.

Chamberlain. Then, I have a little to add. When at the sight of his own ring the king remembered that he had indeed secretly married the lady Śakuntalā, and had rejected her under a delusion, from that time the king was struck with remorse. Thus

> He abhors everything pleasurable ; he is not daily waited upon by his ministers as in former times ; spends sleepless nights in tossing about on the edge of his bed and when by courtesy he addresses suitable words to the ladies of his palace, he blunders in their names and becomes for a long while abashed with shame. (5)

Sānumatī. This is very pleasing to me.

कञ्चुकी—अस्मात्प्रभवतो वैमनस्यादुत्सवः प्रत्याख्यातः।

उभे—जुज्जइ। युज्यते।

(नेपथ्ये।)

एदु एदु भवं। एतु एतु भवान्।

कञ्चुकी—(कर्णं दत्त्वा।) अये, इत एवाभिवर्तते देवः। स्वकर्मानुष्ठीयताम्।

उभे—तह। (इति निष्क्रान्ते) तथा।

(ततः प्रविशति पश्चात्तापसदृशवेषो राजा विदूषकः प्रतीहारी च।)

कञ्चुकी—(राजानमवलोक्य।) अहो सर्वास्ववस्थासु रमणीयत्वमाकृतिविशेषाणाम्। एवमुत्सुकोऽपि प्रियदर्शनो देवः। तथाहि।

प्रत्यादिष्टविशेषमण्डनविधिर्वामप्रकोष्ठार्पितं
बिभ्रत्काञ्चनमेकमेव वलयं श्वासोपरक्ताधरः।
चिन्ताजागरणप्रताम्रनयनस्तेजोगुणादात्मनः
संस्कारोल्लिखितो महामणिरिव क्षीणोऽपि नालक्ष्यते॥ ६॥

सानुमती—(राजानं दृष्ट्वा।) ठाणे क्खु पच्चादेसविमाणिदा वि इमस्स किदे सउन्दला किलम्मदि। स्थाने खलु प्रत्यादेशविमानिताप्यस्य कृते शकुन्तला क्लाम्यति

राजा—(ध्यानमन्दं परिक्रम्य)।

प्रथमं सारङ्गाक्ष्या प्रियया प्रतिबोध्यमानमपि सुप्तम्।
अनुशयदुःखायेदं हतहृदयं संप्रति विबुद्धम्॥ ७॥

CHAMBERLAIN. By reason of this deep mental derangement the festival has been forbidden.

BOTH. It is proper.

(*Behind the scenes*).

Let your Majesty come.

CHAMBERLAIN (*Listening*). Ah, his Majesty is coming here. Attend to your duties.

BOTH. All right. (*Exeunt.*)

(*Enter the king in a dress indicative of remorse; the Vidūṣaka and a portress.*)

CHAMBERLAIN (*Observing the king*). How charming are noble forms under all conditions! Thus his Majesty has a pleasing appearance even in his affliction. For

Rejecting special modes of decoration, he wears but one golden bracelet fastened on the left fore-arm; his lip is faded by sighs; his eyes are very red from sleeplessness caused by thought (of Śakuntalā). Yet through the excellence of his own lustre, though he has grown emaciate he is scarcely observed to be so, even like a magnificent diamond ground away on the polishing-stone. (6)

SĀNUMATĪ (*Looking at the king*). No wonder Śakuntalā languishes for him even though he dishonoured her by his repudiation of her.

KING. (*Walking round slowly in meditation*).

This my blighted heart which previously slept even when it was wakened from sleep by my fawn-eyed beloved is now broad awake to feel the anguish of remorse. (7)

सानुमती—णं ईदिसाणि तवस्सिणीए भाअहेआणि । नन्वीदृशानि तपस्विन्या भागधेयानि ।

विदूषकः—(अपवार्य ।) लङ्घिदो एसो भूओ वि सउन्दलावाहिणा । ण आणे कहं चिकिच्छिदव्वो भविस्सदि त्ति ।

कञ्चुकी—(उपगम्य ।) जयतु जयतु देवः । महाराज, प्रत्यवेक्षिताः प्रमदवनभूमयः । यथाकाममध्यास्तां विनोदस्थानानि महाराजः ।

राजा—वेत्रवति, मद्वचनादमात्यमार्यपिशुनं ब्रूहि । चिरप्रबोधान्न संभावितमस्माभिरद्य धर्मासनमध्यासितुम् । यत्प्रत्यवेक्षितं पौरकार्यमार्येण तत्पत्रमारोप्य दीयतामिति ।

प्रतीहारी—जं देवो आणवेदि । (इति निष्क्रान्ता ।) यद्देव आज्ञापयति ।

राजा—वातायन, त्वमपि स्वं नियोगमशून्यं कुरु ।

कञ्चुकी—यदाज्ञापयति देवः । (इति निष्क्रान्तः ।)

विदूषकः—किदं भवदा णिम्मच्छिअं । संपदं सिसिरातवच्छेअरमणीए इमस्सिं पमदवणुद्देसे अत्ताणं रमइस्ससि । कृतं भवता निर्मक्षिकम् । सांप्रतं शिशिरातपच्छेदरमणीयेऽस्मिन्प्रमदवनोद्देश आत्मानं रमयिष्यसि ।

राजा—वयस्य, रन्ध्रोपनिपतिनोऽनर्था इति यदुच्यते तदव्यभिचारि वचः । कुतः ।

मुनिसुताप्रणयस्मृतिरोधिना
मम च मुक्तमिदं तमसा मनः ।
मनसिजेन सखे प्रहरिष्यता
धनुषि चूतशरश्च निवेशितः ॥ ८ ॥

विदूषकः—चिट्ठ दाव । इमिणा दण्डकट्ठेण कन्दप्पवाणं णासइस्सामि । (इति दण्डकाष्ठमुद्यम्य चूताङ्कुरं पातयितुमिच्छति ।) तिष्ठ तावत् । अनेन दण्डकाष्ठेन कन्दर्पबाणं नाशयिष्यामि ।

SĀNUMATĪ. Such is also the fate of the poor girl.

VIDŪṢAKA (*Aside*). He is again seized by his Śakuntalā sickness; and I hardly know a remedy for his illness.

CHAMBERLAIN (*Advancing*). Victory to your Majesty! The grounds of the pleasure-park have been inspected. Your Majesty may visit its pleasure-spots at will.

KING. Vetravati, tell the minister, the noble Piśuna, in my name, that owing to long sleeplessness, it was not possible for me to sit in the tribunal to-day. Whatever business of the citizens the worthy sir may have investigated, should be written down and dispatched to me.

PORTRESS. As your Majesty commands. (*Exit.*)

KING. And you, Vātāyana, attend to your business.

CHAMBERLAIN. As my king commands. (*Exit.*)

VIDŪṢAKA. You have not left a fly in this place. Now you will amuse yourself in this part of the pleasure-park which is cool and delightful by the mitigation of heat.

KING. Friend, the proverb 'Misfortunes rush through the weak spot' is an infallible one. For

> No sooner does the darkness that clouded the remembrance of my love for the sage's daughter, lift from my mind, than the God of Love, preparing to strike, puts the shaft of mango blossom to his bow. (8)

VIDŪṢAKA. Wait a bit, while I destroy Love's arrow with my stick. (*He raises his stick and desires to strike down the mango-shoot.*)

राजा—(सस्मितम् ।) भवतु । दृष्टं ब्रह्मवर्चसम् । सखे, क्वोपविष्टः प्रियायाः किंचिदनुकारिणीषु लतासु दृष्टिं विलोभयामि ।

विदूषकः—णं आसण्णपरिआरिआ चदुरिआ भवदा संदिट्ठा—माहवीमण्डवे इमं वेलं अदिवाहिस्सं । तहिं मे चित्तफलअगदं सहत्थलिहिदं तत्तहोदीए सउन्दलाए पडिकिदिं आणेहित्ति । नन्वासन्नपरिचारिका चतुरिका भवता संदिष्टा । माधवीमण्डप इमां वेलामतिवाहयिष्ये । तत्र मे चित्रफलकगतां स्वहस्तलिखितां तत्रभवत्याः शाकुन्तलायाः प्रतिकृतिमानयेति ।

राजा—ईदृशं हृदयविनोदस्थानम् । तत्तमेव मार्गमादेशय ।

विदूषकः—इदो इदो भवं । इत इतो भवान् ।

(उभौ परिक्रामतः । सानुमत्यनुगच्छति ।)

विदूषकः—एसो मणिसिलापट्टअसणाहो माहवीमण्डवो उवहाररमणिज्जदाए णिस्संसअं साअदेण विअ णो पडिच्छदि । ता पविसिअ णिसीददु भवं । एष मणिशिलापट्टकसनाथो माधवीमण्डप उपहाररमणीयतया निःसंशयं स्वागतेनेव नौ प्रतीच्छति । तत्प्रविश्य निषीदतु भवान् ।

(उभौ प्रवेशं कृत्वोपविष्टौ ।)

सानुमती—लदासंस्सिदा देक्खिस्सं दाव सहीए पडिकिदिं । तदो से भत्तुणो बहुमुहं अणुराअं णिवेदइस्सं । (इति तथा कृत्वा स्थिता ।) लतासंश्रिता द्रक्ष्यामि तावत्सख्याः प्रतिकृतिम् । ततोऽस्या भर्तुर्बहुमुखमनुरागं निवेदयिष्यामि ।

राजा—सखे, सर्वमिदानीं स्मरामि शकुन्तलायाः प्रथमवृत्तान्तम् । कथितवानस्मि भवते च । स भवान्प्रत्यादेशवेलायां मत्समीपगतो नासीत् । पूर्वमपि न त्वया कदाचित्संकीर्तितं तत्रभवत्या नाम । कच्चिदहमिव विस्मृतवानसि त्वम् ।

विदूषकः—ण विसुमरामि । किंतु सव्वं कहिअ अवसाणे उण तुए परिहासविअप्पओ एसो ण भूदत्थोत्ति आचक्खिदं । मए वि मिप्पिण्डबुद्धिणा तह एव्व गहीदं । अहवा भविदव्वदा

KING (*Smiling*). Enough ! I have seen a Brahmin's power. Now, friend, where shall I sit and recreate my sight with the slender shrubs which bear a faint resemblance to my beloved ?

VIDŪṢAKA. Well, have you not told Caturikā, your attendant, that you would be spending this hour in the Mādhavī bower, and that she should bring you there the picture of the lady Śakuntalā which you yourself painted on a tablet ?

KING. Will such a place divert me ? Well, lead the way to the same place.

VIDŪṢAKA. This way, your Majesty, this way.

(*Both walk round ; Sānumatī follows them.*)

VIDŪṢAKA. This Mādhavī bower furnished with a marble slab with its lovely flower-offerings appears to bid us welcome. Let your Honour enter and sit.

(*Both enter and seat themselves.*)

SĀNUMATĪ. Concealed behind the creepers I will just see the dear girl's picture. Then I shall be able to tell her how sincere her husband's love is.

(*Does so, and pauses.*)

KING. Friend, I now remember all the previous affair with Śakuntalā. And I have spoken to you (about it.) You, however, were not present near me at the time I disavowed her. Nor did you ever before mention her ladyship's name. Had you forgotten her even as I did ?

VIDŪṢAKA. No, I did not forget. But after telling the whole story, you said at the end that it was all a joke and that there was no truth in it. And I who

क्खु बलवदी । न विस्मरामि । किंतु सर्वं कथयित्वावसाने पुनस्त्वया परिहासविजल्प एष न भूतार्थ इत्याख्यातम् । मयापि मृत्पिण्डबुद्धिना तथैव गृहीतम् । अथवा भवितव्यता खलु बलवती ।

सानुमती—एव्वं णेदं । एवमेवैतत् ।

राजा—(ध्यात्वा ।) **सखे, त्रायस्व माम् ।**

विदूषकः—भो, किं एदं । अणुववण्णं क्खु ईदिसं तुइ । कदा वि सप्पुरिसा सोअपत्तप्पाणो ण होन्ति । णं पवादे वि णिक्कम्पा गिरीओ । भोः, किमेतत् । अनुपपन्नं खल्वीदृशं त्वयि । कदापि सत्पुरुषा शोकपात्रात्मानो न भवन्ति । ननु प्रवातेऽपि निष्कम्पा गिरयः ।

राजा—वयस्य, निराकरणविक्लवायाः प्रियायाः समवस्थामनुस्मृत्य बलवदशरणोऽस्मि । सा हि

इतः प्रत्यादेशात्स्वजनमनुगन्तुं व्यवसिता
मुहुस्तिष्ठेत्युच्चैर्वदति गुरुशिष्ये गुरुसमे ।
पुनर्दृष्टिं बाष्पप्रसरकलुषामर्पितवती
मयि क्रूरे यत्तत्सविषमिव शल्यं दहति माम् ॥ ९ ॥

सानुमती—अम्महे । ईदिसी सकज्जपरदा । इमस्स संदावेण अहं रमामि । अहो । ईदृशी स्वकार्यपरता । अस्य संतापेनाहं रमे ।

विदूषकः—भो, अत्थि मे तक्को । केण वि तत्तहोदी आआसचारिणा णीदेत्ति । भोः, अस्ति मे तर्कः । केनापि तत्रभवत्याकाशचारिणा नीतेति ।

राजा—कः पतिदेवतामन्यः परामर्ष्टुमुत्सहेत । मेनका किल सख्यास्ते जन्मप्रतिष्ठेति श्रुतवानस्मि । तत्सहचारिणीभिः सखी ते हृतेति मे हृदयमाशङ्कते ।

सानुमती—संमोहो क्खु विम्हअणिज्जो ण पडिबोहो । संमोहः खलु विस्मयनीयो न प्रतिबोधः ।

विदूषकः—जइ एव्वं अत्थि क्खु समाअमो कालेण तत्तहोदीए । यद्येवमस्ति खलु समागमः कालेन तत्रभवत्या ।

have no more intelligence than a lump of clay believed it. Or rather fate is powerful.

SĀNUMATĪ. It is even so.

KING (*Meditating*). Friend, help me!

VIDŪṢAKA. Oh, what is it? This is indeed unbecoming in you. Never do great men give themselves up to grief; the mountains are calm even in a tempest.

KING. When I remember my beloved's condition who was greatly affected by my desertion I feel quite forlorn.

> When I rejected her from here, she made an attempt to follow her kinsfolk; and when her father's pupil, revered as her father himself, repeatedly cried "stay" in a loud voice, then once more she fixed on me, who had become inexorable, a glance bedimmed with gushing tears; (the idea of) it all burns me like an envenomed shaft. (9)

SĀNUMATĪ. Dear me! Such is one's regard for one's own interest that I delight in his pain.

VIDŪṢAKA. O I have a guess that her ladyship was carried away by some heavenly being.

KING. Who else would dare to touch rudely a wife to whom her husband is a divinity? I have heard that Menakā gave birth to your friend. And her companions have, I imagine, carried her away.

SĀNUMATĪ. His delusion is, to be wondered at, not the awakening from it.

VIDŪṢAKA. If that is so, you will meet her again after a time.

राजा—कथमिव ।

विदूषकः—ण क्खु मादापिदरा भत्तुविओअदुक्खिदं दुहिदरं देक्खिदुं पारेन्ति । न खलु मातापितरौ भर्तृवियोगदुःखितां दुहितरं द्रष्टुं पारयतः ।

राजा—वयस्य,

स्वप्नो नु माया नु मतिभ्रमो नु
क्लिष्टं नु तावत्फलमेव पुण्यम् ।
असंनिवृत्त्यै तदतीतमेव
मनोरथा नाम तटप्रपाताः ॥ १० ॥

विदूषकः—मा एव्वं । णं अङ्गुलीअअं एव्व णिदंसणं अवस्सं-भावी अचिन्तणिज्जो समाअमो होदि त्ति । मैवम् । नन्वङ्गुलीयकमेव निदर्शनमवश्यंभाव्यचिन्तनीयः समागमो भवतीति ।

राजा—(अङ्गुलीयकं विलोक्य ।) अये, इदं तावदसुलभ-स्थानभ्रंशि शोचनीयम् ।

तव सुचरितमङ्गुलीय नूनं
प्रतनु ममेव विभाव्यते फलेन ।
अरुणनखमनोहरासु तस्या-
श्च्युतमसि लब्धपदं यदङ्गुलीषु ॥ ११ ॥

सानुमती—जइ अण्णहत्थगदं भवे सच्चं एव्व सोअणिज्जं भवे । यद्यन्यहस्तगतं भवेत्सत्यमेव शोचनीयं भवेत् ।

विदूषकः—भो, इअं णाममुद्दा केण उग्घदेण तत्तहोदीए हत्थ-संसग्गं पाविदा । भोः, इयं नाममुद्रा केनोद्घातेन तत्रभवत्या हस्तसंसर्गं प्रापिता ।

सानुमती—मम वि कोदूहलेण आआरिदो एसो । ममापि कौतू-हलेनाकारित एषः ।

राजा—श्रूयताम् । स्वनगराय प्रस्थितं मां प्रिया सबाष्पमाह । कियच्चिरेणार्यपुत्रः प्रतिपत्तिं दास्यतीति ।

विदूषकः—तदो तदो । ततस्ततः ।

KING. How so?

VIDŪṢAKA. No father and mother can (long) endure to see their daughter separated from her husband.

KING. Friend,

> Was it a dream? or an illusion? or the infatuation of my mind? Or was it that my merit having borne me that much fruit, was exhausted? It is gone, never to return: these my hopes are like falls from a precipice. (10)

VIDŪṢAKA. Do not speak thus. Is not the ring itself a proof that there may be an unexpected meeting with that which must necessarily happen?

KING. (*Looking at the ring*). This, indeed, which has fallen from a station hard to gain, deserves my pity.

> Verily, O ring, thy merit like mine is proved to be but slight from (thy) reward; since after finding a place on her lovely pink-nailed fingers thou hast suffered a fall. (11)

SĀNUMATĪ. Had it found a way to any other hand, its lot would have been truly deplorable.

VIDŪṢAKA. With what object was the ring placed in her ladyship's hand?

SĀNUMATĪ. He, too, seems to be impelled by the curiosity I feel.

KING. Listen: when I started for the capital, my darling wept and said: After how long will my lord send me news?

VIDŪṢAKA. Well, what then?

राजा—पश्चादिमां मुद्रां तदङ्गुलौ निवेशयता मया प्रत्यभिहिता।

एकैकमत्र दिवसे दिवसे मदीयं
नामाक्षरं गणय गच्छसि यावदन्तम्।
तावत्प्रिये मदवरोधगृहप्रवेशं
नेता जनस्तव समीपमुपैष्यतीति ॥ १२ ॥

तच्च दारुणात्मना मया मोहान्नानुष्ठितम्।

सानुमती—रमणीओ क्खु अवही विहिणा विसंवादिदो। रमणीयः खल्ववधिर्विधिना विसंवादितः।

विदूषकः—कहं धीवलकप्पिअस्स लोहिअमच्छस्स उदलब्भन्तले आसि। कथं धीवरकल्पितस्य रोहितमत्स्यस्योदराभ्यन्तर आसीत्।

राजा—शचीतीर्थं वन्दमानायाः सख्यास्ते हस्ताद्गङ्गास्रोतसि परिभ्रष्टम्।

विदूषकः—जुज्जइ। युज्यते।

सानुमती—अदो एव्व तवस्सिणीए सउन्दलाए अधम्मभीरुणो इमस्स राएसिणो परिणए संदेहो आसि। अहवा ईदिसो अणुराओ अहिण्णाणं अवेक्खदि। कहं विअ एदं। अत एव तपस्विन्याः शकुतलाया अधर्मभीरोरस्य राजर्षेः परिणये संदेह आसीत्। अथवेदृशोऽनुरागोऽभिज्ञानमपेक्षते। कथमिवैतत्।

राजा—उपालप्स्ये तावदिदमङ्गुलीयकम्।

विदूषकः—(आत्मगतम्।) गहीदो णेण पन्था उम्मत्तआणं। गृहीतोऽनेन पन्था उन्मत्तानाम्।

राजा—

कथं नु तं बन्धुरकोमलाङ्गुलिं
करं विहायासि निमग्नमम्भसि।

अथवा।

अचेतनं नाम गुणं न लक्षये-
न्मयैव कस्मादवधीरिता प्रिया ॥ १३ ॥

KING. Then, fixing this ring on her finger, I said:

> Count one by one every day the letters of my name on this (ring); as soon as you reach the end, my darling, the messenger who is to lead you to the entrance of the inner apartment, will come into your presence. (12)

And hard-hearted that I am, I failed to carry it out in my madness.

SĀNUMATĪ. A charming interval, indeed which was, however, marred by fate.

VIDŪṢAKA. How did it get inside the maw of the carp cut up by the fisherman?

KING. While your friend was worshipping Śacītīrtha, it must have slipped from her hand into the stream of the Ganges.

VIDŪṢAKA. It is explained

SĀNUMATĪ. It was hence that the king, who is afraid of doing anything unrighteous, doubted his marriage with poor Śakuntalā. And yet such love does not require a token. How could it be?

KING. Well, I will now reproach the ring.

VIDŪṢAKA (*To himself*). (So) he is (again) going the the way of madmen!

KING.

> How couldst thou leave that hand with its slender delicate fingers and fall into the water? Or a lifeless thing may well not appreciate excellence. But how could I scorn my beloved? (13)

विदूषकः—(आत्मगतम् ।) **कहं बुभुक्खाए खादिदव्वो म्हि** कथं बुभुक्षया खादितव्योऽस्मि ।

राजा—अकारणपरित्यक्ते अनुशयतप्तहृदयस्तावदनुकम्प्यतामयं जनः पुनर्दर्शनेन ।

(प्रविश्यापटीक्षेपेण चित्रफलकहस्ता ।)

चतुरिका—इअं चित्तगदा भट्टिणी । (इति चित्रफलकं दर्शयति ।) इयं चित्रगता भट्टिनी ।

विदूषकः—साहु वअस्स, महुरावत्थाणदंसणिज्जो भावाणुप्पवेसो । क्खलदि विअ मे दिट्ठी णिण्णुण्णअप्पदेसेसु । साधु वयस्य, मधुरावस्थानदर्शनीयो भावानुप्रवेशः । स्खलतीव मे दृष्टिर्निम्नोन्नतप्रदेशेषु ।

सानुमती—अम्मो एसा राएसिणो णिउणदा । जाणे सही अग्गदो मे वट्टदित्ति । अहो एषा राजर्षेनिपुणता । जाने सख्यग्रतो मे वर्तत इति ।

राजा—

यद्यत्साधु न चित्रे स्यात्क्रियते तत्तदन्यथा ।
तथापि तस्या लावण्यं रेखया किंचिदन्वितम् ॥ १४ ॥

सानुमती—सरिसं एदं पच्छादावगुरुणो सिणेहस्स अणवलेवस्स अ । सदृशमेतत्पश्चात्तापगुरोः स्नेहस्यानवलेपस्य च ।

विदूषकः—भो, दाणिं तिण्णि तत्थहोदीओ दीसन्ति । सव्वाओ अ दंसणीआओ । कदमा इत्थ तत्तहोदी सउन्दला । भोः, इदानीं तिस्रस्तत्रभवत्यो दृश्यन्ते । सर्वाश्च दर्शनीयाः । कतमात्र तत्रभवती शकुन्तला ।

सानुमती—अणभिण्णो क्खु ईदिसस्स रूवस्स मोहदिट्ठी अअं जणो । अनभिज्ञः खल्वीदृशस्य रूपस्य मोघदृष्टिरयं जनः ।

राजा—त्वं तावत्कतमां तर्कयसि ।

विदूषकः—तक्केमि जा एसा सिढिलकेसबन्धणुव्वन्तकुसुमेण केसन्तेण उब्भिण्णसेअबिन्दुणा वअणेण विसेसदो ओसरीआहिं बाहाहिं अवसेअसिणिद्धतरुणपल्लवस्स चूअपाअवस्स पासे इसिपरिस्सन्ता विअ आलिहिदा सा सउन्दला । इदराओ सहीओत्ति ।

VIDŪṢAKA (*To himself*). How ? must I be devoured by hunger ?

KING. O (My darling) abandoned without reason, let me, whose heart is stung with remorse, be once more blessed with a sight of thee ?

(*Entering with a toss of the curtain, tablet in hand*).

CATURIKĀ. Here is our lady in the picture. (*She shows the tablet.*)

VIDŪṢAKA. Excellent, my friend ! How beautifully are the feelings represented in this lovely posture ! mine eyes stumble as it were over its uneven parts.

SĀNUMATĪ. What great skill the virtuous king possesses ! My friend seems to stand before my eyes.

KING.

Whatever is not well executed in the picture may be (retouched and) improved; and yet (even then) her loveliness will be possessed by the picture in some measure only. (14)

SĀNUMATĪ. This is befitting an affection increased by remorse, and absence of conceit.

VIDŪṢAKA. There are to be seen three ladies now, and all are beautiful. Which one is the lady Śakuntalā ?

SĀNUMATĪ What use are his eyes to this man who is ignorant of such beauty ?

KING. Which one do you think ?

VIDŪṢAKA. I think that she who is represented as if a little fatigued by the side of the mango-tree whose young leaves are glistening after her watering, with

तर्कयामि यैषा शिथिलकेशबन्धनोद्वान्तकुसुमेन केशान्तेनोद्भिन्नस्वेदबिन्दुना वदनेन विशेषतोऽपसृताभ्यां बाहुभ्यामवसेकस्निग्धतरुणपल्लवस्य चूतपादपस्य पार्श्वे ईषत्परिश्रान्तेवालिखिता सा शकुन्तला । इतरे सख्याविति ।

राजा—निपुणो भवान् । अस्त्यत्र मे भावचिह्नम् ।

स्विन्नाङ्गुलिविनिवेशो रेखाप्रान्तेषु दृश्यते मलिनः ।
अश्रु च कपोलपतितं दृश्यमिदं वर्तिकोच्छ्वासात् ॥ १५ ॥

चतुरिके, अर्धलिखितमेतद्विनोदस्थानम् । गच्छ । वर्तिकां तावदानय ।

चतुरिका—अज्ज माठव्व, अवलम्ब चित्तफलअं जाव आअच्छामि । आर्य माठव्य, अवलम्बस्व चित्रफलकं यावदागच्छामि ।

राजा—अहमेवैतदवलम्बे । (इति यथोक्तं करोति ।)

(निष्क्रान्ता चेटी ।)

राजा—अहं हि

साक्षात्प्रियामुपगतामपहाय पूर्वं
चित्रार्पितां पुनरिमां बहु मन्यमानः ।
स्रोतोवहां पथि निकामजलामतीत्य
जातः सखे प्रणयवान्मृगतृष्णिकायाम् ॥ १६ ॥

विदूषकः—(आत्मगतम् ।) **एसो अत्तभवं णदिं अदिक्कमिअ मिअतिण्हिआं संकन्तो ।** (प्रकाशम् ।) **भो, अवरं किं एत्थ लिहिदव्वं ।** एषोऽत्रभवान्नदीमतिक्रम्य मृगतृष्णिकां संक्रान्तः । भोः, अपरं किमत्र लिखितव्यम् ।

सानुमती—जो जो पदेसो सहीए मे अहिरूवो तं तं आलिहिदुकामो भवे । यो यः प्रदेशः सख्या मेऽभिरूपस्तं तमालिखितुकामो भवेत् ।

राजा—श्रूयताम् ।

arms drooping in a peculiar manner; with a face on which drops of perspiration have broken out; with locks of her hair the flowers of which have dropped down from the loosened braid; that is Śakuntalā. The others are her friends.

KING. You are clever. Here are proofs of my love.

At the edges of the drawing is seen the soiled impression of my perspiring fingers; and here is to be observed this tear that fell from my cheek from the swelling of the paint. (15)

CATURIKĀ, this source of my consolation is but half finished. Therefore, go, get me a brush.

CATURIKĀ. Worthy Māṭhavya, hold the picture tablet till I get back.

KING. I will myself hold it. (*Does as said.*)

(*Exit maid.*)

KING. I, now,

Having first rejected my darling who had approached me in person, and now again and again doing homage to her drawn in this picture, have become, O friend, possessed of a longing for the mirage, after passing by a river on my way having plenty of water. (16)

VIDŪṢAKA (*To himself*). Here is his honour, having passed by a river, gone to a mirage. (*Aloud*). Oh what else is to be painted here?

SĀNUMATĪ. He may be desirous of painting every spot that the dear girl loved.

KING. Listen—

कार्या सैकतलीनहंसमिथुना स्रोतोवहा मालिनी
पादास्तामभितो निषण्णहरिणा गौरीगुरोः पावनाः ।
शाखालम्बितवल्कलस्य च तरोर्निर्मातुमिच्छाम्यधः
शृङ्गे कृष्णमृगस्य वामनयनं कण्डूयमानां मृगीम् ॥ १७ ॥

विदूषकः—(आत्मगतम् ।) जह अहं देक्खामि पूरिदव्वं णेण चित्तफलअं लम्बकुच्चाणं तावसाणं कदम्बेहिं । यथाहं पश्यामि पूरितव्यमनेन चित्रफलकं लम्बकूर्चानां तापसानां कदम्बैः ।

राजा—वयस्य, अन्यच्च शकुन्तलायाः प्रसाधनमभिप्रेतं विस्मृतमस्माभिः ।

विदूषकः—किं विअ । किमिव ।

सानुमती—वणवासस्स सो उमारस्स अ जं सरिसं भविस्सदि । वनवासस्य सौकुमार्यस्य च यत्सदृशं भविष्यति ।

राजा—

कृतं न कर्णार्पितबन्धनं सखे
शिरीषमागण्डविलम्बिकेसरम् ।
न वा शरच्चन्द्रमरीचिकोमलं
मृणालसूत्रं रचितं स्तनान्तरे ॥ १८ ॥

विदूषकः—भो, किं णु तत्तहोदी रत्तकुवलअपल्लवसोहिणा अग्गहत्थेण मुहं आवारिअ चइदचइदा विअ ठिआ । (सावधानं निरूप्य दृष्ट्वा ।) आ, एसो दासीए पुत्तो कुसुमरसपाडच्चरो तत्तहोदीए वअणं अहिलङ्घदि महुअरो । भोः, किं नु तत्रभवती रक्तकुवलयपल्लवशोभिनाग्रहस्तेन मुखमावार्य चकितचकितेव स्थिता । आः, एष दास्याः पुत्रः कुसुमरसपटच्चरस्तत्रभवत्या वदनमभिलङ्घति मधुकरः ।

राजा— ननु वार्यतामेष धृष्टः ।

The stream of Mālinī ought to be drawn with a pair of swans resting on its sands ; and on both its sides must appear the sacred hills at the base of the Himālayan ranges, where the deer are squatting ; and I wish to draw, underneath a tree that bears some bark-garments suspended from its boughs, a doe that rubs her left eye on the horn of a black antelope. (17)

VIDŪṢAKA (*To himself*). As I imagine, he will fill up the picture with multitudes of long-bearded hermits.

KING. Friend, I have forgotten to draw another of Śakuntalā's ornament which I had intended to draw.

VIDŪṢAKA. What is it ?

SĀNUMATĪ. Such as becomes her forest life and her delicacy.

KING.

A Śirīṣa-flower with its stalk fastened over her ear, and its filaments waving over her cheek, has been omitted, O friend ; nor has a necklace of lotus fibres, soft like the rays of the moon of autumn, been drawn between her breasts. (18)

VIDŪṢAKA. But why does the lady stand, as if she is very much frightened, covering her face with the palm of her hand glowing like the petal of a red-lotus ? (*Looking closely*). Ah ! Here is this bee, this son of a slave, this thief who robs the flowers of their honey, attacking her ladyship's face.

KING. Drive off this impudent (bee).

विदूषकः—भवं एव्व अविणीदाणं सासिदा इमस्स वारणे पहविस्सदि। भवानेवाविनीतानां शासितास्य वारणे प्रभविष्यति।

राजा—युज्यते। अयि भोः, कुसुमलताप्रियातिथे, किमत्र परिपतनखेदमनुभवसि।

एषा कुसुमनिषण्णा तृषितापि सती भवन्तमनुरक्ता।
प्रतिपालयति मधुकरी न खलु मधु विना त्वया पिबति॥ १९॥

सानुमती—अज्ज अभिजादं क्खु एसो वारिदो। अद्याभिजातं खल्वेष वारितः।

विदूषकः—पडिसिद्धा वि वामा एसा जादी। प्रतिषिद्धापि वामैषा जातिः।

राजा—एवं भोः, न मे शासने तिष्ठसि। श्रूयतां तर्हि संप्रति।

अक्लिष्टबालतरुपल्लवलोभनीयं
पीतं मया सदयमेव रतोत्सवेषु।
बिम्बाधरं स्पृशसि चेद्भ्रमरप्रियाया-
स्त्वां कारयामि कमलोदरबन्धनस्थम्॥ २०॥

विदूषकः—एव्वं तिक्खदण्डस्स किं ण भाइस्सदि। (प्रहस्य। आत्मगतम्।) एदो दाव उम्मत्तो। अहं पि एदस्स सङ्गेण ईदिसवण्णो विअ संवुत्तो। (प्रकाशम्।) भो, चित्तं क्खु एदं। एवं तीक्ष्णदण्डस्य किं न भेष्यति। एष तावदुन्मत्तः। अहमप्येतस्य सङ्गेनेदृशवर्ण इव संवृत्तः। भोः, चित्रं खल्वेतत्।

राजा—कथं चित्रम्।

सानुमती—अहं पि दाणिं अणवगदत्था, किं उण जहालिहिदाणुभावी एसो। अहमपीदानीमनवगतार्था, किं पुनर्यथालिखितानुभाव्येषः।

राजा— वयस्य, किमिदमनुष्ठितं पौरोभाग्यम्।

VIDŪṢAKA. Your honour alone, that punishes all offenders, has the power to drive him off.

KING. True. O welcome guest of flowering-plants, why undergo the trouble of hovering round here?

> There, perched on a flower, is the female bee who loves thee, and though athirst, is waiting for thee still, nor without thee will she taste its honey. (19)

SĀNUMATĪ. For once now is he kept off quite in a courteous manner.

VIDŪṢAKA. This kind is perverse, however it may be warned off.

KING. Thus, then, thou wilt not obey my command. Well then listen;

> Shouldst thou touch, O bee, the bimba-lip of my darling, sweet as a virgin leaf on a tree, the lip from which I drank delight in love-feasts, then I will make thee imprisoned in the hollow of a lotus. (20)

VIDŪṢAKA. How should he not be afraid of one who gives so severe a punishment? (*Laughing, to himself*). As for him, he is quite crazy, and I too am just as bad, from keeping him company! (*Aloud*). O, it is only a picture.

KING. How? A picture?

SĀNUMATĪ. I, too, did not realise the fact; how much less he who is experiencing what he has painted!

KING. Friend, why have you done such a wicked thing?

दर्शनसुखमनुभवतः साक्षादिव तन्मयेन हृदयेन।
स्मृतिकारिणा त्वया मे पुनरपि चित्रीकृता कान्ता॥ २१॥

(इति बाष्पं विहरति ।)

सानुमती—पुव्वावरविरोही अपुव्वो एसो विरहमग्गो । पूर्वापरविरोध्यपूर्व एष विरहमार्गः ।

राजा—वयस्य, कथमेवमविश्रान्तदुःखमनुभवामि ।

प्रजागरात्खिलीभूतस्तस्याः स्वप्ने समागमः।
बाष्पस्तु न ददात्येनां द्रष्टुं चित्रगतामपि॥ २२॥

सानुमती—सव्वहा पमज्जिदं तुए पच्चादेसदुक्खं सउन्दलाए। सर्वथा प्रमार्जितं त्वया प्रत्यादेशदुःखं शकुन्तलायाः ।

(प्रविश्य ।)

चतुरिका—जेदु जेदु भट्टा । वट्टिआकरण्डअं गेण्हिअ इदोमुहं पत्थिदम्हि । जयतु जयतु भर्ता । वर्तिकाकरण्डकं गृहीत्वेतोमुखं प्रस्थितास्मि ।

राजा—किं च ।

चतुरिका—सो मे हत्थादो अन्तरा तरलिआदुदीआए देवीए वसुमदीए अहं अज्जउत्तस्स उवणइस्सं त्ति सबलक्कारं गहीदो । स मे हस्तादन्तरा तरलिकाद्वितीयया देव्या वसुमत्याहमेवार्यपुत्रस्योपनेष्यामीति सबलात्कारं गृहीतः ।

विदूषकः—दिट्ठिआ तुमं मुक्का । दिष्ट्या त्वं मुक्ता ।

चतुरिका—जाव देवीए विडवलग्गं उत्तरीअं तरलिआ मोचेदि ताव मए णिव्वाहिदो अत्ता । यावद्देव्या विटपलग्नमुत्तरीयं तरलिका मोचयति तावन्मया निर्वाहित आत्मा ।

While I was enjoying the rapture of beholding her as if she stood before my eyes, with my heart completely wrapped up in her, you have, by reviving my memory, again transformed my darling into a picture. (21).

(*Sheds tears.*)

SĀNUMATĪ. Quite without a precedent is this way of (one in a state of) separation, involving as it does an inconsistency between what preceded and what followed.

KING. Friend, why do I thus experience unremitting grief ?

Union with her is prevented by my sleeplessness ; and my tears will not suffer me to view her even in this picture. (22).

SĀNUMATĪ. You have completely atoned for the pain you caused Śakuntalā by repudiating her.

(*Entering*) CATURIKĀ. Victory victory, to your Majesty ! I had started in this direction with the box of paint-brushes——

KING. Well ?

CATURIKĀ. When on the way it was forcibly snatched from my hand by queen Vasumatī who was accompanied by Taralikā ; (the queen) saying " I will take it to my lord myself."

VIDŪṢAKA. Fortunately you were let off.

CATURIKĀ. While Taralikā was disengaging the queen's upper garment which had been caught by the branch of a shrub, I took myself off.

राजा—वयस्य, उपस्थिता देवी बहुमानगर्विता च भवानिमां प्रतिकृतिं रक्षतु।

विदूषकः—अत्ताणं त्ति भणाहि। (चित्रफलकमादायोत्थाय च।) **जइ भवं अन्तेउरकालकूडादो मुञ्चीअदि तदो मं मेहप्पडिच्छन्दे पासादे सद्दावेहि।** (इत्ति द्रुतपदं निष्क्रान्तः।) आत्मानमिति भण। यदि भवानन्तःपुरकालकूटान्मोक्ष्यते तदा मां मेघप्रतिच्छन्दे प्रासादे शब्दापय।

सानुमती—अण्णसंकन्तहिअओ वि पढमसंभावणं अवेक्खदि। सिढिलसोहदो दाणिं एसो। अन्यसंक्रान्तहृदयोऽपि प्रथमसंभावनामपेक्षते। शिथिलसौहार्द इदानीमेषः।

(प्रविश्य पत्रहस्ता।)

प्रतीहारी—जेदु जेदु देवो। जयतु जयतु देवः।

राजा—वेत्रवति, न खल्वन्तरा दृष्टा त्वया देवी।

प्रतीहारी—अह इं। पत्तहत्थं मं देक्खिअ पाडिणिउत्ता। अथ किम्। पत्रहस्तां मां प्रेक्ष्य प्रतिनिवृत्ता।

राजा—कार्यज्ञा कार्योपरोधं मे परिहरति।

प्रतीहारी—देव, अमच्चो विण्णवेदि। अत्थजादस्स गणणाबहुलदाए एक्कं एव्व पोरकज्जं अवेक्खिदं तं देवो पत्तारूढं पच्चक्खीकरेदु त्ति। देव, अमात्यो विज्ञापयति। अर्थजातस्य गणनाबहुलतयैकमेव पौरकार्यमवेक्षितं तद्देवः पत्रारूढं प्रत्यक्षीकरोत्विति।

राजा—इतः पत्रिकां दर्शय।

(प्रतीहार्युपनयति।)

राजा—(अनुवाच्य।) **कथम्। समुद्रव्यवहारी सार्थवाहो धनमित्रो नाम नौव्यसने विपन्नः। अनपत्यश्च किल तपस्वी। राज-**

KING. Friend, the queen is come, and she is rendered arrogant by (my) great attentions to her. Do you take care of this picture.

VIDŪṢAKA. Say " yourself." (*Taking the picture-board and rising*). If your honour is freed from the bane of the inner apartments then call me in the Meghapraticchanda palace.

(*Goes out with hurried steps.*)

SĀNUMATĪ. Although his heart is transferred to another he yet cares for his first love. His love has very much lost its ardour now.

(*Entering, letter in hand*) PORTRESS. Victory to your Majesty.

KING. Vetravati, did not you meet the queen on the way ?

PORTRESS. Yes, I did. But she turned back when she saw me carrying a letter in my hand.

KING. She knows (the importance of state) business, and avoids interrupting my duty.

PORTRESS. Your Majesty, the minister requests : On account of the heavy work of counting the various items of revenue, only one citizen's suit has been attended to ; let your Majesty consider the same which is committed to writing.

KING. Give me the letter.

(*The portress brings it.*)

KING. (*Reading*). How ! The merchant Dhanamitra who had (extensive) commerce at sea had been lost in a

गामी तस्यार्थसंचय इत्येतदमात्येन लिखितम् । (सविषादम् ।) कष्टं खल्वनपत्यता । बहुधनत्वाद्बहुपत्नीकेन तत्रभवता भवितव्यम् । विचार्यतां यदि काचिदापन्नसत्त्वा तस्य भार्यासु स्यात् ।

प्रतीहारी—देव, दाणिं एव्व साकेदअस्स सेट्ठिणो दुहिआ णिव्वुत्तपुंसवणा जाआ से सुणिअदि । देव, इदानीमेव साकेतस्य श्रेष्ठिनो दुहिता निर्वृत्तपुंसवना जायास्य श्रूयते ।

राजा—ननु गर्भः पित्र्यं रिक्थमर्हति । गच्छ एवममात्यं ब्रूहि ।

प्रतीहारी—जं देवो आणवेदि । (इति प्रस्थिता) यद्देव आज्ञापयति ।

राजा—एहि तावत् ।

प्रतीहारी—इअम्हि । इयमस्मि ।

राजा—किमनेन संततिरस्ति नास्तीति ।

येन येन वियुज्यन्ते प्रजाः स्निग्धेन बन्धुना ।
स स पापादृते तासां दुष्यन्त इति घुष्यताम् ॥ २३ ॥

प्रतीहारी—एव्वं णाम घोसइदव्वं । (निष्क्रम्य । पुनः प्रविश्य ।) काले पवुट्ठं विअ अहिणन्दिदं देवस्स सासणम् । एवं नाम घोषयितव्यम् । काले प्रवृष्टमिवाभिनन्दितं देवस्य शासनम् ।

राजा—(दीर्घमुष्णं च निःश्वस्य ।) एवं भोः संततिच्छेदनिरवलम्बानां कुलानां मूलपुरुषावसाने संपदः परमुपतिष्ठन्ति । ममाप्यन्ते पुरुवंशश्रियः एष वृत्तान्तः ।

shipwreck. And they say that the poor man had no child. All his accumulated wealth reverts to the king; thus the minister writes. (*Sorrowfully*). It is indeed dreadful to be childless. He had great riches, he must have wedded several wives; let an inquiry be made whether any one among his wives is with child.

PORTRESS. Your Majesty, it is reported that his wife, the daughter of a merchant from Sāketa, has even now gone through the Puṁsavana ceremony.

KING. Surely the child in the womb has a title to its father's property. Go, say so to the minister.

PORTRESS. As your Majesty commands.

(*Starts to leave.*)

KING. Come for a while.

PORTRESS. I am here.

KING. What does it matter whether he has or has not left offspring?

> Let it be proclaimed that whatever dearly loved kinsman any one of my subjects may lose, Duṣyanta will supply the place of that kinsman to them, the wicked excepted. (23)

PORTRESS. Thus surely it shall be proclaimed (*Going out and returning*). The royal decree was welcomed (by the people) like a timely shower.

KING. (*Heaving a deep and hot sigh*). O, thus it is that the wealth of families which are bereft of support through the failure of progeny passes on the death of the representative of the progenitor, to a stranger. When I die, such will be the fate of the wealth of Puru's line.

प्रतीहारी—पडिहदं अमङ्गलम् । प्रतिहतममङ्गलम् ।

राजा—धिङ्मामुपस्थितश्रेयोऽवमानिनम् ।

सानुमती—असंसअं सहिं एव्व हिअए करिअ णिन्दिदो णेण अप्पा । असंशयं सखीमेव हृदये कृत्वा निन्दितोऽनेनात्मा ।

राजा—

संरोपितेऽप्यात्मनि धर्मपत्नी
त्यक्ता मया नाम कुलप्रतिष्ठा ।
कल्पिष्यमाणा महते फलाय
वसुंधरा काल इवोप्तबीजा ॥ २४ ॥

सानुमती—अपरिच्छिण्णा दाणिं दे संददी भविस्सदि । अपरिच्छिन्नेदानीं ते संततिर्भविष्यति ।

चतुरिका—(जनान्तिकम् ।) अए इमिणा सत्थवाहवुत्तन्तेण दिउणुव्वेओ भट्टा । णं अस्सासिदुं मेहप्पडिच्छन्दादो अज्जं माठव्वं गेण्हिअ आअच्छ । अयि, अनेन सार्थवाहवृत्तान्तेन द्विगुणोद्वेगो भर्ता । एनमाश्वासयितुं मेघप्रतिच्छन्दादार्यं माठव्यं गृहीत्वागच्छ ।

प्रतीहारी—सुट्ठु भणासि । (इति निष्क्रान्ता ।) सुष्ठु भणसि ।

राजा—अहो दुष्यन्तस्य संशयमारूढाः पिण्डभाजः । कुतः ।

अस्मात्परं बत यथाश्रुति संभृतानि
को नः कुले निवपनानि नियच्छतीति ।
नूनं प्रसूतिविकलेन मया प्रसिक्तं
धौताश्रुशेषमुदकं पितरः पिबन्ति ॥ २५ ॥

(इति मोहमुपगतः ।)

चतुरिका—(ससंभ्रममवलोक्य ।) समस्ससदु भट्टा । समाश्वसितु भर्ता

PORTRESS. Heaven avert the calamity!

KING. Fie on me who despised the happiness that had offered itself.

SĀNUMATĪ. Surely he has the dear girl in mind when he thus reproaches himself.

KING.

> Verily my lawful wife, the glory of my family was forsaken by me, although my own self was implanted (in her) like the earth sown with seed at the right season, when she promises the richest fruit. (24)

SĀNUMATĪ. Now your line will never be interrupted.

CATURIKĀ (*Aside*). The merchant's story has doubled our lord's remorse. Go to the Meghapraticchanda palace and fetch the noble Māṭhavya to comfort him.

PORTRESS. A good idea. (*Exit.*)

KING. Ah me! Duṣyanta's ancestors, who claim a share in the funeral offering, are brought to a critical situation. For,

> Thinking "who indeed after this (man) in our family will offer us the libations prepared according to scriptural precept?" my ancestors verily drink such of the water offered by me, who am destitute of progeny, as remains to them after washing their tears. (25)

(*Faints.*)

CATURIKĀ (*Looking about in haste*). Take heart, my lord.

सानुमती—हद्धी हद्धी। सदि क्खु दीवे ववधाणदोसेण एसो अन्धआरदोसं अणुहोदि। अहं दाणिं एव्व णिव्वुदं करोमि। अहवा सुदं मए सउन्दलं समस्सासअन्तीए महेन्दजणणीए मुहादो जण्णभाओस्सुआ देवा एव्व तह अणुचिट्ठिस्सन्ति जह अइरेण धम्मपदिणिं भट्टा अहिणन्दिस्सदित्ति। ता जुत्तं एदं कालं पडिपालिदुं। जाव इमिणा वुत्तन्तेण पिअसहिं समस्सासेमि। (इत्युद्भ्रान्तकेन निष्क्रान्ता।) हा धिक् हा धिक्। सति खलु दीपे व्यवधानदोषेणैषोऽन्धकारदोषमनुभवति। अहमिदानीमेव निर्वृत्तं करोमि। अथवा श्रुतं मया शकुन्तलां समाश्वासयन्त्या महेन्द्रजनन्या मुखाद्यज्ञभागोत्सुका देवा एव तथानुष्ठास्यन्ति यथाऽचिरेण धर्मपत्नीं भर्ताभिनन्दिष्यतीति। तद्युक्तमेतं कालं प्रतिपालयितुम्। यावदनेन वृत्तान्तेन प्रियसखीं समाश्वासयामि।

(नेपथ्ये।)

अब्बम्हण्णं अब्बम्हण्णं। अब्रह्मण्यम्, अब्रह्मण्यम्।

राजा—(प्रत्यागतप्राणः कर्णं दत्त्वा।) **अये, माठव्यस्येवार्तस्वरः। कः कोऽत्र भोः।**

(प्रविश्य।)

प्रतीहारी—(ससंभ्रमम्।) **परित्ताअदु देवो संसअगदं वअस्सं।** परित्रायतां देवः संशयगतं वयस्यम्।

राजा—केनात्तगन्धो माणवकः।

प्रतीहारी—अदिट्ठरूवेण केण वि सत्तेण अदिक्कमिअ मेहप्पडिच्छन्दस्स पासादस्स अग्गभूमिं आरोविदो। अदृष्टरूपेण केनापि सत्त्वेनातिक्रम्य मेघप्रतिच्छन्दस्य प्रासादस्याग्रभूमिमारोपितः।

राजा—(उत्थाय।) **मा तावत्। ममापि सत्त्वैरभिभूयन्ते गृहाः। अथवा।**

अहन्यहन्यात्मन एव ताव-
ज्ज्ञातुं प्रमादस्खलितं न शक्यम्।
प्रजासु कः केन पथा प्रयाती-
त्यशेषतो वेदितुमस्ति शक्तिः॥ २६॥

(नेपथ्ये।)

भो वअस्स, अविहा अविहा। भो वयस्य, अविहा अविहा।

SĀNUMATĪ. Alas, alas! Though the light is there he is suffering the evil effects of darkness by reason of the intervening screen. I can make him happy even now. But I have heard from the mouth of the mother of the great Indra as she was consoling Śakuntalā, that the Gods themselves, longing for their portions of the sacrifice, will so devise it that before long the husband will welcome his true wife. It is, therefore, proper to wait for this period. In the meanwhile, I will comfort the dear girl with the news. (*Exit by flying through the sky.*)

(*Behind the scenes*)

Help, help!

KING (*Coming to himself and listening*). Ah, that sounds like the distressed cry of Māṭhavya. Who is there, ho!

(*Entering*) PORTRESS (*Confusedly*). Let your Majesty save your friend who is fallen into danger.

KING. Who has humbled Māṇavaka?

PORTRESS. Some invisible spirit, who having overpowered him took him to the top-most floor of the Meghapraticchanda palace.

KING. (*Rising*). This must not be. How, even my house is infested by evil spirits! Or,

> Even when the mischiefs occasioned by one's own negligence from day to day are scarcely known, how then can one have the power to know fully what path each of my subjects is treading? (26)

(*Behind the scenes.*)

O friend, alas! alas!

राजा—(गतिभेदेन परिक्रामन् ।) **सखे, न भेतव्यं न भेतव्यम् ।**

(नेपथ्ये ।)

(पुनस्तदेव पठित्वा ।) **कहं ण भाइस्सं । एस मं को वि पच्छावणदसिरोहरं इक्खुं विअ तिण्हभङ्गं करेदि ।** कथं न भेष्यामि । एष मां कोऽपि पश्चादवनतशिरोधरमिक्षुमिव त्रिभङ्गं करोति ।

राजा—(सदृष्टिक्षेपम् ।) **धनुस्तावत् ।**

(प्रविश्य शार्ङ्गहस्ता ।)

यवनी—**भट्टा, एदं हत्थावावसहिदं सरासणं ।** भर्तः, एतद्धस्तावापसहितं शरासनम् ।

(राजा सशरं धनुरादत्ते ।)

(नेपथ्ये ।)

एष त्वामभिनवकण्ठशोणितार्थी
शार्दूलः पशुमिव हन्मि चेष्टमानम् ।
आर्तानां भयमपनेतुमात्तधन्वा
दुष्यन्तस्तव शरणं भवत्विदानीम् ॥ २७ ॥

राजा—(सरोषम् ।) **कथं मामेवोद्दिशति । तिष्ठ कुणपाशन, त्वमिदानीं न भविष्यसि ।** (शार्ङ्गमारोप्य ।) **वेत्रवति, सोपानमार्गमादेशय ।**

प्रतीहारी—**इदो इदो देवो ।** इत इतो देवः ।

(सर्वे सत्वरमुपसर्पन्ति ।)

राजा—(समन्ताद्विलोक्य ।) **शून्यं खल्विदम् ।**

(नेपथ्ये ।)

अविहा अविहा । अहं अत्तभवन्तं पेक्खामि । तुमं मं ण पेक्खसि । बिडालग्गहीदो मूसओ विअ णिरासो म्हि जीविदे संवुत्तो । अविहा अविहा । अहमत्रभवन्तं पश्यामि । त्वं मां न पश्यसि । बिडालगृहीतो मूषिक इव निराशोऽस्मि जीविते संवृत्तः ।

राजा—**भोस्तिरस्करिणीगर्वित, मदीयं शस्त्रं त्वां द्रक्ष्यति । एष तमिषुं संदधे,**

यो हनिष्यति वध्यं त्वां रक्ष्यं रक्षति च द्विजम् ।
हंसो हि क्षीरमादत्ते तन्मिश्रा वर्जयत्यपः ॥ २८ ॥

KING. (*Moving round with an altered gait*). Fear not, my friend, fear not. (*Behind the scenes.*)

(*After repeating the same*).. Fear not? There is some one trying to break me into pieces violently like a sugarcane having bent back my neck.

KING. (*Looking about*). Hola! my bow—

(*Entering, bow is hand*) YAVANI. My lord, here is the bow with the arm-guard.

(*The King takes the bow and arrows.*)

(*Behind the scenes*) Now, thirsting for the fresh blood from the neck, I will slay thee struggling as a tiger (slays) a beast. Let Duṣyanta now, who takes his bow to remove the fear of the oppressed, be thy protector. (27)

KING. (*Angrily*). How, he even refers to me! Stay, carrion-eater; you shall die now. (*Stringing his bow*). Vetravati, show the way to the stairs.

PORTRESS. This way, this way, your Majesty.

(*All advance in haste.*)

KING (*Looking around*). There is, indeed, no one here.

(*Behind the scenes.*)

Alas! Alas! I see your honour, but you see me not. I despair of my life like a mouse caught by a cat.

KING. You, who pride yourself on your power which renders you invisible, my weapon will see you; here I will fix an arrow,

Which will slay you that deserve death and save the Brahmin who deserves to be saved. The swan drinks up the milk and leaves the water which has been mingled with it. (28)

(इत्यस्त्रं संधत्ते ।)

(ततः प्रविशति विदूषकमुत्सृज्य मातलिः ।)

मातलिः—

कृताः शरव्यं हरिणा तवासुराः
शरासनं तेषु विकृष्यतामिदम् ।
प्रसादसौम्यानि सतां सुहृज्जने
पतन्ति चक्षूंषि न दारुणाः शराः ॥ २९ ॥

राजा—(अस्त्रमुपसंहरन् ।) अये मातलिः । स्वागतं महेन्द्रसारथये ।

(प्रविश्य ।)

विदूषकः—अहं जेण इट्ठिपसुमारं मारिदो सो इमिणा साअदेण अहिणन्दीअदि । अहं येनेष्टिपशुमारं मारितः सोऽनेन स्वागतेनाभिनन्द्यते ।

मातलिः—(सस्मितम् ।) आयुष्मन्, श्रूयतां यदस्मि हरिणा भवत्सकाशं प्रेषितः ।

राजा—अवहितोऽस्मि ।

मातलिः—अस्ति कालनेमिप्रसूतिर्दुर्जयो नाम दानवगणः ।

राजा—अस्ति । श्रुतपूर्वं मया नारदात् ।

मातलिः—

सख्युस्ते स किल शतक्रतोरजय्य-
स्तस्य त्वं रणशिरसि स्मृतो निहन्ता ।
उच्छेत्तुं प्रभवति यन्न सप्तसप्ति-
स्तन्नैशं तिमिरमपाकरोति चन्द्रः ॥ ३० ॥

स भवानात्तशस्त्र एव इदानीं तमैन्द्ररथमारुह्य विजयाय प्रतिष्ठताम् ।

राजा—अनुगृहीतोऽहमनया मघवतः संभावनया । अथ माठव्यं प्रति भवता किमेवं प्रत्युक्तम् ।

(*Aims his arrow.*).

(*Then enter Mātali leaving the Vidūṣaka.*)

MĀTALI.

The demons are made by Indra thy mark; against them let thy bow be drawn. The good cast not cruel shafts, but eyes soft with kindness on their friends. (29)

KING. (*Withdrawing his arrow*). Ah, Mātali! Welcome to the charioteer of the great Indra.

(*Entering*) VIDŪṢAKA. What, he by whom I was being butchered like a sacrificial animal, is greeted by him with a welcome!

MĀTALI (*Smiling*). Hear, long-lived one, on what errand I am dispatched to you by Indra.

KING. I am attentive.

MĀTALI. There is a host of demons, called Durjaya —the brood of Kālanemi.

KING. Yes; I have heard so from Nārada.

MĀTALI. Thy friend Indra, it is said, is unable to quell them; but that thou wouldst smite them in the front of battle. That nocturnal darkness, which the Sun is not able to dispel, is scattered by the Moon. (30)

Therefore, grasping thy weapon thus, mount the car of Indra, and set forth for victory.

KING. I am grateful for the honour which Indra shows me. But why did you act thus towards Māthavya?

मातलिः—तदपि कथ्यते । किंचिन्निमित्तादपि मनःसंतापादायुष्मान्मया विक्लवो दृष्टः । पश्चात्कोपयितुमायुष्मन्तं तथा कृतवानस्मि । कुतः ।

ज्वलति चलितेन्धनोऽग्निर्विप्रकृतः पन्नगः फणां कुरुते ।
प्रायः स्वं महिमानं क्षोभात्प्रतिपद्यते हि जनः ॥ ३१ ॥

राजा—(जनान्तिकम् ।) वयस्य, अनतिक्रमणीया दिवस्पतेराज्ञा । तदत्र परिगतार्थं कृत्वा मद्वचनादमात्यपिशुनं ब्रूहि ।

त्वन्मतिः केवला तावत्परिपालयतु प्रजाः ।
अधिज्यमिदमन्यस्मिन्कर्मणि व्यापृतं धनुः ॥ ३२ ॥

इति ।

विदूषकः—जं भवं आणवेदि । (इति निष्क्रान्तः ।) यद्भवानाज्ञापयति ।

मातलिः—आयुष्मान्रथमारोहतु ।

(राजा रथाधिरोहणं नाटयति ।)

(इति निष्क्रान्ताः सर्वे ।)

षष्ठोऽङ्कः ।

MĀTALI. I will tell that. I perceived that by some inner sorrow caused by one thing or another, the long-lived one was distressed. Thereafter I acted thus to provoke the wrath of the long-lived one. For

The fire blazes when the fuel is stirred ; the serpent, when provoked, expands its hood ; for a man generally regains his proper greatness, under some provocation. (31)

KING. (*Aside*). Friend, inviolable is the command of heaven's lord. So acquaint the minister Piśuna with the matter and tell him in my name—

Let thy wisdom alone secure my people from harm, (while) this braced bow has a different employment. (32)

VIDŪṢAKA. As your Honour commands. (*Exit.*)

MĀTALI. Let the long-lived one mount the chariot. (*The king acts mounting the chariot.*)

Exeunt Omnes

End of Act VI

सप्तमोऽङ्कः ।

(ततः प्रविशत्याकाशयानेन रथाधिरूढो राजा मातलिश्च ।)

राजा—मातले, अनुष्ठितनिदेशोऽपि मघवतः सत्क्रियाविशेषादनुपयुक्तमिवात्मानं समर्थये ।

मातलिः—(सस्मितम् ।) आयुष्मन्, उभयमप्यपरितोषं समर्थये ।

प्रथमोपकृत मरुत्वतः
 प्रतिपत्त्या लघु मन्यते भवान् ।
गणयत्यवदानविस्मितो
 भवतः सोऽपि न सत्क्रियागुणान् ॥ १ ॥

राजा—मातले, मा, मैवम् । स खलु मनोरथानामप्यभूमिर्विसर्जनावसरसत्कारः । मम हि दिवौकसां समक्षमर्धासनोपवेशितस्य

अन्तर्गतप्रार्थनमन्तिकस्थं
 जयन्तमुद्वीक्ष्य कृतस्मितेन ।
आमृष्टवक्षोहरिचन्दनाङ्का
 मन्दारमाला हरिणा पिनद्धा ॥ २ ॥

मातलिः—किमिव नामायुष्मानमरेश्वराम्नार्हति । पश्य ।

ACT VII

(Then enter king seated in a chariot that flies through the air, and Mātali.)

KING. Mātali, although I have executed the mission which Indra gave me, yet considering the special welcome he accorded me, I think myself to have been of very little service to him.

MĀTALI (*Smiling*). Long-lived one, I think neither of you is satisfied.

> Your Highness considers the prior benefit (conferred by you) on Indra as trifling (in comparison) with the honour (done by him to you); while he reckons as of little account the special honours (bestowed) on your Highness, being filled with wonder at your heroic achievement. (1)

KING. Mātali, no, say not so ; for the honour done me at parting surpassed my warmest expectations. For making me sit on half of his throne before the eyes of the gods,

> And smiling to see Jayanta, who stood near him, filled with an inward longing (for the same honour), a wreath of Mandāra flowers, marked with the yellow-sandal from its rubbing on his breast, was by Indra placed about my neck. (2)

MĀTALI. But what does not the long-lived one deserve from the king of the gods ? See

सुखपरस्य हरेरुभयैः कृतं
त्रिदिवमुद्धृतदानवकण्टकम् ।
तव शरैरधुना नतपर्वभिः
पुरुषकेसरिणश्च पुरा नखैः ॥ ३ ॥

राजा—अत्र खलु शतक्रतोरेव महिमा स्तुत्यः ।

सिध्यन्ति कर्मसु महत्स्वपि यन्नियोज्याः
संभावनागुणमवेहि तमीश्वराणाम् ।
किंवाभविष्यदरुणस्तमसां विभेत्ता
तं चेत्सहस्रकिरणो धुरि नाकरिष्यत् ॥ ४ ॥

मातलिः—सदृशमेवैतत् । (स्तोकमन्तरमतीत्य ।) आयुष्मन्, इतः पश्य नाकपृष्ठप्रतिष्ठितस्य सौभाग्यमात्मयशसः ।

विच्छित्तिशेषैः सुरसुन्दरीणां
वर्णैरमी कल्पलतांशुकेषु ।
विचिन्त्य गीतक्षममर्थजातं
दिवौकसस्त्वच्चरित लिखन्ति ॥ ५ ॥

राजा—मातले, असुरसंप्रहारोत्सुकेन पूर्वेद्युर्दिवमधिरोहता न लक्षितः स्वर्गमार्गः । कतरस्मिन्मरुतां पथि वर्तामहे ।

मातलिः—

त्रिस्रोतसं वहति यो गगनप्रतिष्ठां
ज्योतींषि वर्तयति च प्रविभक्तरश्मिः ।

The heaven of ease-loving Indra has been made free from the thorns of Danu's race by two (means) : now by your smooth-jointed shafts, and formerly by the claws of the man-lion. (3)

KING. In the present case, really, the greatness of Indra alone deserves praise.

That servants succeed even in great enterprises—know that to be the effect of the honour shown to them by their masters. Could Aruṇa dispel the shades of night if the thousand-rayed one had not placed him in front (of his chariot ?) (4)

MĀTALI. That is quite worthy (of you). (*Going a little distance*). Long-lived one, see the full exaltation of your glory, which (now) rides on the back of heaven !

With the residue of colours used by nymphs of heaven to adorn their persons, these dwellers of heaven are writing your exploits on vestments of the heavenly trees, thinking out verses suitable for singing. (5)

KING. Mātali, In my eagerness for battle with the demons, I did not observe the way to heaven, while ascending the sky the other day. In what path of the winds are we now journeying ?

MĀTALI.

They call this the way of the wind Parivaha, which is freed from all darkness by being the second step of Viṣṇu, and which bears the

तस्य द्वितीयहरिविक्रमनिस्तमस्कं
वायोरिमं परिवहस्य वदन्ति मार्गम् ॥ ६ ॥

राजा—मातले, अतः खलु सबाह्यान्तःकरणो ममान्तरात्मा प्रसीदति। (रथाङ्गमवलोक्य।) मेघपदवीमवतीर्णौ स्वः।

मातलिः—कथमवगम्यते।

राजा—

अयमरविवरेभ्यश्चातकैर्निष्पतद्भि-
र्हरिभिरचिरभासां तेजसा चानुलिप्तैः।
गतमुपरि घनानां वारिगर्भोदराणां
पिशुनयति रथस्ते सीकरक्लिन्ननेमिः ॥ ७ ॥

मातलिः—क्षणादायुष्मान्स्वाधिकारभूमौ वर्तिष्यते।

राजा—(अधोऽवलोक्य।) वेगावतरणादाश्चर्यदर्शनः संलक्ष्यते मनुष्यलोकः। तथाहि।

शैलानामवरोहतीव शिखरादुन्मज्जतां मेदिनी
पर्णाभ्यन्तरलीनतां विजहति स्कन्धोदयात्पादपाः।
संतानैस्तनुभावनष्टसलिला व्यक्तिं भजन्त्यापगाः
केनाप्युत्क्षिपतेव पश्य भुवनं मत्पार्श्वमानीयते ॥ ८ ॥

मातलिः—साधु दृष्टम्। (सबहुमानमवलोक्य।) अहो, उदाररमणीया पृथिवी।

triple-streamed river flowing through the sky, and causes the luminaries to roll in a circle diffusing their beams. (6)

KING. Mātali, that is why my inner self, with the internal and external senses, feels a pleasurable repose. (*Looking at the wheel of the chariot*). We have descended to the region of the clouds.

MĀTALI. How is that perceived ?

KING.

This your chariot, with the rims of its wheels bedewed with spray indicates by the Cātakas flying through the interstices of its spokes, and by the horses lapped in lightning-flashes that we are now moving over clouds pregnant with showers. (7)

MĀTALI. In a moment, the long-lived one will be in the land under his rule.

KING. (*Looking down*). Through our quick descent, the world of men appears a wonderful sight. For

The earth appears to descend from the summits of mountains that emerge upwards ; the trees no longer appear to be enveloped in their foliage, as their trunks heave in sight ; the rivers whose waters were lost to view from their narrowness become visible from the expansion (of their waters). Behold the earth is being brought near me as if by some one throwing it upwards. (8)

MĀTALI. Well-observed. (*Looking with reverence*) How grand, how noble is the earth !

राजा—मातले, कतमोऽयं पूर्वापरसमुद्रावगाढः कनकरसनिस्यन्दी सांध्य इव मेघपरिघः सानुमानालोक्यते ।

मातलिः—आयुष्मन्, एष खलु हेमकूटो नाम किंपुरुषपर्वतस्तपःसंसिद्धिक्षेत्रम् । पश्य ।

स्वायंभुवान्मरीचेर्यः प्रबभूव प्रजापतिः ।
सुरासुरगुरुः सोऽत्र सपत्नीकस्तपस्यति ॥ ९ ॥

राजा—तेन ह्यनतिक्रमणीयानि श्रेयांसि । प्रदक्षिणीकृत्य भगवन्तं गन्तुमिच्छामि ।

मातलिः—प्रथमः कल्पः ।

(नाट्येनावतीर्णौ ।)

राजा—(सविस्मयम् ।)

उपोढशब्दा न रथाङ्गनेमयः
प्रवर्तमानं न च दृश्यते रजः ।
अभूतलस्पर्शतया निरुन्धत-
स्तवावतीर्णोऽपि रथो न लक्ष्यते ॥ १० ॥

मातलिः—एतावानेव शतक्रतोरायुष्मतश्च विशेषः ।

राजा—मातले, कतमस्मिन्प्रदेशे मारीचाश्रमः ।

मातलिः—(हस्तेन दर्शयति ।)

वल्मीकार्धनिमग्नमूर्तिरुरसा संदष्टसर्पत्वचा
कण्ठे जीर्णलताप्रतानवलयेनात्यर्थसंपीडितः ।

KING. Mātali, what mountain is seen yonder, that dives into the eastern and western sea, dripping with liquid gold, like a bank of evening cloud ?

MĀTALI. Long-lived one, this is the mountain Hema-Kūṭa of the Kiṁpuruṣas—a place where the powers of penance are fully attained. See,

> That Prajāpati who sprang from Mārīci, the son of the self-existent, father of the gods and demons, practises penance here along with his wife. (9)

KING. Well then (opportunities for obtaining) blessings must not be neglected. It is my desire to proceed after walking humbly round the holy sage.

MĀTALI. An excellent idea.

(*Gesticulate descending.*)

KING. (*Wonderingly*).

> The rims of the chariot-wheels produce no sound ; nor does dust appear to be raised ; and the chariot, as you rein-in (the steeds), is scarcely marked to have descended to the earth, when it has really done so, on account of its not touching the surface of the earth. (10)

MĀTALI. That is all the difference between Indra and the long-lived one.

KING. Mātali, where is the holy retreat of Mārīca ?
MĀTALI (*Pointing with his hand*).

> There where stands yonder sage, facing the Sun's orb, inmovable as a pollard half buried in an ant-hill, with his breast closely encircled by the

अंसव्यापि शकुन्तनीडनिचितं बिभ्रज्जटामण्डलं
यत्र स्थाणुरिवाचलो मुनिरसावभ्यर्कबिम्बं स्थितः ॥ ११ ॥

राजा—नमस्ते कष्टतपसे ।

मातलिः—(संयतप्रग्रहं रथं कृत्वा ।) महाराज, एतावदितिपरिवर्धितमन्दारवृक्षं प्रजापतेराश्रमं प्रविष्टौ स्वः ।

राजा—स्वर्गादधिकतरं निर्वृतिस्थानम् । अमृतह्रदमिवावगाढोऽस्मि ।

मातलिः—(रथं स्थापयित्वा ।) अवतरत्वायुष्मान् ।

राजा—(अवतीर्य ।) मातले, भवान्कथमिदानीम् ।

मातलिः—संयन्त्रितो मया रथः । वयमप्यवतरामः । (तथा कृत्वा ।) इत आयुष्मन् । (परिक्रम्य ।) दृश्यन्तामत्रभवतामृषीणां तपोवनभूमयः ।

राजा—ननु विस्मयादवलोकयामि ।

प्राणानामनिलेन वृत्तिरुचिता सत्कल्पवृक्षे वने
तोये काञ्चनपद्मरेणुकपिशे धर्माभिषेकक्रिया ।
ध्यानं रत्नशिलातलेषु विबुधस्त्रीसंनिधौ संयमो
यत्काङ्क्षन्ति तपोभिरन्यमुनयस्तस्मिंस्तपस्यन्त्यमी ॥ १२ ॥

मातलिः—उत्सर्पिणी खलु महतां प्रार्थना । (परिक्रम्य आकाशे ।) अये वृद्धशाकल्य, किमनुतिष्ठति भगवान्मारीचः । किं

slough of a serpent : his neck is heavily squeezed by a coil of the tendrils of old creepers ; and he has a mass of matted hair that covers his shoulders and is filled with the nests of birds. (11)

KING. Bow to thee of such austere devotion.

MĀTALI (*Drawing in the reins of the chariot*). O king, here now we have entered the sanctuary of the Prajāpati, in which the Mandāra-trees are reared by Aditi.

KING. It is place more delightful than heaven ; I seem plunged in a pool of nectar.

MĀTALI (*Stopping the chariot*). Let the long-lived one descend.

KING. (*Descending*). But what of you, now Mātali ?

MĀTALI. I have stopped the chariot. I too will alight. (*Doing so*). This way, long-lived one. (*Walking round*). Behold the holy retreat of the revered sage.

KING. Indeed I am looking on with amazement.

Here in this forest of Kalpa-trees, they draw from air life's necessary sustenance ; in waters yellow with the golden dust of the lotus, they perform ablutions for religious vows ; on jewelled slabs, they meditate ; and restrain their passions in the midst of celestial nymphs : they practise penance in a place which other sages by their austerities seek to win. (12)

MĀTALI. Verily the aspirations of the great ever mount upwards. (*Walking about ; in the air*). O Vṛdhaśākalya how is the holy Mārīca occupied ? What do you say ? Being questioned by Aditi respecting the

ब्रवीषि। दाक्षायण्या पतिव्रताधर्ममधिकृत्य पृष्टस्तस्यै महर्षिपत्नी-सहितायै कथयतीति।

राजा—(कर्णं दत्त्वा।) अये, प्रतिपाल्यावसराः खलु मुनयः।

मातलिः—(राजानमवलोक्य।) अस्मिन्नशोकवृक्षमूले तावदास्तामायुष्मान्, यावत्त्वामिन्द्रगुरवे निवेदयितुमन्तरान्वेषी भवामि।

राजा—यथा भवान्मन्यते। (इति स्थितः।)

मातलिः—आयुष्मन्, साधयाम्यहम्। (इति निष्क्रान्तः।)

राजा—(निमित्तं सूचयित्वा।)

मनोरथाय नाशंसे किं बाहो स्पन्दसे वृथा।
पूर्वावधीरितं श्रेयो दुःखं हि परिवर्तते ॥ १३ ॥

(नेपथ्ये।)

मा क्खु चावलं करेहि। कहं गदो एव्व अत्तणो पकिदिं। मा खलु चापलं कुरु। कथं गत एवात्मनः प्रकृतिम्।

राजा—(कर्णं दत्त्वा।) अभूमिरियमविनयस्य। को नु खल्वेष निषिध्यते। (शब्दानुसारेणावलोक्य। सविस्मयम्।) अये, को नु खल्वयमनुबध्यमानस्तपस्विनीभ्यामबालसत्त्वो बालः।

अर्धपीतस्तनं मातुरामर्दक्लिष्टकेसरम्।
प्रक्रीडितुं सिंहशिशुं बलात्कारेण कर्षति ॥ १४ ॥

(ततः प्रविशति यथानिर्दिष्टकर्मा तपस्विनीभ्यां बालः।)

बालः—जिम्भ सिङ्घ, दन्ताइं दे गणइस्सं। जृम्भस्व सिंह, दन्तांस्ते गणयिष्ये।

duties of a faithful wife, he is explaining them to her in company with the wives of the great sages?

KING (*Listening*). Ah! We must await the leisure of saints.

MĀTALI (*Looking at the king*). Let the long-lived one rest at the foot of the Aśoka tree; in the meanwhile I will wait for an opportune moment to announce your arrival to the father of Indra.

KING. As your Honour thinks. (*Stands.*)

MĀTALI. Long-lived one, I will depart. (*Exit.*)

KING (*Indicating an omen*).

I do not hope to obtain my desire; why, O my arm, dost thou vainly throb? Happiness that was scorned before, surely turns into pain. (13).

(*Behind the scenes*)

Do not be so wild. What! Gone already to your own nature!

KING (*Listening*). This is no place, surely, for any rudeness. Who can be thus rebuked? (*Looking in the direction of the sound; in surprise*). Who is this child, closely attended by two female-ascetics—a child that possesses not the strength of a mere child?

He forcibly drags towards him, for sport, a lion's whelp that has but half-sucked its mother's dug, and has its mane ruffled by pulling. (14)

(*Enter a boy acting as described, and two female ascetics.*)

BOY. Open thy mouth, lion, that I may count thy teeth.

प्रथमा—अविणीद, किं णो अपच्चणिव्विसेसाणि सत्ताणि विप्पअरेसि। हन्त, वड्ढइ दे संरम्भो। ठाणे क्खु इसिजणेण सव्वदमणो त्ति किदणामहेओ सि। अविनीत, किं नोऽपत्यनिर्विशेषाणि सत्त्वानि विप्रकरोषि। हन्त, वर्धते तव संरम्भः। स्थाने खलु ऋषिजनेन सर्वदमन इति कृतनामधेयोऽसि।

राजा—किं नु खलु बालेऽस्मिन्नौरस इव पुत्रे स्निह्यति मे मनः। नूनमनपत्यता मां वत्सलयति।

द्वितीया—एसा क्खु केसरिणी तुमं लङ्घेदि जइ से पुत्तअं ण मुञ्चेसि। एषा खलु केसरिणी त्वां लङ्घयिष्यति यदि तस्याः पुत्रकं न मुञ्चसि।

बालः—(सस्मितम्।) अम्हहे, बलिअं क्खु भीदो म्हि। (इत्यधरं दर्शयति।) अहो, बलीयः खलु भीतोऽस्मि।

राजा—

महतस्तेजसो बीजं बालोऽयं प्रतिभाति मे।
स्फुलिङ्गावस्थया वह्निरेधापेक्षा इव स्थितः॥ १५॥

प्रथमा—वच्छ, एदं बालमिइन्दअं मुञ्च। अवरं दे कीलणअं दाइस्सं। वत्स, एनं बालमृगेन्द्रं मुञ्च। अपरं ते क्रीडनकं दास्यामि।

बालः—कहिं। देहि णं। (इति हस्तं प्रसारयति।) कुत्र। देह्येतत्।

राजा—कथं चक्रवर्तिलक्षणमप्यनेन धार्यते। तथा ह्यस्य

प्रलोभ्यवस्तुप्रणयप्रसारितो
विभाति जालग्रथिताङ्गुलिः करः।
अलक्ष्यपत्रान्तरमिद्धरागया
नवोषसा भिन्नमिवैकपङ्कजम्॥ १६॥

द्वितीया—सुव्वदे, ण सक्को एसो वाआमेत्तेण विरमाविदुं। गच्छ तुमं। ममकेरए उडए मक्कण्डेअस्स इसिकुमारअस्स वण्णचित्तिदो मित्तिआमोरओ चिट्ठदि। तं से उवहर। सुव्रते, न शक्य एष वाचामात्रेण विरमयितुम्। गच्छ त्वम्। मदीय उटजे मार्कण्डेयस्यर्षिकुमारस्य वर्णचित्रितो मृत्तिकामयूरस्तिष्ठति। तमस्योपहर।

प्रथमा—तह। (इति निष्क्रान्ता) तथा।

FIRST. Naughty boy, why dost thou torment the animals whom we cherish as if they were our own offspring? Ha! thou art getting more wild. Aptly have the sages named thee Sarvadamana.

KING. Ah, what means it that my heart inclines to this boy as if he were my own son? No doubt my childlessness makes me soft-hearted.

SECOND. This lioness will surely attack thee, if thou release not her whelp.

BOY (*Smiling*). Oh, I am indeed dreadfully scared! (*Pouts his under-lip.*)

KING. This boy appears to me to be the germ of heroic valour and looks like fire in a tiny spark waiting only for fuel (to blaze up). (15)

FIRST. Child, set at liberty this little lion; and I will give thee another plaything.

BOY. Where is it? Give it me. (*Extends his hands.*)

KING. How, he bears the marks of universal royalty! Thus his

Hand extended in eagerness to grasp the coveted object, with fingers connected by a web, appears like a single lotus, the interspaces of whose petals are not visible, blown open by the early dawn with its glow enkindled. (16)

SECOND. Suvratā, it is not possible to stop him by mere words. Go; in my cottage you will find a painted clay peacock that belongs to the hermit-boy Mārkandeya. Give that to him.

FIRST. As you say. (*Exit.*)

बालः—इमिणा एव्व दाव कीलिस्सं । (इति तापसीं विलोक्य हसति ।) अनेनैव तावत्क्रीडिष्यामि ।

राजा—स्पृहयामि खलु दुर्ललितायास्मै ।

आलक्ष्यदन्तमुकुलाननिमित्तहासै-
रव्यक्तवर्णरमणीयवचःप्रवृत्तीन् ।
अङ्काश्रयप्रणयिनस्तनयान्वहन्तो
धन्यास्तदङ्गरजसा मलिनीभवन्ति ॥ १७ ॥

तापसी—होदु । ण मं अअं गणेदि । (पार्श्वमवलोकयति ।) को एत्थ इसिकुमाराणं । (राजानमवलोक्य ।) भद्दमुह, एहि दाव । मोएहि इमेणा दुम्मोअहत्थग्गहेण डिम्भलीलाए बाहीअमाणं बालमिइन्दअं । भवतु । न मामयं गणयति । कोऽत्र ऋषिकुमाराणाम् । भद्रमुख, एहि तावत् । मोचयानेन दुर्मोकहस्तग्रहेण डिम्भलीलया बाध्यमानं बालमृगेन्द्रम् ।

राजा—(उपगम्य । सस्मितम् ।) अयि भो महर्षिपुत्र ।

एवमाश्रमविरुद्धवृत्तिना
संयमः किमिति जन्मतस्त्वया ।
सत्त्वसंश्रयसुखोऽपि दूष्यते
कृष्णसर्पशिशुनेव चन्दनम् ॥ १८ ॥

तापसी—भद्दमुह, ण क्खु अअं इसिकुमारओ । भद्रमुख, न खल्वयं ऋषिकुमारः ।

राजा—आकारसदृशं चेष्टितमेवास्य कथयति । स्थानप्रत्ययात्तु वयमेवंतर्किणः । (यथाभ्यर्थितमनुतिष्ठन्बालस्पर्शमुपलभ्य । आत्मगतम् ।)

अनेन कस्यापि कुलाङ्कुरेण
स्पृष्टस्य गात्रेषु सुखं ममैवम् ।
कां निर्वृतिं चेतसि तस्य कुर्या-
द्यस्यायमङ्कात्कृतिनः प्ररूढः ॥ १९ ॥

Boy. In the meanwhile, I will play with this. (*Looks at the hermit-woman and laughs.*)

King. How my heart goes out to this unmanagable child!

Blessed are they who, carrying their sons that fondly seek their laps, with bud-like teeth that slightly appear in their causeless smiles, lisping their charming inarticulate prattle, are soiled by the dust of their limbs. (17)

Hermit-woman. Well, he does not mind me. (*Looks back*). Which one of the hermit-boys is here? (*Looking at the king*). Come, gentle sir, and free this lion-cub being tormented in childish sport by this child from whose grasp it is difficult to disengage it.

King. (*Approaching; smilingly*). O son of some great sage,

Why is it, that by thee acting in a way opposed to the hermitage is befouled, from thy very birth that virtue of forbearance which delights in the protection of animals like the sandal tree by the black-serpent's brood? (18)

Hermit-woman. But, good sir, he is not the son of a sage.

King. His actions, indeed, which are conformable to his appearance bespeak it. But I took that view from the evidence of the place. (*Acting as requested, and feeling the boy's touch, to himself*).

If it gives me such delight to touch the limbs of the child who is the scion of some stranger's family, what rapture will arise in the heart of that happy man from whose body he sprang? (19)

तापसी—(उभौ निर्वर्ण्य ।) अच्छरिअं अच्छरिअं । आश्चर्यमाश्चर्यम् ।

राजा—आर्ये, किमिव ।

तापसी—इमस्स बालअस्स दे वि संवादिणी आकिदी त्ति विम्हाविदम्हि । अपरिइदस्य वि दे अप्पडिलोमो संवुत्तो त्ति । अस्य बालकस्य तेऽपि संवादिन्याकृतिरिति विस्मापितास्मि । अपरिचितस्यापि तेऽप्रतिलोमः संवृत्त इति ।

राजा—(बालकमुपलालयन् ।) नचेन्मुनिकुमारोऽयम्, अथ कोऽस्य व्यपदेशः ।

तापसी—पुरुवंसो । पुरुवंशः ।

राजा—(आत्मगतम् ।) कथमेकान्वयो मम । अतः खलु मदनुकारिणमेनमत्रभवती मन्यते । अस्त्येतत्पौरवाणामन्त्यं कुलव्रतम् ।

भवनेषु रसाधिकेषु पूर्वं
क्षितिरक्षार्थमुशन्ति ये निवासम् ।
नियतैकयतिव्रतानि पश्चा-
त्तरुमूलानि गृहीभवन्ति तेषाम् ॥ २० ॥

(प्रकाशम् ।) न पुनरात्मगत्या मानुषाणामेष विषयः ।

तापसी—जह भद्दमुहो भणादि । अच्छरासंबन्धेण इमस्स जणणी एत्थ देवगुरुणो तवोवणे पसूदा । यथा भद्रमुखो भणति । अप्सरःसंबन्धेनास्य जनन्यत्र देवगुरोस्तपोवने प्रसूता ।

राजा—(अपवार्य ।) हन्त, द्वितीयमिदमाशाजननम् । (प्रकाशम् ।) अथ सा तत्रभवती किमाख्यस्य राजर्षेः पत्नी ।

तापसी—को तस्स धम्मदारपरिच्चाइणो णाम संकीतिदुं चिन्तिस्सदि । कस्तस्य धर्मदारपरित्यागिनो नाम संकीर्तयितुं चिन्तयिष्यति ।

HERMIT-WOMAN (*gazing at both*). Oh wonderful!

KING. What is it, holy woman?

HERMIT-WOMAN. I am astonished to mark the resemblance between your form and the child's. And although he had no (former) acquaintance with you, yet he did not take any dislike to you.

KING (*Fondling the child*). If he is not the son of a hermit, what is his family?

HERMIT-WOMAN. The family of Puru.

KING. (*To himself*). How, he belongs to the same family as mine? That is how the lady thinks he resembles me. For this is the last family-vow of the descendants of Puru.

> To them who dwell at first in palaces which abound in all the pleasures of sense, for protecting the world, the roots of trees where the one vow of asceticism is rigidly observed serve as homes afterwards. (20)

(*Aloud*) But the place is inaccessible to mortals by their own power.

HERMIT-WOMAN. As the good sir says. But in consequence of her relationship to a nymph, his mother brought him forth in the pious grove of the father of the gods.

KING (*To himself*). Ah, this is a second ground of hope. (*Aloud*). What is the name of the virtuous monarch who claims the noble lady for his wife?

HERMIT-WOMAN. Who, indeed, would think of speaking his name who rejected his lawful wife?

राजा— (स्वगतम् ।) **इयं खलु कथम मामेव लक्ष्यीकरोति । यदि तावदस्य शिशोर्मातरं नामतः पृच्छामि । अथवानार्यः परदारव्यवहारः ।**

(प्रविश्य मृण्मयूरहस्ता ।)

तापसी—सव्वदमण, सउन्दलावण्णं पेक्ख । सर्वदमन, शकुन्तलावण्यं प्रेक्षस्व ।

बालः—(सदृष्टिक्षेपम् ।) **कहिं वा मे अज्जू** । कुत्र वा मम माता ।

उभे—णामसारिस्सेण वञ्चिदो माउवच्छलो । नामसादृश्येन वञ्चितो मातृवत्सलः ।

द्वितीया—वच्छ, इमस्स मित्तिआमोरअस्स रम्मत्तणं देक्ख त्ति भणिदो सि । वत्स, अस्य मृत्तिकामयूरस्य रम्यत्वं पश्येति भणितोऽसि ।

राजा—(आत्मगतम् ।) **किंवा शकुन्तलेत्यस्य मातुराख्या । सन्ति पुनर्नामधेयसादृश्यानि । अपि नाम मृगतृष्णिकेव नाममात्रप्रस्तावो मे विषादाय कल्पते ।**

बालः—अज्जुए, रोअदि मे एसो भद्दमोरओ । (इति क्रीडनकमादत्ते ।) मातः, रोचते म एष भद्रमयूरः ।

प्रथमा—(विलोक्य सोद्वेगम् ।) **अम्हहे, रक्खाकरण्डअं से मणिबन्धे ण दीसदि** । अहो, रक्षाकरण्डकमस्य मणिबन्धे न दृश्यते ।

राजा—अलमलमावेगेन । नन्विदमस्य सिंहशावविमर्दात्परिभ्रष्टम् । (इत्यादातुमिच्छति ।)

उभे—मा क्खु एदं अवलम्बअ । कहं गहिदं णेण (इति विस्मयादुरोनिहितहस्ते परस्परमवलोकयतः ।) मा खल्विदमवलम्ब्य । कथं गृहीतमनेन ।

राजा—किमर्थं प्रतिषिद्धा स्मः ।

KING. (*To himself*). This story, really, points at me alone. Suppose I ask the name of the child's mother. But it is against good manners to inquire concerning the wife of another man.

(*Entering with the clay peacock in her hand*). HERMIT-WOMAN. Sarvadamana, look at the bird's beauty—the Śakunta-loveliness.

BOY (*Looking about*). Where is my mamma ?

BOTH. Tenderly loving his mother, how he is deceived by the similarity (of the sound) to her name !

SECOND. Dear boy, thou wast asked to see how pretty the clay-peacock was.

KING. (*To himself*). What, his mother's name is Śakuntalā ! But names are alike. Will it be that the mention of a mere name, like some mirage, would in the and lead to bitter disappointment ?

BOY. Mother, I like this fine peacock. (*Takes up the plaything.*)

FIRST (*Looking ; with alarm*). Oh, the amulet is not on his wrist !

KING. Don't get alarmed. It was dropped while he was struggling with the lion's cub. (*Desires to pick it up.*)

BOTH. Don't take it. How he has already picked it up !

(*They lay their hands on their bosom and gaze with surprise at each other.*)

KING. Why was I forbidden ?

प्रथमा—सुणादु महाराओ। एसा अवराजिदा णाम ओसही इमस्स जादकम्मसमए भअवदा मारीएण दिण्णा। एदं किल मादापिदरो अप्पाणं च वज्जिअ अवरो भूमिपडिदं ण गेण्हादि। शृणोतु महाराजः। एषापराजिता नामौषधिरस्य जातकर्मसमये भगवता मारीचेन दत्ता। एतां किल मातापितरावात्मानं च वर्जयित्वापरो भूमिपतितां न गृह्णाति।

राजा—अथ गृह्णाति।

प्रथमा—तदो तं सप्पो भविअ दंसइ। ततस्तं सर्पो भूत्वा दशति।

राजा—भवतीभ्यां कदाचिदस्याः प्रत्यक्षीकृता विक्रिया।

उभे—अणेअसो। अनेकशः।

राजा—(सहर्षम्। आत्मगतम्।) कथमिव संपूर्णमपि मे मनोरथं नाभिनन्दामि। (इति बालं परिष्वजते।)

द्वितीया—सुव्वदे, एहि। इमं वुत्तन्तं णिअमव्वावुडाए सउन्दलाए णिवेदेम्ह। सुव्रते, एहि। इम वृत्तान्तं नियमव्यापृतायै शकुन्तलायै निवेदयावः।

(इति निष्क्रान्ते।)

बालः—मुञ्च मं। जाव अज्जुए सआसं गमिस्सं। मुञ्च माम्। यावन्मातुः साकाशं गमिष्यामि।

राजा—पुत्रक, मया सहैव मातरमभिनन्दिष्यसि।

बालः—मम क्खु तादो दुस्सन्दो। ण तुमं। मम खलु तातो दुष्यन्तः। न त्वम्।

राजा—(सस्मितम्।) एष विवाद एव प्रत्याययति।

(ततः प्रविशत्येकवेणीधरा शकुन्तला।)

शकुन्तला—विआरकाले वि पकिदित्थं सव्वदमणस्स ओसहिं सुणिअ ण मे आसा आसि अत्तणो भाअहेएसु। अहवा जह साणुमदीए आचक्खिदं तह संभावीअदि एदं। विकारकालेऽपि प्रकृतिस्थां सर्वदमनस्यौषधिं श्रुत्वा न म आशासीदात्मनो भागधेयेषु। अथवा यथा सानुमत्याख्यातं तथा संभाव्यत एतत्।

राजा—(शकुन्तलां विलोक्य।) अये, सेयमत्रभवती शकुन्तला। यैषा

वसने परिधूसरे वसाना
नियमक्षाममुखी धृतैकवेणिः।

FIRST. Listen, your Majesty. This is the herb Aparājitā given at his birth-rites by the holy Mārīca. They say, that in case it fell to the earth no one but the parents or the boy himself may touch it.

KING. And supposing he takes it?

FIRST. It becomes a serpent and bites him.

KING. Did you ever see it thus transformed?

BOTH. Several times.

KING. (*With joy; to himself*). Why then do I not welcome my hope fulfilled at last? (*Embraces the boy.*)

SECOND. Suvratā, come let us carry the news to Śakuntalā who is engaged in the observance of her vows. (*Exeunt.*)

BOY. Leave me that I might go to my mother.

KING. My child, thou shalt go with me to greet thy mother.

BOY. My father is Duṣyanta, not you.

KING. (*Smiling*). Even this contradiction convinces me.

(*Enter Śakuntalā wearing her hair twisted into a single braid.*)

ŚAKUNTALĀ. Hearing that Sarvadamana's amulet remained in its natural form, even when there was an occasion when it ought to have changed its form, I could scarcely trust my fortunes. Or perhaps as Sānumatī told me, this is possible.

KING. (*Looking at Śakuntalā*). Ah, here is the lady Śakuntalā. She who,

Wearing two dark-grey garments, having a face worn by her vows, and wearing a single

अतिनिष्करुणस्य शुद्धशीला
मम दीर्घं विरहव्रतं बिभर्ति ॥ २१ ॥

शकुन्तला—(पश्चात्तापविवर्णं राजानं दृष्ट्वा ।) ण क्खु अज्जउत्तो विअ । तदो को एसो दाणिं किदरक्खामङ्गलं दारअं मे गत्तसंसग्गेण दूसेदिं । न खल्वार्यपुत्र इव । ततः क एष इदानीं कृतरक्षामङ्गलं दारकं मे गात्रसंसर्गेण दूषयति ।

बालः—(मातरमुपेत्य ।) अज्जुए, एसो कोवि पुरिसो मं पुत्तेत्ति आलिङ्गदि । मातः, एष कोऽपि पुरुषो मां पुत्र इत्यालिङ्गति ।

राजा—प्रिये, क्रौर्यमपि मे त्वयि प्रयुक्तमनुकूलपरिणामं संवृत्तम् । यदाहमिदानीं त्वया प्रत्यभिज्ञातमात्मानं पश्यामि ।

शकुन्तला—(आत्मगतम्) हिअअ, समस्सस समस्सस । परिच्चत्तमच्छरेण अणुअम्पिअम्हि देव्वेण । अज्जउत्तो क्खु एसो । हृदय, समाश्वसिहि समाश्वसिहि । परित्यक्तमत्सरेणानुकम्पितास्मि दैवेन । आर्यपुत्रः खल्वेषः ।

राजा—प्रिये,

स्मृतिभिन्नमोहतमसो दिष्ट्या प्रमुखे स्थितासि मे सुमुखि ।
उपरागान्ते शशिनः समुपगता रोहिणी योगम् ॥ २२ ॥

शकुन्तला—जेदु जेदु अज्जउत्तो । (इत्यर्धोक्ते बाष्पकण्ठी विरमति ।) जयतु जयत्वार्यपुत्रः ।

राजा—सुन्दरि,

बाष्पेण प्रतिषिद्धेऽपि जयशब्दे जितं मया ।
यत्ते दृष्टमसंस्कारं पाटलोष्ठपुटं मुखम् ॥ २३ ॥

बालः—अज्जुए, को एसो । मातः, क एषः ।

शकुन्तला—वच्छ, दे भाअहेआइं पुच्छेहि । वत्स, ते भागधेयानि पृच्छ ।

braid of hair, and pure in her conduct, is undergoing a long vow of separation from me who have been exceedingly cruel to her. (21)

ŚAKUNTALĀ (*Observing the king pale with remorse*). Certainly he does not look like my husband. Who then could he be that sullies with the contact of his body my child protected by an auspicious amulet?

BOY (*Advancing to his mother*). Mother, who is this man who calls me son and embraces me?

KING. Oh my beloved, even the cruelty I showed to you has come to have a happy conclusion, since I find that you have recognized me.

ŚAKUNTALĀ (*To herself*). Be comforted, my heart; fate, no longer envious, has taken pity on me. This is indeed my husband.

KING. Darling,

By the kindness of heaven, O lovely faced one, thou standest again before me, the darkness of whose delusion has been dispelled by recollection. The star Rohiṇī at the end of an eclipse rejoins her (beloved) Moon. (22)

ŚAKUNTALĀ. Victory to my noble lord! (*Tears choke her voice when this is half-said.*)

KING. Lovely one,

Though the word victory be suppressed by thy tears, yet have I gained victory since I see thy unadorned face with its red lips. (23)

BOY. Mother, who is he?

ŚAKUNTALĀ. Ask thy fate, my child.

राजा—(शकुन्तलायाः पादयोः प्रणिपत्य ।)

सुतनु हृदयात्प्रत्यादेशव्यलीकमपैतु ते
किमपि मनसः संमोहो मे तदा बलवानभूत् ।
प्रबलतमसामेवंप्रायाः शुभेषु प्रवृत्तयः
स्रजमपि शिरस्यन्धः क्षिप्तां धुनोत्यहिशङ्कया ॥ २४ ॥

शकुन्तला—उट्ठेदु अज्जउत्तो । णूणं मे सुअरिअप्पडिबन्धअं पुराकिदं तेसु दिअहेसु परिणाममुहं आसि जेण साणुक्कोसो वि अज्जउत्तो मइ विरसो संवुत्तो । उत्तिष्ठत्वार्यपुत्रः । नूनं मे सुचरितप्रतिबन्धकं पुराकृतं तेषु दिवसेषु परिणाममुखमासीद्येन सानुक्रोशोऽप्यार्यपुत्रो मयि विरसः संवृत्तः ।

(राजोत्तिष्ठति ।)

शकुन्तला—अह कहं अज्जउत्तेण सुमरिदो दुक्खभाई अअं जणो । अथ कथमार्यपुत्रेण स्मृतो दुःखभाग्ययं जनः ।

राजा—उद्धृतविषादशल्यः कथयिष्यामि ।

मोहान्मया सुतनु पूर्वमुपेक्षितस्ते
यो बाष्पबिन्दुरधरं परिबाधमानः ।
तं तावदाकुटिलपक्ष्मविलग्नमद्य
बाष्पं प्रमृज्य विगतानुशयो भवेयम् ॥ २५ ॥

(इति यथोक्तमनुतिष्ठति ।)

शकुन्तला—(नाममुद्रां दृष्ट्वा ।) **अज्जउत्त, एदं तं अङ्गुलीअअं ।** आर्यपुत्र, एतत्तदङ्गुलीयकम् ।

राजा—अस्मादङ्गुलीयोपलम्भात्खलु स्मृतिरुपलब्धा ।

शकुन्तला—विसमं किदं णेण जं तदा अज्जउत्तस्स पच्चाअकाले दुल्लहं आसि । विषमं कृतमनेन यत्तदार्यपुत्रस्य प्रत्ययकाले दुर्लभमासीत् ।

KING (*Falling at Śakuntalā's feet*).

> O fair one let the unpleasantness caused by my desertion of thee depart from thy heart ; for at that time a violent frenzy somehow overpowered my soul. Such, for the most part, is the attitude towards good of those in whose minds the darkness of illusion prevails. A blind man shakes off even a wreath of flowers thrown over his head, mistaking it for a snake. (24)

ŚAKUNTALĀ. Rise, my husband ; surely some (evil) deed of mine in a former existence coming in the way (of the action) of my virtue, was in those days approaching fruition ; since my husband, who is so kind at heart became unfeeling towards me. (*The king rises.*) Śakuntalā. But how did my husband remember this unfortunate woman ?

KING. I will tell thee when I shall have plucked the dart of sorrow.

> Fair one, the anguish of my heart shall cease by wiping off the tears that now cling to thy slightly curved eye-lashes--the tears which formerly paining thy under-lip were neglected by me through mental delusion. (25)

(*Does as said.*)

ŚAKUNTALĀ (*Seeing the signet-ring*). My husband, this is the ring.

KING. It was the recovery of this ring that restored my memory.

ŚAKUNTALĀ. It has acted wickedly, since it was not found at the time of convincing my husband.

राजा—तेन ह्यृतुसमवायचिह्नं प्रतिपद्यतां लता कुसुमम् ।

शकुन्तला—ण से विस्ससामि । अज्जउत्तो एव्वं णं धारेदु । नास्या विश्वसिमि । आर्यपुत्र एवैतद्धारयतु ।

(ततः प्रविशति मातलिः ।)

मातलिः—दिष्ट्या धर्मपत्नीसमागमेन पुत्रमुखदर्शनेन चायुष्मान् वर्धते ।

राजा—अभूत्संपादितस्वादुफलो मे मनोरथः । मातले, न खलु विदितोऽयमाखण्डलेन वृत्तान्तः स्यात् ।

मातलिः—(सस्मितम् ।) किमीश्वराणां परोक्षम् । एत्वायुष्मान् । भगवान्मारीचस्ते दर्शनं वितरति ।

राजा—शकुन्तले, अवलम्ब्यतां पुत्रः । त्वां पुरस्कृत्य भगवन्तं द्रष्टुमिच्छामि ।

शकुन्तला—हिरिआमि अज्जउत्तेण सह गुरुसमीवं गन्तुं । जिह्रेम्यार्यपुत्रेण सह गुरुसमीपं गन्तुम् ।

राजा—अप्याचरितव्यमभ्युदयकालेषु । एह्येहि ।

(सर्वे परिक्रामन्ति ।)

(ततः प्रविशत्यदित्या सार्धमासनस्थो मारीचः ।)

मारीचः—(राजानमवलोक्य ।) दाक्षायणि,

पुत्रस्य ते रणशिरस्ययमग्रयायी
दुष्यन्त इत्यभिहितो भुवनस्य भर्ता ।
चापेन यस्य विनिवर्तितकर्म जातं
तत्कोटिमत्कुलिशमाभरणं मघोनः ॥ २६ ॥

अदितिः—संभावणीआणुभावा से आकिदि । संभावनीयानुभावास्याकृतिः ।

KING. Then let the creeper receive her flower as a sign of her union with spring.

ŚAKUNTALĀ. I do not trust it. Let my husband alone wear it.

(*Then enter Mātali.*)

MĀTALI. I congratulate the long-lived one on reunion with his lawful wife, and on seeing the face of his son.

KING. My desire has come to attain a sweet fruit. Mātali, was not this event really known to Indra ?

MĀTALI (*Smiling*). What is unknown to the Gods ? Come, long-lived one. The divine Mārīca gives you an audience.

KING. Śakuntalā, take our son by the hand ; I wish to see the holy one, leading thee into his presence.

ŚAKUNTALĀ. I am ashamed to go before my elders with my husband.

KING. But that is the custom on (such) happy occasions. Come, come.

(*All walk round.*)

(*Then enter seated Mārīca and Aditi.*)

MĀRĪCA (*Looking at the king*). Aditi,

This is he that marches foremost in the front of thy son's battles, named Duṣyanta, the ruler of the earth, through whose bow that edged thunder-bolt of Indra, all its work being accomplished, has become (a mere) ornament. (26)

ADITI. His greatness may be inferred from his appearance.

मातलिः—आयुष्मन्, एतौ पुत्रप्रीतिपिशुनेन चक्षुषा दिवौकसां पितरावायुष्मन्तमवलोकयतः। तावुपसर्प।

राजा—मातले एतौ

प्राहुर्द्वादशधा स्थितस्य मुनयो यत्तेजसः कारणं
भर्तारं भुवनत्रयस्य सुषुवे यद्यज्ञभागेश्वरम्।
यस्मिन्नात्मभवः परोऽपि पुरुषश्चक्रे भवायास्पदं
द्वन्द्वं दक्षमरीचिसंभवमिदं तत्स्रष्टुरेकान्तरम्॥ २७॥

मातलिः—अथ किम्।

राजा—(उपगम्य।) उभाभ्यामपि वासवानुयोज्यो दुष्यन्तः प्रणमति।

मारीचः—वत्स, चिरं जीव। पृथिवीं पालय।

अदितिः—वच्छ अप्पडिरहो होहि। वत्स अप्रतिरथो भव।

शकुन्तला—दारअसहिदा वो पादवन्दणं करेमि। दारकसहिता वां पादवन्दनं करोमि।

मारीचः—वत्से,

आखण्डलसमो भर्ता जयन्तप्रतिमः सुतः।
आशीरन्या न ते योग्या पौलोमीसदृशी भव॥ २८॥

अदितिः—जादे, भत्तुणो अभिमदा होहि। अवस्सं दीहाऊ वच्छओ उहअकुलणन्दणो होदु। उवविसह। जाते, भर्तुरभिमता भव। अवश्यं दीर्घायुर्वत्स उभयकुलनन्दनो भवतु। उपविशत।

(सर्वे प्रजापतिमभित उपविशन्ति।)

मारीचः—(एकैकं निर्दिशन्।)

दिष्ट्या शकुन्तला साध्वी सदपत्यमिदं भवान्।
श्रद्धा वित्तं विधिश्चेति त्रितयं तत्समागतम्॥ २९॥

MĀTALI. Long-lived one, these parents of the gods are gazing upon you with an eye that betrays parental affection. Approach them.

KING. Mātali,

Are those the pair, sprung from Dakṣa and Mārīci, at one remove from the Creator, whom sages pronounce the fountain of glory apparent in the twelve forms (of the sun) ; who begot the lord of the triple world, the lord of the (gods who are the) sharers of every sacrifice, the pair whom Viṣṇu, who is higher than the self-existent himself, chose as the source of his birth ? (27)

MĀTALI. Yes, quite so.

KING. (*Approaching*). Duṣyanta, Indra's servant, bows to you both.

MĀRĪCA. Child, mayest thou live long ! Protect the earth.

ADITI. Be thou a matchless hero.

ŚAKUNTALĀ. I salute your feet along with my son.

MĀRĪCA. Like Indra is thy husband ; and like Jayanta thy son ; no other blessing would be suitable to thee. Mayest thou be like Paulomī ! (28)

ADITI. Child, be thou highly honoured by thy husband. May thy child be long-lived and unfailingly be the joy of both the families. Sit down.

(*All sit down around Prajāpati.*)

MĀRĪCA (*Pointing to each of them by turns*).

The virtuous Śakuntalā, her noble child and your Honour—here fortunately are combined faith, fortune, and action. (29)

राजा—भगवन्, प्रागभिप्रेतसिद्धिः। पश्चाद्दर्शनम्। अतोऽपूर्वः खलु वोऽनुग्रहः। कुतः।

उदेति पूर्वं कुसुमं ततः फलं
घनोदयः प्राक्तदनन्तरं पयः।
निमित्तनैमित्तिकयोरयं क्रम-
स्तव प्रसादस्य पुरस्तु संपदः ॥ ३० ॥

मातलिः—एवं विधातारः प्रसीदन्ति।

राजा—भगवन्, इमामाज्ञाकरीं वो गान्धर्वेण विवाहविधिनोपयम्य कस्यचित्कालस्य बन्धुभिरानीतां स्मृतिशैथिल्यात्प्रत्यादिशन्नपराद्धोऽस्मि तत्रभवतो युष्मत्सगोत्रस्य कण्वस्य। पश्चादङ्गुलीयकदर्शनादूढपूर्वां तद्दुहितरमवगतोऽहम्। तच्चित्रमिव मे प्रतिभाति।

यथा गजो नेति समक्षरूपे
तस्मिन्नपक्रामति संशयः स्यात्।
पदानि दृष्ट्वा तु भवत्प्रतीति-
स्तथाविधो मे मनसो विकारः ॥ ३१ ॥

मारीचः—वत्स, अलमात्मापराधशङ्कया। संमोहोऽपि त्वय्यनुपपन्नः। श्रूयताम्।

राजा—अवहितोऽस्मि।

मारीचः—यदैवाप्सरस्तीर्थावतरणात्प्रत्यक्षवैक्लव्यां शकुन्तलामादाय मेनका दाक्षायणीमुपगता तदैव ध्यानादवगतोऽस्मि दुर्वाससः

KING. Holy one, First came the fulfilment of my desires, and afterwards, the sight of you; thus the favour you showed me is without parallel. For

First appears the flower, then the fruit ; first the clouds and then come the showers ; such is the regular course of cause and effect ; but fortunes came before your grace. (30)

MĀTALI. That is how the creators of all beings show favour.

KING. Holy sir, I married this your hand-maid by the Gāndharva ceremony and when after a time she was brought to me by her kindred, my memory failing me, I rejected her and thus committed a grievous offence against the venerable Kaṇva who is kin to you. But afterwards on seeing the ring, I perceived that I had married his daughter. This strikes me as very wonderful.

As if a man were to say 'This is not an elephant' when its form was before his eyes ; and when it has marched past him, were to doubt (what animal it could be) ; but conviction were to take place on seeing its foot-prints ; of such a kind has been the change that had come over my mind. (31)

MĀRĪCA. Cease, my son to charge thyself with an offence ; nor is infatuation explicable in thee. Listen.

KING. I am all attention.

MĀRĪCA. Even when Menakā took Śakuntalā whose distress was so evident, from the steps of the Apsaras-tirtha, and brought her to Aditi, at that very time I

शापादियं तपस्विनी सहधर्मचारिणी त्वया प्रत्यादिष्टा नान्यथेति। स चायमङ्गुलीयकदर्शनावसानः।

राजा—(सोच्छ्वासम्।) एष वचनीयान्मुक्तोऽस्मि।

शकुन्तला—(स्वगतम्।) दिट्ठिआ अकारणपच्चादेसी ण अज्जउत्तो। ण हु सत्तं अत्ताणं सुमरेमि। अहवा पत्तो मए स हि साबो विरहसुण्णहिअआए ण विदिदो। अदो सहीहिं संदिट्ठम्हि भत्तुणो अङ्गुलीअअं दंसइदव्वं त्ति। दिष्टयाकारणप्रत्यादेशी नार्यपुत्रः। न खलु शप्तमात्मानं स्मरामि। अथवा प्राप्तो मया स हि शापो विरहशून्यहृदयया न विदितः। अतः सखीभ्यां संदिष्टास्मि भर्तुरङ्गुलीयकं दर्शयितव्यमिति।

मारीचः—वत्से, चरितार्थासि। सहधर्मचारिणं प्रति न त्वया मन्युः कार्यः। पश्य।

शापादसि प्रतिहता स्मृतिरोधरूक्षे
भर्तर्यपेततमसि प्रभुता तवैव।
छाया न मूर्च्छति मलोपहतप्रसादे
शुद्धे तु दर्पणतले सुलभावकाशा॥ ३२॥

राजा—यथाह भगवान्।

मारीचः—वत्स, कच्चिदभिनन्दितस्त्वया विधिवदस्माभिरनुष्ठितजातकर्मा पुत्र एष शाकुन्तलेयः।

राजा—भगवन्, अत्र खलु मे वंशप्रतिष्ठा। बालं हस्तेन गृह्णाति

मारीचः—तथा भाविनमेनं चक्रवर्तिनमवगच्छतु भवान्। पश्य।

रथेनानुद्धातस्तिमितगतिना तीर्णजलधिः
पुरा सप्तद्वीपां जयति वसुधामप्रतिरथः।

perceived through my powers of contemplation that this thy poor dutiful wife was repudiated by thee in consequence of Durvāsas' curse, and through no other cause; that curse was to terminate at the sight of the ring.

KING. (*With a sigh*). So I am free from blame.

ŚAKUNTALĀ (*To herself*). Happy am I that my husband did not repudiate me without cause. But, indeed I don't remember I was cursed. Or I did not know I was cursed as I was absent-minded through separation; for my friends advised me to show the ring to my husband.

MĀRĪCA. Thou knowest, my daughter, the whole truth and must not give way to anger against thy rightful husband. Remember

Thou wast rejected in consequence of the curse, thy husband being cruel to thee through the obstruction of his memory; but now when his mind is freed from darkness, thou alone wilt rule him. As an image has no effect on a mirror whose surface is sullied with dirt, but on a clean one finds an easy access. (32)

MĀRĪCA. Child, have you greeted this son whom Śakuntalā bore (to you) whose birth-rites have been duly performed by us?

KING. Holy one, in him is the hope of my family.

MĀRĪCA. Know that he will be a universal monarch in days to come.

First, a matchless warrior, he will cross the ocean in a chariot whose motion would be steady and free from jolts and conquer the earth consisting of her seven islands; here

इहायं सत्त्वानां प्रसभदमनात्सर्वदमनः
पुनर्यास्यत्याख्यां भरत इति लोकस्य भरणात् ॥ ३३ ॥

राजा—भगवता कृतसंस्कारे सर्वमस्मिन्वयमाशास्महे ।

अदितिः—भअवं, इमाए दुहिदुमणोरहसंपत्तीए कण्णो वि दाव सुदवित्थारो करीअदु । दुहिदुवच्छला मेणआ इह एव्व उपचरन्ती चिट्ठदि । भगवन् अनया दुहितृमनोरथसंपत्त्या कण्वोऽपि तावच्छ्रुतविस्तारः क्रियताम् । दुहितृवत्सला मेनाकेहैवोपचरन्ती तिष्ठति ।

शकुन्तला—(आत्मगतम् ।) मणोरहो क्खु मे भणिदो भअवदीए । मनोरथः खलु मे भणितो भगवत्या ।

मारीचः—तपःप्रभावात्प्रत्यक्षं सर्वमेव तत्रभवतः ।

राजाः—अतः खलु मम नातिक्रुद्धो मुनिः ।

मारीचः—तथाप्यसौ प्रियमस्माभिः प्रष्टव्यः । कः कोऽत्र भोः ।

(प्रविश्य ।)

शिष्यः—भगवन् , अयमस्मि ।

मारीचः—गालव, इदानीमेव विहायसा गत्वा मम वचनात्तत्रभवते कण्वाय प्रियमावेदय । यथा पुत्रवती शकुन्तला तच्छापनिवृत्तौ स्मृतिमता दुष्यन्तेन प्रतिगृहीतेति ।

शिष्यः—यदाज्ञापयति भगवान् । (इति निष्क्रान्तः ।)

मारीचः—वत्स, त्वमपि स्वापत्यदारसहितः सख्युराखण्डलस्य रथमारुह्य ते राजधानीं प्रतिष्ठस्व ।

राजा—यदाज्ञापयति भगवान् ।

he is called Sarvadamana, because he forcibly tames all animals ; but (later) he shall acquire the name of Bharata, because he shall sustain the world. (33)

KING. I anticipate all (this) from him for whom the purificatory-rites were performed by the holy one.

ADITI. Holy one, let Kaṇva also be apprised of all the circumstances of the attainment by his daughter of all that her heart desired. Menakā, who is (so) fond of her daughter, is here in attendance upon me.

ŚAKUNTALĀ (*To herself*). The holy one has, indeed, given expression to my heart's desire.

MĀRĪCA. But the holy one knows the whole matter through the power of his devotions.

KING. Hence it is that the sage was not very much angry with me.

MĀRĪCA. Nevertheless, he must be questioned by me about this happy event. Ho, who is there ?

(*Entering*) Pupil. Holy one, here I am.

MĀRĪCA. Gālava, fly through the air at once, and inform the holy Kaṇva of the happy event, in my name : That Śakuntalā with her son is accepted by Duṣyanta when his memory revived on the termination of her curse.

PUPIL. As the holy one commands. (*Exit.*)

MĀRĪCA. My son, thou too now ascend the chariot of thy friend Indra along with this wife and child, and set out for thy capital.

KING. As the holy one commands.

मारीचः—अपि च ।

तव भवतु बिडौजाः प्राज्यवृष्टिः प्रजासु
त्वमपि विततयज्ञः वज्रिणं प्रीणयस्व ।
युगशतपरिवर्तानेवमन्योन्यकृत्यै-
र्नयतमुभयलोकानुग्रहश्लाघनीयैः ॥ ३४ ॥

राजा—भगवन्, यथाशक्ति श्रेयसे यतिष्ये ।

मारीचः—वत्स, किं ते भूयः प्रियमुपकरोमि ।

राजा—अतः परमपि प्रियमस्ति । यदिह भगवान्प्रियं कर्तुमिच्छति तर्हीदमस्तु । (भरतवाक्यम् ।)

प्रवर्ततां प्रकृतिहिताय पार्थिवः
सरस्वती श्रुतमहतां महीयताम् ।
ममापि च क्षपयत नीललोहितः
पुनर्भवं परिगतशक्तिरात्मभूः ॥ ३५ ॥

(इति निष्क्रान्ताः सर्वे)

सप्तमोऽङ्कः ।

समाप्तमिदमभिज्ञानशाकुन्तलं नाम नाटकम् ॥

MĀRĪCA. Moreover,

May Indra send copious rain for (the benefit of) thy subjects; and mayest thou with frequent sacrifices please him. Thus pass periods of hundreds of ages with reciprocal friendly offices laudable on account of the benefits conferred on both the worlds. (34)

KING. Holy one, I shall strive, as far as I can, to attain (that) felicity.

MĀRĪCA. My son, what other favours can I bestow on thee?

KING. Can there be any favour greater still than this? As (however) the holy one desires to bestow a favour then let this be (fulfilled). (*Epilogue*).

May the king apply himself to the attainment of the happiness of his subjects. May the speech of those who stand high in their knowledge of the Veda be honoured, and may the self-existent Siva whose energy is immanent in all things put an end to my rebirth. (35)

(*Exeunt Omnes.*)

End of Act VII

Here ends the drama Abhijnāna-Śākuntala.

ABHIJNĀNA-ŚĀKUNTALAM

NOTES

ACT I

P. 1. From the Nāṭyaśāstra we learn that before the commencement of a drama, an elaborate series of preliminaries (पूर्वरङ्ग) had to be performed, consisting chiefly of the प्रत्याहार which would announce the beginning of the performance, the अवतरण, when the musicians enter and take their places, the आरम्भ when the chorus try their voices, and the आश्रवण when the musicians try their instruments, and so on up to Nāndi. All these preliminaries are performed by the सूत्रधार, who then leaves the stage and his place is immediately taken by another similar person called स्थापक who introduces the play to the audience. This elaborate practice, was however given up later on, and we find that the सूत्रधार alone performed both the functions of the preliminaries and of the prologue. Cf. पूर्वरङ्गं विधायादौ सूत्रधारे विनिर्गते । प्रविश्य तद्वदपरः काव्यमास्थापयेन्नटः ॥ ...सूचयेद्वस्तु बीजं वा मुखं पात्रमथापि वा ॥ दशरूपक० III. 2–3.

I. 1. This benedictory stanza praises god Śiva and invokes his blessing and protection. He manifests himself through his eight different forms, for the support of this universe. These eight visible forms corresponded to the eight different manifestations of god Śiva called Rudras, viz. रुद्र, भव, सर्व, ईशान, पशुपति, भीम, उग्र and महादेव. " Brahmā assigned to them their respective stations: water, the sun, earth, fire, air, ether, the officiating Brāhmaṇa, and the moon; these are termed their visible forms (तनवः) "—विष्णुपुराण. Cf. अष्टाभियस्य कृत्स्न जगदपि तनुभिर्बिभ्रतो नाभि-

मानः । माल० I. 1. Also कुमा० V. 26. विदितं वो यथा स्वार्था न मे काश्चित् प्रवृत्तयः । ननु मूर्तिभिरष्टाभिरित्थंभूतोऽस्मि सूचितः ॥ Also कलितान्योन्यसामर्थ्यैः पृथिव्यादिभिरात्मभिः । येनेदं ध्रियते विश्वं धुर्यैर्यानमिवाध्वनि ॥ ibid. V. 76. या स्रष्टुः आद्या सृष्टिः—Which was the first creation of the Creator i. e. water. According to the Paurāṇic conception of the creation of the universe, water was created first. Cf. अप एव ससर्जादौ तासु वीर्यमवासृजत् । तदण्डमभवद्धैमं सहस्रांशुसमप्रभम् ॥ मनु० I. या विधिहुतं हविः वहति–Which carries the oblations (to the various gods), offered with due rites. Agni does the duty of delivering the offerings to the various gods. He is thus a carrier of oblations–a veritable portman. The significance of the adjective विधिहुत is best understood when it is known that the offerings not so given are not delivered unto the gods, but are reduced to ashes. (अविधिहुतं भस्मीभवति). ये द्वे कालं विधत्तः–The two, who make time viz. the sun and the moon. The Time or Kāla is infinite, but then the divisions of Time and its reckoning are possible because of the two luminaries. The day and night, the fortnight, the month, the seasons, the year etc, into which Time could thus be divided, are to be calculated by the sun and the moon, and therefore, they make (विधत्तः) Time. श्रुति...गुणा –श्रुतेः विषयः (शब्दः) गुणः यस्याः सा–Characterised by the object of hearing viz. thc sound. आकाश or ether, invisible as it is, has its characteristic गुण of conveying sound from the place of origin to the sense of hearing. Cf. अथात्मनः शब्दगुणं गुणज्ञः पदं विमानेन विगाहमानः । रघु० XVIII. सर्वबीजप्रकृतिः–The source of all seeds viz. the Earth, प्रकृति is the उत्पत्तिस्थान or the source. Cf. इयं भूमिर्हि भूतानां शाश्वती योनिरुच्यते ॥ मनु० IX. 37. Note the other reading सर्वभूतप्रकृतिः, which is also good. यया प्राणिनः प्राणवन्तः–By which, the living beings are endowed with प्राण i. e. vital breaths. Beings have life in them because of these five vital breaths in the body. They are:—प्राण, अपान, व्यान, उदान and समान. प्राण is the all-in-all of a living being, the essence of life, as is illustrated by the Upaniṣadic parable in the form of the dialogue between the various senses and Prāṇa, in the छांदोग्योपनिषद्. प्रपन्नः– उपेतः, Endowed with, i. e. manifested in those eight visible forms. 'Known i. e. inferred to exist. The existence of ईश is inferred from his eight forms (अष्टाभिः तनुभिः) which are directly perceived (प्रत्यक्षाभिः)'—Ray. Note the other reading, प्रसन्नः 'Pleased'. With this reading, the meaning would be 'May god Śiva, pleased, protect you with his eight manifested forms.

नान्द्यन्ते. At the end of the Nāndi or benediction. The verse, explained above, constitutes the नान्दी, which is defined thus–आशीर्नमस्क्रियारूपः श्लोकः काव्यार्थसूचकः i. e. 'a verse or verses of the form of a salutation or a benediction and suggestive of the story of the drama. It is called नान्दी, because by the praise which it contains and is a source of delight to the gods. Cf. नन्दन्ति देवता यस्यां तस्मान्नान्दीति कीर्तिता। Its another characteristic of suggesting the Kāvyārtha has led commentators into ingenious attempts to find out far-fetched fantastic allusions to the elements or the various characters in the drama. Thus the expression या सृष्टिः etc. refers to that páragon of beauty, शकुन्तला, who has been described as अपरा स्त्रीरत्नसृष्टिः in the II Act, or in the terms of the Meghaduta, may be described as सृष्टिराद्येव धातुः। while the expression ये द्वे etc. refers to the two friends of शकुन्तला.

सूत्रधारः–The principal stage-manager who arranges the cast of characters, instructs them in their different roles, and is thus responsible for the successful performance of the drama–"The threads of which he holds in his hands, as it were." According to मातृगुप्ताचार्य he must have the following accomplishments:–

चतुरातोद्यनिष्णातोऽनेकभाषासमावृतः । नानाभाषणतत्त्वज्ञो नीतिशास्त्रार्थतत्त्ववित् ॥ नानागतिप्रचारज्ञो रसभावविशारदः । नाट्यप्रयोगनिपुणो नानाशिल्पकलान्वितः ॥ छन्दोविधानतत्त्वज्ञः सर्वशास्त्रविचक्षणः । तत्तद्गीतानुगलयकलातालावधारणः ॥ अवधानप्रयोक्ता च योक्तृणामुपदेशकः । एवंगुणगणोपेतः सूत्रधारोऽभिधीयते ॥

नेपथ्याभिमुखम्–Towards the tiring or the dressing room. The word नेपथ्य means 'the Dress or Costume' (Cf. विरलनेपथ्ययोः

पात्रयोः प्रवेशोऽस्तु । माल० I), or the dressing room, the space where the actors attire themselves, which is always behind the curtain. नेपथ्यविधानम्–Arrangements in the tiring room or the dressing. अवसितम्–finished, P. P. of √अव+सो. नियोग.–Task, duty assigned. अभिरूपभूयिष्ठा–अभिरूपाः भूयिष्ठाः यस्यां सा or आभिरूपैः भूयिष्ठा–Mostly consisting of wise men. आभिरूप means here 'Learned, enlightened'. परिषद्–An assembly, audience. कालिदास...वस्तु–कालिदासेन ग्रथितं वस्तु यस्य तत्–The story of which has been woven into the plot (of this drama) by Kālidāsa. अभिज्ञानशकुन्तलाख्ये–called the 'Token–Śakuntalā' or 'Ring–(recognised) Śakuntalā.' The word is thus explained:–अभिज्ञानेन स्मृता शकुन्तला–अभिज्ञानशकुन्तला, a compound of the शाकपार्थिव type, where we get the elision of the second member, and which has to be supplied while dissolving the compound. अभिज्ञानशकुन्तलां आधिकृत्य कृतं (नाटकं)–अभिज्ञानशकुन्तलं; अभि...न्तलं आख्या यस्य तद्–अभिज्ञानशकुन्तलाख्यम् । उपस्थातव्यम्–Pot. pass. part. of उप + स्था 'To wait upon, to serve'. प्रतिपात्रम्–पात्रे पात्रे–For every part or character. आधीयतां यत्नः–Care should be taken, effort should be made. सुविहितप्रयोगतया–on account of the fact that the performance (प्रयोग) has been well-arranged. न किमपि परिहास्यते. Nothing will be found to be amiss or wanting. If the Sūtradhāra is overcareful in his eagerness to see that nothing goes wrong, his wife Natī is in a self-complacent mood and wants to compliment her husband on his efficient management. भूतार्थः–सत्यार्थः–the truth, the true state of the case. Cf. कः श्रद्धास्यति भूतार्थं सर्वो मां तुलयिष्यति । मृच्छ० III.

I. 2. प्रयोगविज्ञानम्–the profound knowledge of acting. बलवत्–Adv. greatly. Lit. mightily ; to be construed with शिक्षितानाम् । आत्मनि अप्रत्ययम्–diffident in itself, wanting in one's own confidence. The सूत्रधार means that it is no good flattering oneself with the thought of one's own proficiency, which must stand the test of public criticism, which alone proves the inherent merit, if there is any. It is for this reason, that even the wisest men tremble in their shoes with feelings of diffidence, when they have to face the general public.

P. 2. अनन्तरकरणीयं–what has to be done next i. e. immediately (अनन्तरं). श्रुतिप्रसादनतः–श्रवणेन्द्रियतर्पणात्–besides pleasing the ears (of the audience); the Abl. governed by अन्य acc. to the सूत्र-अन्यारादितरर्ते । पा० II. 3. 29. उपभोगक्षमं–Fit to be enjoyed, suited to the enjoyment of pleasures. आधिकृत्य–Lit. 'Having placed over; having made the prominent object'; about, with reference to.

I. 3. सुभगसलिलावगाहाः (दिवसाः)–सुभगः सलिले अवगाहः येषु ते–On which a plunge (अवगाह) in water is so delightful. पाटल...वाताः–पाटलानां संसर्गेण सुरभयः वनवाताः येषु–When the forest-breezes are (rendered) fragrant by their contact with the trumpet flowers. The flower has a red hue and possesses sweet fragrance. प्रच्छायसुलभनिद्राः–प्रच्छाये सुलभा निद्रा येषु–When slumber is easily induced in a thick shady-place. प्रच्छायं–प्रकृष्टा छाया यत्र तत् स्थानं or प्रकृष्टा छाया–प्रच्छायम् । परि...णीयाः–परिणामे रमणीयाः–Charming at the close. परिणाम–Lit. means ' Ripening, development, ' here it means ' evening, the close of the day. ' Cf. प्रचण्डसूर्यः स्पृहणीयचन्द्रमाः सदावगाहक्षमवारिसंचयः । दिनान्तरम्योऽभ्युपशान्तमन्मथो निदाघकालोऽयमुपागतः प्रिये ॥ ऋतु० I ।

I. 4. ईषद्...चुम्बितानि–Very gently kissed (by the bees). They sip the honey very softly without harming the flower. सुकुमार......शिखानि–सुकुमाराः केसराणां शिखाः (अग्रभागाः) येषु तानि (शिरीषकुसुमानि)–With tender tips of the filaments, अवतंसयन्ति–A denominative verbal form from अवतंस meaning 'an ear-ornament.' दयमानाः–Compassionate, tender-hearted ; a present Part. from... दय् I. A. ' To take pity on. ' प्रमदा–A youthful lady. Note that the verse is a Prākrit song, a द्विपदी or a couplet, having thirty मात्राs in each line. It is being sung by the नटी, ' to the tunes of the सारङ्ग melody, which has proved highly captivating. ' राग... वृत्तिः–रागेण बद्धा चित्तवृत्तिर्यस्य सः–With all its mental activity arrested by the melody (of the song). The Com. राघवभट्ट solves the compound thus—रागे बद्धा चित्तवृत्तिर्यस्य सः–, ' Having all mental activity fixed on the melody. ' आलिखितः–Painted, drawn in a picture. रङ्गः–The audience, the assembly. प्रकरणम्–A topic, a subject of representation; a play in general. The word is usually used with reference to a particular type of a drama, like the मृच्छकटिक, or मालतीमाधव, which has a fictitious plot. आर्यमिश्रैः–' By your reverence, your respectable self.' It should however be taken as an epithet of the audience meaning the noble men in the audience.' Cf. यावदिदानीं आर्यमिश्रान् विज्ञापयामि ॥ विक्र० I. मिश्र is a honorific title, (usually affixed to the names of great men and scholars, e. g. वसिष्ठमिश्रः, मण्डनमिश्रः). अनुबोधितः–Reminded.

I. 5. हारिणा—(i) With reference to गीतरागेण–' ravishing, captivating' (ii) With reference to सारङ्गेण–' luring, drawing away' (into the forest). प्रसभं–forcibly. अतिरंहसा–अतिशयितं रंहः यस्य सः तेन–Having a great speed (रंहस्). सारङ्गेण–By the antelope or the spotted deer; " by the सारङ्ग melody of the song (गीतरागेण)." Prof. Ranade's सुशिक्षितांचें संगीत P. 4.

Here ends the प्रस्तावना or the Prologue called also आमुख, which generally consists of an introductory dialogue between the सूत्रधार and नटी or one of the actors. After giving an account of the author and his qualifications, it introduces the incidents of the drama. Cf. सूत्रधारो नटीं ब्रूते मार्षं वाथ विदूषकम् । स्वकार्यं प्रस्तुताक्षेपि चित्रोक्त्या यत्तदामुखम् । प्रस्तावना वा ॥ दश. III. 8. Also नटी विदूषको वापि पारिपार्श्वक एव वा । सूत्रधारेण सहिताः संलापं यत्र कुर्वते ॥ चित्रैर्वाक्यैः स्वकार्योत्थैः प्रस्तुताक्षेपिभिर्मिथः । आमुखं तत्तु विज्ञेयं नाम्ना प्रस्तावनापि वा ॥ Of the प्रस्तावना there are three varieties, according to दशरूपक (or five according to साहित्यदर्पण) of which प्रयोगातिशय or particular presentation is one in which a character is introduced by a remark of the stage-manager. एषोऽयमित्युपक्षेपात् सूत्रधारप्रयोगतः । पात्रप्रवेशो यत्रैष प्रयोगातिशयो मतः ॥ ३ ॥ Thus the प्रस्तावना of our drama also is of the प्रयोगातिशय type. आयुष्मन्–A respectable mode of addressing kings. Cf. 'आयुष्मन्' इति वाच्यस्तु रथी सूतेन सर्वदा '–Com.

I. 6. अधिज्यकार्मुके (त्वयि)–Having a strung bow, अधिज्यं कार्मुकं यस्य सः तस्मिन् । The word अधिज्य means 'having the string up'; ज्यामधिगतं or अधिरूढा ज्या यत्र तद् (पिनाकिन् is an epithet of god Śiva armed as he is with his bow called पिनाक. मृगानुसारिणम् The expression has a reference to the following mythological episode. ' Śiva, not having been invited to दक्ष's celebrated horse-sacrifice, was so indignant, that with his wife, he suddenly presented himself, confounded the sacrifice, dispersed and mutilated the gods, and chasing यज्ञ, ' the lord of sacrifice', who fled in the form of a fleet deer, overtook and decapitated him. ' Cf. तत्प्रसुप्तभुजगेन्द्र-भीषणं वीक्ष्य दाशरथिराददे धनुः । विद्रुतक्रतुमृगानुसारिणं येन बाणमसृजद्वृषध्वजः ॥ रघु० XI. 44.

I. 7. The verse gives a fine description of the pursued antelope. ग्रीवा......रामं–To be construed with बद्धदृष्टिः–In a charming manner because of the bending. of the neck (ग्रीवा). अनुपतति–Loc. Sing. of अनुपतत्–a Pres. Part. of √ अनु + पत्–' to rush behind, to pursue.' Cf. कथमनुपतत एव प्रयत्नप्रेक्षणीयः संवृत्तः ।. बद्धदृष्टिः,–With his eyes fixed (upon the chariot). Note V. L. दत्तदृष्टिः, which, with the word मुहुः suggesting frequent interruption in the steadfast look, is to be preferred. For बद्धदृष्टि, compare– स्यन्दनाबद्धदृष्टिषु । रघु० I. 40. पश्चार्धेन–by hinder half (of the body) अपरः अर्धः पश्चाधः । Cf. वार्तिक ' अपरस्यार्धे पश्चभावो वक्तव्यः । पूर्वकायम्–पूर्वं कायस्य–The fore-part of the body. श्रम...भ्रंशिभिः (दर्भैः)–dropping from his mouth forced open (विवृत) through exhaustion. कीर्णवर्त्मा–कीर्णं वर्त्म यस्य सः–whose path was strewn (with grass). उदग्रप्लुतत्वात्. By reason of his lofty bounds (प्लुत) in the air. स्तोकम्–अल्पम्–Very little. उर्व्याम्–Loc. Sing. of उर्वी 'the earth'. The poet means that because of his high boundings, he appears to be traversing the distance mostly through the air, and very little on the earth, which he has to touch while taking leaps one after another. प्रयत्नप्रेक्षणीयः–To be seen with effort. उद्घातिनी–Bumpy, giving shocks, causing jolting (of the chariot). The reading उत्खातिनी–would mean 'Having ups and downs, uneven.' विप्रकृष्टान्तरः–विप्रकृष्टं अन्तरं यस्य सः–Separated by a long interval or distance.

I. 8. निरायतपूर्वकायाः–नितरां आयतः पूर्वकायः येषाम्–the fore-part of whose bodies has been fully stretched out. निष्कम्पचामरशिखाः–निष्कम्पाः चामराणां शिखा येषाम्–With the (decorative) chowrie–crests (between the two ears) standing motionless. The great speed taken by the horses had made them stiff and unmoving. Cf. चित्रारम्भविनिश्चलं हयशिरस्यायामवच्चामरम् । विक्र॰ I. 4. निभृतोर्ध्वकर्णाः–With their ears erect (ऊर्ध्व) and steady (निभृत).

P. 8. आत्मोद्धतैः Raised (उद्धत) by themselves. Pischel reads–स्वेषामपि प्रसरतां रजसामलभ्याः ।. मृग...मया मृगजवस्य अक्षमया।–Out of impatience. or intolerant jealousy of the deer's speed. For this line Pischel reads–धावन्ति वर्त्मनि तरन्ति नु वाजिनस्ते । " These horses, they gallop on the road, no, (I should say) they swim along. " हरितः–Acc. plu. of हरित् a bay horse of the sun. हरिः–A horse of Indra.

I. 9. This verse gives a realistic description of the king's experience in a fast–moving chariot—an experience, the like of which every one gets while going in a train. अर्धे विच्छिन्न cut in half; Note V. L. अद्धा विच्छिन्नं ' really (अद्धा) disconnected कृतसंधानम्–कृतं संधानं यस्य तत् which is joined. समरेखम्–समा रेखा यस्य तद्–Straight. बाणपथवर्तिनः–standing within the range (पथ) of the arrow. V. L. बाणपातवर्तिनः which is not good.

I. 10. संनिपात्यः–which should be allowed to descend upon. पुष्पराशौ V. L. तूलराशौ. The reading पुष्पराशौ–is to be preferred. क्व...क्व–implies great incongruity between the two viz. the frail tender life of the deer and the hard-hitting arrows. अतिलोलम्–Extremely frail. निशितानिपाताः–निशितः निपातः येषाम्–coming down with piercing sharpness. वज्रसाराः–वज्रस्य इव सारः येषाम् ते–Having the strength (सार) of a thunderbolt.

I. 11. आर्तत्राणाय–For the protection (त्राण) of the distressed (आर्त) अनागसि–Loc. Sing. of अनागस्–' One who has not offended, harmless, innocent.

युक्तरूपम्-अतिशयेन युक्तं-युक्तरूपम् । 'प्रशंसायां रूपम् प्रत्ययः' highly befitting. अनुमालिनीतीरम्=मालिनीनदीतीरे ; 'विभक्त्यर्थेऽव्ययीभावः। On the bank of the Mālini river. अन्य...पात-अन्यकार्यस्य अतिपातः-A transgression of other (more important) duty, आतिथेयः-अतिथिषु साधुः-good for guests, cf. पथ्यतिथिवसतिस्वपतेर्ढञ्। पा० सू०

I. 13. प्रतिहतविघ्नाः-The disturbance from which has been removed. मौर्वीकिणाङ्कः (भुजः)-मौर्व्याः किणः अङ्कं यस्य सः-Having a mark of the bow-string (मौर्वी). दैवं प्रतिकूलं शमयितुम्-Herein we get the first inkling of the tragic situation in V Act. सोमतीर्थम्-modern प्रभास, acc. to some, a holy place in the Kathiawar, near the temple of Somnāth. Others, however, locate it near Pānipat, 'between कुरुक्षेत्र and गंगाह्रद, a holy place near कुरुक्षेत्र.' P. 12 आभोगः-Premises, precincts.

I. 14. शुक...भ्रष्टाः-शुकाः गर्भे येषाम्-तादृशानां कोटराणां मुखेभ्यः भ्रष्टाः-dropped down from the mouths of the hollowtrunks with parrots inside. इङ्गुदीफलभिदः-used in crushing the Ingudi fruit. This fruit was commonly used by the ascetics for extracting oil, which was used for lamps and also for toilet. अभिन्नगतयः without breaking their (slow) gait into a run. They are not disturbed by the noise of the chariot, because of the sence of security created in them by the affectionate behaviour of the sages. तोयाधारपथाः-The paths leading to the reservoirs of water. वल्कल... ङ्किताः-वल्कलानां शिखाभ्यः यः निष्यदः, तस्य याः रेखाः, ताभिः अङ्किताः (°पथाः)-Marked by the lines of dripping water from the fringes (शिखाः) of the barkgarments.

I. 15. कुल्यांभोभिः-by the waters of canals (कुल्या). धौतमूलाः-with their roots washed (धौत). किसलयरुचां रागः भिन्नः-The red tint of sprouts is diversified. The smoke has partially obscured the red lustre. अर्वाक्-अग्रतः-In front, near. छिन्नदर्भाङ्कुरायां, where the stalks of Darbha grass have been mown (by the grazing fawns). नष्टाशङ्काः-Free from timidity (आशङ्का). This fine verse has been rejected by annotators like Ray, on the ground that it does not suit the context, and gives a repetition of the features already noted in the preceding verse. The latter describes, however, the तपोवनाभोग, or the precincts of the forest-grove. May we not suppose that the king has moved on further in his chariot, and has now come nearer the hermitage, though not actually in it, and that in this verse he describes the features of the vicinity of the hermitage ? The verse has this justification and should not be rejected.

उपरोध:–Disturbance. The hermits are sure to be disturbed in their daily routine by the unusual advent of the king in his chariot. प्रग्रहा:–Reins. P. 14. विनीतवेषेण–In a dress of a humble ordinary gentleman ; दुष्यन्त would not like to enter as a king in state having a gaudy attire, but as an ordinary gentleman. Note his regard for the feelings of ascetics. आर्द्रपृष्ठा:–Lit. 'wet-backed' i. e. watered and refreshed. निमित्तं–An omen ; it is the throbbing of the right arm, which, in the case of man, indicates union with a beautiful woman.

I. 16. The king means that a tranquil hermitage is certainly the last place where such romantic omens prove effective ; and yet, who knows, how fate will work to find out openings for predestined events. They are to be had everywhere. भवितव्यानाम्— of things or events that are to happen. दक्षिणेन वृक्षवाटिकां–To the right of the grove of trees. दक्षिणेन governs the accusative as also the genitive. Cf. एनपा द्वितीया । एनपेति योगविभागात् षष्ठ्यपि । दक्षिणेन ग्रामं ग्रामस्य वा । स्वप्रमाणानुरूपै:–Suited to their own size or stature (प्रमाण) ; or better still 'suited to their strength' Cf. पयोघटैराश्रमबालवृक्षान् संवर्धयन्ती स्वबलानुरूपै: । रघु० XIV. 78. पयो दातुम्–Cf. the Marathi idiom पाणी देणें.

I. 17. The king gives expression to his feelings of wonder and admiration in a figurative manner. He never expected such beauty of form to reside in forests, their proper resort being the secluded harem in the city, where alone, like creepers in a garden, beauty is developed and nourished. If, therefore, such forms are met with in the woodland retreats, then it clearly signifies a defeat of the garden-creepers by the forest ones, untended and uncared for by human beings, as they are. शुद्धान्तः-Harem. दूरीकृताः-Surpassed, excelled. The figure is निदर्शना, which is defined as अभवन्वस्तुसंबन्ध उपमापरिकल्पकः ।

P. 16. नव...पेलवा-Delicate (पेलवा) like a Jasmine flower. आलवालं-A basin. सोदरस्नेहः-A sisterly affection असाधुदर्शी-one who sees not aright; wanting in discrimination.

I. 18. The king explains why कण्व, according to him, lacks discretion. अव्याजमनोहरं-Artlessly (अव्याजं) beautiful. तपःक्षमं-Fit to undergo penance. शमीलता-The शमी tree, which is very tough, and which is supposed to conceal fire within. Cf. शमीमिवाभ्यन्तरलीनपावकाम् । रघु० III. 9. This verse is a fine example of निदर्शना. अतिपिनद्धेन-fastened too tightly. पिनद्ध P. P. of √अपि+नह् पयोधरविस्तारयितृ-which swells the bosom.

P. 18. I. 19. The king means that the bark-garment is not a fitting apparel for such a lovely form whose charms are definitely marred by it. उप...ग्रन्थिना-secured with delicate knots (ग्रन्थि). स्तन...च्छादिना-covering the fully developed orbs of her two breasts. अभिनवं-Fresh, in her prime of youth. स्वां शोभां न पुष्यति-does not develop the fulness of its own charms. पाण्डु...दरेण पिनद्धं-Enveloped by a calyx (उदर) of pale (पाण्डु) leaves. अथवा-The particle introduces the other alternative, or पक्षान्तर. काम...पुष्यति-In the preceding verse, he has given it as his opinion that she does not look charming with the bark-garment on. He changes his mind, and reverts to the other alternative. 'Although the bark-garment is certainly not a suitable apparel for such a form, I cannot say that in her case it does not heighten her physical charm; indeed she does look beautiful even with a bark-garment.'

I. 20. शैवलेन अनुविद्धम्-Intertwined or overspread with moss (शैवल, Cf. Mar शेवाळें). लक्ष्मन n.-the speck or spot. लक्ष्मीं तनोति-

Increases the glory. मनोज्ञा–Lovely, charming. Lit. मनो जानाति सा–One who knows the mind; a clever, attractive woman. मण्डनम्–Decoration, ornament, embellishment. This is a fine illustration of अर्थान्तरन्यास, wherein we get a generalisation based upon particular instances or vice versa. वाते...लीभिः-वातेन ईरिताः पल्लवाः एव अङ्गुल्यः-ताभिः–With his sprout-like fingers moved by the breeze. संभावयामि–I shall honour him (by granting his request). The suggestion, in this sentence, is that of a loving friend beckoning her to come near and do him a good turn. Cf. इदं चैकदेशविवर्ति रूपकम् । तेन केसरवृक्षस्य वयस्यत्वमपि रूपितं भवति । तेनायमर्थः । यथा कश्चन सखाऽत्यन्तमुत्कण्ठितोऽङ्गुलीचालनेन मित्रं त्वरयति तद्वदिति । Com. लतासनाथः–In the company (सनाथ) of a creeper. शकुन्तला is imagined to be a creeper, and the two together thus present the sight of a pretty couple. This idea lends greater charm if we believe that दुष्यन्त is standing just behind the केसर tree all along, and was associated with the tree in beckoning her to him and grant him his request. प्रियंवदा–one who talks sweet.

I. 21. शकुन्तला was likened to a creeper, and the idea has caught the king's fancy. He, therefore, tries to analyse her charms to see in what respects they agree with the creeper's charms. किसलयरागः-किसलयस्य इव रागः यस्य सः—Having the red glow of a tender sprout (किसलय). कोमल...कारिणौ–Resembling tender twigs (विटप). लोभनीयं–Alluring, covetable, bewitching. अङ्गेषु संनद्धम्–Pervades her limbs, is fully developed in all parts of the body; 'is arrayed in the limbs'–Ray. अत्राङ्गेष्विति बहुवचनेन वदने कान्तिमत्ता नयनयोस्तरलता कण्ठे कम्बुत्रिरेखावत्त्वं वक्षसि स्तनोज्जृम्भणं नाभौ गभीरता नितम्बे मध्यनिम्नत्वमुभयभागे चतुरस्रत्वं जघनजङ्घाजानुमण्डलोरुदेशानां मांसलत्वं गतौ सविलासत्वमित्यादि ध्वनितम् ।

P. 20. स्वयंवरवधूः-स्वयं वृणीते इति स्वयंवरा-सा च वधूश्च–who has elected herself to be the (bride of the Mango tree), self-elected. कृतनामधेया–Named. कृतं नामधेयं यस्याः सा । Cf. मिथुनं परिकल्पितं त्वया सहकारः फलिनी च नन्विमौ । अविधाय विवाहसत्क्रियामनयोर्गम्यत इत्यसांप्रतम् ॥ रघु॰ VIII. 61. व्यतिकरः–Union, blending, intertwining, intermingling.

अपि नाम–would that ! How I wish that ! एष नूनं...मनोरथाः–The joke of प्रियंवदा has really gone home, and hence such a reply. For we cannot believe that Śakuntalā had no such romantic thoughts of love and union. Her appreciation of the pretty couple of the सहकार and वनजोत्स्ना clearly indicates how in her mind youthful charm is associated with the pleasure of union. असवर्ण...भवा–असवर्णं क्षेत्रं संभवः यस्याः सा–Born of a wife belonging to a caste not his own; sprung from a wife dissimilar in caste. If शकुन्तला were कण्व's daughter born from a Brahmin wife, दुष्यन्त, a क्षत्रिय, cannot marry her as she is ineligible as क्षत्रिय's wife. If, on the other hand, she is his daughter sprung from a wife the क्षत्रिय class–a custom sanctioned in those days–then दुष्यन्त had no legal or religious difficulty in marrying her. Cf. मनु० III. 13. शूद्रैव भार्या शूद्रस्य सा च स्वा च विशः स्मृते । ते च स्वा चैव राज्ञश्च ताश्च स्वा चाग्रजन्मनः ॥

I. 22. क्षत्र...क्षमा–क्षत्रस्य परिग्रहः (कलत्रत्वेन अङ्गीकारः)–तस्य क्षमा (योग्या)–Fit to be accepted as a wife by a क्षत्रिय. आर्यं मनः–My noble heart, my honourable soul. अभिलाषि–filled with a longing. सतां हि etc. The meaning is 'That I was conscious of a sudden liking for her is a clean proof of the fact that she is eligible for me a क्षत्रिय ; since such a feeling of sympathy could only arise towards a legitimate object. The inner voice or the secret prompting of the heart is always decisive, in the case of men of a higher and nobler mind.' तत्वतः–In reality, in her true nature. उपलप्स्ये–ज्ञास्ये–I shall ascertain. P. 22 सलिल...द्रुतः–dislodged by the disturbance caused in the sprinkling of water.

I. 23. प्रेरितलोलल्लोचना–प्रेरिते लोले लोचने यया– Directing her tremulous eyes. विवर्तितभ्रूः–who has bent or curved her eye-brows (through fear). अकामा–uninfluenced by love. The poet means that the coquettish movements of the eyes are due to the inspiration of amorous feelings. In the case of शकुन्तला, that was impossible. It appears, however, that she is taking lessons in that art, which she has very soon to exhibit. दृष्टिविभ्रमः–The playful movements of the eyes.

I. 24. The king is jealous of the bee and addresses this verse to him who is taking so much liberty with her. The bee is represented as an aggressive lover, having no scruples, and paying little heed to the delicate sentiments of his beloved. Such a type has succeeded, however, while he, a cool calculating rational lover is left in the lurch to witness their amours taking place before his very eyes. चलापाङ्गां (दृष्टिं)–चलः अपाङ्गः (प्रान्तभागः) यस्याः सा ताम्–With its tremulous outer corner. वेपथुमतीम्–Trembling, possessed of a tremor (वेपथुः) रहस्याख्यायीव etc. Cf. कर्णे लोलः कथयितुमभूदाननस्पर्शलोभात् । मेघ० II. रतिसर्वस्वं–(the lip) which has the all-in-all of amorous pleasure. व्याधुन्वत्याः (अस्याः) of her who is waving (her hand). Pres. Part. of √ वि + आ + धु–तत्वान्वेषात्–In our attempt to ascertain the truth viz. the real character of शकुन्तला. Cf. तथापि तत्त्वत एनामुपलप्स्ये । हताः–Undone, ruined, frustrated (in our desires). कृती–कृतं यस्यास्तीति–One who has done i. e. accomplished his purpose; successful. धृष्टः–P. P. of √धृष्–Impudent, presumptuous. The Prākrit is धिट्ठो, corresponding to the Marathi धीट. दुर्विनीत–ill-trained, ill-behaved. अभिभूयमानाम्–Being assailed or overpowered. के आवां परित्रातुं–' who are we to protect? We are as weak and helpless as you are'. Apparently they make slight of the fright of शकुन्तला caused by a mere bee.

P. 24. I. 25. पौरवे शासति (सति)–Loc. Absolute construction. ' While a descendant of Puru is governing.' Note how he refers to himself in an indirect manner. कोऽयमविनयं आचरति–'Who is this that practises rudeness.' The king tries to show that he had just come on the scene, having casually heard of Śakuntalā's cry, and that he knew nothing of the bee episode. किंचिदिव संभ्रान्ताः–They are slightly confused, because the king entered as an ordinary humble man. अत्याहितं–A great calamity or danger. अपि तपो वर्धते--'Does your piety thrive?' This was a regular form of salutation on meeting a Brahmin. साध्वसात्-Through nervous excitement. अवचना-Without speaking a word. Note that throughout the whole interview, she has not exchanged one single word with the king. इदानीं...लम्भेन-When Śakuntalā gave no reply to the king's question, she has filled in the gap by coming forward to answer the king's question. " Yes ; now indeed, does Tapas prosper by the acquisition of a distinguished guest. " Observe how Anasūyā, elderly and senior amongst the three, directs the interview on their side. अर्घ or अर्घ्यम्-A respectful offering to a guest of rice, Dūrvā grass, flowers, fruit etc. with water in a small boat-shaped vessel. ' The rites of hospitality were enforced amongst the Hindus by very stringent regulations. The observance of them ranked as one of the five great sacraments (महायज्ञ) under the title of नृयज्ञ or मनुष्ययज्ञ, the man-sacrament.' Brahmā, Prajāpati, Indra, Fire, the Vasus and the Sun were supposed to be present in the person of a guest and to partake of the food that was given to him. If a guest departed disappointed from any house, his sins were to be transferred to the house-holder, and all the merits of the house-holder were to be transferred to him. " Monier Williams. इदं (पादोदकं) This water (brought by us for watering the trees). सूनृतया गिरा-By your kind yet sincere language ; complimentary and friendly words without flattery. (प्रियं सत्यं च वचनम्). सप्तपर्णवेदिकायाम्-On the raised-seat under the सप्तपर्ण tree. It is quite an ancient custom to construct platforms or raised-seats (Cf. Mar. पार) round the trunk of big trees. परिश्रम-विनोद:-Removal of fatigue. पर्युपासनम्-Lit. sitting by the side, waiting upon. तपोवनविरोधिन: विकारस्य गमनीया-Susceptible to an emotion which is out of place in this forest-grove devoted to piety. A particular attraction she has felt for the king at his first sight and impulse the like of which she never felt for any man in the hermitage so far. This is the first awakening of love, which has unnerved and excited her a little. Innocent as she is, however, she is not able to explain her feeling. सम...रमणीयं-Pleasing because of equal age and beauty of form. सौहार्दम्-Friendship, abstract, noun from सुहृद्. P. 26. चतुरगम्भीराकृतिः-Possessed of a form, smart (चतुर) and dignified. प्रभाववान्-Possessed of majestic glory (प्रभाव). Pischel reads this sentence differently thus:—को णु क्खु एसो दुरवगाववगंभीराकिदी महुरं आलवंतो पहुत्तदक्खिण्णं वित्थारेदि । विरह...जनः (देशः)-विरहेण पर्युत्सुकाःजनाः यत्र-The people in which are left in anxiety on account of your separation. °परिश्रमस्य आत्मा पदं उपनीतः-' You have exposed yourself to the hardship of the journey, etc.' मा उत्ताम्य-' Be not impatient.' त्वया चिन्तितानि-She too was very eager to know these details about the king. She, however, kept silent, lest her emotion should be detected. आत्मापहारः-concealment of (my) identity. पौरवेण राज्ञा may as well refer to his father as to himself. He would like, however, to introduce himself as king Dusyanta's official, appointed to supervise the penance-forests and guard them from disturbances. In case he is found out to be the king, it is open to him to say, that in speaking thus about himself he has not spoken a lie because had not his father entrusted him with the sacred duty of looking after the sages ? सनाथाः-Possessed of a lord and protector (नाथ). A very clever suggestion is made by अनसूया in this her remark—सनाथा इदानीं धर्मचारिणः । शकुन्तला devoted to the observance of piety, has now found one who could be a नाथ-also meaning ' husband ' to her. This शकुन्तला fully understands, and hence the stage-remark शकुन्तला शृङ्गारलज्जां निरूपयति । आकारं विदित्वा-Understanding the gestures of both who appeared to be enamoured of each other. आकार-means ' the outward appearance, accompanied with various gestures, which indicates the inner state of mind. जीवितसर्वस्वेन-With the all-in-all, the most valuable treasure of his life, i. e. Śakuntalā. Cf. सा भगवतः कण्वस्य कुलपतेरुच्छ्वसितम् । Act III. Anasūyā suggests that their mutual love is apparent; and if only father काश्यप had been here, this guest would have been made happy with the gift of शकुन्तला.

P. 28. युवां अपेतम्-' Get off with you!' As a girl would say in Marathi. चला चालत्या व्हा ! सखीगतं-About or relating to (गतं) your friend. Cf. आत्मगतम् ।. शाश्वते ब्रह्मणि-In perpetual celibacy (ब्रह्मणि = ब्रह्मचर्ये). तदात्मजा–तस्य (कण्वस्य) आत्मजा–His own daughter ; born of himself. गोत्रनामधेयः–गोत्रेण नामधेयं यस्य सः–Having a family name of कौशिक. i. e. The famous royal sage विश्वामित्र. किमपि जातशङ्कैः–Frightened, for what reason we cannot tell (किमपि). अन्यसमाधिभीरुत्वं The dread of the devotion (समाधि) of others. वसन्तोदारसमये–' During the charming (उदार) Spring–time. Prākrit expression वसंतोदारसमए may also be translated as वसन्तावतारसमये–' During the season of the advent of spring'. उन्मादयितृ–Maddening, exhilerating.

P. 30 I. 26. मानुषीषु–Amongst mortal females. प्रभातरलं ज्योतिः–The tremulously radiant–flash i. e. lightning. लब्धावकाशः–लब्धः अवकाशः येन–Which has found scope (अवकाश). He has ascertained now that she is eligible, and therefore he feels he could entertain a desire for her hand. धृत...कातरं–धृतः द्वैधीभावः–तेन कातरम्–Nervous or anxious because of the suspense. The king refers to what प्रियंवदा said before, viz. अपि नामैवमहमप्यात्मनोऽनुरूपं वरं लभेयेति ।, and he apprehends the possibility of her marriage having been not only contemplated but perhaps fixed up already. Hence, says he, his mind is in suspense. वक्तुकामः–वक्तुं कामः यस्य सः–With a desire to speak. This was more or less intended to tease Śakuntalā, and hence the stage-remark 'शकुन्तला सखीमङ्गुल्या तर्जयति । सच्चरित...लोभात्–' out of a keen desire to hear the life of the pious people.' Really speaking, the king only wanted to know whether Śakuntalā was likely to be married, and if so, to whom. अनि...योगः–न विद्यते नियन्त्रणा यस्य–तादृशः अनुयोगः यस्य सः (तपस्विजनः)–To whom a question (अनुयोग) may be asked without any restraint or reserve (नियंत्रणा).

I. 27. वैखानसं–Relating to a विखानस or hermit. तेन कृतं प्रोक्तं वा व्रतं वैखानसं, तत्तु नियतारण्यवासरूपम् । 'A vow which is performed by him or enjoined on him is called वैखानस, and that consists in always living in the woods.' आप्रदानात्–प्रदानपर्यन्तम् i. e. आविवाहात्–Up to the period of her marriage. मदनस्य

व्यापाररोधि कामाकथानिवारकम्-Prohibiting indulgence in the ways of love. अत्यन्तम्-For all time, for ever. आत्म...वल्लभाभिः (हरिणाङ्गनाभिः)-dear (वल्लभा) to her because of their eyes like her own (आत्मसदृश). आत्मसदृशे ईक्षणे यासां ताः °क्षणाः-अत एव वल्लभाः-ताभिः । It may be optionally resolved into आत्मसदृशेक्षणवल्लभा: आभिः । In that case it would mean 'with these (female deer), of whom she is a favourite for having eyes like their own. आहो-A particle of doubt, is used पक्षान्तरे or विकल्पे i. e. antithetically, in stating an opposite alternative. परवशः-dependent on another, under the control of another i. e. the sage कण्व. संकल्पः-Intention, thought. दुःखापा-Difficult to obtain. दुःखेन अवाप्तुं शक्या । प्रार्थना Desire, longing (for शकुन्तला).

I. 28 स्पर्शक्षमं-That bears a touch, fit to be touched. He means the lustre of this gem-like शकुन्तला first dazzled his eyes, and made him suspect that she was beyond his reach and like fire must remain untouched by human hands. It transpires now that he can reasonably covet her hand, which if touched will not only not burn him, but will prove a veritable Kohinoor in his possession.

P. 32 असंबद्धप्रलापिनी-Prattling nonsense or absurdly (असंबद्ध). She refers to the action of प्रियंवदा in volunteering information regarding her marriage etc. स्वच्छन्दतः-At (your) sweet will. ग्रहीतु...त्मानम्-V. L. उत्थाय जिघृक्षुरिव इच्छां निगृह्य-' Rising up as if desirous of holding her (and then) restraining his intention.' चेष्टाप्रतिरूपिका प्रतिगतं रूपं अस्यां सा प्रतिरूपा-प्रतिरूपा एव प्रतिरूपिका-A reflector, a counter-part. चेष्टा प्रतिरूपिका यस्याः सा-रूपिका (कामि...वृत्तिः) Having a physical action (चेष्टा) for its counter-part; presenting itself as reflected in a physical action. As the stage-direction informs us, when शकुन्तला left the place, the king almost felt impelled by an inward powerful impulse, to go after her and bring her back. That would have looked highly improper and absurd, if not actually indecent. He has therefore restrained himself, and in his cooler moment, reviews what happened a few seconds before. The mental inclination of a lover is found reflected in a physical action. 'The desire to restrain शकुन्तला was so powerful that I feel what I desired has been actually translated in physical action (चेष्टा).'

I. 29. अनुयास्यन्–Future Part. of √अनु + या–'About to or on the point of following.' वारितप्रसर :–वारितः प्रसरः यस्य सः–Whose movement was checked. वृक्षसेचने–'Two waterings of trees.' 'You owe me the labour, according to our agreement, of watering two more shrubs.' The delicate शकुन्तला, on a former occasion, could not complete the watering of a certain number of trees, fixed for each one of them. प्रियंवदा, therefore, helped her, on the understanding that शकुन्तला was to pay back, on demand, this debt of labour. Very cleverly therefore, प्रियंवदा has thought of that, with a view to detain her on this pretext, when even Anasūyā's reasoning of propriety failed to stop her. आत्मानं मोचयित्वा–Releasing yourself (from this debt).

I. 30. अति...तलौ (बाहू)–With the palms (तलौ) excessively red (लोहित). प्रमाणाधिकः–स्वाभाविकमानादधिकः–More than usual or natural; abnormal P. 34. बद्धम्–formed. जालकम्–Lit. A net-work, a collection. Cf. तस्य कर्कशविहारसंभवं स्वेदमाननविलग्नजालकम् । रघु० IX. 68. बन्धे स्रंसिनि–The knot (binding the hair) getting loose. पर्याकुल–Dishevelled. अनृणा–Free from debt.–(अविद्यमानं ऋणं यस्याः सा). परिग्रहः–V. L. प्रतिग्रहः–A gift. राजपुरुषं...गच्छथ–He means that the ring should not be taken as evidence for his identity as दुष्यन्त. It is a gift he has received in his capacity as a राजपुरुष, which would thus have a two-fold meaning. राजपुरुष–(i) राज्ञः पुरुषः–A King's official. (ii) राजा चासौ पुरुषश्च–A royal person, which दुष्यन्त is, while the ring he obtained was a gift from his kingly father. अथवा महाराजेन shows clearly that the king has not succeeded in deceiving प्रियंवदा at least. यद्यात्मनः...प्रभविष्यामि–She means that the king's company has so much hypnotised her that she has no power left over her body to move away. Cf. भवतु कोपिष्यामि यद्यात्मनः प्रभवामि । उत्तर० I. विस्रष्टव्यस्य रोद्धव्यस्य वा–(To decide) what should be allowed to go and what should be restrained.

I. 31. कर्णं ददाति— i. e. अवहिता, तत्परा अस्ति–is very attentive. Cf. Mar. कान देते. अन्यविषया–अन्यः विषयः यस्याः सा–Having a different object (to observe).

P. 36. I. 32. विटप...वल्कलेषु (० द्रुमेषु)–विटपेषु विषक्तानि जलार्द्राणि वल्कलानि येषां तेषु । (The trees) on the branches of which were suspended (विषक्त) the bark garments wet with water. परि...प्रकाशः (रेणुः)–Shining (प्रकाश) like the twilight glow. अरुण्य is the glow either of sun–rise or sun–set, more usually the former.

I. 33. स्कन्ध...दन्तः–स्कन्धे लग्नः एकदन्तः यस्य–One of whose tusks was fixed in a tree–trunk. The Bengali Mss. read तीव्राघातादभिमुखतरुस्कन्धभग्नैकदन्तः । ' with a violent blow, having broken one tusk against the trunk of a tree standing in his way. ' पादा...पाशः–पादेन आकृष्टानि व्रततिवलयानि–तेषां आसङ्गेन संजातः पाशः यस्य सः–with fetters formed by the clinging (आसङ्ग) of creeper–coils dragged along by his feet. आरण्यकवृत्तान्तेन–By this forest incident viz. of the wild–elephant. असंभा...सत्कारं–To whom the due (rites of) hospitality were not profferred. पुरस्कृतः–सत्कृतः—Hospitably entertained; received. कुशसूचिः–The needle–like point of the Kuśa grass. परिपालयत–wait. सव्याजम्–With some pretext (व्याज) For lingering. Cf. अहो लता विटपे ममैकावली लग्ना । विक्र० I.

P. 38 मन्दौत्सुक्यः–मन्दं औत्सुक्यं यस्य सः–Whose eagerness (to return) has slackened ; grown indifferent. अनुयात्रिक–A follower. निवेशयामि–Causal of √ नि + विश्–meaning ' to enter, to take up a station, to encamp ' as an army. शकुन्तला०व्यापारात्–From busying or occupying myself with thoughts regarding शकुन्तला.

I. 34. असंस्तुतं–अपरिचितं–Unacquainted, unrelated. He means, the connection between the mind and the body is severed as it were, both going in diverse ways and not working in harmony. The word also means अवश i. e. not under the control (of the body); V. L. असंस्थितं meaning ' restless, unstable. ' चीनांशुकं–A silken cloth from China. Even in those days, there was great export of silk from China. प्रतिवातं–Against the wind–current.

ACT II

P. 40. भो दिष्टम्–'Oh my (evil) destiny, my fate!' Some translate दिट्ठं by दृष्टं, to mean almost the same thing, दृष्ट and अदृष्ट being two kinds of fate, one referring to its visible working, and the other to its secret or invisible working. निर्विण्णः–Tired, disgusted. वयस्यभावः–Friendship. शार्दूलः–A tiger. आहिण्ड्यते–Pres. Passive, III sing. of √आ + हिण्ड्–'to wander about'. पत्रसंकरकषायाणि–Astringent (कषाय) from the mixture (संकर) of leaves. कटूनि–Pungent, bad-smelling. अनियतवेलम्–न नियता वेला यस्मिन् कर्मणि यथा तथा–At irregular hours. शूल्यमांसभूयिष्ठः–mostly consisting of roast-meat, i.e. meat cooked or roasted on spits. शूल्य is explained as शूले संस्कृतम्। तुरगा...सन्धेः–with my joints bruised or dislocated (कण्डित) by having to ride in pursuit on horse-back. निकामं शयितव्यम्–enough sleep, comfortable lying down (in bed). महति प्रत्यूषे–At the very earliest (महति) dawn. Cf. Mar. मोठ्या पहांटेस. दास्याः पुत्रैः–is the same as दासीपुत्रैः, being one compound. The genitive in this compound is used in reviling and abusing (आक्रोशे). शकुनिलुब्धकः–Bird-hunter, a fowler. वनग्रहणं–Beating the forest; surrounding and taking possession of a wood for the purpose of hunting the animals it contains. इयता–एतावता–'with this much'. गण्डस्य...संवृत्ता–Note this Sanskrit idiom. It means 'A small boil or a pimple (पिण्डिका or पिटका) has grown on the (old) boil (गण्ड).' पिण्डिका or according to some पिटका means 'a pustule, a pimple, a small boil.' Cf. 'To add misery to misfortune.' अवहीनेषु–पश्चात् पतितेषु–Left behind; dropped behind. अधन्यतया–Through ill–luck or misfortune. मनः न करोति–Does not form or fix up his mind. अक्ष्णोः प्रभातमासीत्–i.e. जाग्रतः एव or दृशोः उन्मीलतोः सतोः रजनी निर्गता। The day dawned on his eyes (wide awake). कृता...क्रमं–कृतः आचारप्राप्तः परिक्रमः येन सः–who has finished the usual or customary routine (of the morning duties). V. L. °परिकर्माणम्–परिकर्म–Toilet, decoration after bath! बाणासनं–शरासनं–A bow. यवनी–A native woman of यवन or Arabia.

The word is also applied to the Greek or Ionian maiden. Wilson remarks that Tartarian or Bactrian women may be intended. The business of these attendants was to act as the bearers of the king's bow and arrows, and during war-time, she gives weapons to the king. अङ्गभङ्गविकलः—Crippled by palsy or paralysis of the limbs.

P. 42. II. 1. तद्भाव...श्वासि – Deriving encouragement from the observance of her gestures. V. L. °दर्शनायासि—' Exerting to observe her (favourable) gestures' is not so good, as it implies that the favourable indication in the form of gestures may not exist, in which case, whatever he says later on—' स्मितं कृत्वा...स्वतां पश्यति, has no proper justification, based as these remarks are on the assumption of the existence of the favourable gestures. अकृतार्थे मनसिजे—Even if love has not achieved its object viz. union with the beloved. उभयप्रार्थना—Longing for both, love felt by both. रतिं कुरुते–gives delight; Cf. अनातुरोत्कण्ठितयोः प्रसिध्यता समागमेनापि रतिर्न मां प्रति। परस्परप्राप्तिनिराशयोर्वरं शरीरनाशोऽपि समानुरागयोः॥ माल० III. 15. आत्मा...वृत्तिः (प्रार्थयिता)—आत्मनः आभिप्रायेण संभाविता इष्टजनस्य चित्तवृत्तिः येन सः—Who judges of the state of feeling of his beloved one, by his own desires (अभिप्राय). विडम्ब्यते—Is deluded (to find that he was wandering in a fool's paradise.)

II. 2. स्निग्धं—Adverb going with वीक्षितं—Tenderly, softly, full of love. विलासादिव—As if through dalliance. It is one of the Bhāvās caused by love and is thus explained:—विलासोऽङ्गे विकारो यः प्रियाप्तावासनादिषु। मा गाः–' Do not go.' गाः–Aorist form √ इ, with the augment dropped because of the particle मा. उपरुद्धया–V. L. अवरुद्धया. By her who was obstructed. सासूयम्–Angrily, disdainfully. मत्परायणम्–अहमेव परं अयनं यस्य तत्। Chiefly meant for me. He means that all these gestures like the soft look, the graceful slow gait, the disdainful remark were all intended for me, to convey to me her inner feeling. अहो–denotes wonder (आश्चर्यं). कामी स्वतां पश्यति–How a lover sees himself everywhere. In every movement of his beloved, he tries to discover the influence of his own love. न प्रसरति–Do not move i. e. are paralysed. वाङ्मात्रेण–By words merely (and not by the usual Anjali, or the joining of two hands and raising them to the forehead). जाप्यसे–Causal, Pass. II sing. of √ जि. स्वयं...पृच्छसि. विदूषक–speaks by a turn of the speech, probably quoting some proverb. The Com. शंकर explains it thus:—यथा कोऽपि कस्यचिन्नयनयोरङ्गुल्यादिकं प्रवेश्य पृच्छति, 'भवतश्चक्षुषोरश्रु कथमायाति तथा त्वमपि पृच्छसि। भिन्नार्थम्–स्फुटार्थम्–Distinctly, clearly; V. L. वेतसः—Reed; कुब्जलीलाम्–The gait or character of the hunch-backed, कुब्ज means 'hump-backed (cf. Mar. कुबडा); it is also a name for a crooked aquatic plant, also called वारि° or जलकुब्ज. 'To appreciate विदूषक's pleasantry in comparing himself to an upright reed, accidentally transformed into a crooked plant, we must bear in mind that his natural form was that of a lame hump-backed man. '–Monier Williams. विडम्बयति–Imitates, copies. P. 44. आकुलप्रदेशे–In a wild region. Some read in addition अमानुषसंचारे–' Unfrequented.' यत्सत्यं–To tell you the truth, to speak the truth. सन्धिबन्धः–' The tendon or ligament binding the joints together.' अनीशः–अप्रभुः–Not a master, i. e. one who has lost all control. प्रसादयिष्यामि–Causal, Future I sing. of √ प्र+ सद्. It means 'I beg of you to favour me.' मृगयाविक्लवं–Disinclined or averse to hunting.

II. 3. आहितसायकम्–आहितः सायकः यस्मिन्–With an arrow (सायक) fixed upon it मुग्धविलोकित–A lovely glance. अरण्ये...सीत्–(It means:) I have cried in wilderness (where nobody listens or replies); a kind of a proverbial phrase. Cf. तदलमधुनारण्यरुदितैः। अमरु॰ 76. अनतिक्रमणीयं–which cannot be set aside or disregarded सावशेषम्–अवशेषेण सहितं–With a remnant, with something left (unspoken yet). अनायासे (कर्मणि)–न विद्यते आयासः यस्मिन्–Where no physical exertion is involved, which would give no physical trouble. मोदकखण्डिका–Bits of sweet–meats. V. L. मोदकखादिकायाम्–' In eating sweet-meats.' सुगृहीतः क्षणः–I have pledged my word, I accept the invitation. ' The phrase has origin in a formula; used in connection with the श्राद्ध ceremony. A Brahmin is duly invited to attend the ceremony, and he uses this expression, when he accepts the invitation. गृहीत्वामुकसंज्ञस्यामुकगोत्रस्य चामुके । श्राद्धे तु वैश्वदेवार्थं करणीयः क्षणस्त्वया ॥ इत्येवं श्राद्धकृद् ब्रूयात् तं प्राप्नोतु भवानिति। स वदेत् प्राप्नवानीतीतरस्तं प्रति द्विजः ॥ Cited by Pandit from शौनक॰ 16.—' The person who addresses in the words of the formula (the श्राद्धकृत्) is said to give the क्षण, and the Brahmin to whom it is addressed) to take the क्षण, in the language of ignorant priests. Hence because the word क्षण is so often used in the formula, so has come, in the common parlance of Brahmanas, who subsist mostly upon, occasional dinners at Śrāddhas, and to which class our विदूषक belonged, to signify 'an engagement at Srāddha, which, when once begun, must be carried out, on pain of incurring sin.' It may be observed that Vidūṣaka's way of expressing his obligation to accomplish what he has undertaken is perfectly in keeping with his character. 'क्षण घेणें' is still used in Marathi in the sense of 'pledging one's self for the performance of a thing'– Pandit.

P. 46. आज्ञावचनोत्कण्ठः–eager (to speak out) words of command. दृष्टदोषा–दृष्टाः दोषाः यस्यां सा (मृगया)। Found fault with, observed to have evil effects. मृगया is looked as one of the ten vices which a king has to avoid. Cf. पानमक्षाः स्त्रियश्चैव मृगया च यथाक्रमम् । एतत्कष्टतमं विद्याच्चतुष्कं कामजे गणे ॥ मनु॰ VII. 50.

II. 4. अनवरत...पूर्वं (गात्रं)–अनवरतं धनुर्ज्यायाः आस्फालनं तेन क्रूरः पूर्वः (पूर्वभागः) यस्य तत्–The fore-part of which was tough because of the incessant friction (आस्फालन) of the bow-string. सहिष्णु–capable of enduring. Read क्लेशलेशैः–By the slightest fatigue. The reading स्वेद° is possibly a misreading of खेद in the Mss. अपचितम्–Reduced in bulk व्यायतत्वात्–कृतव्यायामत्वात्–दृढत्वात्–Because of the muscular development; व्यायाम–coming from the same root means this. प्राणसारं (गात्रं)–which is all life and energy. प्राणः सारः स्थिरांशः यत्र तत्–with vatality alone left behind. अपवादिन्–one who speaks ill. or censures. स्थिरप्रतिबन्धः–Persisting in opposition, persevering in throwing obstacles in the way. वैधेयः–मूर्खः–A fool, blockhead.

निदर्शनम्–Illustration, example. Cf. हिमसेकविपत्तिरत्र मे नलिनी पूर्वनिदर्शनं मता ।

II. 5. मेद...दरं–मेदसः छेदेन कृशं उदरं यस्य तद्–With the waist attenuated by the cutting down of fat. उत्थानं–Activity, exertion. सत्वानाम्–जन्तूनां सिंहादीनाम्–of creatures. भयक्रोधयोः विकृतिमत् चित्तं–Their minds undergoing various changes (विकृति) or affected by various emotions under the influence of fear and anger. P. 48. उत्कर्षः Excellence, glory. चले लक्ष्ये सिध्यन्ति. Succeed in hitting a moving target. (लक्ष्यं). Men practising shooting will realise how difficult it is to shoot a moving target and what delight it gives when they succeed in doing so. उत्साहहेतुक–' one who incites or encourages one to action viz. hunting. ' प्रकृतिमापन्न–Has come back to his normal, healthy state of the mind, (hunting mood being looked upon as an aberration). प्रकृति is the natural quiescent state of the soul, as opposed to विकृति, explained above. जीर्णऋक्षस्य–of an old bear Cf. भल्लूका मनुष्याणां नासिकां गृह्णन्ति । दशकुमार०

II. 6. निपातं...आहावः–A reservoir or trough near a well. छाया...म्बकं–छायायां बद्धः कदम्बकः येन–Forming a group in the shade. रोमन्थः–भुक्तस्य पुनः पुनराकृष्य or उद्गीर्य चर्वणम्–Ruminating, chewing the cud. वराहततिभिः–By the herd (तति) of the boars. V. L. वराहपतिभिः ।. मुस्ताक्षतिः–Destroying or uprooting (क्षति) of the मुस्ता grass. ' मुस्ता–is a sort of fragrant grass, eaten by swine and hence are they called ' मुस्ताद. ' शिथिल...बन्धम्–शिथिलः ज्यायाः बन्धः यस्मिन्–With the bow-string loosened.

II. 7. शमप्रधानेषु–शमः प्रधानः येषाम् ते । °प्रधानाः तेषु–By whom self-control or exemption from all passion and feeling is regarded as the summum bonum or everything. स्पर्शानुकूल–agreeable to the touch. सूर्यकान्तः–The sun-gem, a shining stone, a sun-crystal. It is supposed to emit lustre, when touched by the sun's rays. Its properties thus resemble those of a glass lens. It is also called सूर्यमणि or दीप्तोपल ; and corresponding to it, there is the चन्द्रकान्त or चन्द्रमणि which is believed to be oozing drops of water when the moon's rays fall on it. Cf. यदचेतनोऽपि पादैः स्पृष्टः प्रज्वलति सवितुरतिकान्तः ।

तत्तेजस्वी पुरुषः परकृतनिकृतिं कथं सहते ॥ भर्तृ० ii. 30. अन्य...भवात् Through the opposition of other forces or lustre (तेजस्). वमन्ति–Emit. The root वम् 'to vomit' is one of those objectionable ones which should not be used in good poetry, unless in a secondary or figurative sense. Cf. निष्ठ्यूतोद्गीर्णवान्तानि गौणवृत्तिव्यपाश्रयम् । अतिसुन्दरमन्यत्र ग्राम्यकक्षां विगाहते ॥ काव्या० I. The Bengali reading is—स्पर्शानुकूला अपि सूर्यकान्तास्ते ह्यन्यतेजोऽभिभवाद्दहन्ति । He means that the sages, though outwardly calm and quiet, and given to the subduing of passions, have a latent destructive energy with them; and if they are provoked by wanton insults, will not fail to destroy those who molest them.

50. ध्वंसतां...वृत्तान्तः–Let all your agreement to (provoke the king) to action prove futile. स्वं...अशून्यं कुरु–Fulfil your office or post of duty i. e. Stand at the door. निर्मक्षिकम्–मक्षिकाणां अभावः clear of the flies i. e. free from all people. विरचित...नीयायाम् (छायायां) pleasant with the canopy of creepers formed above. अनवाप्त...फलः–न अवाप्तं चक्षुषः फलं येन सः–Who has not obtained the fruit i. e. the benefit of the eyes. दर्शनीयं–A worthy object of sight, V. L. द्रष्टव्यानां परं. The best of things worthy to be seen! He means that unless and until शकुन्तला is observed by him, he may consider his eyes to have been created in vain. Cf. यदृच्छया त्वं सकृदप्यवन्ध्ययोः । पथि स्थिता सुन्दरि यस्य नेत्रयोः । विक्र० I. ननु...वर्तते. विदूषक retorts saying that he has observed the most handsome person in दुष्यन्त and thus has obtained the reward of his eyes. आश्रमललामभूता–who serves as an embellishment of the hermitage. ललाम-अलंकारः ornament, decoration अवसरं न दास्ये I shall give him no opportunity (अवसरं) (to speak about शकुन्तला). ते तापसकन्यका...दृश्यते. He means that a hermit's daughter can never be a proper object of his love–a fact which it seems he has overlooked in his ardour for शकुन्तला. परिहार्य–Fit to be avoided.

II. 8. किल 'So goes the report, so I hear' (किलेति ऐतीह्ये). तदु...गतम् तया आदौ उज्झितं पश्चात् (मुनिना) अधिगतम् Found by the sage after having been deserted by her i. e. by the celestial nymph मेनका. अर्कस्योपरि On the sun-plant. It is a large vigorous plant with medicinal sap and rind (Mar. रुई). शिथिलं-वृन्तात् च्युतं--severed from the stem. नवमालिका is a tender delicate plant, which as a creeper requires some other tree for support. Note the correspondence of words in the first line with those in the second. सुरयुवति with नवमालिका, मुनि with अर्क, अपत्य with कुसुम, उज्झित with शिथिल, and अधिगत with च्युत. पिण्डखर्जूरैः उद्वेजितः वैमनस्यं प्रापितः Disgusted or tired of eating the dates; तिन्तिणी or V. L. तिन्तिडिका Tamarind. Mar. चिंच. स्त्रीरत्नपरिभाविन् slighting the jewels amongst women.

II. 9. The king imagines that in creating शकुन्तला, either of these two methods must have been used by the Creator. चित्रे... योगा–Having first of all painted a faultless figure on the canvas, he breathed the principle of life in it. परि...योगा–परिकल्पितः सत्वेन योगः यस्याः–Who was endowed with life (सत्व). सत्वयोग–A combination of the various properties of being and life. रूपो...नु–Or may it be that having collected into one ideal model all excellent forms, she was created by mind (without the touch of hands). रूपोच्चयेन–चन्द्राद्युपमानवस्तुसमुच्चयेन–By a collection of all exquisite forms, or models of beauty like the moon etc, for the creation of one ideal perfect Beauty. मनसा (करणेन) कृता–Formed by means of the mind. अत एव करस्पर्शाद्यभावात्तादृशं कान्तिमत्त्वमेतादृग्लक्षणत्वादिकमिति भावः। Com. राघव°. Cf. मन्ये च मातङ्गजातिस्पर्शदोषभयादस्पृशतेयमुत्पादिता प्रजापतिना; अन्यथा कथमियमक्लिष्टता लावण्यस्य। न हि करतलस्पर्शक्लेशितानामीदृशी भवति कान्तिः। कादं° I. विधिना–By the Creator. अपरा स्त्रीरत्नसृष्टिः–A matchless or extra-ordinary (अपरा) creation of the loveliest of women. अपरा–is also interpreted to mean 'last'; the idea would be that by creating शकुन्तला, the Creator has said the last word in the matter. विभुत्वं–Omnipotence. प्रत्यादेशः–The eclipser, the supplanter; one who throws into the back-ground. Cf. प्रत्यादिश्यन्त इव मे दृष्टलक्ष्यभिदः शराः। रघु° I. उर्वशी प्रत्यादेशो रूपगर्वितायाः श्रियः। विक्र° I.

II. 10. The verse gives beautiful Rūpakas or metaphors for the beautiful form of शकुन्तला. कररुहैः-By the nails. अलूनं-शाखावस्थितं -Not cut, unplucked. लून-P. P. of √ लू ' to cut'. अनाविद्धं असमुत्कीर्णं- Unperforated, not pierced (by a diamond pin) Cf. मणौ वज्रसमुत्कीर्णे सूत्रस्येवास्ति मे गतिः । रघु० 1. 3. अना...रसम्-(Honey) whose flavour is yet untasted. पुण्यानां अखण्डं फलं-Unimpaired or complete and perfect reward of the meritorious actions (done in former life.) He means the beauty of शकुन्तला represents a full and perfect development of all the merits of her former birth. अनघं- Faultless इह i. e. अस्मिन् रूपविषये-With reference to this form.

P. 54 इङ्गुदी...शीर्षस्य. इङ्गुदीतैलेन चिक्कणं शीर्षं यस्य-whose head is greasy (चिक्कण) with the Ingudī oil (applied to the head). तपस्विनः-of some hermit ; ' of some wretched rustic'-M. Williams. दृष्टिरागः or चक्षूरागः means ' love as betrayed or displayed by the eyes.' भवन्तमन्तरेण-About you, with reference to (अन्तरेण) you. अन्तरेण governs the Accusative. अप्रगल्भः-Not bold, shy, modest, reserved.

II. 11. अन्य...दयम् (हसितं)-अन्येन निमित्तेन कृतः उदयः यस्य तत्- (feigned to be) raised from some other cause (than love). As a matter of fact, says the king, love's influence was the cause of her smile. विनय...वृत्तिः (मदनः)-विनयेन वारिता वृत्तिः यस्य सः-Love which was checked in its manifestation by modesty. न विवृतः न च संवृतः-(Love) was neither fully manifested (विवृतः) nor was it fully concealed (संवृतः). Note how cleverly has the poet delineated love's manifestation in a typically Indian girl. न खलु... आरोहति-विदूषक means that it is just the way in which girls normally would behave under the influence of love. Surely he i. e. दुष्यन्त never expected that at his very first sight, she will come straightway and sit in his lap ! मिथःप्रस्थाने-At our mutual departure, when both of us took leave of one another and departed. शालीनतया-Through modesty (शालीनता). Cf. सखे, कुतूहलवानपि निसर्गशालिनः स्त्रीजनः । माल० IV. The word शालीन is generally explained as शालाप्रवेशमर्हतीति–one who is fit to enter an apartment of a house i. e. well-behaved, shy.

II. 12. अकाण्डे–अकस्मात्–Suddenly. विवृत्तवदना–Having turned her face back (towards me). The verse has a reference to Act I. अनसूये, अभिनवकुशसूच्या परिक्षतं मे चरणम् । कुरबकशाखापरिलग्नं च वल्कलम् । तावत् परिपालयतं मां यावदेतन्मोचयामि । and the stage-remark इति राजानमवलोकयन्ती सव्याजं विलम्ब्य सह सखीभ्यां निष्क्रान्ता । गृहीतपाथेयः–गृहीतं पाथेयं येन सः–One who has supplied himself with the provisions of the journey. पाथेय–a stock of provender. विदूषक means that the king will have now to stay for a longer time. He should, therefore, make provision for this lengthened stay. Note how विदूषक is anxious mainly about the provision. उपवनं–A pleasure-garden. A place of piety has been turned into a pleasure-resort by the king. P. 56 अपदेशः–Pretext, excuse. नीवारषष्ठभागं–The sixth portion of the produce of the forest-grain. A king was entitled to receive as tax, a sixth part of liquids, flowers, roots, fruit, grass etc. But from a Brahmin, learned in the Vedas, he was not to receive anything although dying of want. Cf. मनु॰ vii. 131–133. भागधेयः–यं–Share, tribute. भाग एव भागधेयः । Cf. भागरूपनामभ्यो धेयः ।. वर्णेभ्यः–From the four classes of people viz. ब्राह्मण, क्षत्रिय, वैश्य and शूद्र. क्षयि–Perishable अक्षय्यं–अविनाशि, Impossible to perish. Cf. क्षय्यजय्यौ शक्यार्थे ।. सिद्धार्थौ–who have accomplished their object viz. the king's interview. दीप्तिमतः–Resplendent, possessed of majestic lustre. He means that the king's form, although endowed with kingly glory, does not repel but inspires confidence in the minds of those who approach him. Cf. भीमकान्तैर्नृपगुणैः स बभूवोपजीविनाम् । अधृष्यश्चाभिगम्यश्च यादोरत्नैरिवार्णवः ॥ रघु॰ I. उपपन्नं–योग्यम्. Proper. ऋषिभ्यः नातिभिन्न–Who is not much different (in character) from the sages. V. L. ऋषिकल्पे–' Resembling a ऋषि, but with a degree of inferiority.'

P. 58. II. 14. सर्वभोग्ये आश्रमे–गार्हस्थ्ये–In the order (of house-holder) which is open to every one for enjoyment.

अभ्याक्रान्ता–Taken up, accepted. Like the sage the king also abides in an आश्रम. रक्षायोगात्– By reason of (योगात्) the protection he offers to the subjects. This is a form of penance which he observes. चारणद्वन्द्वगीतः–गन्धर्वमिथुनगीतः–Sung by a pair of Gandharvas, or celestial–choristers. 'These beings were the musicians or minstrels of Indra's heaven, just as the Apsarasas were the dancers and actresses; and their business was to amuse the inhabitants of Svarga by singing the praises of gods, saints and heroes.'—M. W. राजपूर्वः–Preceded by the word राजन्. He is therefore राजमुनि a राजर्षि. Cf. दशपूर्वरथं यमाख्यया दशकण्ठारिगुरुं विदुर्बुधाः । रघु० XI. बलभित्सखः–The friend of बलभिद् i. e. Indra who crushes armies with his thunderbolt.

II. 15. उदधि......सीमां–उदधिभिः श्यामाः सीमाः यस्याः सा– With its boundaries darkened by the oceans. नगर...बाहुः–नगरस्य परिघः इव प्रांशू बाहू यस्य सः–Having long arms like the iron-bar of a city (gate). परिघ–अर्गल–The iron-bar to secure a gate. 'In a city-gate it was both massive and long (स्त्यान and दीर्घ), and therefore an object of comparison highly significant of muscular strength. It should be borne in mind that length and vigour of arm were prime requisites in the ancient hero, whose fame depended on his skill and power in managing a bow. Hence the appropriateness of such epithets as महाबाहु and प्रांशुबाहु.' M. W. आशंसन्ते–expect, long for (victory). सुरसमितयः–Groups of Gods. दैत्यैः बद्धवैराः–In constant enmity with the demons. V. L. समितिषु सुराः सक्तवैराः etc. where समितिषु would mean 'in battles.' Another reading is सुरयुवतयः बद्धवैराः etc. of the Com. राघवभट्ट, who remarks thus 'सुरयुवतयः इति युवतिग्रहणं तासामतिभीरुत्वाद्वन्दीदुःखाद्यनुभवात् स्त्रीत्वेन युद्धाभिमानाद्यभावाच्च । पौरुहूते वज्रे–On the thunderbolt of पुरुहूत i. e. Indra (lit. invoked by many पुरुभिः बहुभिः हूतः). आश्रमसद्–आश्रमवासिन्–The inhabitant of the hermitage. Note the construction of this sentence, where विदित is used with the genitive. कतिपयरात्रं–for a few nights. The demons caused trouble during night.

P. 60. II. 16. पूर्वेषां–Of (your) predecessors. आप...त्रेषु–आपद्गतानां भयत्राणे–In the sacrifices (सत्रेषु) viz. giving security to the distressed. दीक्षिताः–consecrated, initiated. सपरिवाहम्–परिवाहेण सहितं–overflowing, flooded. Cf. पुरोत्पीडे तडागस्य परीवाहः प्रतिक्रिया। उत्तर० III. मा भैषीः–Aorist II sing. of √ भी 'to fear,' with the augment अ dropped, because of the prohibitive particle मा. एष राक्षसात् etc. V. L. एष तव चक्ररक्षीभूतोऽस्मि। 'Here I will guard the wheel of your chariot.' विजयप्रस्थानः–A march unto victory. आज्ञाप्तिहरः–Bearing a message of command.

P. 62. पुत्रपिण्डपालनः–(The ceremony of) cherishing the body of a son ; this ceremony seems to be akin to the birth-day ceremony and on this occasion, as the commentator काटयमेव observes, various presents are to be given to the son, in the form of sweet-meats, clothes etc. The V. L. प्रवृत्तपारणो मे उपवासो भविष्यति। 'My fast will be coming to an end (on the fourth day)' is not so satisfactory as our reading, which mentioning the definite ceremony, proves the importance of the king's presence for it. संभावयितव्या–Should be honoured by (your) presence. त्रिशङ्कुरिव–Like त्रिशङ्कु–' a just and a pious prince who aspired to celebrate a great sacrifice, hoping thereby to ascend the heaven in his mortal body. He first requested the sage वसिष्ठ to officiate for him ; but being refused, he then applied to the sage's hundred sons, by whom he was cursed and degraded to the condition of a Cāndāla. In this pitiable state, he had recourse to विश्वामित्र, who undertook to conduct the sacrifice and invited all the gods to be present; they however, refused to attend. Upon this, the enraged विश्वामित्र transported त्रिशङ्कु to the skies, whither he had no sooner arrived than he was hurled down again, head foremost, by Indra and the gods; but being arrested in his downward course by विश्वामित्र, remained suspended, between heaven and earth, forming a constellation in the southern hemisphere.'—M. W. अन्तराले–between the two.

II. 17. भिन्नदेशत्वात्–On occount of a difference or divergence in place (देश) शैले प्रतिहतं–Driven back, made to recoil by a hill

(शैल) in front (पुरः). स्रोतोवहः Gen. Sing of स्रोतोवह् 'a river.' तपोवनापरोध: Disturbance to the penance grove. Very cleverly has दुष्यन्त done away with his retinue which was a source of disturbance to him also. चपल: Restive, fickle, lacking control over his tongue. बटुः 'A lad, chap.'

II. 18. परोक्षमन्मथः To whom the (ways of) love are foreign, one who has had no experience of love. मृगशाव: A young one of a deer, a fawn. एधितः वर्धितः Bred up. He means, the association of such young creatures as fawns has left her thoroughly innocent of the working of love. परिहासविजल्पितं (which amounted to) mere prattling in joke हास्यभाषितं । परमार्थेन न गृह्यताम् should not be taken in earnest i. e. as representing the true state of things (परमार्थ).

ACT III.

P. 66. महानुभावः-महान् अनुभावः यस्य सः । Of great prowess. निरुपप्लवानि–free from obstacles ; some have निरुपद्रवाणि which gives the same meaning. उपप्लव an obstruction. Cf. जीवन्पुनः शश्वदुपप्लवेभ्यः प्रजाः प्रजानाथ पितेव पासि ॥ रघु॰ II. 48.

III. 1. का कथा what talk, or mention ; what account i. e. where is the need of fitting the arrow to the bow when the mere twanging of the bow is enough to expel the demons who impede their rites, in the same way as the roar (हुंकार) of some fierce animal suffices to scare away those who hear it. Cf. वसुधाधरकन्दराभिसर्पी प्रतिशब्दोऽपि हरेर्भिनत्ति नागान् ॥ विक्रमो॰ I. अपोहति from अप+ऊह्–dispels, removes. ऋत्विज्–ऋतौ यजतीति formed with the affix क्विन् of which nothing remains; one sacrificing at prescribed times, also means a priest who officiates at a sacrifice. आकाशे–this is an example of आकाशभाषितम्–a speech addressed to some person off the stage, the actor at the time fixing his eyes in the air ; the answer which is supposed to be given is also आकाशभाषितम् and is not heard by the audience–the actor on the stage pretending to hear it (श्रुतिमभिनीय) repeats the imaginary reply with the words किं ब्रवीषि. Cf. किं ब्रवीष्येवमित्यादि विना पात्रं ब्रवीति यत् । श्रुत्वेवानुक्तमप्येकस्तत्स्यादाकाशभाषितम् ॥ दशरू॰. उशीर is a kind of fragrant grass called वाळा in Marathi. आतपलङ्घनात्–from injury caused by the heat. लङ्घ to leap over also signifies as here "to inflict some injury." निर्वापणाय–for cooling, from निर्वप् to extinguish ; after this Monier Williams gives प्रियंवदे यत्नात् उपचर्य्यताम् । Let her be nursed with care '. उच्छ्वसितम्–life-breath—as precious to him as his own life. वैतानिक–वितानसम्बन्धि pertaining to a sacrifice (वितान). शान्त्युदकं–शान्त्यर्थं उदकम् । water which has the power to allay fever, to soothe and comfort. विष्कम्भः an introductory monologue or dialogue so called from its compressing (वि+स्कम्भ्) into a short space an account of those secondary incidents of the story which are not enacted before the audience, but a knowledge of which is essential for comprehending the action of the play. Cf. वृत्तवर्तिष्यमाणानां कथांशानां निदर्शकः । संक्षिप्तार्थस्तु विष्कम्भः ।. It is two-fold- शुद्ध when in Sanskrit by a middling character or characters (मध्यपात्र) and मिश्र when in mixed Sankrit and Prākrit by characters belonging to the middling or lower rank (नीचमध्यमैः). It may come at the beginning of any act, even the first, immediately after the प्रस्तावना. When, however, the characters are exclusively of an inferior class, and speak Prākrit only, it is called a प्रवेशक, which can come at the beginning of any act except the first. कामयमानावस्थः–others give समदनावस्थः । कामयानावस्थः । The form कामयानः is used by Kālidāsa elsewhere : राजयक्ष्मपरिहानिरायर्यौ कामयानसमवस्थया तुलाम् ॥ कामयते विषयान् इच्छति इति कामयानः । Although the regular form is कामयमान, yet this form can be defended on the ground that the rule prescribing the augment म् (मुमागम) is not universal.

III. 2. V. L. अलमस्मि ततो हृदयं तथापि नेदं निवर्तयितुम् । etc. I am not able to turn my heart from her. The reading we have chosen is न च निम्नादिव सलिलं निवर्तते मे ततो हृदयम् । This reading is supported by the commentators.

P. 68. विश्वसनीयाभ्याम्—Because the one has only flowers for his arrows and the other has cool rays that distil nectar. Stanza 3. अयथार्थम्–is explained as विपरीतक्रियम् having a contrary effect. The five arrows of Cupid are अरविन्दमशोकं च चूतं च नवमालिका । नीलोत्पलं च पञ्चैते पञ्चबाणस्य सायकाः । Some substitute other flowers in the list ; while sometimes other kinds of arrows are mentioned : उन्मादनस्तापनश्च शोषणः स्तम्भनस्तथा । संमोहनश्च कामस्य पञ्च बाणाः प्रकीर्तिताः ॥ In erotic poetry, the cooling rays of the moon or the cooling objects such as sandal or Southern breeze etc. are often spoken of as having a heating effect. Cf. in this connection Urvśai's love-song in act II–नन्दनवनवाता अपि भवन्ति अत्युष्णाः शरीरे । or the king's remark towards the end of Act III. पादास्त एव शशिनः सुखयन्ति गात्रम् । etc.

III. 4. The story of the burning of Kāmadeva from a scorching flame issuing from the third eye of Śiva is well–known and given fully by our poet in the Kumāra, Canto III. For the idea. Cf. कर्पूर इव दग्धोऽपि शक्तिमान्यो जने जने । नमोऽस्त्ववार्यवीर्याय तस्मै मकरकेतवे ॥ बालरामायण–act III. और्वः Submarine fire also called वाडव; according to the legend given in the Harivaṁśa और्व is the son of the sage उर्व who had gained great power by his austerities, and who was requested by the gods to beget children to perpetuate his race. He consented but warned them that his offspring would consume the world. So from his thigh he created a devouring fire which would have consumed the world, had not Brahma assigned to it the ocean as its habitation and the waters as its food–उर्वस्य मुनेरपत्यं पुमान् और्वः ।

III. 4. मकरकेतुः The God of love so called because of the मकर or sea–monster, subdued by him, painted on his banner (केतु). यदि मदिरायत etc. anything, even affliction and restlessness are welcome to him if they are caused by Śakuntalā or have a reference to her. After this Stanza the following is given by some editions:–भगवन् कन्दर्प । एवमुपालब्धस्य ते न मां प्रत्यनुक्रोशः । वृथैव सङ्कल्पशतैरजस्रमनङ्ग नीतोऽसि मया विवृद्धिम् । आकृष्य चापं श्रवणोपकण्ठे मय्येव युक्तस्तव बाणमोक्षः ॥–The passage, however, is not supported by many of the Devanāgarī Mss. although it is found in a few, and in all Bengali Mss. संस्थिते कर्मणि–after the sacrificial rites are concluded, finished. सदस्यैः–सदसि साधवः सदस्याः । तैः उपद्रष्टृभिः । The superintending priests or simply those who took part in the rites. P. 70. after तत्रैव तावद् गच्छामि, some read अनया बालपादपवीथ्या सुतनुर चिरं गतेति तर्कयामि । कुतः–सम्मीलन्ति न तावद् बन्धनकोषास्तयावचितपुष्पाः । क्षीर–स्निग्धाश्चामी दृश्यन्ते किसलयच्छेदाः ॥ This is a beautiful example of अनुमानालंकार which is frequently used by भास and कालिदास but it is not supported by all Devanāgarī Mss. प्रवातः–प्रकृष्टः वातः ।

III. 6. शक्यम् etc. used impersonally. पवनः आलिङ्गितुं शक्यम् is equal to पवनस्य आलिङ्गनं शक्यम्–where the act of embracing (आलिङ्गनं) implied in the infinitive goes with the predicate शक्यम्–

hence the neu. Cf. एवं हि प्रणयवती सा शक्यमुपेक्षितुं कुपिता। मालव॰ III. 22 or शक्यं श्वमांसादिभिरपि क्षुत् प्रतिहन्तुम्।. The full significance of the stānza which is here implied is clearly brought out in the following from भवभूति's मालति॰. तामीषत्प्रचलविलोचनां नताङ्गीमालिङ्गन् पवन मम स्पृशाङ्गमङ्गम् ॥ I. 41.

III. 7. Here again is an instance of अनुमानालंकार. The idea is also found in विक्रमो॰ IV. पश्चान्नता गुरुनितम्बतया ततोऽस्या दृश्येत चारुपदपङ्क्तिरलक्तकाङ्का ॥. नेत्रनिर्वाणम् = The full bliss of my eyes. निर्वाण lit. 'What is blown out' refers to the state of release, to the Vedāntic idea that each who seems a separate whole fuses all the skirts of self and again remerges in the Absolute. That is the highest happiness, the "Summum Bonum." Cf. प्रसक्ते निर्वाणे हृदय परितापं वहसि किम् ॥ मालवि॰ III. 1. सुखयति Denom. from सुख in the sense of giving comfort.

P. 72. III. 8. स्तनन्यस्तोशीरं and शिथिलित...वलयं are to be taken adjectivally with वपुः. एकवलयम्–implies the extreme tenderness of the wearer; a single lotus-bracelet was all she could bear, so weak she had grown. किमपि indescribably—hence, exquisitely. प्रसरः–action, influence. There is figure व्यतिरेक as मनसिज and निदाघ are compared and then the superiority of मनसिज over निदाघ is pointed out in the last line. सुभगं अपराद्धं=affecting a person in such a charming manner. पर्युत्सुका–greatly affected by love. Cf. पर्युत्सुकां कथयसि प्रियदर्शनां तामार्तं न पश्यसि पुरूरवसं तदर्थे ॥ विक्रमो॰ II. 16. आतङ्कः–anguish, malady, painful condition. अनभ्यन्तरे –not acquainted with, perfectly ignorant about; lit. not inside. Cf. अहो प्रयोगाभ्यन्तरः प्राश्निकः। मालविका॰ II. प्रतीकारस्य or प्रतिकारस्य–both forms are correct. प्रतिकारः = प्रतिकरणम् from प्रतिकृ + the affix घञ्. The ending vowel of a preposition when following by a word formed with the affix घञ् and not denoting 'man' is optionally lengthened–उपसर्गस्य घञ्यमनुष्ये बहुलम्। So we have परिवाहः or परीवाहः परिपाकः or परीपाकः. अनसूयामपि अनुगतः–Some read अनुसूययापि अवगतः। which we have followed in the translation–but which through mistake was not printed in the text. The former means, "my guess has also occurred to Anasūyā." अभिनिवेशः–firm attachment.

परिहीयसे अङ्गैः–mark the idiom thou art abandoned by thy limbs–hence thou art wasting away. लावण्यमयी छाया–your exquisite beauty-छाया here means कान्तिः complexion, your lovely complexion. P. 74. अवितथम्–thus derived : विगतं तथा सत्यं यस्मात् तत् वितथम्, न वितथमवितथम् ।

III. 9. क्षामक्षाम॰ अतिकृश–the repetition implies excess. It may also imply the idea of becoming gradually more and more emaciate. काठिन्यमुक्त–the Bengali has युक्त–but that is not correct because the loss of firmness is a sign of weakness. शोषणेन means शोषकेण–that dries up.

III. 10. समदुःखसुखेन–Cf. समदुःखसुखः सखीजनः । रघु॰ VII. 65. Cf. also समदुःखः पिबतीव मां नयनाभ्याम् । विक्रमो॰. I. बाला properly a girl sixteen years of age. अत्रान्तरे is अस्मिन् अवसरे ।. स्निग्धवीक्षित is one of the four ways by which a maiden encourages the advances of her lover. According to भरत they are लेखप्रस्थापन, स्निग्धवीक्षित, मृदुभाषित and दूतीसंप्रेषण. Now he was encouraged by Śakuntalā by स्निग्धवीक्षित because she again and again turned round and looked longingly at the king. But now that she is actually going to confess what she felt, the king's mind is in an agonising suspense. मम दर्शनपथमागतः Came across the path of my sight–quite a common idea; Cf. यदृच्छया त्वं सकृदप्यवन्ध्ययोः पथि स्थिता सुन्दरि यस्य नेत्रयोः । विक्रमो॰ I. 9.

P. 76. III. 11. निर्वापयिता lit. the extinguisher; hence allaying the fever. तपात्यये at the end of Summer ग्रीष्मान्ते. अभ्रश्यामः–Some read अर्धश्यामः partially-dark, half-obscured which is not quite good. The days are very sultry when the clouds come; but these clouds allay the heat by their grateful showers. Thus we have in रत्नावली–तपति प्रावृषि नितरामभ्यर्णजलागमो दिवसः ॥. तिलोदकम्–Water with sesamum seed–she means that her friends will have to celebrate her funeral obsequies–for these, such water is poured out. दूरगतमन्मथा Cf. दूरारूढः प्रणयः असहनः । विक्रमो॰ IV. किमत्र चित्रं... विशाखे etc. the two friends of शकुन्तला are here compared to the two stars in the constellation विशाखा and शकुन्तला herself who has grown so emaciated to शशाङ्कलेखा. Cf. the remark of रम्भा in विक्रमो० Act I. एष चित्रलेखाद्वितीयां प्रियसखीमुर्वशीं गृहीत्वा विशाखासमीपगत इव भगवांश्चन्द्र उपस्थितो राजर्षिः ॥. The union of the moon with the constellation of विशाखा is described as particularly charming by our poet ; so also with चित्रा as in हिमनिर्मुक्तयोर्योगे चित्राचन्द्रमसोरिव ॥ रघु० I. 46. because in summer the चित्रा and विशाखा shine very brightly. एतान् दिवसान्–According to " कालाध्वनोरत्यन्तसंयोगे " we have the accu. indicating that the king did not sleep even for a moment.

P. 78. III. 12. This gives a picture of the king as pensively he rests his head upon the palm of his hand sideways, so that the tears which trickle down from the corner of his eye (अपाङ्गप्रवर्तिभिरश्रुभिः) soil the gems in the golden bracelet which constantly slips down from his wrist (मणिबन्धनात्) and is not prevented from slipping down because the callosities on the forearm are not sufficiently prominent. This is a favourite idea with Kālidāsa Cf. कनकवलयभ्रंशरिक्तप्रकोष्ठः। मेघ० २. मणिबन्धन is " the wrist " so called because it is a place round which jewels are bound. देवताशेषापदेशेन–The remains of an offering of flowers presented to some deity. It was usual to offer these in the way mentioned. आत्मनः उपन्यासपूर्वं–preceded by a reference or allusion to yourself. ललितपदबन्धनम्–Cf. ललितार्थबन्धम् in विक्रमो० II. 14.

III. 13. श्रीः Lakṣmi or fortune ; when she herself seeks a man, how could she fail ? A man seeking fortune may or may not find her. Similarly the suitor may or may not win the beautiful maiden he loves–but if he is loved by her, how can she have any difficulty in gaining him ? Cf. the same idea in कुमार० V. 45 न रत्नमन्विष्यति मृग्यते हि तत्। आत्मगुणावमानिनी one who undervalues, scorns her own virtues or merits. क इदानीं etc. This is characteristic of Kālidāsa's style. An apt parallel to the situation in question which constitutes an illustration or (निदर्शनम्) and gives the figure of speech निदर्शना or ललितं according to some rhetoricians.

P. 80. नियोजिता so now I am directed by you–I do this by your orders—so that you will be responsible for the consequences विस्मृतनिमेषेण–which has forgotten winking–very expressive of an earnest longing gaze. Cf. पपौ निमेषालसपक्ष्मपङ्क्तिरुपोषिताभ्यामिव लोचनाभ्याम् ॥ रघु० II. 19.

III. 14. उन्नमित० =उन्नमिता एका भ्रूलता यस्य तत् । कण्टकितेन having the hair erect like thorns, the same as पुलकित–the hair starting up erect on the body is a sign of exquisite delight or some pleasurable emotion. Cf. उद्यत्कठोरपुलकाङ्कितकण्टकाग्रैर्यत् खिद्यते तव पदं ननु सा व्यथा मे ॥ अलंकारसर्वस्व. Cf. also स्पृष्टः सरोमविक्रियमङ्कुरितं मनसिजेनेव ॥ कण्टकाः संजाताः अस्य । कण्टक+इत (च्). गीतवस्तु–the subject-matter of the song. निक्षिप्तवर्ण–निक्षिप्ताः वर्णाः यस्य तत् । the syllables of which are transcribed. संगतार्थम्–well–connected in sense.

III. 15. रत्तिंमि–better read रत्तिम्पि which gives रात्रिमपि–which is better than रात्रावपि, for the accusative implies the ceaselessness of her torments by the rule कालाध्वनोरत्यन्तसंयोगे द्वितीया । वृत्तमनोरथानि–Monier Williams reads वृत्तमनोरथायाः । I whose desires are centred on thee.

III. 16. Here is a beautiful दृष्टान्त ; naturally therefore, there is बिम्बप्रतिबिम्बभाव–the king and शकुन्तला aud मदन are compared respectively to शशाङ्क ; कुमुद्वती and दिवसः He means that he is affected by love far more violently than Śakuntalā herself. So in विक्रमो० the king says पर्युत्सुकां कथयसि प्रियदर्शनां तां आर्तं नं पश्यसि पुरूरवसं तदर्थे । She is filled with anxious longing but he is distracted on her account. अविलम्बिनः मनोरथस्य ' the desire of the heart, which does not delay ' refers to Dusyanta by लक्षणा–Cf. अत्यायतं नयनयोर्मम जीवितमेतदायाति ॥ मालविका. III. 7. where the king refers to मालविका as his very life जीवितम् ।

P. 82. III. 17. संदष्ट from संदंश् to press the teeth closely together, bite, hence " press closely, come in close contact". Cf. संदष्टवस्त्रेष्वबलानितम्बेषु० रघु. XVI. 16. Cf. also the word संदंशः which means " a pair of tongs ". आशु० आशुक्रान्ताः ये बिसभङ्गाः तैः

सुरभीणि । उपचारम्–is the usual salutation, आचार; she need not give up her recumbent posture and rise to receive him. पुनरुक्तवादिनी–She was going to tell him how her dear friend was affected by love on his account; but their love for one another was too evident; her words, therefore, were superfluous–i. e. simple repetition of what was already well-known; Cf. प्रहर्षचिन्हानुमितं प्रियायै शशंस वाचा पुनरुक्तयेव । पुनरुक्त lit. what is said again, repeated, has further acquired the sense of "what is superfluous," or "unnecessary," and hence at times simply 'additional.' Cf. अभिव्यक्तायां चन्द्रिकायां किं दीपिकापौनरुक्त्येन । विक्रमो॰ III. मुक्तावलीविरचनापुनरुक्तमसैः ॥ विक्रमो॰ V. विषयनिवासिनो जनस्य–engaged in the affairs of life as M. Williams translates it; but the proper meaning is those living within his territory—hence his subjects. आर्तिः distress. अवस्थान्तरम् आरोपिता reduced to this altered condition; अन्या अवस्था अवस्थान्तरम् ।—an alteration from her normal healthy condition. अभ्युपपत्त्या–By favouring her; Cf. रतिमभ्युपपद्यमातुरां मधुरात्मानमदर्शयत्पुरः ॥ कुमार॰ IV. 25 साधारणोऽयं प्रणयः–Cf. विक्रमो॰ II. 16 साधारणोऽयमुभयोः प्रणयः ॥ किं... उपरोधेन ।–Mark this sly remark of Śakuntalā; "Tax not his courtesy too much–for he must be eager to join the bright ladies at his court".

III. 18. अनन्य॰ न अन्यत् परायणं यस्य–which has nothing else as its highest object, which is devoted to no other. हृदयसन्निहिते O thou that abidest in my heart. मदिरेक्षणे–माद्यति अनेन इति मदिरा–is properly wine–hence by लक्षणा–intoxicating like wine; मदिरे ईक्षणे यस्याः–Having eyes intoxicating like wine–hence fascinating or bewitching eyes; an epithet of common occurrence–and thus defined सौष्ठवेनापरित्यक्ता स्मेरापाङ्गमनोहरा । वेपमानान्तरा दृष्टिर्मदिरा परिकीर्तिता ॥. He was already killed by love's shaft; and this her unkind remark, therefore, slays him again. बहुवल्लभा etc. kings are prodigal to many of their love–hence this request with which Cf. चित्रलेखा's request to पुरूरवस् in act III. of विक्रमो॰. For निर्वर्तय some read निर्वाहय.

III. 19. How naturally in the ardour of his love does the king give this promise—not as in the original Mahābhārata story–is there a bargaining for her future. प्रतिष्ठे–प्रतिष्ठा–a cause of stability–but here cause of renown, " chief glory. " समुद्रवसना– V. L. समुद्ररशना–the sea girdled, the sea-girt earth. संयोजयावः–lit. let us cause it to join its mother–lead it to its mother; obviously this is a mere pretext. They want to leave the lovers to themselves–Cf. निर्यातश्शनकैरलीकवचनोपन्यासमालीजनः । अमरु; also बकुलावलिके एष बालाशोकवृक्षस्य पवल्लानि हरिणो लङ्घितुमागच्छति । एहि निवारयावः एनम् । माल० IV. आराधयिता–your adorer, worshipper of a deity, hence implying adoration as well as service.

P. 86. III. 20. करभोरु–करभ is the part of the hand between the wrist and the fingers; it is better however to understand करभ to mean by लक्षणा a part of करभ an elephant; i. e. the trunk of an elephant, so that the thighs are rounded and tapering like the trunk of an elephant. करभ इव ऊरू यस्याः सा । the affix ऊ (ऊङ्) is applied to ऊरु when it is the second member of a compound, and resemblance is implied. Cf. कुमार० I. 36. or द्विरदनासोरूः of भट्टि० IV. 17. न माननीयेषु etc. I will not make myself in fault with those who are worthy of respect i. e. with father Kaṇva and the elders. अपरिनिर्वाणः Lit. quite extinguished–not yet cool; it was still very hot.

III. 21. परिबाधापेलवैः–'incapable of bearing hardships.' M. W.; but the proper meaning is " rendered languid through suffering. कोमलैः is substituted for पेलवैः in the Bengali. रक्ष अविनयम्–some read रक्ष विनयम्. न आत्मनः प्रभवामि–she was not mistress of herself विदितधर्मा–who knows the law. धर्म because धर्मन् at the end of a बहुव्रीहि compound.

III. 22. गान्धर्वेण etc. the गान्धर्व is one of the eight forms of marriage which are ब्राम्हो दैवस्तथैवार्षः प्राजापत्यस्तथा ऽऽसुरः । गान्धर्वो राक्षसश्चैव पैशाचश्चाष्टमोऽधमः॥. गान्धर्व is thus defined इच्छयान्योन्यसंयोगः कन्यायाश्च वरस्य च । गान्धर्वः स तु विज्ञेयो मैथुन्यः कामसंभवः ॥ मनु० III 32. It is the marriage of a maiden and a young man at their sweet will concluded without any ceremony and without the consent of the elders

अनुमानयिष्ये–from the causal of अनुमन् to cause or induce to assent –hence take counsel with, to ask the consent of.

P. 88. III. 23. अपरिक्षत etc. a flower untouched, uninjured and fresh. The reference here is to the दन्तक्षतं which is often spoken of in Sanskrit erotic poetry–Cf. दन्तक्षतं कपोले वध्वाः वेदना सपत्नीनाम् । अधरस्य पिपासता etc. पिपासता–पान्तु इच्छता. Desid. from पा to drink. Cf. पिबसि रतिसर्वस्वमधरम् । Act I. 24. Mark how in his depiction of love-passages Kālidāsa does not go beyond aesthetic bounds– "A kiss unkissed is all beyond which the affair does not pass." चक्रवाकवधूः–How delicately and cleverly are the lovers warned ! The Cakrawākas are models of constancy and connubial affection. They keep together during the day, but are doomed to pass the night apart. There are frequent allusions to the habits of these birds in Sanskrit literature. Cf. सरसि नलिनीपत्रेणापि त्वमावृतविग्रहां ननु सहचरीं दूरे मत्वा विरौषि समुत्सुकः ।। विक्रमो॰ IV. 20. दूरीभूते मयि सहचरे चक्रवाकीमिवैकाम् । मेघ॰. शशिनं पुनरेति शर्वरी दयिता द्वंद्वचरं पतत्रिणम् । रघु॰ VIII. 56. शरीरवृत्तान्तोपलम्भाय–to inquire after my health, ascertain the state of my bodily health. लघु॰ लघुः संतापः येषां तानि Whose fever is abated. अस्ति मे विशेषः is idiomatic–there is a change for the better in me. सानुशयविघटितस्य–is contrasted with सुखोपनत–the desire of her heart came so readily and brought with it सुख happiness (सुखेन सह उपनत) but the separation comes and brings अनुशय repentance, or regret with it. लतावलय etc. A double entendre is intended, one meant for गौतमी, and the other for the king.

P. 90. III. 24. The first two lines are to be construed adjectivally with मुखं in the third line. अङ्गुलिभिः संवृतः अधरोष्ठः यस्य तत् । प्रतिषेधा॰– प्रतिषेधस्य यानि अक्षराणि तेषु विक्लवं अत एव अभिरामम्–looking beautiful as it simply stammered forth, could not utter distinctly the words of prohibition. अंसे विवर्तते इति अंसविवर्ति । पक्ष्मल is पक्ष्म + the affix ल (च्) having soft, beautiful eyelashes. परिभुक्तमुक्ते-आदौ परिभुक्तः पश्चात् मुक्तः तस्मिन् । शरीरलुलिता–crushed by her body. आसज्यमानं ईक्षणं यस्य–whose eyes are rivetted or fixed. III. 25. सायंतन

-belonging to the evening-तन is applied in this sense to adverbs of time. Cf. चिरंतन, प्राक्तन. परितः governs the accusative अभितः परितः-समयानिकषाहाप्रतियोगेऽपि । सवनकर्म-sacrificial rite, sacrifice. As the demons were stalking about, their shadows, dark-brown like evening-clouds, fell on the altar where the sacred fire was kindled. पिशिताशनानाम्-the eaters of raw flesh (पिशित raw flesh + अशन). अयमयं etc.-Observe the use of अयं " this one " with the verb in the first person. Some read however अयमहमागच्छामि ।

ACT IV

92. कुसुमावचयम्–according to पाणिनि III. 3–40 हस्तादाने चेरस्तेये। The root चि takes the affix घ (ञ्) when the sense is "taking something with the hand" except when the thing is stolen. Thus the proper form is अवचाय because घ (ञ्) causes Vṛddhi in the root-vowel. However the rule implies that the thing so taken is quite within reach; and so the commentator defends the form अवचय by supposing that the flowers were not quite within the reach of the girls. The defence, however, is evidently very weak. This is rather a case of poetic license. निर्वृत्तकल्याणा–निर्वृत्त p. p. of निर्+वृत्–effected, accomplished. कल्याणम् is happiness, good–fortune; here used in the sense of marriage on which so much of man's happiness depends; "having her nuptials celebrated." निर्वृतम्–Happy, comforted–p. p. of निस्+वृ. आकृतिविशेषाः etc.–Distinguished excellent forms; आकृतीनां विशेषाः or आकृतिविशेषो येषां ते–Whose distinction lies in their noble form. This prepossession in favour of beautiful, excellent persons is pretty commonly expressed by Sanskrit poets–the outward form is an index to inward worth. Cf. न ह्याकृतिः सुसदृशं विजहाति वृत्तम्। मृच्छ० IX. 16 यत्राकृतिस्तत्र गुणा वसन्ति।. घोणोन्नतं मुखमपाङ्गविशालनेत्रं नैतद्धि कारणमकारणदूषणानाम्॥ मृच्छ० किं प्रतिपत्स्यते–किं अभिधास्यति–What he would say, what reply he would make; or किं अवधारयिष्यति–what he would think. प्रथमः संकल्पः–The first desire of his heart, hence the best desire as in प्रथमः कल्पः—than which he can wish nothing better.

P. 94. सौभाग्यदेवता–The deity that presides over her fortune and welfare; the tutelary deity. निवेदितम्–निवेदनम् नपूंसके भावे क्तः। The p. p. is used as an abstract noun and is neuter. अतिथीनां–the plural to show respect; some honoured guest announcing himself. Some read अदिधिणा (अतिथिना) but that is not the Devnāgarī reading. हृदयेनासन्निहिता–With her heart, she is not near, her heart is far away with Dusyanta. अतिथिपरिभाविनि–One who slights, scorns, or is disrespectful to a guest. No punishment was thought too severe for one who violated the rites of hospitality.

IV. 1. अनन्यमानसा–अविद्यमानं अन्यत् यस्य तद् अनन्यं च तत् मानसं यस्याः सा । One whose mind is regardless of everything else, thinking of him to the exclusion of all other objects. बोधितोऽपि–the full significance of this word comes home to us in the fifth act where Śakuntalā tries to revive the king's memory by reporting to him of some of the incidents of their privacy. वेगबलोत्फुल्लया गत्या उत्फुल्ल from उद् + स्फुल् to leap–hence bounding through its impetuosity. The other reading is वेअचहुलुप्फुल्लदुव्वाराए = वेगचटुलोत्फुल्लदुर्वारया–with a step (गत्या) tremulous, bounding and difficult to be checked through its impetuosity. Some have अविरलपादतुवराए = अविरलपादत्वरया–but it is too tame a description of the choleric saint bounding away in anger कोऽन्यो हुतवहात् etc.–a fine दृष्टान्त. The wrath of a Brahmin is frequently compared to fire.

P. 96. आवेगस्खलितया गत्या–owing to her steps stumbling through her excitement. अग्रहस्तात्–a very puzzling compound explained thus: अग्रश्चासौ हस्तश्च–where one is अवयव and the other अवयवी ; but these are not identical while in a कर्मधारय such as नीलोत्पलं–नीलं च तत् उत्पलम् च–both the members of the compound refer to one and the same object. The defence, however, is that both अग्र and हस्त may be regarded as identical on account of the relation of the part and the whole between them ; and thus the compound is a कर्मधारय. Some however explain–हस्तस्य–अग्रम्–हस्ताग्रम् and account for the पूर्वनिपात of अग्र by putting the compound in the आहिताग्न्यादि class, but this rule of पूर्वनिपात applies to बहुव्रीहि compounds, hence the first explanation is better. Here is an ill omen ; the poet is preparing the ground for the tense feeling of this and the tragedy of the next act. अन्यथाभवितुं must not be falsified, hence must not be recalled. शापो निवर्तिष्यते–curse and its modification are altogether so common in the Paurāṇic tales.

P. 98. आश्वसितुम्–it is possible to take cheer or comfort–feel confident. स्वाधीनोपाया–She will be possessed of a resource or remedy in her own power. द्वयोरेव ननु नौ मुखे etc. mark the tragic irony ; with the best of intentions the friends resolve on a course of action which only helps on the tragedy. Had they revealed the incident, Śakuntalā would have been more careful about the ring and perhaps the tragedy may have been averted. विष्कम्भः Really speaking this is मिश्रविष्कम्भ with its Sanskrit and Prākrit. But perhaps the characters are all middling मध्य, while मिश्र– requires मध्य and नीच characters. प्रकाशं-विवृतप्रदेशम्–Open spot, open air. हन्त–Here shows surprise.

IV. 1. अस्त–It is believed that there are two mountains the अस्ताचल in the West and the उदयाचल in the East–and the rising and setting of the sun and the moon depends upon their going behind the अस्ताचल and coming from behind the उदयाचल. पतिरोषधीनाम्–One of the names of the moon is ओषधीपतिः। औषधी is explained as फलपाकान्ता a plant which dies after the ripening of its fruit, hence any medicinal plant. These are supposed to thrive under the influence of the moon hence the moon is ओषधीपतिः. Really speaking the सोम plant is described in the Veda as the king of plants ; but when later सोम became the appellation of the moon,—the latter too received the epithet ओषधीपतिः. Even the lord of medicinal herbs which revive and help to live–dies–such is the beautiful suggestion. आविष्कृतारुण etc. V. L. आविष्कृतोऽरुणपुरः etc. But this requires us to suppose that आविष्कृतः is used in an active sense–आवीर्भूतः अरुणः पुरःसरः यस्य एतादृशः अर्कः एकतः दृश्यते। We have to supply this word दृश्यते. अरुण the herald of the sun is the dawn personified ; according to the Purānās अरुण is the son of कश्यप and विनता and the elder brother of गरुड. His mother is said to have prematurely broken the egg which was to be hatched for a thousand years, and so the child was born thighless: later on he became the charioteer of the sun ; hence the latter is called अनूरुसारथिः. लोको नियम्यते इव– people are guided as it were ; restrained or governed i. e. people are taught the lesson that when even the highest suffer rise and fall how can mortals escape it. The stanza beautifully suggests the reverse of fortune which is to come over Śakuntalā. The दशान्तराणि–the various vicissitudes of life are alluded to in the well-known verse नीचैर्गच्छत्युपरि च दशा चक्रनेमिक्रमेण ।–मेघदूत० ।

IV. 2. संस्मरणीयशोभा–Whose beauty is now a matter of remembrance. The poet here beautifully refers to the condition of the heroine in the absence of दुष्यन्त. The last two lines give a generalisation, and so the figure is अर्थान्तरन्यास. अपटीक्षेप–A hurried toss of the curtain–a stage-direction indicating the sudden entrance of a character who is flurried through joy or sorrow etc. एवं नाम–etc. the passage is very corrupt and variously read. She is referring to herself by the word जनस्य–विषयपराङ्मुख–she was पराङ्मुख averse to, withdrawn from all विषय worldly concerns ; one unacquainted with them. अनार्यं–as a noun–ungentlemanly conduct–what is unworthy of an आर्य. उचितेषु–The usual duties, from " usual " the word came to mean "proper". कामः इदानीं etc. Cf. अलब्धफलनीरसान्मम विधाय तस्मिञ्जने। समागममनोरथान् भवतु पञ्चबाणः कृती ॥ विक्रमो० II. 11. शुद्धहृदया–V. L. शून्यहृदया । पदं कारिता–caused to have dealings with, repose confidence in. Cf. हञ्जे पश्य पश्य । कारितैवैतस्मिन् बकुलावलिकया पदं मालविका । मालवि० III. 14. 3. also धर्मेणापि पदं शर्वे कारिते पार्वती प्रति। पूर्वापराधभीतस्य कामस्योच्छ्वसितं मनः ॥ कुमार० VI. 14. एतावत्कालस्य the genitive irregularly for the accusative. दुःखशीले–they are inured to hardships–hence either it would not be proper to trouble them any more–or they would not be able to sympathise with Śakuntalā and her friends as they are rendered callous to sufferings. Or, who are hard to please, bad-tempered and hence cannot be easily induced. व्यवसिताऽपि–although I am resolved, have made up my mind. आपन्नसत्त्वा–आपन्नः सत्त्वः (गर्भः) अनया । A pregnant woman.

P. 102. प्रस्थानकौतुकम्–कौतुक festive solemnities auspicious ceremonies that attend the departure. Cf. अथ तस्य विवाहकौतुकं ललितं

बिभ्रत एव पार्थिवः । रघु० VIII. 1 ; where कौतुक is explained as मङ्गलम्– or as हस्तसूत्र. " कौतुकं मङ्गले हर्षे हस्तसूत्रे कुतूहले–इति शाश्वतः । In the स्वप्न. III we have both कौतुक and मङ्गल combined–अद्यैव कौतुकमङ्गलं कर्तव्यमत्यस्माकं भट्टीनी भणति ।–where the reference is to the auspicious ceremony of the tying of the nuptial thread सुखशयन-पृच्छिका–रात्रौ तव सुखशयनं जातं इति या पृच्छति सा । सुखशयन + पृच्छ् + the affix ण्वुल् (अक) + आ. There is also the form सौखशायनिक– Raghu X. 14. धूमाकुलितस्य etc. Both the comparisons are very appropriate in the mouth of Kaṇva. सुशिष्यपरिदत्ता–a common idea. Cf. the Nirukta passage विद्या ह वै ब्राह्मणमाजगाम । गोपाय मां शेवधिस्तेऽहमास्मि । etc. अग्निशरणं the fire sanctuary–the house (शरणं=गृहं) where the sacred fire is kept. Cf. later अग्निशरणालिन्द in Act V.

IV. 3. भूतये भुवः for earth's prosperity, suggesting that the child would be सार्वभौम. अग्निगर्भां शमीमिव । for the idea Cf. शमीमिवाभ्यन्तरलीनपावकाम् । रघु० III. 9. Agni who bore the seed of Śiva at the request of the gods felt a consuming fire spreading through his body–so he entered the Śami tree ; when the gods discovered him there, they assigned the tree to him as his permanent abode; the story is told in the अनुशासनपर्व chap. 35. उत्कण्ठासाधारणम्–mingled or mixed with anxiety. Cf. वीज्यते स हि संसुप्तः श्वाससाधारणानिलैः । कुमार० II. 42.

P. 104. तपस्विनी–the poor girl, the helpless one ; one deserving pity. समुद्गकः A small box or casket. मृगरोचना– yellow ointment, the concrete bile of deer used as such. समालंभनानि–Here decorations ; properly समालम्भनं is besmearing the body with ointments–समालंभो विलेपने इत्यमरः । शार्ङ्गरवमिश्राः–मिश्र At the end of a compound has the sense of पूज्य respectable–as also the additional sense " and others " हस्तिनापुर– So called because it was founded by हस्तिन् the great grandson of भरत ; thus it is an anachronism to call दुष्यन्त's capital by that name. शिखामाज्जिता–meaning with her hair (शिखा) combed or cleansed. प्रतिष्ठित–Consecrated or hallowed–or placed in i. e. carrying, having in their hands. स्वस्तिवाचनिकाभिः–invoking blessings on her, wishing to pronounce blessing on her. स्वस्तिवाचनाय हिताभिः । स्वस्तिवाचन

also means a present given to Brahmins for blessings from him–but that sense is not appropriate here.

P. 106. गौतमीवर्जम्–गौतमीं वर्जयित्वा an instance of the gerund in अम् (णमुल्) ; leaving Gautami, except Gautami. आभरणोचितं etc. आभरण and प्रसाधन are contrasted–the former meaning rich costly ornaments from the root आ + भृ implying opulence–the latter simple decorations such as garlands etc. मानसी सिद्धिः a creation of his mind–created through the superhuman power (सिद्धि) acquired through Yaugic practices.

P. 108. IV. 4. क्षौमम्–क्षुमायाः विकारः–क्षुमा is flax or silk. माङ्गल्यम्–auspicious–it is explained as मङ्गले साधुः but the form would be मङ्गल्यम् ।; so it may be explained thus मङ्गल्यं एव माङ्गल्यं–by applying the affix अ (ण्) स्वार्थे i. e. without any change of meaning. निष्ठ्यूतः distilled–lit. vomited; but it is not अश्लील when used by लक्षणा in a secondary sense (गौणवृत्तिव्यपाश्रयात् अतिसुन्दरमन्यत्र ग्राम्यकक्षां विगाहते ।) लाक्षारसः "A red dye prepared from an insect analogous to the cochineal insect" आपर्व॰ पर्वभागं मर्यादीकृत्य–as far as the wrists. किसलय॰ किसलयोद्भेदाः उद्भिद्यमानपल्लवाः तत्प्रतिद्वंद्विभिः–तत्प्रतिस्पर्धिभिः ।–The hands of the fairies were as red as the fresh sprouts of trees. अणुवजुत्त–V. L. अणुवहुत्त=अनुपभुक्त॰ The girls were taught the art of painting or perhaps they would put the ornaments on her person even as they have seen them in pictures.

IV. 5. संस्पृष्टम्–not simply touched, but smitten powerfully, affected. स्तम्भित etc. स्तम्भिता या बाष्पस्य वृत्तिः प्रवृत्तिः तया कलुषः स्वरभङ्गवान् ।. दर्शनम् lit. the sight, the sense of vision–better तत्तदिन्द्रियजं ज्ञानम् । hence he felt all his senses paralysed. अरण्यौकसः–अरण्यं ओकः यस्य–Cf. दिवौकस्, वनौकस्. The argument employed is what is called कैमुतिकन्याय–a fortiori and the figure of speech is अर्थापत्तिः–आनन्दपरिवाहिणा–आनन्दस्य परिवाहः अस्यास्तीति–overflowing with joy–with tears of joy.

IV. 6. ययाति was an ancient king the father of पुरु from whom Duṣyanta himself derived his descent. He had two wives देवयानी and शर्मिष्ठा the daughter of वृषपर्वन्. शर्मिष्ठा by her superior charms won the heart of ययाति. She like शकुन्तला had married ययाति by the गांधर्व form–the simile is thus appropriately chosen. प्रदक्षिणीकुरुष्व is a च्वि form. प्रगतो दक्षिणं प्रदक्षिणं । अव्ययीभावः । अप्रदक्षिणं प्रदक्षिणं संपद्यमानं करोति प्रदक्षिणीकरोति ।. Cf. प्रदक्षिणीकृत्य हुतं हुताशम् । रघु॰ II. 71. walking round an object worthy of one's veneration keeping it to one's right. ऋक्छन्दसा–the metre is त्रिष्टुप् which is so common in Ṛgveda; it consists of 11 syllables to a पाद and is irregular in arrangements.

IV. 7. क्लृप्तानि धिष्ण्यानि येषां–whose places are fixed round the altar. प्रान्त॰ the दर्भ grass was strewn round their margins to give additional sanctity. हव्यगन्धैः etc. for this virtue of the smell Cf. पुनानं पवनोध्दूतैर्धूमैराहुतिगन्धिभिः । रघु. 1. 53. घ्रात्वा हविर्गन्धि रजोविमुक्तः समश्नुते मे लघिमानमात्मा ॥ रघु. XIII. 37. भगिन्याः the genitive is to be taken objectively; show thy sister her way.

P. 112. IV. 8-9 अपीतेषु–when you were not watered–lit. before you have had your fill of water–or when you have not drunk. This describes how dearly this daughter of the forest loved her brothers and sisters–the trees; they were her वनवासबन्धु–the friends or kinsfoik that surrounded her in forest-life. Cf. उत्तर॰ III. 8. यत्र द्रुमा अपि मृगा अपि बन्धवो मे ।. परभृत–परे or परैः भृत–the koil, so called because the female is supposed to leave her eggs in the nest of a crow which unknowingly hatches them. Cf. प्रागन्तरिक्षगमनात्स्वमपत्यजातमन्यैर्द्विजैः परभृताः खलु पोषयन्ति । Act. V. 22. Cf. for a similar idea उदीरयामासुरिवोन्मदानामालोकशब्दं वयसां विरावैः ॥ रघु॰ II. 9.

IV. 10. The four lines beautifully describe her path. रम्यान्तरः–रम्यं अन्तरं यस्य । "Having its intervening spaces delightful or charming, " छायाद्रुमैः–छायाप्रधानैः द्रुमैः–मध्यम॰ तत्पुरुष. कुशेशय॰–with the dust (रेणुः) soft like the pollen (रजः) of lotuses. कुशे जले शेते इति । कुश + शी + the affix अ (च्) according to अधिकरणे शेते । पाणिनि॰ III. 2. 15. It is an अलुक् समास. There is some difficulty with regard to the construction. If the आशंसा is to be taken as repeated with each attribute--thus अस्याः पन्थाः रम्यान्तरः भूयात्–नियमितार्कमयूखतापः भूयात् and so on as the commentators do, then the 'च' would have to be repeated every time and not twice only. This shows therefore that there is समुच्चय of two आशंसाs only–may her path–described as above–be शान्तानुकूलपवनः and शिवः । So that the first three lines give the उद्देश्य only and the last line the विधेय. शान्तानुकूल॰ Cf. पवनस्यानुकूलत्वात् प्रार्थनासिद्धिशंसिनः ॥ रघु॰ I. 42. because such a wind is a good augury for the future fulfilment of the desired object. शिवश्च पन्थाः ।–a phrase commonly used as a parting benediction; the usual phrase is शिवास्ते पन्थनः सन्तु ।. जातिजनास्निग्धाभिः–Dear to these (स्निग्ध) as thy own kinsfolk–the same idea as expressed by वनवासबन्धुभिः– । of Stz. 9. P. 114. समवस्था = समावस्था–the same condition. Cf. रघु॰ VIII. 41.

IV. 11. उद्गलित॰–उद्गलिताः दर्भाणां कवलाः यासां ताः । उद्गलित means the same as उद्गीर्ण of the Bengali–ejected from the mouth, dropped from the mouth. Cf. with this रघु॰ XIV 69. which expresses the same sentiment नृत्यं मयूराः कुसुमानि वृक्षाः दर्भानुपात्तान् विजहुर्हरिण्यः । तस्याः प्रपन्ने समदुःखभावमत्यन्तमासिद्रुदितं वनेऽपि ॥ सोदर्यस्नेहम् sisterly affection समाने उदरे शयितः सोदर्यः–she looked upon her as her sister. Cf. लताभगिनी शाखाबाहाभिः–बाहा is the same as बाहुः–the feminine form as M. W. observes is more appropriately joined with शाखा.

IV. 12. वीतचिन्तः–वीता चिन्ता यस्य । Mark how Kaṇva not only has no resentment that Śakuntalā should have not consulted him but that he had in mind दुष्यन्त as the husband who was in every way worthy of Śakuntalā.

P. 116. स्थिरीकर्तव्या–rendered firm, hence cheered. उटजपर्यन्तचारिणी–grazing about the hut–in the neighbourhood (पर्यन्त) of the hut, अनघप्रसवा–अनघः प्रसवः यस्याः सा । Will have happily brought forth, safely delivered of her young. Cf. अनघप्रसूतिः in इतो भविष्यत्यनघप्रसूतेरपत्यसंस्कारमयो विधिस्ते ॥ रघु॰ XIV. 75. प्रियनिवेदयितृ-

कम्–the same as प्रियनिवेदयितारम्–One who conveys the good tidings.

IV. 13. व्रणविरोपणम्–qualifies तैलं–that which heals a wound–causes a scar to cicatrize–hence healing oil. व्रणं विरोपयतीति । from the causal of विरुह्+the affix अन (ल्युट्) in the sense of the agent. परिवर्धितकः–the affix क used in the sense of अनुकम्पा–or in endearment. अनुकम्पया परिवर्धितः–tenderly reared. पुत्रकृतकाः–कृत्रिमः पुत्रः । Adopted son.

IV. 14. The first two lines should be thus construed उत्पक्ष्मणोः नयनयोः उपरुद्धवृत्तिं बाष्पं स्थिरतया विरतानुबन्धं कुरु ।. firmly make the tears cease to rise or cling continuously in thy eyes with their upturned eye-lashes–obstructing their action. विरतः अनुबन्धः यस्य–whose continuity i. e. continuous flow has stopped. उत्पक्ष्मणोर्नयनयोः this is to be connected with वृत्ति in the compound उपरुद्धवृत्तिम्–which is rather loose–the action (वृत्ति) of the eyes is impeded by the rising tears. अलक्षिताः नतोन्नताः भूमिभागाः यस्य तस्मिन् qualifies मार्गे–विषमीभवन्ति–become unequal, are liable to trip or stumble.

P. 118. ओदकान्तं–आ+उदकान्तम् । as far as the water's brink. श्रूयते–It is enjoined by श्रुति i. e. scripture–it is a scriptural rule. क्षीरवृक्ष lit. milk–tree–a kind of fig–tree which yields a milky juice and is large enough to afford abundant shade. युक्तरूपम्–Cf. युक्तरूपमिदं तव Act I. 12 ; II. 16. रूप is here a प्रत्यय, the word is not a compound. नलिनीपत्रान्तरितमपि–Precisely the same sentiment is to be found in the विक्रमोर्वशीय–सरसि नलिनीपत्रेणापि त्वमावृतविग्रहां ननु सहचरीं दूरे मत्वा विरौषि समुत्सुकः । A few lines before this passage the cry is compared to the sound कः कः–it is possible that the harsh expression दुष्करं करोमि may refer to this peculiar cry. " Hard is the lot I suffer " " Hard is my lot."

IV. 15. विषाददीर्घतरां–Cf. अविनोददीर्घयामा कथं नु रात्रिर्गमयितव्या ॥ विक्रमो॰ III. 4. आशाबन्धः साहयति–causal–the bond of hope causes, helps us to bear. Cf. the parallel passage in मेघ॰ 12. आशाबन्धः कुसुमसदृशं प्रायशो ह्यङ्गनानां सद्यःपाति प्रणयि हृदयं विप्रयोगे रुणद्धि ॥

IV. 16. संयमधनान्–thinking well of us who are rich in self-control. विचिन्त्य–He asks दुष्यन्त to think of three circumstances–think of him who was self-controlled–implying by it that he was worthy of respect ; think of his own family–implying tha, he would acquit himself well and worthily ; and her love for him which was spontaneous–implying, therefore, that he should be very kind to her. सामान्यप्रतिपत्तिपूर्वकम्–प्रतिपत्ति is respect ; साधारणगौरव पुरःसरम्–the word पूर्व at the end of a compound often denotes the manner in which anything is done–so the meaning is सामान्यप्रतिपत्त्या–with equal respect. दारेषु–the word is mas. plu. लौकिकज्ञाः–Acquainted with worldly affairs. न खलु धीमतां–This is a generalisation–which supports the previous remark of काश्यप–the figure would be thus अर्थान्तरन्यास. Such generalisations are in the characteristic manner of कालिदास and भास.

IV. 17. गुरून् not only father or father-in-law, but elders ; any male relation that is entitled to respect. प्रियसखीवृत्तिं–acting the part of a dear friend towards them treating them as dear friends. सपत्नी०–समानः पतिः यासां ताः । according to पत्युर्नो यज्ञसंयोगे । पा० V. I. 33. the word पति takes the augment न् before the fem. affix ई when participation in a sacrifice is meant–hence पत्नी is one who is entitled to join her husband in the performance of religious rites. भाग्येषु अनुत्सेकिनी–Cf. अनुत्सेको लक्ष्म्याम् भर्तृहरि II. 54. वामाः–Perverse, those of an opposite character. प्रतीपदर्शिनी वामा । अमरः । प्रदेये–" the प्र implies that the thing is given once for all and cannot be taken back. " P. 122. मलयतटो०–How very appropriate the simile ; the sandal-tree transplanted from its native–soil—the slopes of Malaya, may not thrive in another place ; that is the image for Śakūntala leaving her forest–home.

IV. 18. अभिजनवतः possessed of a noble birth, nobly born. विभवगुरुभिः Important from his dignity or greatness ; so that every moment she will be fully occupied with them. प्राची–is often poetically represented as the mother of the sun and the moon. प्रत्यभिज्ञानमन्थरः slow to recognize. Mark that the incident of the curse was kept a secret by the friends. But they are careful enough to warn Śakuntalā about the ring, who unfortunately could not understand the full significance of the warning. अतिस्नेहः पापशङ्की–Cf. प्रेम पश्यति भयान्यपदेऽपि । किराता॰ IX. 70. Love sees causes of alarm although without foundation. P. 124. युगान्तरं–युग is according to some equal to a प्रहर " a division of the day comprising one eighth of the sun's diurnal revolution, or three hours ; according to others हस्तचतुष्टयम्–a space of four cubits.

IV. 19. चतुरन्तमहीसपत्नी–the earth bounded by the four (quarters), the entire earth. चत्वारः अन्ताः यस्याः सा । दौष्यन्ति–दुष्यन्तस्य अपत्यं पुमान् । अप्रतिरथम्=अप्रतिराथिकम्–रथ by लक्षणा means a रथिक warrior who fights from a chariot ; having no rival, having no antagonist. निवेश्य–Having caused to marry, having settled in marriage. Cf. तान्निवेश्य चतुरोऽपि तत्र सः । रघु॰ XI. 57. अहमपि तव सूनावायुषि न्यस्तराज्यः । विचरितमृगयूथान्याश्रयिष्ये वनानि । अहवा चिरेण वि पुणो etc. How beautifully the same thought is expressed in the प्राकृत verse, vide intro. XX. मा उत्कण्ठितुं–gives the sense of मा उत्कण्ठस्व the infinitive is thus combined with मा and idiomatically used in the sense of the imperative. This use of the infinitive is rare ; but in भास it is common enough.

IV. 20. उटजद्वारविरूढं etc. " बलि or गृहबलि is a particular kind of offering identical with the भूतयज्ञ–i. e. a sacrifice for all creatures, but especially in honour of those demigods and spiritual beings called गृहदेवताः household deities–which are supposed to hover round and protect house-holds–(मनु॰ III. 80). This offering was made by throwing up into the air (मनु॰ III. 90) in some part of the house generally at the door (मनु॰ III. 88) the remains of the morning and evening meal of rice or grain." M. W. The reference here, however, is not necessarily to the भूतयज्ञ ; as Kaṇva speaks of the germination of the seeds, it must be uncooked grains scattered about the threshold. Generally this is consumed by crows, dogs or insects ; hence बलिभुज्–बलिपुष्ट

as the names of a crow, or a crane; such of the grains as escaped being devoured by them would be likely to germinate about the threshold. Cf. यासां बलिः सपदि मद्गृहदेहलीनां हंसैश्च सारसगणैश्च विलुप्तपूर्वः । तास्वेव संप्रति विरूढतृणाङ्कुरासु बीजाञ्जलिः पतति कीटमुखावलीढः ॥. मृच्छ० I.

P. 126. सहधर्मचारिणी–Rather unusual–"friend in religious duties;" it means a wife. स्नेहप्रवृत्ति० etc. the course of affection views it thus—thus your love interprets. हन्त–is an exclamation of joy. स्वास्थ्यं—natural serenity of mind–I feel as if a load of anxiety is taken off my mind.

IV. 21. परिग्रहीतुः–परिग्रहीतृ is the husband and परिग्रह is the wife. Lit. one who accepts; while a wife is one who is accepted. विशदः–Serene, clear, tranquil. प्रकामं=अत्यर्थम्–the Bengali reading is जातोऽस्मि सम्यग्विशदान्तरात्मा । चिरस्यनिक्षेपमिवार्पयित्वा ॥ A deposit is a source of very great anxiety because it is another's property held in trust. Cf. सुखमर्थो भवेद् दातुं सुखं प्राणाः सुखं तपः । सुखामन्यद्भवेत्सर्वं दुःखं न्यासस्य रक्षणम् ॥ स्वप्न० I. 10.

ACT V

कलविशुद्ध–Soft and clear. कल is generally explained as अव्यक्त-मधुर, sweet and indistinct. स्वरसंयोग:–A combination of harmonious sounds. The blending of harmonious notes required by a particular Rāga or melody. वर्णपरिचय–Acquaintance with the Varṇās; practice in singing. The word वर्ण means 'The order or arrangement of a subject in a song (गीतक्रम्).' Cf. उपात्तवर्णे चरिते पिनाकिन:....। कुमार० V. 56. Where मल्लिनाथ quotes हलायुध–'गीतक्रमे स्तुतौ वेदे वर्णशब्द: प्रयुज्यते।. It may also mean 'a musical mode.' Cf. गीतिषु चत्वारो वर्णा भवन्ति। यदाह भरत:–स्थायी तथैव संचारी तथा रोहावरोहिणौ। वर्णाश्चत्वार एवैते कथिता: सर्वगीतिषु। Com. शंकर.

V. 1. अभि......लोलुप:–Eagerly longing (लोलुप) for fresh honey. तथा परिचुम्ब्य–Having kissed in such a manner i. e. so ardently. कमल...निर्वृत:–कमले वसति: एव-कमलवसतिमात्रं-तेन निर्वृत:–Being altogether contented or satisfied by merely dwelling (may be, without enjoyment) in the lotus. विस्मृत:–Past Passive Participle used actively. The song of हंसपदिका, as the king remarks, has a veiled reproof for the king, who after a brief period of amours with her, left her in favour of his Queen. The king has been represented by her as the bee who flies from flower to flower in his eager search for fresh honey. चूतमञ्जरी is her own self who has been the victim of his momentary passion (Cf. परिचुम्ब्य), while the lotus, his usual resort in the evening after the day's wandering is over, represents the Queen वसुमती. Observe how skilfully the poet prepares the audience to face the tragic catastrophe of the repudiation of शकुन्तला, that is soon to follow. रागपरिवाहिणी–Impassioned, overflowing with feeling or passion. Cf. प्रथमं सपरिवाहमासीत्। Act II. अक्षरार्थ:–The meaning of words, (lit. of the letters.). (सकृत्) कृतप्रणय:–कृत: प्रणय: येन स:–Who made love. (to her). If अयं जन:–this person is taken to refer to हंसपदिका, then it would mean 'who was once loved' (कृत: प्रणय: यस्या:स:). उपालम्भं गत:–Become an object of taunt or censure. परकीयैः हस्तैः–By the hands of others i. e. through her servants. शिखण्डके–(seized) by the tuft of hair. Mar शेण्डी. अप्सरसा (गृहीतस्य) वीतरागस्य–Like a sage who was free from passions, but who has been ensnared by a celestial nymph. This reference ordinarily ought to suggest to the king the name of शकुन्तला, who owes her birth to such an incident. The hint falls flat, however, since it rouses no such recollection. मोक्षः–(i) Escape; (ii) liberation of the soul from further transmigration. नागरिकवृत्त्या– In a polite or courtly manner. नागरिक ‘ a city-bred man, who has developed politeness of manners. It also implies ‘insincerity, as a man shows exaggerated attention to his first mistress, while he is courting some one else. ’—M. W. इष्टजनविरहादृतेऽपि Even without (ऋते) the separation from a beloved person. Note how cleverly the poet suggests by the expression that the curse of the sage Durvāsas has proved effective in obliterating all trace of शकुन्तला from the mind of दुष्यन्त.

V. 2. पर्युत्सुकीभवति—Becomes filled with ardent longing. सुखितः–Happy in every respect अबोधपूर्वं (स्मरति)–without any definite knowledge of the particular details of the object of recollections. Cf. विषयविशेषज्ञानाभावपूर्वम् । Com. राघव० भावस्थिराणि–Which remains clinging (to the soul) in the forms of impressions भावैः वासनाभिः स्थिराणि ।. जननान्तरसौहृदानि–Friendships of the other i. e. former births. The doctrine of पुनर्जन्म or the transmigration of the soul is an essential dogma of the Hindu religion, according to which, the soul migrates from one body to another, taking with it, in the form of impression, all associations of its former life, and its deeds, good or bad. The present condition of every person derives its character from the virtues or vices of his previous life, while very often vague recollections of occurrences and associations do cross his mind dimly, without his being aware of them in a definite form. Our present ties of friendship could also be thus traced to the former associations of intimacy existing between the two souls. Kālidāsa refers to these ideas very often. Cf. उन्मनाः प्रथमजन्मचेष्टितान्यस्मरन्नपि बभूव राघवः । रघु० XI. 22. फलानुमेयाः

प्रारम्भाः संस्काराः प्राक्तना इव ॥ रघु० I. 20. मनो हि जन्मान्तरसंगतिज्ञम् । रघु० VII. 15. कंचुकिन् or a chamberlain is an attendant in the royal harem, an old man, a Brahmin endowed with numerous good qualities. He is to enter the stage as a decrepit old man, tottering with age and lamenting his hard lot in the harem. आचार इति–Thinking it to be customary, or a matter of form. अवरोधगृहेषु–in the harem or the inner apartments. वेत्रयष्टिः–A cane staff with a gold or silver knob, used as a symbol or badge of office. बहुतिथे–बहूनां पूरणः बहुतिथः ।. The affix तिथ (तिथुक्) indicates measure or length of time. Cf. बहुपूगगणसंघस्य तिथुक् ।. प्रस्थानविक्लवगतेः–प्रस्थाने विक्लवा गतिर्यस्य–With a faltering or tottering step while walking. V. L. वृद्धस्य विक्लवगतेः । अवलम्बनार्थो–अवलम्बनाय इयम्–(Become indispensable) for support. अनतिपात्यम्–Which ought not to be neglected or set aside. Cf. न चेदन्यकार्यातिपातः etc. Act I. धर्मासनं–The seat or judgment where the king sits to hear the grievances or complaint of the people and administer justice. अविश्रमः–न विद्यते विश्रमः यस्य सः–Knowing no rest or repose. लोकतन्त्राधिकारः–The office (आधिकार) of governing (तन्त्र) the people–Cf. प्रजाः प्रजाः स्वा इव तन्त्रायित्वा । V. 5.

V. 4. युक्ततुरङ्गः-युक्ताः तुरङ्गाः येन सः । who has yoked the horses (to his chariot) once for all, (सकृत्) and he knows no rest, but drives on eternally. रात्रिंदिवम्-रात्रौ च दिवा च–day and night. गन्धवहः–Lit. the carrier of fragrance; the wind. आहितभूमिभारः–आहितः भूमेः भारः येन सः–who has placed (on his head) the burden of the earth. शेषः–' i. e. अनन्त, a mythological serpent, the personification of eternity (अनन्तता) and king of the Nāgas or snakes who inhabit the lowermost of the seven Pātālas or infernal regions. His body formed the couch of विष्णु, reposing on the waters of Chaos, whilst his thousand heads were the god's canopy. He is also said to uphold the world on one of his heads. He has become incarnate at various times, especially in the god बलराम, the elder brother of कृष्ण'. M. W. षष्ठांशवृत्तिः-षष्ठांशेन वृत्तिः यस्य सः–The king who lives on the tribute given by the people viz. one-sixth of the produce.

V. 5. स्वाः प्रजाः इव–Like his own children. तंत्रयित्वा–Having ruled or governed. √तंत्र्–has also the sense of 'Maintaining or supporting (as a family)'. श्रान्तमनाः–with a wearied mind. V. L. शान्तमनाः–'with a peaceful or composed mind' is not so good. विविक्तं–A secluded or solitary place. यूथानि संचार्य–Having led or conducted the herds (यूथ); Lit. 'Having caused to move about or graze.' दिवा–i. e. मध्याह्ने–At mid-day. उपत्यका–अद्रेरासन्ना भूमिः the slope of the mountain, a lowland at the foot of the mountain. सस्त्रीकाः–with (two) women (accompanying). श्रौतेन विधिना–According to the form prescribed by the scriptures (श्रुति). चरितार्थता–The state of having obtained everything desired by them (i.e. kings). दुःखोत्तरा–खेदसंवलिता–V. L. दुःखान्तरैव 'painful, encompassed with trouble or worry.' He means that the interval between the desire and its attainment, accompanied as it is with keen effort to win the object and its phases of hope and disappointment, is indeed a very lively period in man's life. This is however denied to a king who has everything at his disposal, and has nothing to wish for. This very condition, however, is positively painful to him.

V. 6. प्रतिष्ठा–The high position, the (royal) glory, the dignity –सर्वोत्कृष्टं गौरवम् ।. M. W. Understands it in the sense of 'the attainment of the object of ambition' agreeing with प्रार्थितार्थाधिगम or चरितार्थता. अवसादयति–satisfies. अवसाययति—V. L. Terminates, finishes; he means that the dignity of a king, by which he gets everything the moment he desires it, destroys even the eagerness or the anxious longing (औत्सुक्यं) for that object, because it is so easily attainable. Cf. अन्यजनस्य तु यत्किंचिद्विषयिणी समुत्पन्नोत्कण्ठा तथैव तिष्ठति तत्ताद्विषयालाभात् । राज्ञस्तु–फल्लाभादुत्कण्ठापरिपूर्तिः । राघव० लब्ध... वृत्तिः—The duty or the (King's) function of preserving whatever he has obtained. नातिश्रमापनयनाय–' Not so much conducive to the removal of fatigue–' The king's position, because of its accompanying worries of preserving his kingdom intact, is not calculated to give him any physical or mental relief. 'Uneasy lies the head that wears a crown.' यथा श्रमाय–As it is (positively) for causing fatigue or exhaustion (by its cares and anxieties). Note the other reading–नातिश्रमापनयनाय न च श्रमाय. ' Is not for the removal of great fatigue and not for fatigue i.e. royalty does lead to fatigue. ' स्वहस्त...दण्डम्–स्वहस्ते धृतः दण्डः यस्य तत्—The handle of which is held in one's own hand आतपत्रम्–A parasol, umbrella. ' The Indian parasol or छत्र, from the shelter it affords, has been chosen as one of the insignia of royalty. It is very heavy and being fixed on a long pole, greatly fatigues the person holding it. It is always borne by a servant; but here the king is figuratively made to bear it himself, so that he cannot give shelter to himself and others, without undergoing great personal fatigue.' M. W. वैतालिकः–A herald, bard, a panegyrist. ' He was a kind of a herald or crier whose duty was to announce, in measured verse, the fixed periods, into which the king's day was divided. '

V. 7. स्वसुखनिरभिलाषः–स्वसुखे निर्गतः अभिलाषः यस्य सः– Having no desire for personal happiness indifferent to your own ease. खिद्यसे–(you) exert, toil. A fine illustration of दृष्टान्त.

V. 8. नियमयसि–(You) restrain, curb, punish. आत्तदण्डः–आत्तः दण्डः येन सः–Who has assumed the sceptre, the symbol of punishment and justice. विवादः–Dispute, quarrel. कल्पसे–You are fit for or adequate to (the protection). अतनुषु विभवेषु–In great (अतनु) prosperity, in affluent circumstances. नाम–in the sense of प्राकाश्ये ' as it is well known. ' त्वयि परिसमाप्तं–In you is perfected, is fully comprehended. ' बन्धुकृत्यं–The duty of a kinsman. He means that the king stands as the chief kinsman to his subjects, the so–called relatives being with man only during his prosperous time. Compare the king's declaration at the end of the VI Act–येन येन वियुज्यन्ते प्रजाः स्निग्धेन बन्धुना । स स पापादृते तासां दुष्यन्त इति घुष्यताम् ॥ Cf. also प्रजानां विनयाधानाद्रक्षणाद्भरणादपि । स पिता पितरस्तसां केवलं जन्महेतवः ॥ रघु० 1. 24. नवीकृतः–Refreshed. आभि...सश्रीकः–अभिनवेन संमार्जनेन सश्रीकः (श्रिया सहितः) Beautiful after its recent purification by the sprinkling of water. अग्नि...लिन्दः–A terrace (अलिन्द) of the fire–sanctuary.

V. 9. व्रतिन्–An ascetic, a hermit. उपोढतपस्–उपोढं तपः यस्य सः–who has accumulated or hoarded (a store of) penitential merit. दूषितं–marred, frustrated. For this idea, compare आपाद्यते न व्ययमन्तरायैः कच्चिन्महर्षेस्त्रिविधं तप स्तत्। रघु० V. 5. असत्–wrong, harm, injury. आहोस्वित्–used in introducing generally a third alternative. अपचरितं–A misdeed, a sinful action वीरुधां प्रसवः–The flowering or the blossoming of creepers. विष्टम्भितः–Paralysed, checked. The line (आहोस्वित् etc.) has a reference to the belief that the king's sins are visited on his subjects in the form of various calamities. Cf. न राजापचारमन्तरेण प्रजास्वकालमृत्युश्चरति। उत्तर० II. Also. राज्ञोऽपचारात् पृथिवी स्वल्पसस्या भवेत्किल। अल्पायुषः प्रजाः सर्वा दरिद्रा व्याधिपीडिताः॥ Quoted by राघ० आरूढ...तर्क (मनः) आरूढाः (संजाताः) बहवः प्रतर्काः यस्मिन् तत्–In which various conjectures had arisen. अपरिच्छेदाकुलं–Perplexed with an inability to decide. अपरिच्छेदः–want of decision. सभाजयितुं–To congratulate, to greet. Cf. स्नेहात् सभाजयितुमेत्य दिनान्यमूनि। उत्तर० I.

V. 10. Kanva's pupil शार्ङ्गरव feels extremely out of sorts, when he finds himself in the midst of the swarming multitudes of the palace, and he tries to discover the causes thereof. महाभागः–eminent in virtues. अभिन्नस्थितिः–न भिन्ना स्थितिः येन सः–who has not broken away from the right path, not swerved from rectitude. He means that this uneasy feeling of his cannot certainly be attributed to the unrighteous policy of the king's behaviour, which is absolutely correct. अपकृष्टोऽपि–Even the lowest (of the four classes—वर्णानां). अपथं–The wrong path. The word is always neuter. हुतवहपरीतं–enveloped in the flames of fire. इदं–i. e. पुरोवर्ति नृपाङ्गणं–This royal court before my eyes. He explains his feelings. Accustomed as he was to seclusion, the crowd of the palace has made him restless, and he feels something out of the way has happened; the palace is as it were on fire and hence the throng of people.

V. 11. The other pupil शारद्वत has a similar experience. He feels, he is in an atmosphere of sin, impurity, uncleanliness of mind and body, of moral depravity. अभ्यक्तं–Anointed with oil. He is regarded as unclean until he has bathed. Cf. तैलाभ्यङ्गे चिताधूमे मैथुने क्षौरकर्मणि । तावद्भवति चाण्डालो यावत् स्नानं समाचरेत् ॥ –Kale. प्रबुद्ध इव सुप्तम्–Men who rise early in the morning have generally the tendency to look down upon those who get up late after sun-rise. सुखसंगिनम्–Addicted to pleasures. It is this fond attachment to or thirst for material pleasures that characterises the city people and that gives him this feeling of sin and impurity. While शार्ङ्गरव has taken a horror of the city-life and would like to run away far from the madding crowd, शारद्वत only pities them for their insatiable thirst for happiness which involves them in sin. निमित्तं–The bad omen viz. the throbbing of the right eye, which is most inauspicious and evil-foreboding in the case of woman. Cf. अङ्गविस्फुरणं नृणां दक्षिणं सर्वकामदं । तदेव शस्यते सद्भिर्नारीणामप्रदक्षिणम् ॥ Cf. जुगूह तस्याः पथि लक्ष्मणो यत् सव्येतरेण स्फुरता तदक्ष्णा । आख्यातमस्यै गुरु भावि दुःखमत्यन्तलुप्तप्रियदर्शनेन ॥ रघु० XIV. 49, where सीता too had a similar omen before she was cast away by लक्ष्मण. प्रतिहतं etc.–The sentence is commonly used to express the speaker's desire that the evil be averted. Cf. Mar. इडा पिडा टळो, अमंगळ पळो. वितरन्तु–May give. वर्णाश्रमाणां रक्षिता–The protector of the four classes (वर्ण) and the four orders or stages of human life viz. ब्रह्मचर्य, गार्हस्थ्य, वानप्रस्थ and संन्यास. महाब्राह्मण–There is a tinge of sarcasm in this expression, which we do get when the word महत् is prefixed to such words as ब्राह्मण,, वैद्य, implying निन्दा or censure which amounts to the absence of the real qualities. शार्ङ्गरव is slightly provoked by the Purohita's flowery description of the king as the protector of the Varnas and Āśramas and as one who favours them, as it were, with an interview. मध्यस्थाः–Unconcerned, indifferent. He means he has nothing to ask of the king, no suit to urge, no petition to present. This benevolent trait in the king is therefore more to the advantage of the पुरोहित than of him.

V. 11. फलागमैः –better than V. L. फलोद्गमैः. दूरविलम्बिनः–Hanging far (too low). दूरं विलम्बन्ते इत्येवंशीलाः । V. L. भूरिविलंबिनः.

अनुद्धताः-Not elated, not puffed up. प्रसन्नमुखवर्णाः-प्रसन्नः मुखवर्णः येषाम् ते-Having a serene, pleased facial expression. विश्रब्धकार्याः-Having a quiet and easy business, (Lit. which inspires confidence).

V. 12. का स्वित्-'who possibly'. स्वित्-a particle of question and doubt. स्विदिति वितर्के । अवगुण्ठनवति-Possessed of a veil (अवगुण्ठन)-It shows that ladies of high family used the veil in ancient days. नाति...लावण्या-न अतिपरिस्फुटं शरीरस्य लावण्यं यस्याः सा-whose loveliness of the body is not fully displayed (being obscured by the veil). कुतूहलगर्भोपहितः-कुतूहलेन गर्भे (मध्ये) उपहितः-Full of curiosity, being hindered (by the veil etc.). अनिर्वर्णनीयम्-अदर्शनीयम्-ought not to be gazed at. भावमवधार्य-Having reflected i. e. called to mind, the (intensity of) the feeling.

V. 14. तपति घर्मांशौ-Loc. Abs. when the sun is blazing. Cf. सूर्ये तपत्यावरणाय दृष्टेः कल्पेत लोकस्य कथं तमिस्रा । रघु० V. अर्थवान्-Full of significance. Cf. यथा प्रल्हादनाच्चन्द्रः प्रतापात्तपनो यथा । तथैव सोऽभूदन्वर्थो राजा प्रकृतिरञ्जनात् ॥. रघु० IV. 12. लोकानुग्रहाय-For the welfare of the world. The sage's health is conducive to the world's welfare. स्वाधीनकुशलाः-who have prosperity in their power. अनामयप्रश्नपूर्वकम्-अनामयप्रश्नः पूर्वं यस्मिन् तत्-preceded by the question of health (अनामय-Lit. Absence of disease). Cf. ब्राह्मणं कुशलं पृच्छेत् क्षत्रं पृच्छेदनामयम् । मनु० II. 127. मिथः समयात्-By mutual agreement (समय). उपायंस्त-Aorist III. Sing. of √उप+यम् 'to marry'.

V. 15. अर्हतां प्राग्रसरः-The chief of the respectable (अर्हत्). नःस्मृतोऽसि-is esteemed by us. मूर्तिमती सत्क्रिया-Virtue incarnate or in person. समानयन्-Bringing together, uniting. तुल्यगुणं-तुल्याः गुणाः यस्य तत्-(The two) of equal merit. वधूवरं-वधूश्च वरश्च (एतयोः समाहारः) तत्-वधूवरं-a समाहारद्वन्द्व compound. चिरस्य-After a long time. वाच्यं न गतः-Has not been exposed to censure, has incurred no blame. He means that so long every marriage was a union of two incompatibles, there being some flaw either in the bride or in the bride-groom. No couple was found to be a happy one in all respects. In the present union, however, the creator has succeeded in bringing two suitable persons together–an event which has saved him from blame for the first time after such a long period. आपन्नसत्वा–गर्भवती–Quick with child. Cf. आपन्नसत्वा स्याद् गुर्विण्यन्तर्वत्नी च गर्भिणी । अमर० सहधर्मचरणाय–For the joint discharge of religious obligations. A wife has to take part in all religious rites that the husband performs. The rites here may be certain संस्कारs to be done conjointly for the child before and after birth. किमपि etc. गौतमी's speech conveys a veiled censure for the king's action in secretly marrying शकुन्तला, without consulting her who was almost a mother to her. न मे...सरोऽस्ति–'There is no occasion for me to put in a word on behalf of शकुन्तला, when on a former occasion neither you nor she herself thought it fit to consult me.'

V. 16. न अपेक्षितः–Not referred to. एकैकं एव चरिते–when the affair was transacted quite privately (एकैकं–Lit one with the other, and no third person was there) भणामि किमेकैकं–what can I say to any one of you i. e. either to शकुन्तला or to you also. V. L. भणदु एक्क एक्कस्स = भणतु एकः एकस्य । 'what has each one to say to the other.' वचनोपन्यासः–The import of the speech लोकनिष्णाताः–well versed or fully acquainted with the ways of the world.

V. 17. ज्ञाति...संश्रयां–ज्ञातिकुलं (एव) एकः संश्रयः यस्याः सा–who solely resides in the family of her kinsmen ज्ञाति–relatives of the family ofbirth–अन्यथा विशङ्कते–suspect (her) to be otherwise i. e. unchaste. प्रियाप्रिया वा–Liked or disliked (by him) ; V. L. तदप्रियापि 'although disliked by him. सांप्रतं–Correct, proper, justified.

V. 18. कृतकार्यद्वेषात्–' Through dislike of a thing done !' He means that the king seems to be repenting of his sojourn in the hermitage that led to a marriage with शकुन्तला , and hence has he turned his face away (विमुखता) from Duty viz. the acceptance of his lawful wife. उचिता राज्ञः–Is it befitting a King ? V. L. कृतकार्यद्वेषो धर्मं प्रति विमुखता कृतावज्ञा । कृतावज्ञा–a wilful disregard. असत्कल्पनः प्रश्नः–A question based upon a fabrication of false-hood. ' The very assumption of marriage is a great fraud being falsely invented. What of this question based upon this false-hood?' मूर्छन्ति–Take effect, grow strong. ऐश्वर्यमत्त–Intoxicated with sovereignty. विशेषेण अधिक्षिप्तोऽस्मि–The अधिक्षेप or censure though worded in general terms is especially aimed at me. I am the especial target of this censorious remark viz. ऐश्वर्यमत्त. It may also mean 'I am greatly censured or rebuked.'

V. 19. एवं उपनतं–Thus presented to me (without any effort on my part). अयत्नप्राप्तम्। Or एवं–i. e. in a pregnant condition' to correspond with अन्तस्तुषारं। अक्लिष्टकान्ति (रूपं)–Of unblemished loveliness. प्रथमपरिगृहीतं–Accepted (in marriage) before अन्यवस्यन्° Unable to decide ($\sqrt{}$वि+अव+सो). V. L. व्यवस्यन्–' Deliberating, trying to decide.' अन्तस्तुषारं–अन्तर्गतः तुषारः यस्य तत्–' With the dew-drop inside.' The dew-drop covers the honey and keeps off the bee by its cold. The king also has to keep his hands off शकुन्तला, because she is now pregnant. विभाते–Cf. अत्र विभात इत्युक्तस्तदनन्तरं रविकिरणैर्हिमे नीते मकरन्दभोगोऽत्रश्यः। एवमिहाप्यभिज्ञानदर्शनेन शापे गते तत्स्वीकारोऽत्रश्य इति द्योतयन्त्योपमया रतेः स्थायित्वदाढर्यं ध्वनितम्। धर्मापेक्षिता–consideration or regard for virtue. जोषम्–Silent. अभि...लक्षणां–अभिव्यक्तानि सत्वस्य (गर्भस्य) लक्षणानि यस्याः–Whose signs of pregnancy are clearly manifested. क्षेत्रिणमाशङ्कमानः–Suspecting myself (with regard to her) to be only a क्षेत्रिन्. क्षेत्रिन् the owner of the field, as opposed to बीजिन् i. e. one who sows the seed in the field, The figurative language was used in the law-books to refer to woman as क्षेत्र ' Field ', while the man who begets children from her was called बीजिन्–in cases where the husband differed from procreator of the child, there arose the controversy as regards the child's ownership, and the position of the क्षेत्रिन् who claimed the child simply because he happened to be the legal husband of the woman, was greatly deprecated. The king, in this case, therefore, has his own scruples about the similar relation he would bear to the child and hence he hesitates to accept her. Cf. भर्तुः पुत्रं विजानन्ति श्रुतिद्वैधं तु भर्तरि। आहुरुत्पादकं केचिदपरे क्षेत्रिणं विदुः।...बीजस्य चैव योन्याश्च

बीजमुत्कृष्टमुच्यते । सर्वभूतप्रसूतिर्हि बीजलक्षणलक्षिता ॥ मनु० IX. 32 ff. दूराधिरोहिणी. High-soaring.

V. 20. मा तावत्—May be taken with विमान्यः in the verse. 'May not the sage be insulted by you ?—Why, yes, he must be insulted etc.' Cf. मा तावदिति श्लोकेन संबध्यते ।...नामेति क्रोधे । मा विमान्यः न विमाननीयः । अपि तु विमाननीय एव । राघव० It may also be taken separately; 'enough, no more of this vow.' In that case the first line will have sarcastic twist, meaning 'The sage forsooth deserved to be thus disrespected by you, since he consented to your dastardly outrage on the modesty of his own daughter etc." The second interpretation is certainly preferable. कृताभिमर्शा—कृतः अभिमर्शः बलाद्धर्षणं यस्याः सा—Who was seduced or ravished. मुष्टं...येन—Construe :—येन (मुनिना) स्वं मुष्टं (अपि त्वां) प्रतिग्राहयता दस्युः इव त्वं पात्रीकृतः असि । The sage's action could be thus compared to that of a man who, finding his treasure robbed, invites the robber, and honourably makes him a gift of that very stolen treasure. पत्ययप्रतिवचनम्—A convincing reply; a reply calculated to produce conviction. शोचनीयः—To be sorrowed for. V. L शोधनीयः 'I myself am now to be cleared (justified) by myself; I have to vindicate the purity of my conduct." संशयिते—In doubt. समुदाचारः—Mode of address. स्वभावोत्तानहृदयं—स्वभावतः उत्तान हृदयं यस्य—तम्—(This person) who by nature is open-hearted. उत्तान—unreserved, frank. समयपूर्वम्—After a formal agreement (समय).

V. 21. व्यपदेश—व्यपदिश्यते अनेन सः—कुलं नाम वा । The designation, the litle or the name (of the family). The family is of शकुन्तला and not of the king, as is clear from the simile of the river making its own waters turbid. पातयितुम्—To bring down, to ruin. कूलंकषा—कूलं कषतीति सा तटसंघर्षिणी—Scratching the banks. उदारः कल्पः—A capital idea, a good proposal. शक्रावताराभ्यन्तरे—Within the शक्रावतार. शक्र is an epithet of Indra, and शक्रावतार is, therefore, some sacred place of pilgrimage where he descended upon the earth. अवतार—means also a descent into the river, a landing-place of stony steps (Mar. घाट). शचीतीर्थं-A holy bathing place, sacred to शची, wife of Indra. इदं तत् etc.-The king thinks the reply of गौतमी to be the work of a quick flash of imagination, and a masterly example of woman's instinctive ready wit. प्रत्युत्पन्नमति-प्रत्युत्पन्ना मतिः यस्य तत्-Ready-witted. स्त्रैणम्-स्त्रीणां समूहः-i. e. स्त्रीजातिः-Womanhood. प्रभुत्वम्-Power, sovereignty. श्रोतव्यमिदानीं संवृत्तम-What was to be seen (द्रष्टव्य) just a minute before, has now turned into what has to be heard (श्रोतव्य). Evidence of the eyes has changed into that of hearing.' Note the tone of contempt and mockery in the words of the king, who feels now fully convinced that he is tried to be duped by this pack of scoundrels in the garb of ascetics, who want to force this pregnant woman into the seclusion of his harem, and father the illegitimate child on him. शृणुमस्तावत्-'Let us hear; (go on).' Clearly indicating that he is not going to believe a single word of what she will say. पुत्रकृतकः-Adopted as a child. पुत्रश्चासौ कृतकश्च-Lit. 'made a son.' स मृगपोतकः-The fawn, (mentioned in IV. यस्य त्वया etc.). उपच्छन्दितः उदकेन-प्रलोभितः, जलपानाय प्रेरितः-Was coaxed or enticed to drink water. √उपछन्द्-To conciliate privately by flattering or coaxing language.' Cf. तस्मादुपच्छन्दयति प्रयोज्यं मयि त्वया न प्रतिरोधरौक्ष्यम्। रघु० V. 58. हस्ताभ्यासं-हस्तसमीपं-Near your hand; M. W. understands the word to mean 'Lit. the use of the hand. i. e. stroking with the hand, caressing,' with उपगम्, 'to approach for fondling, to allow to be caressed, to entrust one's self into any one's hands." प्रणयः कृतः-Showed a favourable disposition; evinced his desire. प्रहसितः-Laughed in a joke. सगन्ध-सदृश°-or संबन्धिजनः-Relative, kith and kin. आत्मकार्यनिर्वर्तिनी-'Accustomed to accomplish one's own purpose.' M. W. takes it to mean 'Turning (voluptuaries) away form their own duty.' अनृतमयवाङ्मधु-The honey of false words. कैतवस्य अनभिज्ञः-Unfamiliar or unacqainted with roguery. तापसवृद्धा-वृद्धा तापसी-वृद्धतापसी-or as we have it तापसवृद्धा according to पाणिनि० II. 2. 38., although the former form would be more usual. Note the king's harsh and jeering tone in the use of this expression with reference to गौतमी.

V. 22. अशिक्षितपटुत्वं-Untaught cleverness or inborn cunning. Cf. स्त्रियो हि नाम खल्वेता निसर्गादेव पण्डिताः । पुरुषाणां तु पाण्डित्यं शास्त्रेणैवोपदिश्यते ॥ मृच्छ० IV. अमानुषीषु-Among non-human species of creatures, i. e. in lower creatures. किमुत-'How much more'. प्रतिबोधवत्यः-ज्ञानिन्यः चैतन्यभाजः-gifted with intellect, endowed with reason. प्राक् 'Before', governs ablative. परभृता-A female cuckoo. In this verse, the king has unconsciously alluded to the story of शकुन्तला's birth, by the use of words which have a double meaning. i. e. अमानुषीषु-may refer to the celestial nymph, मेनका, the mother of शकुन्तला. प्रागन्तरिक्षगमनात्-would refer to her flight to heaven, after the birth of शकुन्तला, her अपत्यजात which is left in the care of a द्विज i. e. the Brahmin sage, कण्व. The expression that refers to her mother, is परभृता i. e. 'fed by others, a courtezan,' which in reality the Apsarasas are. All these invidious suggestions must have been read by शकुन्तला, who was exasperated to find that the king knowingly refers in this to her own story heard in that very आश्रम, and still repudiates her having full well recognised her; that he goes to the indecent length of almost abusing her own mother by calling her a harlot (परभृता), and further he reaches a climax in insulting her by suggesting, even शकुन्तला, who too is no better than a परभृता, has come down here, in imitation of her mother's conduct, to father her own prospective offspring on him. It is here that she feels convinced of the fact that the king is a liar and a scoundrel, and hence in her next sentence, she bursts out in a temper to call him an अनार्य. हृदयानुमानेन-By the measure of your own heart, by an inference drawn in comformity with the (wicked and villainous feelings and impulses of) your own heart. धर्मकञ्चुकप्रवेशिनः-Putting on (Lit. entering into or hiding himself underneath) the cloak or garb of virtue. तृणच्छन्नकूपोपम-Resembling a well covered or concealed underneath the grass, calculated to entrap innocent and unsuspecting creatures. अनुकृतिं प्रतिपत्स्यते-will act in imitation of your conduct; will be so low and degraded as to act like you. संदिग्धबुद्धिं कुर्वन्–Making me doubt my own judgment. अकैतवः– Unfeigned, genuine. The following passage is read by Ray, before संदिग्धबुद्धिं etc. वनवासादविभ्रमः पुनरत्रभवत्याः कोपो लक्ष्यते । तथाहि- न तिर्यगवलोकितं भवति चक्षुरालोहितं वचोऽपि परुषाक्षरं न च पदेषु संसज्यते । हिमार्त इव वेपते सकल एष बिम्बाधरः स्वभावविपते भ्रवौ युगपदेव भेदं गते ॥.

V. 23. विस्मरण...वृत्तौ–विस्मरणेन दारुणा चित्तवृत्तिर्यस्य सः तस्मिन्–(on me) who exhibited a dreadful state of mind by my loss of memory. वृत्तं रहः प्रणयं–(An affair of) love that happened in secret (रहः). भ्रुवोः भेदात्–By the knitting lit. by the parting of her eye-brows. अतिरुषा–Through excessive anger. स्मरस्य शरासनं मय्येव भग्नम् इव–'It seemed as if the bow of Cupid was snapped asunder even against me.' The two curved eye-brows with the bridge of the nose in between present the appearance of a bow in their normal attitude, and have often been imagined to be Cupid's bow, while the glances are likeness to arrows discharged from it. Cf. तस्याः शलाकाञ्जननिर्मितेव कान्तिर्भ्रुवो- रायतलेखयोर्या । तां वीक्ष्य लीलाचतुरामनङ्गः स्वचापसौन्दर्यमदं मुमोच ॥ कुमा॰ I. 47. Now, when these brows were parted from each other, being knit in a frown, they appeared like two pieces of a bow broken in the centre. Note also the double entendre in the word स्मर, which means 'recollection,' as well as 'the God of love.' इदं–this i. e. wicked treacherous conduct. स्वच्छन्दचारिणी–a self-willed woman, wanton, one who acts on the impulse of the moment. मुखमधोः–मुखे मधु यस्य– सः–तस्य–Who has honey on his lips. Cf. मधु तिष्ठति वाचि योषितां हृदि हालाहलमेव केवलम् । also मधुतिष्ठति जिह्वाग्रे हृदये तु हलाहलम् ॥ आत्मकृतं–Self-committed (without consulting any one else). अप्रतिहतं–When not checked or counter-acted. चापलं–A hasty action, a rash act. दहति Brings on repentance, leads to remorse.

V. 24. The first line is variously interpreted thus:– (i) राघव॰–अतः कारणात् संगतं मैत्र्यं परीक्ष्य कर्तव्यम् । रह एकान्ते संगतं विशेषात् परीक्ष्य कर्तव्यमित्यनुषज्यते । Therefore a union, especially (when) in private, ought to be formed with great circumspection, after having made proper inquiry, and investigating each other's characters and circumstances.' (ii) Ray–' Hence secret union has to be made after having specially (विशेषात्) tested (each other).' अज्ञात...सौहृदम्–' Thus does friendship become enmity, between those who know not each other's hearts.' A fitting advice indeed to those who play with love indiscreetly. It is not, as Kale suggests, a stricture on love-marriage. संभृतदोषैः Accumulated accusations. V. L. संयुतदोषाक्षरैः–सम्यक् न त्वीषत् युतः संपृक्तः न तु स्पृष्टः दोषो येषु तान्यक्षराणि येषु वचनेषु तैर्वचनैरिति विशेष्यमुन्नेयम् ।–With words full of accusation. अधिक्षिपथ–Reproach. V. L. क्षिणुथ–Harm, injure. सासूयम्–Sarcastically, ironically. अधरोत्तरम्–अधरं (हीनं) च तदुत्तरं च–निकृष्टप्राधान्यम्–' Ascendancy of the low, placing that at the top which ought to be at the bottom.' The word occurs in the Manusmriti, where it means ' a confused and contradictory statement. Cf. अदेश्यं यश्च दिशति निर्दिश्याह्नुपते च यः । यश्चाधरोत्तरानर्थान् विगतान्नावबुध्यते ॥ मनु० VIII. 53. It would mean here ' Inversion of the proper order of things, something made topsyturvy, a perversion of things.' The sentence may therefore mean, being addressed to all the people assembled in the sacrificial hall, " Have you heard of such a perversion ? " M. W. understands the sentence as addressed to the king, with reference to the ironical statement in the succeeding verse. Hence the meaning may be ' you have been taught upside down or backwards.' In other words, ' The usual definition of the fourth प्रमाण viz. शब्द as आप्तवाक्य, you would make it अनाप्तवाक्य, the words of an improper person.' Ray takes the expression to mean ' a preposterous suggestion,' remarking that शार्ङ्गरव wants the audience to note how the undeserving दुष्यन्त appears deserving and the deserving शकुन्तला as undeserving. The Com. राघवभट्ट takes it to mean ' a base answer.'

V. 25. परातिसन्धानम्–The deceiving of others. विद्येति–As a fine (honourable) art. He probably refers to the king's study of works like कौटिल्य's अर्थशास्त्र, dealing with politics, wherein the

विजिगीषु is taught to employ even questionable methods to gain his ends. आप्तवाचः–आप्तस्य इव वाक् येषां ते–Whose words are (as authoritative) as those of an आप्त. आप्त is defined as one who is trustworthy and who speaks the truth and is thus reliable. आप्तस्तु श्रद्धेयवचनः यथार्थवक्ता. ते सन्तु...वाचः—Let them, forsooth, be considered as men worthy of belief!' Note the ironical tone of शार्ङ्गरव. He exposes the perversity of the situation, where innocent people are being branded as liars, while professional cheats have the high honour of authoritative worthies. विनिपातः–Ruin, destruction, down-fall. Com. शंकर takes it to mean नरकगमन. किमुत्तरेण–' What is the use of replying, no use bandying words.'

V. 26. तदेषा...कान्ता–Saying this, after all argumentation, शारद्वत has proved that he is not going to believe the king. He has faith in शकुन्तला whom he looks upon as the king's lawful wife. The Bengālī Mss. read पत्नी instead of कान्ता. सर्वतोमुखी–सर्वतः मुखानि यस्याः सा–All-sided, in all respects, of every kind, unlimited. Lit. Facing all directions. करुणपरिदेविनी–Wailing or lamenting piteously. प्रत्यादेशपरुष–Harsh or cruel by his rejection of her. पुरोभागिनि–Voc. of पुरोभागिनी–a wanton, perverse person.' The word पुरोभागिन्–first means 'one who takes the first share or more than his proper share' (पुरो भागः यस्य सः) i. e. a grasping character. Cf. मा मां पुरोभागिनीति समर्थयसि । विक्र० III. Hence secondarily it means 'a censorious, malevolent person.' It has also the sense of 'one who is given to the habit of finding faults with others.' Cf. दोषैकदृक् पुरोभागी । अमर० Even this sense holds good here. शार्ङ्गरव wanting to suggest that शकुन्तला could easily call her own husband a rascal (कितव), while she has absolutely no sense of her wifely duty to abide with him in any circumstances. स्वातन्त्र्यमवलम्बसे–A wife has no independence or initiative of her own in her husband's house. Cf. पिता रक्षति कौमारे भर्ता रक्षति यौवने । पुत्रस्तु स्थाविरे भावे न स्त्री स्वातन्त्र्यमर्हति ॥ मनु० IX. 3.

V. 27. उत्कुला–उत्क्रान्ता कुलात् or उत्क्रान्तं कुलं यया सा–Fallen from the family. व्रतं–चारित्रं marriage-vow, conduct. क्षमम्–योग्यम्–Fit, proper. M. W. takes it to mean 'supportable. किं...विप्रलभसे– Why do you deceive her into the belief that she will be retained by me in my house-hold as my wife, if she persists in staying on here !

V. 28. कुमुदान्येव etc. Cf. विकसति हि पतङ्गस्योदये पुण्डरीकम् । उत्तर० पर...मुखी परस्य परिग्रहः तस्य आश्लेषः तस्मात् पराङ्मुखी–Recoiling or turning away with abhorrence from the embrace of another's wife. गुरुलाघवम्–गुरु च लघु च–तस्य भावः । An abstract noun from गुरुलघु, a द्वंद्व compound, the वृद्धि taking place in the second member of the compound instead of the first. It means 'the greater and the less, the heavier and the lighter (sin).' The king wants to know from the Purohita, which of the two courses, viz. rejection of a lawful wife, or acceptance of another's wife as one's own wife, would involve less sin.

V. 29. मूढः–Infatuated. परस्त्री...पांसुलः–Defiled (पांसुल Lit. soiled with dust) by contact with another's wife. आदिष्टपूर्वः–पूर्वं आदिष्टः–Already informed. V. L. उद्दिष्टः–Declared. चक्रवर्तिन्–A Universal monarch, a sovereign ruler–Lit. One who stands at the head of the circle (चक्र) of princes round–about. M. W. takes it to mean 'one who has the mark of the चक्र (or discus) in his hand.' When the lines of the right hand formed themselves into a circle, this was the mark of the future hero and emperor. The word also means 'one whose empire extends to the horizon (चक्र) or from sea to sea.' मुनिदौहित्रः–मुनिदुहितुः अपत्यं पुमान्–The son of the sage's daughter. Note the argumentative style of Purohita's speech, who is more expected to be well–versed in Nyāya and Vedānta than in Kāvya. विवरं–Entrance, admission. She means, she wishes no longer to live in the land of the living. Cf. तथा विश्वंभरे देवि मामन्तर्धातुमर्हसि । रघु० XV. 81. शापव्यवहितस्मृतिः– Whose memory was obscured by the curse.

V. 30. बाहुत्क्षेपं–बाहू उत्क्षिप्य–An instance of णमुल् gerund. Throwing up her arms.' स्त्रीसंस्थानं–स्त्रियाः इव संस्थानं (आकारः,

अवयवविन्यासः) यस्य तत्–Having the shape or form of a woman. आरात्– 'Near,' governs accusative.

V. 31. Construe:-कामं प्रत्यादिष्टां मुनेस्तनयां परिग्रहं न स्मरामि । I admit (कामं) I do not remember the repudiated sage's daughter to be my wife (परिग्रह). दूयमानं–Being troubled, being agitated. मां प्रत्याययतीव–Forces me as it were to believe her.

ACT VI

प्रवेशकः–See note on विष्कम्भक, Act III, IV. M. W. places this Praveśaka, not at the beginning of the VI Act as is done by almost all the editors, but between the two Acts V and VI. Cf. अथ पञ्चमषष्ठाङ्कमध्ये प्रवेशकः । M. W.'s edition, P. 217. नागरिकः– Superintendent of the city-police; नगरे नियुक्तः or नगराधिकारी । श्याल= राष्ट्रीय, is the (King's) brother-in-law, acting as the Police Superintendent, a character often introduced in the plays. Cf. मृच्छ०राजश्याल or राष्ट्रियश्याल. कुंभीलक–or V. L. कुंभीरक means 'a thief.' Cf. लोप्त्रेण गृहीतस्य कुम्भीलकस्यास्ति वा प्रतिवचनम् । विक्र० II. also अहो कुम्भीलकैः परिहरणीया चन्द्रिका । माल० IV. मणि...धेयं–मणिबंधने उत्कीर्णं नामधेयं यस्य–The setting of which is engraven with his name. 'मणिबन्धन usually meaning a 'wrist' (cf. III) has here the sense of the 'setting or the collet of the Jewel which formed the Mudrā or the seal of the ring. मणिः खच्यते यस्मिन्–इति मणिबन्धनः ।. The name might have been engraven on the stone itself or on the gold in which it was set. उत्कीर्ण–Engraven, excavated, inscribed. V. L. महामणिभासुले उक्किण्णणामाक्खले । Note the dialect spoken by the Policemen. It conforms to the characteristics of the Māgadhī, and is to be distinguished from the language of the श्याल or the other Prakrit-speaking characters, who give us the शौरसेनी dialect. प्रतिग्रहः–A present, gift. पाटच्चरः–A thief, a robber; explained as पाटयन् चरति–one who moves about by breaking open the walls. प्रतिबध्नीतम्–from √प्रति + बन्ध् to interrupt. जालोद्गालादिभिः–With fishing nets (जाल) and hooks (उद्गोल). मत्स्यबन्धनोपायैः–With contrivances to catch fish. विशुद्धः–'very pure'; said, of course, ironically; The निषाद or the fisherman's caste was looked upon as the lowest cf. मनु० x. 46–48. आजीवः–Profession.

VI. 1. सहजं–Lit. born along with (the person), कुलक्रमागतम् । किल–As the saying goes. as they say; he refers possibly to the popular quotations from the भगवद्गीता like स्वधर्मे निधनं श्रेयः परधर्मो

भयावहः । II 35 or better still, सहजं कर्म कौन्तेय सदोषमपि न त्यजेत् ॥ XVIII. 48. विनिन्दितं-censured, found fault with. The sense of अपि is understood after this word. श्रोत्रियः-A learned Brāhmaṇa, one well-versed in sacred learning. Cf. जन्मना ब्राह्मणो ज्ञेयः संस्कारैर्द्विज उच्यते । विद्यया याति विप्रत्वं त्रिभिः श्रोत्रिय उच्यते ॥ पशु...श्रोत्रियः-He means that even a learned Brahmin, although soft-hearted and tender with pity (for creatures in general) has to be cruel or dreadful in his slaughter of the sacrificial animal–a thing which ordinarily is an object of public censure. रोहितः-'Lit. 'Red–fish' is a kind of carp, found in lakes and ponds in the neighbourhood of the Ganges. It grows to the length of three feet, is very voracious, and its flesh, though coarse, is eaten. Its back is olive-coloured, its belly of a beautiful golden hue, its fins and eyes red'–M. W. कल्पितः-Cut. विस्रगन्धि–विस्रस्य–आममांसस्य–गन्ध अस्ति यस्मिन्-Smelling of raw meat (विस्र). गोधादी-An eater of गोधा i. e. an alligator. Some read the Prakrit गोहादी as गोधाती i. e. a cow-killer; and as cow-killing is looked upon as a heinous crime, the word is applied as a reproachful epithet to any rogue or low person. Thus in मृच्छ०, the चाण्डाल is called गोह or गोध्न'. M. W. मत्स्यबन्धः-A fish-catcher, a fisherman. विमर्शयितव्यम्-Ought to be investigated or closely inquired into. ग्रन्थिभेदक-Lit. 'knot-cutter or knot-breaker', a cut purse. V. L. गण्डभेदक which means the same thing. Read प्रतीष्य for प्रतीक्ष्य-Having received'. आवुत्तः-Brother-in-law. 'आवुत्तो भगिनीपतिः' अमर० अवसरोपसर्पणीयाः-That could be approached (only) at the proper time. सुमनसः पिनद्धुम्-to bind flowers into a wreath round the head of the victim. It is evident from works like the मालतीमाधव and the मृच्छकटिक, that a person about to be executed or offered as a victim to a deity like Śiva or Durgā had a wreath of flowers bound round the head. शुनो मुखं द्रक्ष्यसि-'will see the face of a dog'. The two policemen have no doubt about the fact that the fisherman guilty of such a criminal theft of the royal ring will receive capital punishment, and that he is soon to be executed. After the execution is carried out, his body will be thrown out, to be preyed upon by vultures or by dogs. If any doubt exists, it is only in regard to his later disposal by the vultures or by the dogs. ' Dr. Boethlingk has adopted an emendation, शिशुणो मुहं i. e. शिशोर्मुखं, and translated, 'or thou wilt see the face of (thy) child (once more).' There is, however, no authority for such an emendation. According to Ray, this refers to execution in which the condemned man is buried upto the neck under ground and dogs are then let loose to tear him up. The victim can see (द्रक्ष्यसि) the dogs coming because he is not dead yet.' जालोपजीवी-who maintains himself by means of a fishing-net. उपपन्नः-Justified, confirmed, found true. अङ्गु...संमितः-commensurate with the ring's value. दापितः-P. P. of the causal of √दा-' caused to be given, bestowed through me.' एष नाम etc. V. L. एष नामानुग्रहः etc.-' such indeed is the favour.' शूल-' A stake for impaling criminals. ' हस्तिस्कन्धे प्रतिष्ठापितः-Mounted or seated on an elephant i. e. elevated to a high dignity, was given a great honour. Elephants, as we know, were used in triumphal processions. संमत-Highly favoured or prized. V. L. बहुमतेन. Read पर्युत्सुकमनाः instead of पर्युत्सुकनयनः । 'Excited in mind.' The V. L. पज्जस्सुणअणो=पर्यश्रुनयनः-' With tearful eyes' is also very good. मात्स्यिकभर्तुः (कृते)-For the sake of this chief of the fishermen. The Prakrit word can be translated by मात्स्यिकाभर्तुः-'For the sake of the husband of the female fish '-said rather in vulgar joke and smacks of contemptuous envy. V. L. मच्छसत्तुणो=मत्स्यशत्रोः-' For the enemy of the fish.' सुमनोमूल्यम्-Of the value of a flower i. e. as insignificant as a flower; compare the Marathi idiom, फूल नाहीं फुलाची पांकळी M. W. looks upon this utterance, as an ironical remark with reference to their earlier comment on his profession—विशुद्ध इदानीमाजीवः ।. In fact he has taunted them before by his remark भर्तः, अथ कीदृशो म आजीवः । महत्तरः-Bigger, greater. The Mar. word म्हातारा owes its origin to this comparative form of महत्. कादम्बरीसाक्षिकं-कादम्बरी साक्षिणी यस्मिन् तद्-With liquor (कादंबरी) for its (i. e. friendship's) witness. कादम्बरी-Wine distilled from कदम्ब flowers. शौण्डिकापणम्-The liquorshop. Lit. the shop of a wine-seller (शौण्डिक). P. 168. पर्यायनिर्वर्तनीयम्-Which is to be carried out in turns (पर्याय), or rotation. For similar duty assigned to the celestial nymphs, Cf. अप्सरोवारपर्यायेणेह भगवतः सूर्यस्य पादमूलोपस्थानं वर्तते इति बलवत् खल्वर्वश्यामुत्कण्ठितास्मि । वि० III. उदन्तः–News, incident, circumstances. शरीरभूता–A veritable body, my own self. निरुत्सवारम्भं–निर्गतः उत्सवारम्भाः यस्मात्–Bereft of preparations (आरम्भ) to celebrate the the festival (of spring). 'The वसन्तोत्सव or 'the vernal festival' in celebration of the return of spring and said to be in honour of the god Krishna. Originally his son Kāma-deva, the god of love, must have been the object of worship in his festival. It is identified with the Holi or Dolā-yātrā, the Saturnalia, or rather, Carnival of the Hindus, when people of all conditions take liberties with each other, especially by scattering red powder and coloured water on the clothes of persons passing in the street as described in the Ratnāvalī Act I, where syringe and waterpipes are used by the crowd. Flowers and especially the opening blossoms of the mango, would naturally be much used for decorations at this festival, and as offerings to the god of love. It was formerly held on the full moon of the month of Caitra, or about the beginning of April, but now on the full moon of Phālguna, or about the beginning of March.' M. W. प्रणिधानम्–deep mental concentration; profound meditation. विभवः–power. आदरः–Eagerness, keen desire (that I should see the king's condition with my own eyes). तिरस्करिणीप्रतिच्छन्ना–covered by a magic veil. तिरस्करिणी is a magic art known to the divine beings, who employ it for the purpose of making themselves invisible to the mortals. Cf. Com. राघव० who explains this expression thus :– अन्तर्धानविद्यया परिच्छन्ना ।

VI. 2. जीवसर्वस्व–The essence or the all-in-all of life. V. L. जीवितसर्वम् ।. चूतकोरकः–The mango-blossom. ऋतुमङ्गल–The auspicious thing that opens the season. प्रसादयामि–causal of √प्र+सद्–I entreat you to favour (me). परभृतिका–A female cuckoo. मधुकरिका–A female bee. These are also the names of the two garden-maids, and significant as they are, they fit in with the atmosphere of spring which the poet has created and where the cuckoo is prominent with her sweet warbling and the bee by its humming and hovering over the fresh mango blossoms. मदविभ्रमगीतानाम्–Of songs of love and intoxication. अप्रतिबुद्धः–not fully bloomed. बन्धनभङ्गसुरभिः–fragrant after the cutting of the stalk (बन्धन). कपोतहस्तकं–The word कपोत, originally meaning 'a dove or a pigeon,' is technically applied to 'a mode of joining the hands together, in an humble entreaty, respectful representation, or fear.' Cf. सर्वपार्श्वसमाश्लेषात् कपोतः सर्व (सप) शीर्षकः । भीतौ विज्ञापने चैव विनये च प्रयुज्यते ॥. Com. शंकर.

VI. 3. गृहीतधनुषे–The compound correctly should be गृहीतधन्वने. To (the God-of-Love) who has taken up the bow, (now that spring has set in, and he is supplied with his shafts viz. the mango-blossoms). पथिक...लक्ष्यः–पथिकजनानां युवतयः लक्ष्यं यस्य सः–Having young women whose husbands have gone abroad, as the target. पञ्चाभ्यधिकः–The best of the five. पंचसु अभ्यधिकः ।. अनात्मज्ञा–आत्मानं न जानाति सा–One who knows not her own self i. e. a silly thoughtless person. अगृहीतार्था–अगृहीतनिषेधवस्तुस्वरूपा–unacquainted with the incident (of prohibition). वासन्तिक-Belonging to the season वसन्त, i. e blossoming in spring. प्रमाणीकृतं–' Looked upon or admitted as authority, received as a rule.'

VI. 4. चूतानां etc. Cf. ईषद्बद्धरजःकणाग्रकपिशा चूते नवा मञ्जरी । विक्र० II. 7. संनद्धम्–Fully developed and therefore ready to blossom. Cf. यौवनमङ्गेषु संनद्धम् । Act I. रुतं–The warbling. संहरति–withdraws. महाप्रभावः राजर्षिः–The king was believed to have power to direct or prohibit the advent of any season. Cf. मुनयोऽपि व्याहरन्ति राजा कालस्य कारणमिति । तत्किमहं जलदसमयं न प्रत्यादिशामि । विक्र० IV. कति दिवसानि–a few days; to be construed with the predicate गतानि. आगन्तुकता–The condition of being a stranger (आगन्तुक) उत्सवप्रियाः–fond of festivals. बहुलीभूतम्–Spread far and wide; known to all, become notorious. कर्णपथः–The range or the path of ears. कौलीनम्–लोकवादः–A scandal, an evil report; derived from कुल 'a family', and may signify 'report relating to family or private matters,' family scandal. कुल also means 'a group of people' and therefore, what is talked in a group is also very often nothing else but a scandal. (कुले जनसमूहे भवम्).

VI. 5. रम्यं-(everything) delighting or pleasurable. यथा पुरा-As before. शय्याप्रान्तविवर्तनैः-Rolling or tossing about on the edge of the bed अनिद्रः-उद्गता निद्रा यस्य सः-Whose sleep has fled away, sleepless. क्षपा-A night. दाक्षिण्यं-courtesy, politeness. It has also the sense of 'outward politeness lacking in the sincerity of love'. Cf. निषिञ्चन् माधवीमेतां लतां कौन्दीं च नर्तयन् । स्नेहदाक्षिण्ययोर्योगात् कामीव प्रतिभाति मे ॥ विक्र० गोत्रेषु स्खलितः-blundering in the (proper) names. Due to his absence of mind, he calls the particular lady by the name uppermost in his mind ; viz. that of शकुन्तला. This is a common idea with Kālidāsa. Cf. स्मरसि स्मर मेखलागुणैरुत गोत्रस्खलितेषु बन्धनम् ॥ कुमार० III. 8. also आर्य, यन्निमित्तं भर्ता उत्कण्ठितस्तस्याः स्त्रिया नामधेयेन भर्त्रा देवी आलपिता ॥ विक्र० II. पुरुषोत्तमेति भणितव्ये पुरूरवसीति निर्गता वाणी ॥ ibid. III. व्रीडाविलक्षः-Embarrassed by a feeling of inward shame. प्रभवतः-Abl. of प्रभवत्-Arising, overpowering, वैमनस्यम्-Abstract noun from विमनस्-विषण्णं मनः यस्य सः । Dejection, mental depression. सर्वास्ववस्थासु etc. Compare अहो सर्वास्ववस्थासु चारुता शोभां पुष्यति । माल० II.

VI 6. प्रत्यादिष्टवि...विधिः-प्रत्यादिष्टः विशेषमण्डनस्य विधिः येन सः-Who has scorned all special forms of decoration. बिभ्रत्-Pres. Part. of √भृ-to wear. वामप्रकोष्ठार्पित-Placed on or fastened upon the left fore-arm (प्रकोष्ठ). Read श्वासापरक्ताधरः-श्वासैः अपरक्तः अधरः यस्य सः Whose lower lip became discoloured i. e. bloodless on account of (hot) sighs. संस्कारोल्लिखितः-Rubbed or ground on a polishing stone. The word संस्कार refers to the act of polishing as also the polishing stone. The poet means that the king, although attenuated in form, does not appear to be such because of his magnificent majestic lustre, as is the case of a gem, which when polished loses its portion and yet shines brighter by its innate lustre ; similar idea, Cf. अपचितमपि गात्रं व्यायतत्वादलक्ष्यम् । Act II. क्लाम्यति Pines. स्थाने खलु-etc. Sānumatī means that the king is so charming that there is no wonder that शकुन्तला should pine for him, although insulted by his rejection of her. Any woman would feel the loss of such a lovely husband.

VI. 7. हतहृदयम्–This wretched or accursed heart हत. When so prefixed has this sense. Cf. कुर्यामुपेक्षां हतजीवितेऽस्मिन । रघु० XIV. अनुशयः—Remorse, repentance नन्वीदृशानि etc.–' Such is her lot, poor pitiable girl ! ' Sānumati observes how unfortunate was the life of शकुन्तला who was repudiated when she had gone to her husband in person, while now when he remembers everything, she is far away from him, deeply merged in grief. लङ्घितः–Attacked, seized, overpowered. Cf. आतपलङ्घनाद् बलवदस्वस्थशरीरा शकुन्तला । Act III. चिकित्सितव्यः–who should be treated after a diagnosis of his disease. चिकित्सा is diagnosis and cure. प्रत्यवेक्षिताः–Thoroughly examined or inspected. This has to be done to ensure close privacy for the king as also to see that no danger to his life comes from an assassin or a hostile person. पत्रमारोप्य–Putting (it) on paper, committing that to writing. The king was always the final authority to give judgment in cases which the minister would investigate. शिशिरा...रमणीय–शिशिरस्य च आतपस्य च छेदेन रमणीयः–Lovely because of the absence of (excessive) cold and heat. Cf नात्यत्यन्तं शिशिरं नात्यातपः । Com. राघव०. Ray takes it to mean ' lovely in the interval (छेद) between winter and summer, i. e. spring. रन्ध्रोपनिपातिनः–Rushing through the (first) hole (रन्ध्र) they can find ; the word रन्ध्र meaning ' a hole ' signifies ' a weak point in man. ' Cf. छिद्रेष्वनर्था बहुलीभवन्ति । or the English idiom, ' Misfortunes never come single. ' अव्यभिचारि–न व्यभिचरते तत्–which never fails, which is invariably true, having no exception.

VI. 8. Note the use of च-च which signifies simultaneous occurrence. मुनि...रोधिना (तमसा)-which obstructed the memory of my love for the sage's daughter. प्रहरिष्यता-Wishing to strike, desirous of striking, a Future Part. from √प्र+हृ. Compare for a similar sentiment, अये परावृत्तभागधेयानां दुःखं दुःखानुबन्धि ।. अयमेकपदे तया वियोगः प्रियया चोपनतः सुदुःसहो मे । नववारिधरोदयादहोभिर्भवितव्यं च

निरातपत्वरम्यैः ॥ विक्र० IV. 3. अनेन दण्डकाष्ठेन etc.–This reminds us of Śudraka's विदूषक or मैत्रेय in the मृच्छकटिक, who too is ever ready to help his friend with his crooked stick. V. L. कन्दर्पव्याधिम्। ब्रह्मवर्चसम्–ब्रह्मणः वर्चः–The Brahmanic lustre; said ironically in view of his ridiculous attempt to destroy the arrows of love. (वेलां) अतिवाहयिष्ये–I shall pass (my) time. चित्रफलकं–picture tablet. मणिशिलापट्टकसनाथः–furnished with a jewelled marble slab. उपहारः–An offering of flowers. प्रतिकृतिः–A portrait, a picture. परिहासः....भूतार्थः–Note the dramatic irony of these remarks. The very words which he had said to विदूषक to stop him from babbling his affair with शकुन्तला to the inmates of his harem, are being returned to him by विदूषक, in such a tragic manner. मृत्पिण्डबुद्धिः–मृदां पिण्डः इव बुद्धिः यस्य सः–Having intellect like a lump of clay, 'where understanding is as dense and lacking in receptivity, as a clod of earth;' clod-pated, block–head Cf. प्रभवति शुचिर्बिम्बोद्ग्राहे मणिर्न मृदां चयः। उत्तर० II. सखे त्रायस्व माम्–The acute pang of remorseful meditation on शकुन्तला has become unbearable to him. शोकपात्रात्मानः–शोकस्य पात्रं आत्मा येषाम् ते–Whose hearts have become receptacles (पात्र) of grief, who have given themselves up to grief. V. L. शोकवक्तव्याः–yields no sense. Ray incorrectly translates सोअवत्तव्वा as शोकवास्तव्याः–' Abode of grief.' प्रवातेऽपि etc. Cf द्रुमसानुमतां किमन्तरं यदि वायौ द्वितयेऽपि ते चलाः। रघु० VIII. 90. समवस्था–has the same sense as अवस्था, 'plight, miserable condition.'

VI. 9. व्यवसिता–Tried (to follow), made an attempt (only). मुहुस्तिष्ठति etc. refers to the words of शार्ङ्गरव, 'किं पुरोभागिनि, स्वातन्त्र्यमवलम्बसे।' बाष्पप्रसरकलुषां–Bedimmed with the flow of tears. स्वकार्यपरता–' Devotion to one's own cause, absorption in one's own object.' Sānumatī means that her eagerness to accomplish her purpose for which she came, viz. to witness the king's condition after Śakuntalā's rejection, has so much affected her, that she feels actually delighted to observe the king's tragic plight and his outbursts of grief. पतिदेवता–पतिः (एव) देवता यस्याः

सा-'To whom her husband is a god, a chaste, faithful wife.' M. W. translates it with an Englishman's outlook, thus "The idol or the goddess of her husband" or as we should say, 'a wife idolised by her husband.' परिमार्ष्टुम्- To touch, to hold, to outrage the modesty of. जन्मप्रतिष्ठा-जन्मस्थानम् The source of birth. सख्याः ते- of your friend i. e. of शकुन्तला. विदूषक, the king's friend, is being spoken of by the king as his wife's friend. Cf. जाने संख्यास्तव मयि मनः संभृतस्नेहमस्मात् । etc. संमोह...प्रतिबोधः-Śānumatī means that it is indeed a great wonder that this king should have been under such a delusion as to forget everything about Śakuntalā ; that he remembers her now, the cloud of forgetfulness being lifted off his mind, is nothing to be wondered at. न पारयतः- Are not able.

VI. 10. The blissful period in the hermitage in the company of Śakuntalā was so uncommonly delightful that it appears, when recalled to the mind, to be a dream (स्वप्न) as it were. But it cannot be such a vision, since I am sure, I was not under the influence of sleep. Was it magic (माया) practised on me by a juggler ? But it cannot be that, either, since there was not the slightest tinge of unreality in the whole experience, followed by the tragic repudiation of the real Śakuntalā. In the same manner, the idea that it was perhaps some mental delusion or hallucination, has to be dismissed. If then real, it was so short-lived, possibly because the store of my merit which gave me this much reward (तावदेव फलं यस्य-तावत्फलं), was meagre and got exhausted (क्लिष्टं), by this much experience, as a result of it. Cf. अखंडं पुण्यानां फलमिव च तद्रूपमनघम् ॥ Act II. In this strain does the king argue about the nature and the causes of his love's period with Śakuntalā. माया-Magic, illusion ; used in the Vedānta philosophy to signify 'The imagining of something which does not actually exist, super-imposition of one thing upon another.' असंनिवृत्त्यै-For the purpose of never returning, never to come back. मनोरथानामतटप्रपाताः-All the fondest hopes of meeting Śakuntalā once again are veritable crumblings of the river banks (तट) or like falls from a steep precipice, i. e. are to be ruthlessly frustrated and crushed. M. W. reads मनोरथानामतटप्रपातः–' And so (it–तद्) has become the steep precipice (अतट) of my heart's fondest hopes. Ray reads–तदतीतमेते । मनोरथानामतटप्रपाताः । एते, according to him, refers to the four possibilities, like स्वप्न etc. while the last line means, ' These are the precipices for my wishes (मनोरथानि) to drop from. ' The reading and the interpretation given above is supported by the com. राघवभट्ट, who remarks:—अतः परमेते त्वयोच्यमाना मया वाशस्यमाना मनोरथाः । नामेत्यलीके । अलीका मनोरथा इत्यर्थः । ते तटप्रपाता इति भिन्नरूपकम् । यथा वर्षासमये गङ्गादेस्तटा ओघेन पीड्यमाना अहमहमिकया पतन्ति । एकः पतति तदुपर्यन्यस्तदुपरीतरः । एवं मनोरथानामेके विलीयन्तेऽन्य उत्पद्यन्ते तेऽपि विलीयन्ते तदितरे उत्पद्यन्ते इत्यर्थः । निदर्शनम्–Example, illustration. असुलभ°.. भ्रंशि–असुलभात् स्थानात् भ्रश्यति तद्–which slipped away from a place which was ordinarily beyond reach or inaccessible. शोचनीयम्–Fit to be lamented.

VI. 11. सुचरितं-good action, merit. फलेन विभाव्यते–Is to be inferred by its result (फलं). अरुण......मनोहरासु (अङ्गुलीषु)–(The fingers) charming with its rosy nails (अरुण). लब्धपदं-लब्धं पदं येन तद्–which obtained a place.उद्घातः–Reference, allusion; or occasion. विदूषक all innocently wants to know what occasion was there for the king to give her the ring. निवेशयता–(By me) who was putting (the ring on her finger).

VI. 12. मद...प्रवेशं नेता–who will lead you to the entrance of my inner apartment. The ring had the king's name दुष्यन्त engraved on it, and it will not, therefore, take more than three days for the king's servant to come to the hermitage to take away Śakuntalā. अवधिः–Period, interval (of expectation), the appointment of a period. विसंवादितः–made to fail in keeping up the promise, frustrated. शचीतीर्थं वन्दमानायाः–etc.–And these were the very words said by गौतमी in explanation of the loss of the ring, that were jeered at by the king. ईदृशः...वैतत्–' How could it be explained that such (deep) love stands in the expectation of a token-ring, for the beloved to be recognised by her lover. '

VI. 13. बन्धुर...ङ्गुलिं (करं)–बन्धुराः कोमलाश्च अङ्गुल्यः यस्य तम् With its lovely (बन्धुर) delicate fingers. अचेतनं etc. He means that the ring is after all an inanimate object, and is not likely to use any discretion and appreciate excellence (गुणं). He was, however, more to blame since he, endowed with चेतना, rejected her when she had come to him of her own accord. अनुशय...हृदया– Whose heart is scorched with remorse (अनुशय). इयं चित्रगता भट्टिनी– The entrance of चतुरिका with the picture of शकुन्तला just at a time when the king is craving for her sight, is very opportune. मधुरा... प्रवेशः–The representation (अनुप्रवेश) of the various feelings (of fear, bewilderment, curiosity etc.) is very charming because of the lovely posture (अवस्थान) Cf. Com. राघव० मधुरं सुन्दरं यदवस्थान-माकृतिस्तया दर्शनीयो भावस्यानुप्रवेशोऽभ्यन्तरीकरणम् । सुन्दराकारतया भावाविर्भावो रम्यतर इत्यर्थः । M. Williams translates it thus: 'The presence of the prevailing sentiment (love–रति) is delightful by its sweet abiding in every part.' स्खलतीव...प्रदेशेषु–My sight stumbles, as it were, over the uneven parts of the body, Lit. on the depressions and prominences. 'The relief or appearance of projection and depression in the picture is so well managed that my eye is deceived, and seems to follow the inequalities of surface.' M. W.

VI. 14. चित्रे साधु न स्यात्–May not be well drawn in a picture, falls short of the real because of the painter's lack of skill. तदन्यथा क्रियते–Is improved upon, having been retouched. M. W. translates it thus, 'whatever is not well (executed) in the picture, all that is wrongly portrayed). तथापि–In spite of (all the retouching that is done to the picture). तस्या......न्वितम्–Her loveliness is exhibited in the picture, in a slight measure i. e. very faintly. He means that with all his effort and skill that he could bring to bear on this painting, he has failed in bringing out her natural loveliness which could be imitated very faintly. रेखा–लेखनं, The sketch, the delineation. राघवभट्ट quotes the following to define रेखा–शिरोनेत्रकरादीनामङ्गानां मेलने सति । कायस्थितिर्यतो नेत्रहरा रेखा प्रकीर्तिता ॥. अनवलेपः–Absence of conceit. For the remarks of

विदूषक viz. इदानीं तिस्रः etc. compare, वि० विदूषकः—कथं नैषा उर्वशी। तस्यास्तत्रभवत्या अभिमता सहचरी। which shows how विदूषक has no eye for beauty. मोघदृष्टिः—Having eyes in vain, possessed of sight, which serves no purpose. Some read मोहदृष्टिः—' dull-sighted. ' उद्वान्तकुसुमेन—the flowers from which have been thrown out (lit. vomited). विशेषतः अपसृताभ्यां—drooping down very much. अव...... पल्लवस्य—With its fresh foliage glistening with the sprinkling of water. भावचिह्नम्—A sign of love, an indication of passion.

VI. 15. स्विन्ना...वेशः—The impression (विनिवेश) of the perspiring fingers. रेखाप्रान्तेषु—On the edges of the picture. कपोलपतितं अश्रु—A tear-drop fallen on the cheek (of Śakuntalā in the picture). As he was drawing her portrait, the overpowering grief filled his eyes with tears, one of which dropped down on the picture. वार्तिका—A painting brush, a pencil. वर्तिकोच्छ्वासात्—By the swelling (in colour) caused by the brush with which the drop was tried to be removed. V. L. वर्णि (र्ण) कोच्छ्वासात्—from the coming out or puff of the paint; cf. रङ्गस्य उत्फुल्लत्वात्।.

VI. 16. बहुमन्यमानः—Thinking much, showing so much regard. स्रोतोवहा—A river. निकामजला—Having plenty of water. प्रणयवान्—full of love or desire. मृगतृष्णिका मृगाणां तृष्णा अस्यां—सा मृगतृष्णा—सैव मृगतृष्णिका—Mirage. This is a fine illustration of निदर्शना. अभिरूपः—favourite.

VI. 17. The picture was only half-drawn, and these details have to be supplied to make the picture complete. सैकत...मिथुना—With couples of swans resting unnoticed on the sandy bank (सैकत). निषण्णहरिणाः—With the deer sitting or reclining. गौरीगुरोः पादाः—The sloping hills of the mountain Himālaya, lit. the father of Gauri or Pārvati. तामभितः—On both the sides of the river. शाखा...वल्कलस्य शाखासु आलम्बितानि वल्कलानि यस्य—तस्य (तरोः). On whose branches are suspended the bark-garments. वामनयनं कण्डूयमानां—Scratching or rubbing her left eye. Note how the king wants to create an atmosphere of love in the picture. The river Mālini with the mountain by its side, the pairs of swans and last of all, the picture of the female deer rubbing her left eye on the horn of her mate, the black antelope will certainly lend a peculiar charm to this picture of Śakuntalā. लम्बकूर्च–Having long beard. प्रसाधनम्–Decoration.

VI. 18. कर्णार्पितबन्धनं (शिरीषं)–कर्णे अर्पितं बन्धनं यस्य तत् With its stalk (बन्धनं) placed on the ear. आगण्ड...केसरम्–आगण्डं (गण्डपर्यन्तं) विलम्बिनः केसराः यस्य तत्–With its filaments hanging down up to the cheeks. शर...कोमलं– (The lotus-fibre) soft like the ray of the autumnal moon. स्तनान्तरे–Between the two breasts, in the midst of her bosom. Cf. अन्योन्यमुत्पीडयदुत्पलाक्ष्याः स्तनद्वयं चारु तथा प्रवृद्धम् । मध्ये यथा श्याममुखस्य तस्य मृणालसत्रान्तरमप्यलभ्यम् ॥ कुमार॰ I 40. चकितचकितेन–As if greatly frightened or scared. ननु...धृष्टः–Cf. न एष धृष्टो विरमति । Act I. अविनीतानां शासिता–The chastiser of the impudent. विदूषक reminds him, as it were, of his own words (कः पौरवे वसुमतीं शासति शासितरि दुर्विनीतानाम् । Act I.) said by him while introducing himself to the girls. कुसुमलताप्रिय–dear unto the flowering creepers. परिपतनम्–Flying or hovering about.

VI. 19. प्रतिपालयति–Waits (for you). अभिजातं–Politely, nobly, in a courteous manner. वामा–Wanton, perverse.

VI. 20. अक्लिष्ट...नीयः–अक्लिष्टः यः बालः तरुपल्लवः, तदिव लोभनीयः–Alluring or enticing like an unfaded fresh sprout of a tree. Cf. अधरः किसलयरागः etc. Act I. रतोत्सवेषु–During love's festivals or love's banquets. कमलोदरबन्धनस्थं कारयामि–I shall get you thrown in the prison of the hollow of a lotus. A culprit guilty of molesting a woman is punished usually by imprisonment ; and the same punishment will therefore be meted out to the bee as well, both in his capacity of a king and as her husband. In the first Act (Cf. चलापाङ्गां दृष्टिं etc.), the king's position was different. Both of them, were on equal footing, although later, as a king he steps in to ward off his successful rival. एवं तीक्ष्णदण्डस्य–' Of you, giving such a severe punishment '–said, of course, ironically. एष उन्मत्तः...संवृत्तः–विदूषक now realises that he too like the mad king, had transformed himself into the atmosphere of the picture, where the whole scene, he felt, was actually being enacted before his eyes. अनवगतार्था-one who had not understood the thing, viz. that it was a picture. V. L. अनवगतार्था-would mean, 'I too realised it just now.' पौरोभाग्यम्-पुरोभागी दुष्टः-तस्य कर्म पौरोभाग्यम्-Mischief, a wanton, ill-natured act.

VI. 21. तन्मयेन हृदयेन-With a heart fully absorbed (in the picture). चित्रीकृता-Was turned into a picture. He means, he had rescued her from the lifeless picture, by the power of his mental absorption, and made her live and move before his eyes; by reminding him that it is a picture, विदूषक has again turned her into the picture पूर्वापरविरोधी-Involving a contradiction between what preceded (पूर्व) and what followed (अपर). She means that his actions before (i. e. when he did not remember her and consequently most cruelly discarded her) bear a strange contrast to his moping attitude of grief and bereavement. He was stern like steel, before, and soft like wax now. The Com. राघव takes it differently thus:- पूर्वं चित्रस्य चित्रत्वेन ज्ञानं पुनस्तस्योन्मादावस्थायां सत्यत्वेन ज्ञानं पुनरपि चित्रत्वेन ज्ञानमिति पूर्वापरविरोधः।

VI. 22. खिलीभूतः—prevented, barred. द्रष्टुं न ददाति—Do not allow me to see (her in a picture). Note the idiom, which is very much like the Marathi expression, पाहूं देत नाहीं. The tears obstructing the lover's view of his beloved drawn in a picture, is a favourite idea of कालिदास. Cf. त्वामालिख्य प्रणयकुपितां धातुरागैः शिलायां... अस्रैस्तावन्मुहुरुपचितैर्दृष्टिरालुप्यते मे। मे० II. मत्संभोगः कथमुपनमेत् स्वप्नजोऽपीति निद्रामाकाङ्क्षन्तीं नयनसलिलोत्पीडरुद्धावकाशाम्॥ मे० II. हृदयमिषुभिः कामस्यान्तः सशल्यमिदं सदा। कथमुपलभे निद्रां स्वप्ने समागमकारिणीम्। न च सुवदनामालेख्येऽपि प्रियामसमाप्य तां मम नयनोरुद्बाष्पत्वं सखे न भविष्यति॥ विक्र० II. 10. प्रमार्जितं-Wiped away, fully atoned for. अन्तरा-On the way, midway. आत्मा निर्वाहितः-I took myself off. I made my escape. Lit. my own self was carried off (by me). बहुमानगर्विता-Puffed up or elated with vanity, because of the great attention (बहुमान) I show to her. आत्मानं (रक्षतु) इति भण-विदूषक is afraid of his own safety more than that of the picture. अन्तःपुरकालकूटात्– From the bane or the deadly poison (कालकूट) of the harem, (which is full of bitter jealousy and hatred). V. L. अन्तपुरकूट-वागुरातः–' From the noose of perfidy of the harem.' प्रथमसंभावनाम-पेक्षते–Respects or shows his regard to his first love. It is read as one sentence by some. Cf. अन्यसंक्रान्तप्रेमाणो नागरा अधिकं दक्षिणा भवन्ति ॥ विक्र० III. अर्थजातं– The various items of revenue; Ray ' several receipts.' विपन्नः–died. तपस्वी–Poor man ! बहुधनत्वात् बहु-पत्नीकः–Polygamy, especially among the rich, was the rule of the day. He had as it were a right to marry many wives, because he had ample wealth ! साकेतस्य श्रेष्ठी–A merchant from Sāketa i. e. Ayodhyā. पुंसवनं–' The rite performed on the quickening of the foetus' with a view to secure the birth of a male child. It is second of the 16 संस्कारs, coming next after the गर्भाधान ceremony, and performed generally in the third or fourth month after conception. Cf. व्यक्ते गर्भे तृतीये तु मासे पुंसवनं भवेत् । गर्भेऽव्यक्ते तृतीये तु चतुर्थे मासि वा भवेत् ॥ शौनक० The ceremony consists in placing यव grain and two माष grains (representing the male organs of generation on the right palm of the lady, who is to swallow them, along with some cream, to the accompaniment of the sacred Mantrās. रिक्थं–Property, wealth.

VI. 23. पापादृते–(i) except it be a sinful relation; for instance, that of a husband to a widow. (ii) The wicked excepted; i. e. if the man is a sinner and a culprit, and therefore deserves no patronage from the king. सन्तति...लम्बाना– (Of families) that are supportless by the lapse of progeny (that would have maintained the continuity). मूलपुरुषवसाने At the end i. e. the death (अवसान) of the representative of the race or the original stock. मूलपूरुष would properly mean the original proginitor but here it means 'the stock-man, the eldest surviving son.' राघव and M. W. read ममाप्यन्ते पुरुवंशश्रीरकाल इवोप्तबीजा भूरेवंवृत्ता । उपस्थित–...मानिनम्–उपस्थितं श्रेयः अवमन्यते सः–तम् Who despised the bliss that waited on him.

VI. 24. आत्मनि संरोपितेऽपि–' Although myself was implanted (in her womb), she was sown with myself, i. e. she bearing my second self in her womb.' This refers to the belief that a child is an incarnation or a reproduction of one's own self. Cf. अङ्गादङ्गात् संभवसि हृदयादभिजायसे । आत्मा वै पुत्रनामासि स जीव शरदः शतम् ॥. Also पतिर्जायां प्रविशति गर्भो भूत्वेह मातरम् । जायायास्तद्धि जायात्वं यदस्यां जायते पुनः ॥ मनु°. कुलप्रतिष्ठा–The stability of the family. काले–At the proper season; if अकाले–is read, then it has to be construed with त्यक्ता, meaning 'forsaken at a wrong time, when just the harvest was ready.' अपरिच्छिन्ना–' Uninterrupted.' She knows that he has a son from Śakuntalā संशयमारूढाः–' Have reached a critical state, (when they have become apprehensive as regards offerings to them in future, after me.').

VI. 25. यथाश्रुति संभृतानि–prepared in accordance with the scriptural texts. निवपनानि–Libations. नियच्छति–Offers. V. L. करिष्यति । प्रसूतिविकल–destitute of progeny, deficient in offspring. धौताश्रुशेषं–Remaining after being used for washing the tears (caused by this galling thought), मोहमुपगतः–This shows how keen was the king's anxiety, caused by an implicit faith in the prevailing notion of the Śrāddha ceremony and its efficacy. व्यवधानदोषेण–By the fault of the intervening curtain that obscures the view. She means, the king has a son, but because of his ignorance of this fact, he bewails his childless condition, like a man groping in the darkness, the light being obscured by the screen. Read निर्वृतं–Happy, satisfied. यज्ञ...त्सुकाः–Eager to have their share of oblations in a sacrifice. The kings used to perform great sacrifices in celebration of joyful occasions like marriage etc. and Indra as also the other inferior gods were invited to partake of portions intended for them. महेन्द्रजननी The mother of Indra viz. अदिति, who was the wife of कश्यप. आत्तगंधः–आत्तः गन्धः–गर्वः–यस्य सः–Who has his pride removed, humbled, insulted. Cf. पक्षच्छिदा गोत्रभिदात्तगन्धाः । रघु°. XIII. 7. सत्वं–An evil spirit, (भूत). गृहाः–गृह is used in Masc. Plural to denote, 'a house, or a wife.'

VI. 26. प्रमादस्खलितं–'blunder through carelessness, a false step through heedlessness. वेदितुमस्ति शक्तिः–A question asked, with a peculiar change in the tone which is suggestive of the reply. This is called a प्रश्नकाकु. शक्तिरस्ति किम्? नास्तित्यर्थः। अविहा or अविधा–(आक्रोशे) used in calling for assistance. पश्चादवनतशिरोधरं–पश्चात् अवनता शिरोधरा यस्य सः–तम्–Whose neck is bent backwards. V. L. पच्चवणदसिरोहरं = प्रत्यवनतशिरोधरं, which means the same thing. तीक्ष्णभङ्ग–who is being cut violently (तीक्ष्ण) into pieces. V. L. तिण्णभङ्गं = त्रिभङ्गं–cut into three pieces. हस्तावाप–A protection for the hand or fore-arm, a leather band, a handguard.

VI. 27. चेष्टमानम्–Struggling (to escape). शरणं–Refuge, protector. Cf. शरणं गृहरक्षित्रोः। अमर०. कुणपाशनः–कुणपं–शवं–अश्नाति यः–An eater of dead bodies, a carrion-eater.

VI. 28. हंसो हि–A royal swan or a flamingo is supposed to have the power of separating milk from water ; hence we have the हंसक्षीरन्याय. Cf. न त्वस्य दुग्धजलभेदविधौ प्रसिद्धां वैदग्ध्यकीर्तिमपहर्तुमसौ समर्थः ॥ नीति० 18. नीरक्षीरविवेके हंसालस्यं त्वमेव तनुषे चेत् etc. । भा० वि० I. 13. मातलिः–is the name of Indra's charioteer.

VI. 29. शरव्यम्–A mark, a target. हरिणा–By Hari i. e. Indra. प्रसाद etc. Construe सुहृज्जने सतां प्रसादसौम्यानि चक्षुंषि पतन्ति, न दारुणाः शराः (पतन्ति)। प्रसादसौम्यानि–Softened with kindly favour. इष्टिपशुमारम्–A णमुल् gerund used with the उपमान viz. इष्टिपशु–'Beaten like a sacrificial animal.' Cf. कर्मकर्त्रोर्णमुलि...। का० प्र० X. 89. कालनेमिः–'Son of the demon हिरण्यकशिपु. He had hundred arms and as many heads. These दैत्यs were sometimes called दानवs, from their mother दनु, who, as well as दिति, was one of the wives of कश्यप and daughters of दक्ष.' M. W. नारदः–A celebrated divine sage, usually reckoned among the ten प्रजापतिs, first created by ब्रह्मा. He acts as a kind of messenger of the gods.

VI. 30. सः–i. e. The host of demons, called दुर्जयः–अजय्यः–जेतुं अशक्यः–Invincible, unconquerable. Cf. क्षय्यजय्यौ शक्यार्थे ।. It should be distinguished from अजेयः–जेतुं अयोग्यः । शतक्रतुः–An epithet of Indra, meaning 'one who has performed hundred sacrifices (क्रतु).' He is so called because the rank which he occupies is unattainable excepting through a hundred अश्वमेधs or 'horse-sacrifices'. Cf. तथा विदुर्मां मुनयः शतक्रतुं द्वितीयगामी न हि शब्द एष नः ॥ रघु० III. 49. रणशिरसि–In the fore-front (शिरसि) of the battle, at the head of the fight. Read प्रयुक्तम्–Acted, behaved. किंचिन्निमित्त–किंचिद् निमित्तं यस्य सः–Having some reason, (which I did not know).

VI. 31. चलितेन्धनः–चलितं इन्धनं यस्य सः–With its fuel stirred. विप्रकृतः–provoked, molested. फणां कुरुते–expands its hood. V. L. फणं. क्षोभात्–Through provocation. V. L. कोपात्. दिवस्पतिः–The lord of the heaven, i. e. Indra. परिगतार्थं कृत्वा–Having acquainted (the minister) of this circumstance.

VI. 32. केवला–Single, unaided (by my bow). व्यापृतं–Employed, engaged.

ACT VII

P. 210. आकाशयान–The aerial path. यान–also means a 'conveyance'. अनुष्ठितनिदेशः–अनुष्ठितः निदेशः येन सः । ब० । One who has executed or carried out the orders given to him. सत्क्रियाविशेषात्–Because of the high mark of respect or extraordinary honour. अनुपयुक्तम्–i. e. अयोग्यम्. Unworthy, not deserving. The word मघवतः can be construed with both अनुष्ठित° and सत्क्रिया°. Mark the modesty of the king. He is illustrating the saying अनुत्सेकः खलु विक्रमालङ्कारः । उभयमपि–etc. But both are dissatisfied with what they have done. The king feels that the respect shown to him was out of all proportion to the services rendered while Indra feels that he could not adequately reward the king for his timely and generous services.

VII. 1. प्रथमोपकृतं–The previous obligations: i. e, the signal service you rendered to the leader of gods. प्रतिपत्तिः–Honour. अवदानविस्मितः Amazed at (your) heroic deed. अवदानम्–A valorous deed. A feat. मनोरथानामभूमिः etc. the king did expect that he would be honoured by Indra for the great feat of arms achieved by him in vanquishing the demons. And so he was so to say anticipating some reception. But what actually took place far exceeded his imagination and so he says that the reception was beyond even the pale of imagination or expectation. By even the most powerful stretch of my imagination I could not have hoped for the honour I received. अभूमिः–अविषयः–Beyond reach. विसर्जन–Dismissing. Bidding farewell. अर्द्धासनोपवेशित°–etc. Seated on half of the throne of Indra.–Sharing the throne with Indra. This was supposed to be a very high mark of honour for the mortals and many even in the Durbar of Indra craved for it. Cf. अर्द्धासनं गोत्रभिदोऽधितष्ठौ । रघु०

VII. 2. अन्तर्गतप्रार्थनम्–Etc. जयन्त, The son of Indra, who was standing close by, was inwardly–in the heart of his hearts–longing for that garland. Indra knew that and hence जयन्तमुद्वीक्ष्य Etc. He simply cast a glance at his son and smiled. आघृष्ट–Rubbed. हरिचन्दनाङ्क–Marked by the yellow sandal. पिनद्धा–Fastened.

VII. 3. सुखपरस्य–Etc. This explains why Indra often used to take the aid of his mortal friends to oust out the demons. There is of course the other reading सुरसखस्य which absolves him from this draw-back. त्रिदिवं–The heaven. उभयैः–The word उभय is generally used in the singular: here it is a peculiar use उद्धृत॰ Etc. With the thorns in the form of demons extracted. नतपर्वभिः–नतानि पर्वाणि येषाम्–तैः। By the flat–jointed (arrows) or smooth–jointed: पुरुषकेसरिणः–The reference here is to the fourth, Man–lion incarnation of Viṣṇu. The king is compared to this particular Avatāra of Viṣṇu in that both freed the heaven from the tyranny of the demons. The arrows of दुष्यन्त are on a par with the claws of Nara–Siṁha with which he tore to pieces the demon Hiraṇya–Kaṣipu father of Prahlāda.

VII. 4. सिध्यन्ति–Etc. But the king would not admit any such idea. The servants succeed in mighty enterprises only because they have the moral support of their masters. Their ability is only like reflected light. सम्भावनागुणम्—The quality of 'Thinking well of' or honouring giving patronage. धुरि–रथाग्रे–. or पुरोभागे–in the forefront–अरुण or Dawn by himself could never have been able to dispel the darkness but for the patronage it receives at the hands of the sun. Cf. also–वज्रिण एव वीर्यमेतद्विजयन्ते द्विषतो यदस्य पक्ष्याः। विक्रमो॰ नाकपृष्ठगत Etc. The glory of the king had already reached the heaven; and the celestial bards were already busy composing panegyrics about his wonderful feat of arms. सौभाग्यम्–सुभगस्य भावः। Sublimity–beauty or grandeur.

VII. 5. दिवौकसः–द्यौः ओकः येषाम् ते। बहु॰। The denizens of heaven. विच्छित्तिशेष–The remnants or residues of the paints. विच्छित्ति–lit. means 'cutting off.' But it has also the sense of

'Paint' or rogue. कल्पलतांशुकेषु–on garments in the form of the leaves of the desire–yielding tree. The vestments or tapestry. The writing material was provided by the कल्पलता । गीतक्षममर्थजातम् Materials–verses–capable of being sung, or set to music. The V. L. अर्थबन्ध would mean–'पद्s.' They choose only melodious expressions which could be sung. On his way to the heavens, the king was not in a mood to indulge in sight-seeing. And so on his way back he wants to visit all the different charming spots. पूर्वेद्युः–पूर्वस्मिन् दिने । on a previous day. मरुतां पथि–In the course of the wind. "According to Hindu mythology, the heavenly region is divided into seven Paths of Courses, with a particular वायु or wind assigned for each. The first of these seven vāyu–mārgas or vāyu–pathas is identical with the bhuvar–loka, or atmospheric region, extending from the bhur–loka, or terrestrial region, [comprising the earth, and the adhō–lōka, called Pātāla] upwards to the sun. The wind assigned to this Mārga is called āvaha, and its office is to bear along the atmosphere, clouds, meteors lightning, etc. The other six make up the swar-loka or heavenly region with which Swarga is often identified in the following order:—The 2nd Mārga is that of the sun; and its wind, called pravaha or pravāha, causes the sun to revolve; 3rd that of the moon, its wind saṁvaha or saṁvāha impels the moon; 4th that of the nakaṣtra, or lunar constellations; its wind, udvaha, causes the revolution of these asterisms; 5th that of the graha, or planets; its wind vivaha bears along the seven planets 6th that of the Saptarṣi or seven stars of the Great Bear; its wind parivaha bears along these luminaries, as well as the swar-ganga, or heavenly Gangas: [saptarshi–chakram swar-gangam shashthah parivahas tatha : not as Dr. Boehtlingk suggests gaptarshi–chakram swarga-gah, etc.] : it appears from the next verse that this was the Mārga in which Indra's car was at the moment moving; 7th that of dhruva, or the polar star, the pivot or axis of the whole planetary system, to which, according to the Visnu–Purāṇa [pp. 230, 240, Wilson], 'all the celestial luminaries are bound by aerial cords, and are made to travel in their proper orbits, being kept in their places by their respective bands of air. According to the Bramhānda–purāṇa, from which, as quoted by Katavema, the above account is taken, the wind of the 7th Mārga, causing the revolution of the polar-star, is paravāha [or paravaha]."

VII. 6. त्रिस्रोतसम्–त्रीणि स्रोतांसि यस्याः सा त्रिस्रोताः । The triple streamed river–i. e. the Ganges. Cf गङ्गां त्रिपथगां नदीम् । It has three courses (1) Flowing through the Heaven and identical with the Milky way and named Mandākinī. (2) The second is on the Earth named भागिरथी and (3) third is in the Pātāla, the residence of Daityas and Nāgās–and named भोगावती. गगनप्रतिष्ठाम्–गगनस्थाम्. Located in Heaven. It is possible to interpret it as गगनस्य प्रतिष्ठाम् the glory of Heaven. प्रविभक्तरश्मिः-प्रविभक्ता रश्मयः अर्थाद्वायुरूपा एव यत्र कर्माणि । duly distributing their rays. वर्तयति–परिभ्रमति–Revolves. ज्योतीषि–The luminaries. द्वितीयहरिविक्रम्–etc. The reference is to the Dwarf, or वामन incarnation of Viṣṇu. The story is told thus: A particular demon named बलि had become all powerful and reigned over all the three worlds. To relieve Indra of the oppression of बलि. Viṣṇu went to him in the form of a dwarf. बलि was performing a sacrifice and he had declared that he would give इच्छादान to all the suitors. But here was a curious demand of only ' three steps ' which was granted immediately. But then, the dwarf assumed gigantic dimensions and pervaded the whole of the Earth only with his one step. The second pervaded the entire heavenly region. And now he asked बलि for room for the third step. But बलि knew now who the suitor was and in his great joy he offered the Lord his head for the third step. Viṣṇu pressed him down to the nether regions, but being pleased with his devotion, he gave him the Sovereignty of Pātāla and himself remained as his doorkeeper in the form of the dwarf. Thus, the region was rendered absolutely pure–it was in fact consecrated by the second step of Viṣṇu.

विक्रमः-Treading of step. It is for this that Viṣṇu is named as 'त्रिविक्रम' त्रिपाद्. निस्तमस्कं-Com. पापरहितं शोकरहितं च। The third, and fouth lines are read differently—

तस्य व्यपेतरजसः प्रवहस्य वायोर्मार्गो द्वितीयहरिविक्रमपूत एषः ॥

The only difficulty is regarding the name of the wind. According to this reading, the region or Path would belong to the second course and not to the sixth.

सबाह्यान्तःकरणः-With internal as also the external senses. The sense-organ, according to the Sāṁkhya system are divided into two classes-Internal or external. अन्तरिन्द्रिय and बाह्येन्द्रिय. The latter are again subdivided into two-ज्ञानेन्द्रियs and कर्मेन्द्रियs, each having five subdivisions. The Internal organs are three-मनस्, बुद्धि and अहंकार-Individuality or self-consciousness. चित्त-the heart or the organ of feeling, sometimes is added to the list. For the expression Cf. also. त्वद्दर्शनादेव प्रसन्नबाह्यान्तःकरणोन्तरात्मा। वि० IV. मेघपदवी-The path of clouds. But this means that the chariot has descended with the speed of lightning-traversing the four intervening मार्गs within no time. The Bengāli reading 'प्रवहस्य' in the preceding stanza for परिवहस्य removes this difficulty as the transition in that case would be from one मार्ग to the other.

VII. 7. अरविवरेभ्यः Through the interstices of spokes. चातकैः etc. The चातक birds, it appears, could conveniently fly through the interstices of spokes of the chariot. The चातकs are classical rain-birds. हरिभिः-Names of Indra's horses. Cp. I. Act. अचिरभासां etc. अचिरा भा यासां ताः। विद्युताम् इत्यर्थः। The horses were shining because of the flashes of lightning. अनुलिप्तैः-परीतैः or रञ्जितैः Tinged with, covered with. गतम्—गमनम्।.पिशुनयति—Indicates. नेमिः-The rim. शीकरक्लिन्न-Bedewed with drops (of water). वारिगर्भाणि उदराणि येषां ते वारिगर्भोदराः। स्वाधिकारभूमौ-In the land within (your) jurisdiction-which is under (your) control. आश्चर्यदर्शनः-आश्चर्यं दर्शनं यस्य सः। curious to behold.

VII. 8. The king is now giving the description of the earth as he sees from a great height. It is an aerial pen-picture. उन्मज्जताम्–Rising upwards. Shooting up. At first when the king was at a great distance from the earth, the earth and the mountains appeared to be on the same level. But as the king began to descend down rapidly, the earth appeared also to have slipped down from the mountain-tops. स्कन्धोदय:–Because of the rise (i. e. coming into sight) of the trunks. पर्णाभ्यन्तरलीनता–The state of being enveloped in foliage. The trees had worn so to say the veil in the form of thick foliage and so could not be distinguished from a great height. सन्तानात्–From expansion or continuity. व्यक्ति–Manifestation. आपगा: अपां समूह:–आप: । आपेन गच्छन्ति इति आपगा: । Rivers. उत्क्षिपता–By one throwing up. The earth appeared as if it were being thrown upwards by somebody. पूर्वापरसमुद्रावगाढा–Plunging, merging in the eastern and western Seas. Cf. पूर्वापरौ तोयनिधी वगाह्य । कुमार०. सन्ध्यायां भव: सान्ध्य: । Evening cloud. परिघ:–A bar. हेमकूट–Or ' the golden-peaked ' one of the sacred mountains among the Himālaya chain. It is adjacent to Kailāsa and inhabited by किंपुरुषs or the servants of कुबेर. किंपुरुषा:–कुत्सिता: पुरुषा: । तत्पुरुष. । These are so called because they are said to have the body of a man and the head of a horse. They are also called किन्नरs or अश्वमुखs.

VII. 9. स्वायम्भुवात्–स्वयं भवतीति स्वयम्भू: । स्वयम्भुव: अपत्यं स्वायम्भुव: । –From the sun of the self-existent one. Kāṣyapa is the son of मरीचि (and so called मारीच) and the grandson of ब्रह्मन्. He is called प्रजापति–or the lord of creation, but he is not one of the seven original प्रजापतिs nor of the ten mentioned by मनु. He is here said to be one of the प्रजापतिs, who were Brahmā's sons, created by him to supply the universe with inhabitants. He married the thirteen daughters of दक्ष but the eldest one अदिति was his favourite with whom he is practising penance here. तपस्यति like नमस्यति is a denominative from तपस्. अनतिक्रमणीयानि श्रेयांसि–The fortunes or blessings (which can be acquired by paying homage to these revered ascetics) cannot be passed by. In the first act also he just has the same feeling 'पुण्याश्रमदर्शनेन तावदात्मानं पुनीमहे' where he meets Śakuntalā for the first time. Now also, his reunion with her is due to his reverence for these ascetics. प्रथमः कल्पः–A noble resolve, or a fine or capital idea. Cf. उदारः कल्पः ।

VII. 10. उपोढ–P. P. from उप+वह्. Commenced. निरुन्धतः–of thee–checking the speed. The chariot glided down on the earth without making any sound whatsoever. This is the difference between the car of Indra and that of mortal kings.

VII. 11 We get a very vivid description of the sage who is much absorbed in his austerities that he has lost all regard for his body–which is covered over with an anthill. उरसा– The instr. is इत्थंभूतलक्षणे–showing अचलत्व. संदष्ट–closely sticking or encircled by. लताप्रतान–लतासंतान circles of creepers–coils. अंसव्यापि–covering the shoulders. निचितम्–filled with. अभ्यर्कबिम्बम्–We can take it as an अव्ययीभाव or as two separate words. कष्टतपसे–कष्टं तपः यस्य सः । तस्मै । of severe austerities. भवान् कथमिदानीम्–what about you? What do you intend to do?

VII. 12. वृत्तिः–sustenance. उचिता–योग्या i. e. Proper, suitable, habitual. सत्कल्प॰ विद्यमानकल्पवृक्षे । Even when there were desire–yielding trees. कपिश–Brown. संयमः–self–control. The sages already possessed the things which are eagerly sought by others. उत्सर्पिणी–Soaring high, lofty. दाक्षायणी–The daughter of दक्ष–Aditi. प्रतिपाल्यावसराः etc.–The saints must be seen at their leisure: i. e. we must wait till an opportune moment to see the saints–i. e. should not visit them at an odd hour or when they are otherwise engaged. Cf. अवसरोपसर्पणीयाः राजानः ।–The king, therefore, is conscious that others also have their own engagements. There is the reading प्रतिपाल्यावसरः खलु प्रस्तावः—The subject matter deserves some waiting (on our part): i. e. The sage would take some time before he would finish his discourse on the पतिव्रताधर्म–and so it would be better on the part of the king to see him after a while. अन्तरान्वेषी–Seeking an opportune moment. निमित्तं–An omen.

VII. 13. मनोरथाय—मनोरथमाप्तुं–To obtain (my) desire–viz. Śakuntalā. i. e. I cherish absolutely no hopes of obtaining her. पूर्वावधीरितम्–Slighted–spurned before. दुःखं हि परिवर्तते–(1) Misery alone surrounds me or (2) The bliss is turned into misery. चापलं–Naughtiness, wilfulness–Cf. The sense in चपलोऽयं बटुः in II. अनुबध्यमानः–Being closely followed by, from अनु+बन्ध्–'flying after', closely following'.

VII. 14. आमर्द–Rough–handling. Hard pulling. अपत्यनिर्विशेष–Not different from (our) children. Just like (our) children. औरसः–one of the 12 kinds of sons, enumerated by Manu. उरसः जातः औरसः। अनपत्यता Etc. The king is here generalising a great truth. Generally those who have no children crave eagerly for them. They then shower all their affections on the children of other people. Childlessness is a sort of a gap in life which these men try to fill up with small children belonging to strangers even. वत्सलयति–Denominative from वत्सल. अधरं दर्शयति–A very fine touch of child-psychology. The child wants to ridicule the woman who tried to scare it. अधरदर्शन is sign of contempt.

VII. 15. एधापेक्षः–waiting (only) for fuel. महतः तेजसोबीजम्–(The boy) so to say (possesses) the germ of mighty energy (or spirit). The child is the father of man and so the king could judge from the undaunted spirit displayed by the boy that he is destined to be an eminent personality. The child is not to be easily outwitted. It is not prepared to give up the thing in hand for something which is simply a promise. It stretches out its hand to get the toy–when the king gets an opportunity to notice the lines on its hand.

VII. 16. प्रलोभ्यवस्तु०–Desired or coveted object. प्रणय–longing, eagerness or craving. जालग्रथिताङ्गुलिः–जालेषु ग्रथिताः अङ्गुलयः यस्य

(The hand) whose fingers were united together by a web. 'webbed hand' is indicative of great valour. अलक्ष्यपत्रान्तरम्–etc. The hand is compared to a lotus–whose petals cannot be (distinctly) seen–(because of their closeness). इद्धरागया–इद्धः दीप्तः or समृद्धः रागः–लौहित्यम् यस्याः सा तथा । if we take it as an adjective to उषसा, otherwise इद्धो रागो यया–उषस्–which made the lotus red. The redness of the lotus and the hand are to be compared. एकपङ्कजम्–A solitary or single lotus दुर्ललित–दुर्लभं ललितं–इप्सित–यस्य । Unmanageable, difficult to be coaxed or naughty. Cf. विक्रम० where the king applies the adjective to his eye–उपवनलतासु चक्षुर्न बध्नाति धृति तद्रूपालोकदुर्ललितम् ।

VII. 17. Here we get a fine picture of those who are blessed with children. आलक्ष्य°–slightly perceptible. अनिमित्तहासैः–By their innocent smiles : lit. for no reason. अव्यक्त–indistinct. °प्रणयिनः–longing. दुर्मोचहस्तग्राहेण–By the grasp of his hand which is very difficult to loosen.

VII. 18. सत्त्वसंश्रयसुखः (संयमः)–(Forbearance) that takes delight in giving protection to (all) animals. V. L. जन्मनः–of thy father.–Lit. of the source, used for जन्मनः हेतोः. Cf. the word 'कारण' which is also used in this way. न कारणत्स्वाद्बिभिदे कुमारः । etc. The simile in the second line is not, however, quite a happy one. स्थानप्रत्ययात्–owing to the reliance in the place.–Circumstantial evidence. The whole incident–viz दुष्यन्त's seeing the boy–is psychologically very interesting. He experiences a sort of paternal feeling for the boy, but he dare not express it even to himself. He says it only in a round about way. रूपसंवादिनी–'Resembling the form.' अप्रतिलोमः–Not averse. Not untractable. प्रतिलोम–Lit. 'against the course or direction of hair.' व्यपदेशः–Family, pedigree. Cf. व्यपदेशमाविलयितुं etc.

VII. 20. रसाधिकेषु–Abounding in pleasures of senses. V. L. सुधासितेषु–white due to chunam. उशन्ति from वश् to wish. नियतैकयतिव्रतानि–नियतं एकं यतिव्रतं येषु–Where the vows of asceticism alone (are practised). It was a common practice with ancient Indian kings to retire into forest and lead the life of a hermit after they had reigned for a sufficiently long period–entrusting the whole responsibility to their sons. आत्मगत्या–By their own means. विषयः–प्रदेशः । The difficulty is that no mortal could of his own accord, reside in a place like this–viz. the part of heaven. Hence the query. सम्बन्ध–Relationship. अनार्यः परदार० etc. to indulge in a gossip regarding the wife of another is ungentlemanly; Cf. अनिर्वर्णनीयं परकलत्रम् ।. The king was anxious to know the name of the mother of the boy. But his sense of propriety does not allow him to put a blunt question. Now he knows the name–and once more there is reason for him to hope–that after all the boy might be his own son.' नाममात्रप्रस्तावः—mere mention of the name, अंतिका–ज्येष्ठा भगिनी = धात्री । Elder sister. रक्षाकरण्डकम्–The amulet or the talisman. करण्डक also means a herb. This might have been a sort of a locket worn on the wrist. This picking up of the रक्षाबन्ध is the last and convincing incident. Now there remains no doubt whatsoever in the mind of दुष्यन्त–after he is acquainted with the history of the amulet by the two ladies. जातकर्म–The natal ceremony. It is the fourth of the twelve Saṁskāras or purificatory rites described by Manu and the first after the child's birth. It is performed by giving the child honey and clarified butter out of a golden spoon, before separating the navel string. विक्रिया–The change–transformation; विवादः contradiction, dispute. This contradiction is convincing. एकवेणीधरा–The single braid is a sign of mourning. A Hindu woman is supposed not to comb her hair in the absence of her husband. Cf. Megh. V. 90. न मे आशा etc. Śakuntalā had given up all hopes of reunion with दुष्यन्त. Hence, she cherishes no hope even when she learns the रक्षाबन्ध incident. The news is too good to be true for her; प्रकृति–Natural state. विकार–Change. अथवा–etc. सानुमती, it appears, had however prepared the ground.

VII. 21. वसने etc. This shows her absolute indifference to outwardly appearance. ०क्षाम–Emaciated. अतिनिष्करुणस्य–etc. She is observing this 'vow of separation' for me–who was so harsh to her. अनुकूलपरिणामम्–Taking a favourable turn, ending favourably. Śakuntalā at present is in a 'tight corner' so to say. She could not recognise the king in whom remorse had wrought a complete change. Then she had great misgivings regarding her fortune. She, therefore, thinks twice before accepting even facts.

VII. 22. मोहतमस्–Darkness in the form of delusion. उपराग–Eclipse. रोहिणी was the forth of the twenty seven daughters of Dakṣa and most beloved spouse of the Moon.

VII. 23. असंस्कार०–Unadorned. i. e. without any संस्कार i. e. toilet. वत्स etc. Śakuntalā, instead of giving a direct reply, asks the boy to consult his destiny. This is the height of pathos. The king also could not contain himself any longer and so he begs her unconditional, sincere apology–and not content with mere words, even falls prostrate at her feet.

VII. 24. व्यलीक–Grief. Unpleasantness. प्रबलतमसाम्–Those who are completely under the sway of delusion. एवंप्रायाः–प्रायेण एवम् । सुप्सुप् ।. Mostly such, such for the most part. पादयोः पतति–Some commentators make the king fall down at her feet before repeating the stanzas, which would mean that the king repeats the verse falling prostrate at the feet of Śakuntalā and she also listens patiently and then asks him to rise up. But this would be very unnatural. सुचरितप्रतिबन्धकम्–Opposed to virtuous conduct : परिणाममुखम्–Drawing towards its issue, on the point of becoming mature, about to ripen. Śakuntalā is after all a Hindu lady and rather than blame her husband for having repudiated her, she blames her own fate !

VII. 25. पूर्वम्–Formerly, i. e. at the time of repudiating her. आकुटिल–Curved. आ = ईषत् । अनुशय–remorse. बाष्पबिन्दुः–The tear–drop. विषमं कृतम्–It acted adversely. तेन हि etc. the king wants to see the ring once more in its proper place. So he says 'let the creeper bear the fruit as the mark of the union (or advent) of the season (of spring). Here the ring is the fruit, शकुन्तला the creeper and दुष्यन्त–the Vernal Season. But Śakuntalā had enough of the ring. She is not prepared to trust it again !

VII. 26. पुत्रस्य ते i. e. इन्द्रस्य। His bow having accomplished all the work, the thunderbolt of Indra is merely an embellishment for him. विनिवर्तित–Turned away from–resting from its work. अनुभाव–Prowess. °पिशुन indicative of.

VII. 27. द्वादशधा स्थितस्य तेजसः etc. This refers to the solar light: There are supposed to be twelve आदित्यs for twelve months and are described as the sons of अदिति and कश्यप. The gods Viṣṇu and Indra are reckoned amongst their sons : According to the commentator द्वादशधा–refers to the twelve digits of the sun. यज्ञभागेश्वरम्–The lord of a share in (every) sacrifice, or यज्ञभागाः- Gods–those who enjoy a share in sacrifices तेषामीश्वरः–इन्द्रः Indra also is said to be their son. आत्मभुवः परः–Higher even than the self-existent (Brahman). V. L. आत्मभवः–The self-existent one. This seems to be better: i. e. though there was no necessity for him to be born, still he chose this couple as his father and mother. परः पुरुषः The Highest Being. पुरुष–पुरि शेते इति।–That which sleeps or abides in the body. नियोज्यः—The servant, वासव-नियोज्य–The king wants to imply that he is but an humble servant of their son.

VII. 28. पौलोमी–शची। The Wife of Indra.

VII. 29. श्रद्धा–Piety or faith.—Represents Śakuntalā. वित्तम्–Wealth = अपत्यम्–The offspring. विधिः–The Precept, or practice, (represents दुष्यन्त). Cf. the same idea in श्रद्धेव साक्षाद्विधिनोपपन्ना। Raghu II. 16.

VII. 30. निमित्त–The cause. नैमित्तिक–The effect: The cause must always precede the effect. But here the order was reversed. And hence the favour is अपूर्व–unprecedented. विधातारः–Creators, ordainers. आज्ञाकरी–Hand-maid, servant. This also is a विनयोक्ति. Cf.–वासवानुयोज्यः दुष्यन्त etc. कस्यचित्

कालस्य–After some time. युष्मत्सगोत्रस्य of the some गोत्र as you समानं गोत्रं अस्य इति सगोत्रः । But कश्यप was the originator of the race; we have, therefore, to take it as simply 'of your Gotra' i.e. your descendent. दुष्यन्त is all along feeling uneasy for his repudiation of शकुन्तला. Especially the fact that he spurned her when she went to him of her own accord and later on began to pine for her–is inexplicable to him. So at last he asks the sage to enlighten him on this point. प्रत्यक्षवैक्लव्याम्–(1) whose distress was personally witnessed by her (i. e. by मेनका) or (2) who has clear marks of distress (on her face). अवसानः–Terminating with. This removal of misunderstanding was of course very essenrial. Otherwise the memory of it would have haunted them both throughout their life. वचनीय–Blame; चरितार्था–कृतार्था ।

VII. 32. छाया–The image or reflection. न मूर्च्छति–has no effect. Cf. न पादपोन्मूलनशक्ति रंहः शिलोच्चये मूर्च्छति मारुतस्य । Raghu II. 34. सुलभावकाशा–It finds easy access to...Cf. The idea in उत्तर० प्रभवति शुचिर्बिम्बोद्ग्राहे मणिर्न मृदां चयः ।

वंशप्रतिष्ठा–The stability or performance of (my) family. तथा भाविनम्–Destined to be like that.

VII. 33. अनुद्धात–Absence of uneven ground. Cf. ययौ अनुद्धातसुखेन–Raghu. II. 72. पुरा जयति–will conquer. पुरा used with the present tense has the sense of Future. Cf. आलोके ते निपतति पुरा । etc. मेघ० सप्तद्वीपाम्–According to Hindu mythology, the Earth consisted of seven islands; the one inhabited by human beings was called जम्बूद्वीप. भरत so named because of his being the universal supporter. This same भरत was the ancestor of the Kauravas and Pāṇḍavas. आशास्महे–' we expect '–is better than we invoke (all blessings). The news has got to be communicated to कण्व and so an aerial messenger is dispatched.

VII. 34. प्राज्यवृष्टिः–प्राज्या (abundant) वृष्टिः यस्य । very liberal in sending down showers. वितत°–stretched out. Spread over. विस्तृत. °यज्ञः–with long-spread sacrifices. प्रणियस्व–V. L. प्रीणयालम् ।

°परिवर्त–Cycles, revolutions. In this way by reciprocal friendly acts, pass the time etc. Cf. Bhag. देवान् भावयतानेन ते देवा भावयंतु वः। परस्परं भावयंतः श्रेयः परमवाप्स्यथ ॥ III. 11. उभय° The two worlds. Cf. also Raghu. I. 26. भरतवाक्यम्–The (formal) closing stanza of the drama containing blessings to all and put in the mouth of some venerable person entitled to give such blessing; it is named in honour of भरत the founder of the science of dramaturgy and music. He is also supposed to be the author of नाट्यशास्त्र and is said to have superintended the exhibition of the drama Laxmi-Swayaṃvara of Saraswati–in Indra's Heaven.

VII. 35. सरस्वती–The Muse of Learning and Speech. श्रुतमहताम्–great on account of their knowledge of veda. महीयताम्–Be honoured. i, e. Let those, who are masters of learning be properly respected. नीललोहितः–An epithet of Śiva; blue and red. This is variously explained: वामभागे नीलः दक्षिणभागे लोहितः। or नीलः कण्ठे लोहितश्च केशेषु। and so on. परिगतशक्तिः (i) परिगता प्राप्ता शक्तिः–पार्वती–येन सः। 'The wives of the deities were supposed to personify their energy or active powers.' or (2) It might refer to the eight Śaktis of Śiva. or (3) शक्ति–Majesty–prowess in general. So exemption from further transmigration is the Summum bonum–which the writer asks for. The play begins and also ends with a prayer to Śiva–who had a large temple in Ujjayinī–The city of Vikramāditya and the abode of the poet. Both actors and spectators would probably repeat the prayer after the speaker and appropriate it to themselves.' (M. W.).

Metrical Table.

Number of Syllables	Name of the Metre	Where employed	Total	Measure.
8	अनुष्टुप्	I. 5, 6, 11, 12, 26; II. 13, 16, 17; III. 1, 19, 22; IV. 3, 6; V. 14, 24, 26, 29; VI. 14, 22, 23, 28. 32; VII. 9, 13, 14, 15, 23, 28, 29.	29	पञ्चमं लघु सर्वत्र सप्तमं द्विचतुर्थयोः । गुरु षष्ठं च पादानां चतुर्णां स्यादनुष्टुभि ॥
11	त्रिष्टुप्	IV. 7.	1	A Vedic metre consisting of four quarters of 11 syllables, where great liberty is allowed in the matter of rhythm.
,,	इन्द्रवज्रा	IV. 21; V. 4.	2	स्यादिन्द्रवज्रा यदि तौ जगौ गः ।
,,	उपजाति	II. 7; III. 4; V. 5, 20, 25; VI. 10, 24, 26; VII. 2, 5, 19, 31.	12	स्यादिन्द्रवज्रा यदि तौ जगौ गः । उपेन्द्रवज्रा प्रथमे लघौ सा । } इत्यनयोरुपजातिः ।
,,	शालिनी	V. 30.	1	मात्तौ गौ चेच्छालिनी वेदलोकैः ।

11	रथोद्धता	VII. 18.	1	रात्परैर्नरलगैः रथोद्धता ।
12	द्रुतविलम्बित	II. 11; III. 18; V. 27; VI. 8; VII. 3.	5	द्रुतविलम्बितमाह नभौ भरौ ।
,,	वंशस्थ or वंशस्थविल	I. 18, 22, 23; III. 13; IV. 1; V. 12, 15, 17; VI. 13, 18, 29; VII. 10, 16, 30.	14	जतौ तु वंशस्थमुदीरितं जरौ ।
13	प्रहर्षिणी	VI. 27, 30.	2	त्र्याशाभिर्मनजरगाः प्रहर्षिणीयम् ।
,,	रुचिरा	VII. 35.	1	जभौ सजौ गिति रुचिरा चतुर्ग्रहैः ।
14	वसन्ततिलका	I. 8, 27, 31; II. 9, 12; III. 10, 20, 26; IV. 1, 2, 10, 12, 13, 14, 19; V. 2, 3, 6, 22, 23; VI. 12, 16, 20, 25; VII. 4, 6, 17, 25, 26, 32.	30	उक्ता वसन्ततिलका तभजा जगौ गः ।
15	मालिनी	I. 10, 19, 20; II. 4; III. 3; V. 7, 8, 19; VII. 7, 34.	10	ननमयययुतेयं मालिनी भोगिलोकैः ।
17	मन्दाक्रान्ता	I. 15, 33; II. 14, 15.	4	मन्दाक्रान्ताम्बुधिरसनगैर्मो भनौ तौ गयुग्मम् ।

Continued on next page

17	शिखरिणी	I. 9, 24 ; II. 10 ; III. 8 ; V. 10 ; VI. 9 ; VII. 33.	7	रसै रुद्रैश्छिन्ना यमनसभला गः शिखरिणी ।
,,	हरिणी	III. 12 ; IV. 18 ; VII. 24.	3	नसमरसला गः षड्वेदैर्हयैर्हरिणी मता ।
19	शार्दूलविक्रीडित	I. 14, 30 ; II. 2, 5, 6 ; III. 9, 25 ; IV. 4, 5, 8, 16, 17 ; V. 9 ; VI. 4, 5, 6, 17 ; VII. 8, 11, 12, 27 ;	21	सूर्याश्वैर्यदि मः सजौ सततगाः शार्दूलविक्रीडितम् ।
21	स्रग्धरा	I. 1, 7.	2	म्रभ्नर्यानां त्रयेण त्रिमुनियतियुता स्रग्धरा कीर्तितेयम् ।
10/11	वैतालीय or वियोगिनी	II. 18 ; VI. 1 ; VII. 1.	3	विषमे ससजा गुरुः समे सभरा लेऽथ गुरुर्वियोगिनी ।
11/12	अपरवक्त्र	IV. 9 ; V. 1.	2	अयुजि ननरला गुरुः समे तदपरवक्त्रमिदं नजौ जरौ ।
,,	औपच्छन्दसिक	III. 23, 24 ; VII. 20, 21.	4	पर्यन्ते यौं तथैव (वैतालीये इव) शेषमौपच्छन्दसिकं सुधीभिरुक्तम् ।
12/13	पुष्पिताग्रा	I. 32 ; II. 3 ; VI. 11.	3	अयुजि नयुगरेफतो यकारो युजि तु नजौ जरगाश्च पुष्पिताग्रा ।
	आर्या	I. 2, 3, 13, 16, 17, 21, 25, 28, 29, 34 ; II. 1, 8 ; III. 2, 5, 6, 7, 11, 14, 16, 17,	39	यस्याः प्रथमे पादे द्वादश मात्रास्तथा तृतीयेऽपि । अष्टादश द्वितीये चतुर्थके पञ्चदश सार्या ॥

	21 ; IV. 11, 15, 20; V. 11, 13, 16, 18, 21, 28, 31; VI. 2, 3, 7, 15, 19, 21, 31; VII. 22.		
गीति	I. 4; III. 15.	2	आर्यापूर्वार्धसमं द्वितीयमपि भवति यत्र हंसगते । छन्दोविदस्तदानीं गीतिंताममृतवाणि भाषन्ते ॥

(PRINTED AT JAYYED PRESS, BALLIMARAN, DELHI)